# Scratches On Our Minds American Images Of China And India

950 I73s  58-06544
Isaacs
Scratches on our minds...

SCRATCHES ON OUR MINDS

BY HAROLD R. ISAACS

Scratches On Our Minds
No Peace For Asia
The Tragedy of the Chinese Revolution
New Cycle in Asia (editor)

*Contributor to*
As We See Russia
South Asia in the World Today

*Pamphlets*
Two-Thirds of the World
Africa New Crises in the Making

# SCRATCHES ON OUR MINDS

American Images of China and India

HAROLD R. ISAACS

ILLUSTRATED

THE JOHN DAY COMPANY, NEW YORK

© 1958 by Massachusetts Institute of Technology

All rights reserved This book, or parts thereof, must not be reproduced in any form without permission Published by The John Day Company, 62 West 45th Street, New York 36, N Y., and on the same day in Canada by Longmans, Green & Company, Toronto

Library of Congress Catalogue Card Number 58-5692

Manufactured in the United States of America

## The Blind Men and the Elephant

Six blind beggars sitting by a roadside as an elephant passed were told they might touch it so that they would know what an elephant was like. The first one touched only the elephant's side and said, "He is like a wall!" The second one felt only his tusk and said, "No, no, he is like a spear." The third one took hold of his trunk and said, "Surely he is like a snake." "No such thing," cried the fourth, grasping one of his legs, "he is like a tree." The fifth was a tall man and took hold of his ear and said, "All of you are wrong, he is like a fan." The sixth man happened to catch hold of his tail and cried, "O foolish fellows, he is not like a wall, nor a spear, nor a snake, nor a tree, nor a fan, he is exactly like a rope." So the elephant passed on while the six blind men stood there quarreling, each being sure he knew exactly how the elephant looked, and each calling the others hard names because the rest did not agree with him.

—OLD INDIAN FABLE

# PREFACE

I OWE THE OPPORTUNITY to produce this work to the Center for International Studies at the Massachusetts Institute of Technology and its director, Max F. Millikan. The Center is a remarkable institution devoted to inquiry into the current affairs of man, especially of American man and the multitude of new affairs that have pressed so hard and so swiftly in upon him in these years. The Center is not responsible for what appears in this book. Its philosophy as a research organization is based upon the freedom and full responsibility of the individual inquirer I can only hope the work reflects back in some small degree the credit which association with the Center confers upon it.

In addition to a hospitable philosophy, facilities, and support, this setting has provided the opportunity to benefit from discussion with colleagues and associates of many different bents and skills. As a longtime journalist now come among the practitioners of more formal disciplines, I found these encounters almost unfailingly instructive. I have some debt almost to all whom I have met here, but for submitting so patiently to my many impositions on their time and for their contributions to my own thinking, I want to thank especially Raymond Bauer, George Coelho, Karl Deutsch, David Gleicher, Subbiah Kannapan, Suzanne Keller, Daniel Lerner, Howard Perlmutter, Ithiel Pool, Lucian Pye and Paul Rosenstein-Rodan I have also had the advantage of comments from other friends and associates elsewhere who have been concerned in many different ways for many years with Asian affairs. If in thanking them here I abstain from naming names, it is to avoid identifying thereby some of those who were good enough to participate in this inquiry not only by commenting on various chapters of the manuscript but by submitting to interviews in the first place

Throughout I have had the extraordinarily competent aid of my research assistant, Mrs. Leigh R. Kamblu, who made order out of great masses of notes, tracked down scores of elusive references, culled press, periodicals, and the *Congressional Record*, monitored movies, radio, and TV. helped to organize the interview material in many different forms and under many different headings, and generally performed every needful task with rewarding speed and skill, right up to the final careful preparation of the manuscript for publication

Mrs. Dorothy B. Jones made a special study, at our request, of the treatment of Chinese and Indian characters and themes in American films, and the frequent references to her report in my own text indicate the extent of my debt to her. I also have Mrs Jones to thank for the photos from various films which appear as illustrations and the respective studios—Metro-Goldwyn Mayer, Twentieth Century-Fox, R.K.O and Paramount—for their prompt and courteous permission to use them The names of the several newspapers and syndicates and artists whose cartoons I have used are duly credited where they appear in the text and I thank them all for their generous co-operation.

I am indebted to Arnold R. Isaacs for a number of vigilantly gleaned references from sources I might have ignored and of which I have been able to make much good use, to Deborah S. Isaacs for some faithful TV monitoring, and most profoundly of all, as always, to Viola R Isaacs for her indispensable collaboration. The similarity of last names in this group is, happily, no coincidence.

Finally, I want here to thank again the members of the panel, the men and women who submitted with such grace and interest to a difficult interview and who provided the primary raw material on which this report is based. I learned more from them than I have been able to put into this book.

HAROLD R. ISAACS

Cambridge, Massachusetts
September, 1957

# CONTENTS

❀

| | |
|---|---|
| Introduction | 11 |
| I. "ASIA" | 37 |
| II. THE CHINESE | |
|     Introduction | 63 |
|     1. A Panel-Eye View | 72 |
|     2. The Superior People | 89 |
|     3. The Inferior People | 97 |
|     4. "Chink, Chink, Chinaman" | 109 |
|     5. The Wards | 124 |
|     6. The Attractive People | 140 |
|     7. The Heroes Risen | 164 |
|     8. The Heroes Fallen | 176 |
|     9. The Ungrateful Wretches | 190 |
|     10. The Awakened Dragon | 209 |
| III. THE INDIANS | |
|     Introduction | 239 |
|     1. The Fabulous Indians | 243 |
|     2. The Religionists and Philosophers | 249 |
|     3. The Very Benighted Heathen | 259 |
|     4. The Lesser Breed | 271 |
|     5. The Gandhi Image | 290 |
|     6. The Nehru Image | 302 |
|     7. The Indians Encountered | 317 |
|     8. The Gallery Revisited | 366 |
| IV. SOME REFLECTIONS | 379 |
| Index | 409 |

*A section of illustrations from photographs will be found following page 240.*

# INTRODUCTION

---- ✤ ----

I SHALL BE REPORTING in these pages the results of a rather intensive inquiry into some American ideas and impressions of China and India, and particularly of Chinese and Indians as people. A great deal that has turned up in this exploration of minds is new, or at least newly seen; some of it is bound to be pleasantly or unpleasantly controversial. The bulk of this material was gathered by asking a good many people a great many questions during the course of more than a year. To most of their replies I usually rejoined: "And what do you base *that* on?" This is at all times a fair question, even if it is not always easy to answer. I assume that interested readers will want to put it to me in my turn. Those who would prefer to pass at once to the substance of my report can turn immediately to the first chapter that follows, where that story begins. But I hope that many will wait to discover first, as precisely as I can state it, the manner of this inquiry and of the people of whom it was made.

The eruption of the "new" facts of China and India in American national life raises, among a few others, this question: What ideas, notions, and images do Americans have in their heads about these hitherto distant lands and peoples? Insofar as they have *had* to react, what did they have from their past to react *with*? What new or transformed impressions have begun to take shape out of the swift movements and many impacts of these recent years? The public prints and forums have ballooned with controversy and passion, annoyance, anger, and frustration, with fear and wonder, and even sometimes with near panic over images and events dimly seen in places where most people have scarcely ever looked before. Many could only gape at the uproar, absorbing this or that idea almost as they might breathe in rumors about a visitation from Mars.

But what are these ideas that reach them, where do they come from, what do they feed upon? What mental equipment was brought to bear on all the confusion by those expected or required to have opinions or make decisions, those to whom the many publics in the concentric circles of our society listen for cues?

I began, early in 1954, to explore these and other questions with a number of individuals. Some were Asia specialists of one kind or another, some were writers or mass media specialists, and all were personal or professional acquaintances of mine over a considerable period of time. These conversations, we found, took us down paths rarely, if ever, consciously traveled before. As journalists or scholars, students of politics, history, literature, or language, all had been concerned with fact, event, idea, situation, and of course with people, but mostly with people as actors in the dramas that had caught and engaged our interests over the years. I could get the opinions of these individuals on a wide range of affairs, but it quickly developed that these more or less considered opinions stood as only one cluster among many others much less plainly defined. We had, for example, seldom or never critically examined the spontaneous and untutored reactions we had to these countries as countries, to these people as people. What *feelings* about China or India had grown out of years of life there or out of what we had heard or read of what they were like? What *feelings* did we have about the Chinese or Indians we had known, either personally or in the mass, as we lived and moved among them, or encountered them elsewhere, in person, picture, or print? And why?

Some striking and often unexpected answers began to emerge and recur in these talks. It became clear that a variety of unsupported or unsupportable assumptions, indeed all sorts of unticketed and unacknowledged notions about these countries and peoples, floated about, even in such relatively schooled and orderly minds. What were they? Where did they come from? Which ones recurred? How did they resemble each other or differ from person to person, and why? These and a host of similar questions began clamoring for answers. Despite the dismayed surprise some felt over some of the notions that appeared in these exploratory talks, much of what turned up was actually familiar, but as old furniture is familiar, in constant use but unnoticed—stereotyped notions, unexamined generalizations, and, in some cases, hitherto unacknowledged or unspoken prejudices. Some of these turned up unexpectedly around

INTRODUCTION

corners of the conversation, others hid in more obscure mental crannies and had to be drawn out for a look. As a rule, a person had never had to answer for any of these ideas or attitudes because, until now, they had never been questioned. I had begun by seeking out the studied judgments of these people; I had now acquired a brand-new interest in their unstudied notions and a great desire to know more of what might be the relation between the two, and this is what shaped my inquiry. I framed it into a more systematic interview designed to be used with a larger number of more varied people, more varied as to profession and degree of involvement with Asian affairs, but sharing in common some role in the flow of information and ideas through our society. After testing this interview most profitably on some twenty patient and cooperative associates at the Center for International Studies, I set forth on my broader quest.

### THE INTERVIEWEES

This quest led through 181 interviews in the next fourteen months.

Let it be emphasized at once that this group of 181 is *not* a sample in the sample-survey or polling sense of the term. There will be some obvious nose-counting done and some correlations of findings made within the group itself. But there is no intention here to measure these interview results statistically. This study is not a poll in conception, method, or purpose. It is not intended to base any conclusions or predictions on numbers or percentages, as such. The group interviewed is to be regarded as a panel of individual informants, not as a stratified sample.

But on the other hand, let me make it also quite plain that I unhesitatingly regard these individuals as representative examples of American leadership types, products of American education, religion, and politics. On a host of matters—in their childhood associations, in educational experience, and in certain ideas and attitudes—they turned out to share too many common patterns to be regarded on all counts as unique unto themselves. These common holdings will often reinforce me where, on my own responsibility, I make certain generalizations, whether about people of this sort or about the broader meanings and applications of what I have learned from this inquiry.

## By Key Place in a Given Sphere

These 181 individuals were selected as informants, then, and were chosen according to *who* or *what* they were. This is to say that in many cases I went after a particular individual by name In others, I sought out whatever person happened to occupy a particular position, such as high office in a certain type of company, key posts in certain government departments, public bodies, and organizations, or key editorial slots on certain important publications.

As it finally appears here, the panel of 181 includes 32 individuals who can be called nationally prominent, in the sense that their names are well known to wide publics outside their own spheres—in at least half a dozen cases having or approaching the status of household names. There are 77 individuals who are professionally prominent, in the sense that their names would be quite well known to all concerned in their particular fields, professions, or interests. Finally, there are 72 who occupy positions significant for the purposes of this inquiry but who do not command such broader professional or public notice These individuals were sought out in a great variety of places where they perform many different functions in our society. But the primary basis for selection was the one thing they all have in common they all play an important or significant role in what we broadly call the communications process. Each one in some meaningful way influences or has influenced the flow of ideas and information and the patterning of attitudes among one or more of the many publics who compose the people. Thus the first and major category of selection was by key place in a given sphere, and in this respect the group is distributed as follows:

| | | |
|---|---|---:|
| I. | Academic World | 41 |
| II. | Mass Media (Press, Radio-TV, Writers, Publishers) | 40 |
| III. | Government | 28 |
| IV | Ex-Government | 12 |
| V. | Business | 13 |
| VI. | Groups Concerned with Public Opinion and Education | 27 |
| VII. | Church-Missionary Groups | 20 |
| | TOTAL | 181 |

Some of the individual contributors to this study stand by themselves as highly visible names and personalities, but the great bulk derive their special importance from their association in various capacities with all sorts of institutions. Before partially listing them, it may be necessary to state what should be obvious: that these in-

INTRODUCTION

stitutions as such can in no way necessarily be associated with the views or attitudes of these individuals, especially in the form in which these are reported in the present study. They are all large institutions with large numbers of highly varied people in key places on their staffs In some of the most important instances, interviews have been conducted with a number of people in the same organization precisely to tap this variety. In all but a very few such bodies, the guiding or animating ideas are a complex to which many different elements contribute. The members of the present panel are important because they are among these contributing elements, not because they necessarily or decisively shape the outlooks of the institutions to which they belong In a few cases, the identity between a single individual and an institution may be so close and so well known that the association is all but automatic; wherever this fact could endanger the commitment of privacy made in these interviews, the name of the institution has been omitted. With these qualifications and deletions, the list, totaling 86, is as follows:

I. *Academic*
Amherst College
Brooklyn College
Cornell University
Harvard University
Howard University
Massachusetts Institute of Technology
Princeton University
University of California (Berkeley)
University of California (Los Angeles)
University of Chicago
University of Minnesota
University of Pennsylvania
Yale University

Individuals in this category are identified with the following academic disciplines:

Anthropology
Economics
Electrical Engineering
Geography
History
Humanities
International Relations
Political Science
Psychology
Social Psychology
Sociology

II *Mass Media*
Newspapers
  Chicago Daily News
  Chicago Sun-Times
  Christian Science Monitor
  Denver Post
  Minneapolis Star-Tribune
  New York Herald Tribune
  New York Times
  Pittsburgh Courier
  Washington Post
Magazines:
  Life

SCRATCHES ON OUR MINDS

Newsweek
The Reporter
Saturday Review of Literature
Time
U S. News and World Report
Press Services
Associated Press
United Press
Radio TV Networks
   Columbia Broadcasting System
   National Broadcasting Company

III  *Government*
Department of the Army
Department of Commerce
Department of State
Foreign Operations Administration
International Educational Exchange Program
Operations Coordination Board
U S House of Representatives
U S Information Agency
U S Senate

IV  *Ex-Government*
Department of the Army
Department of Commerce
Department of State

V.  *Business*
California-Texas Oil Company
Doubleday & Company, Inc
International General Electric Company
General Motors Overseas Corporation
Irving Trust Company
National City Bank of New York
Standard Vacuum Oil Company
C V Starr Company
Westinghouse International Company

VI.  *Groups Concerned with Public Opinion and Education*
American Institute of Public Opinion
American Universities Field Staff
Carnegie Endowment for International Peace
Congress of Industrial Organizations
Democratic National Committee
Eisenhower Exchange Fellowships
Ford Foundation
Girl Scouts of America
India League of America
International Farm Youth Exchange
International Research Associates
League of Women Voters
The Minnesota Poll
National Association for the Advancement of Colored People
National Opinion Research Center
Republican National Committee
Rockefeller Foundation
Elmo Roper Associates
Washington International Affairs Seminar
Young Women's Christian Association

VII.  *Church and Missionary Groups and Publications*
America
Christian Herald
Christian Medical Council
The Churchman
The Churchwoman
Commonweal
Board of Foreign Missions, Presbyterian Church in the U S A.
Hartford Seminary Foundation
Maryknoll Seminary
Methodist Board of Missions
National Council of Churches of Christ in America
Union Theological Seminary
Yale Divinity School.

## By Degree of Involvement in Asian Affairs

The second and only other major basis for selection of informants was by the degree of their involvement in aspects of Asian affairs. This was classified in three ways.

PRIMARY. The intensive and usually prolonged involvement of the specialist; as a rule, though not always, also including lengthy residence in the country or area of interest, typically, the scholar or educator, journalist, missionary, or government official whose career has been largely or wholly identified with work in Asia or relating to Asia.

SECONDARY: Some degree of professional involvement in an Asian area or problem, either for some brief period in the past or, more typically, during the last six or seven years; often, though not always, including brief visits or sojourns in Asia in connection with this work; e g , the economist concerned in recent years with problems of development, the journalist or publicist who has interested himself in Asian policy problems since these became acute, the government official who has had to make Asia his business, usually since 1949 or even more recently.

INCIDENTAL OR NONE: Shading from some much scantier and peripheral involvement to none at all, except for the impact of day-to-day news and/or the incidental reading of the serious citizen; sometimes, though rarely, individuals in this group have traveled briefly in parts of Asia.

Grouped in this manner, the panel of 181 shows up as follows:

```
Primary . . . . . . . . . . . . . 49
Secondary .   . . . . . . . . . . 59
Incidental or none . . . . . . . . 73
                          TOTAL 181
```

As the panel begins to acquire shape by being grouped under these various headings, certain facts about its members begin to emerge rather strikingly from the initial patterns they tend to form. These are not, as a rule, part of the conscious research design but emerge from it, and they usually turn out to reflect some clearly recognizable realities.

Consider, for example, the group of 49 with primary involvement in Asian affairs. The group includes 25 Indian specialists,[1] 16 China specialists, and 8 others who either were specialists with regard to other countries of Asia or were area "generalists" concerned with wider geographic groupings or problems The fact that there are more India than China specialists is not accidental and will be explained elsewhere But as it stands, the India group turns out to include only 13, or a little more than half, whose involvement in India antedates World War II. Of these all but three are missionaries or businessmen, and even one of these three is the son of a missionary family. There are only two professional scholars whose interest dates back to before 1941, and, characteristically, one deals in the humanities and the other in anthropology Only one of the group comes close to being describable as a journalist, but even his auspices were not primarily journalistic, it is, in fact, impossible to think of any American journalist who made his career primarily by reporting India in the years before the war There is not a single government official or diplomat among these prewar India specialists, for the good and obvious reason that no such specialist-official existed By way of contrast, consider the list of 16 China specialists. They *all* antedate World War II. They include not only missionaries, businessmen, and scholars—the latter in history and political science —but also six journalists and writers, four diplomats, and one army officer, all of whom lived and worked in China for periods ranging from a decade to a lifetime

The lists of those with secondary involvements show similarly meaningful differences. Of the total of 59, 33 have to do with India, and all but one of these postdate World War II, and even the involvement of the single exception was rather scanty and remote. Among the 59, there are only 7 identified with China, and of these five antedate World War II There are 19 others whose involvement tends to cut across various Asian boundaries, all since the war, and

[1] It was estimated in 1953 that there were then "possibly sixty or seventy Americans" in various pursuits with "authoritative knowledge" relating to India (Norman Brown *The United States and India and Pakistan*, Cambridge, 1953, p 265) Even allowing for certain important differences in the criteria used by Professor Brown and those used here, his estimate makes my total of 25 sound like a sizeable proportion of the total number of American specialists on India at the time this study was undertaken

INTRODUCTION 19

many of these are government officials, all of whom encountered Asia as a working problem for the first time in their present jobs, dating back only during the last few years.

These differences illustrate quite sharply the corresponding differences between the degrees and kinds of American involvement with China and India over time, the older, longer, deeper, more varied American preoccupations with the Chinese, and the newer, more recent, more superficial, and more restricted contacts with India. These differences will have a large role to play in the patterns of idea and image which will be unfolded in these pages

## By Travel and Personal Contact

These ideas and images derive in many different ways from the kind and amount of contact these individuals have had with these countries and peoples. Since the relationship between image and contact will be examined in some detail later on, some pains have been taken to group the members of the panel in this respect. Here, again, some rather meaningful facts emerge even from the bare recapitulation of the details

Of the whole panel of 181 only 7 have never been abroad at all.

A total of 112 have traveled or lived in parts of Asia, including 99 who have been in India and 43 in China. Of these, 30 have spent some time in both countries. Within this group also there are 38 who have been in Japan and 48 in Southeast Asia. The periods of time range from a few days to decades, as indicated by this list applying to the China and India groups.

|  | India |  | China |  |
|---|---|---|---|---|
| More than 20 years | 4 |  | 6 |  |
| 10–20 years | 6 | 34% | 3 | 58% |
| 5–10 years | 3 |  | 4 |  |
| 1–5 years | 21 |  | 12 |  |
| 6–12 months | 11 |  | 6 |  |
| 2–5 months | 19 |  | 3 |  |
| 3–6 weeks | 7 |  | 3 |  |
| Less than 3 weeks | 21 |  | 5 |  |
| Duration not given | 7 |  | 1 |  |
| TOTAL | 99 |  | 43 |  |

It is, again, characteristic that of the 34 with more than one year's experience in India, only 13 antedate World War II, while of the 25 in this class in China, all but one go back that far. The larger numbers which show up in the India column for the shorter periods represent, in all but a very few cases, the onset of professional, political, or other interest in India during and since the war. This is especially true of the 30 who have been in India for periods ranging from two to twelve months, and of the 28 whose visits lasted only from a few days to six weeks. For obvious reasons, there are no comparable groups where China is concerned, since Americans stopped going to China after 1949.

Reverting to the panel as a whole, while there are 70 who have never been to any part of Asia at all—corresponding roughly though not precisely to the 73 with incidental or no involvement in Asian affairs—there are only 34 who have never been to Europe. As might be expected of such a group, its travel in the world outside of Asia has been frequent, wide, and often intensive. There are 147 who have been to Europe, of whom 80 record more than a year's time on that continent. There are among them 18 who have also been to Africa, 19 to different parts of the Middle East, and 30 to Latin America.

There are naturally great differences in the kinds and degrees of personal contact these individuals have had with Chinese and Indians, and these obviously influence in many ways the sorts of impressions and ideas they have. In the following listing of the kinds of contact indicated by the members of our panel, it will be noted that only one panelist said he had never encountered any Indian, and 9 had never met any Chinese, and that the great bulk of the contact with both Indians and Chinese has been with visitors and travelers or students in this country. The large number, 51, who noted that they had experienced brief contact with Indians of the official and intellectual classes in India again signals the presence of many panelists who have had recent occasion to travel for short periods to India on various missions.

In the following listing, there are of course panelists who listed more than one kind of contact, and the percentages are added to relate these numbers to the panel-total of 181:

|  | *With Indians* | *With Chinese* |
|---|---|---|
| Extensive, all sorts | (In India) 17 (9%) | (In China) 20 (11%) |
| Extensive, intellectuals, officials, etc. | (In India) 18 (10%) | (In China) 7 (4%) |
| Brief, intellectuals, officials, etc. | (In India) 51 (28%) | (In China) 19 (10%) |

| | | |
|---|---|---|
| Intellectuals, officials, visitors, etc, in U S (or Europe) | 81 (45%) | 57 (32%) |
| Few students in U.S (or Europe) . . | 25 (14%) | 40 (22%) |
| Brief, intellectuals, officials, etc, Formosa only . . . | | 6 (3%) |
| Overseas Chinese only (Southeast Asia) . . . | | 12 (6%) |
| None at all . . . . . . | 1 | 9 (5%) |

## By What They Read

These are all people who work hard at keeping themselves informed. Either in reply to direct questions about what they had read concerning Asia or in passing references, they mentioned over 200 books or authors, 35 newspapers, and 56 American and foreign periodicals. In addition, almost all read their own specialized professional journals and a great variety of special newsletters, bulletins, or reports By far the largest single number, 126, said that they depended for their daily news fare on *The New York Times*. This was a rather remarkable testimonial to the indispensability of that newspaper, since only about half of these individuals actually lived in or near New York.

Besides many scattered mentions of a large number of local dailies in various cities, the other principal newspapers named were the *New York Herald Tribune* (by 37), *Washington Post* (also by 37), and the *Christian Science Monitor* (22) The list of weeklies and periodicals was led by *Time* (43), *Newsweek* (29), *Foreign Affairs* (26), *Harper's* (26), *Atlantic* (25), *Reporter* (23), *Life* (22), and the London *Economist* (17) Although listening to radio news is presumably still an almost universal habit, only a few thought to mention it as a serious source of information about Asia There was no association at all of such information and television.

## By the Vital Statistics

Certain other discernible features of the 181 either follow logically from the major premises of selection or are, in the main, a matter of chance. Again, they form not so much a part of the research design as they are a part of the findings, to which, incidentally, they are often remarkably pertinent.

AGE: Since I have been concerned almost exclusively with people in positions of leadership or importance, it follows that all but a few are of mature age, as follows.

|       |     |
|-------|-----|
| 21–30 | 10  |
| 31–40 | 35  |
| 41–50 | 53  |
| 51–60 | 62  |
| 61–70 | 14  |
| 71–80 | 7   |
| TOTAL | 181 |

ECONOMIC STATUS: An important place in the communications network of our society almost automatically implies a relatively comfortable economic status. Our national sages are more likely nowadays to occupy suites in the Waldorf Towers than a hut on Walden Pond, and to be listened to from a park bench you have to be a millionaire. Almost all the members of this panel unsurprisingly described themselves as belonging to the "middle class." Some, no doubt among the academics, journalists, and government officials, might think of themselves as insufficiently prosperous, but this is a relative state, both of being and of mind. Aside from the missionaries, this panel probably includes very few individuals earning salaries below $9,000 a year, with the bulk of them enjoying, by every indicator, between $10,000 and $20,000, and some moving far, far behind that to the outer regions of pelf. By all the ordinary dollars-and-cents criteria, this must be called an upper-middle to upper group.

EDUCATION: It also follows that with the few usual and notable exceptions of the self-educated, this would tend to be a highly schooled group, and so it turns out to be. Of the 181, only 10 had never gone to college and 12 [2] had attended but not taken degrees. In view of what this study will have to report about the contribution of our educational system to an educated person's knowledge of Asia, it is of more than incidental interest to report that the remaining 159 individuals hold among them, besides a scattering of honorary degrees, a total of 56 Ph.D.'s and 7 other assorted doctoral diplomas, including 2 in medicine, 2 in divinity, and 3 in law, 69 master's degrees, and 173 bachelor's degrees. They hold these from

[2] Four of these, a special subgroup, were still undergraduates when interviewed

116 different institutions of higher learning, including 15 foreign universities and colleges, the largest clusters being: 34 from Harvard, 20 from Columbia, 19 from Yale.

## By the Emergent Profile

The process of bringing together the facts I can use about the contributors to this study has been a process not only of description but of discovery. It has been a little like using the child's drawing board with which, on rubbing a top sheet with finger or pencil, you can bring to light a recognizable likeness hitherto concealed beneath. Although I put this particular board together myself, the features that have been revealed have proved to be even more familiar than I had reason to expect.

I have already given the primary criteria by which individuals were selected for interview. There were certain other bases for deliberate choice. A conscious effort was made, for example, to include some women, some Negroes. Since so many of the informants were well-known public figures, I was obviously aware in advance not only of their professional and public status, but also often of their political complexion and sometimes, in plain cases, of their religious backgrounds. Where I could do so, I made every effort to assure roughly balanced groupings of "liberals" and "conservatives." I made a particularly strenuous effort to include some recognized protagonists of all the most important visible "sides" of public debate on various controversial issues in Asian-American affairs. In some cases, in search of maximum counterbalance to some of the views I was collecting, I deliberately sought out persons from whom I thought I would get views of a different kind—an expectation, I might add, that was not always realized.

These deliberate choices account for some of the distributions in a moderately substantial number of cases. In a great many more, however, the distribution of many of these characteristics was wholly uncalculated. When I approached, say, an officer of an important firm doing business in India, I made no effort to determine in advance whether he was liberal or conservative, Republican or Democrat, Protestant, Catholic, or Jew. I was interested, in effect, in whatever kind of person I found sitting in these places. The result is that by far the larger number of classifications of this kind which appear in the group are a matter of pure chance. This is wholly the case with regard to places of birth; I did conduct a small number of interviews in the Midwest and in California, but I had no interest at all in selecting informants according to their geographic origins.

Despite this large element of the uncontrolled and unchosen, the panel has turned out to have to a remarkable degree many of the more obvious features of our national profile. It is predominantly white (174) and of Protestant background (137) with minorities of Catholics (12), Jews (29)[3], and Negroes (7). In these positions of top and upper-level leadership the panel, like our society, includes along with a large majority of men only a small number of women (13).

Along our national political spectrum, the interviewees distribute themselves likewise in clearly recognizable fashion. By the labels which they used to describe themselves, which I have for 171 of the 181, reading, so to speak, from approximately Right to approximately Left, they emerge as follows

| | |
|---|---|
| "American Nationalist" | 1 |
| "Conservative" | 3 |
| "Republican" | 36 |
| "Progressive Moderate" | 2 |
| "Liberal Conservative" | 2 |
| "Democrat" | 65 |
| "Independent" | 35 |
| "Nonpartisan" | 2 |
| "Earl Warren Republican or Middle-of-the road Democrat" | 1 |
| "Liberal Independent" | 5 |
| "Free Man" | 1 |
| "Liberal" | 11 |
| "Left of Center" | 1 |
| "More repelled by Republicans than by Democrats" | 1 |
| "Socialist" | 2 |
| "Democratic Socialist" | 1 |
| "Independent Social Democrat" | 1 |
| "Radical" | 1 |
| "Don't classify myself" | 1 |
| Unavailable | 9 |
| TOTAL | 181 |

[3] The larger number of Jews as compared to Catholics is, of course, a departure from the national pattern. It is doubtful whether a census of people occupying the positions and levels tapped for this study would justify this difference

INTRODUCTION 25

If we clip off the extremes and prorate the liberals to the three remaining large groups on this list, the result shows roughly 69 Democrats, 47 Republicans, and 44 Independents These proportions come surprisingly close to the national estimates generally used by the major political parties in the 1952 election campaign. As projected by George Gallup, they showed the country to be divided among 22 million Democrats, 17.5 million Republicans, 15.5 million Independents.[4]

There is another and perhaps more meaningful basis for describing the political complexion of the interviewees Besides being asked for the political labels they applied to themselves, they were also asked to register their measure of agreement or disagreement with the views of thirteen important figures in national political life, selected to range along a scale from "liberal" to "conservative," as these terms are used in American politics, i.e., from Chester Bowles, Harry Truman, and Adlai Stevenson through President Eisenhower to John Foster Dulles, Senator Knowland, and General Douglas MacArthur. On this scale the findings are

<pre>
Liberal . . . . . . . . 96
Mixed  . . . . . . . . 36
Conservative . . . . . . . 27
Unavailable . . . . . . 22
</pre>

By laying these indications alongside the self-labels given by the interviewees themselves, I find these interesting juxtapositions

<pre>
96 "Liberals" . . . .  44 "Democrats"
                       13 "Republicans"
                       20 "Independents"
                       12 "Liberals" or "Liberal
                              Independents"
                        4 "Socialists"
                        1 Other

36 "Mixed"    . . . .  13 "Democrats"
                       13 "Republicans"
                        7 "Independents"
                        1 "Liberal"
                        1 "Socialist"
                        1 Other

27 "Conservatives" . .  4 "Democrats"
                       17 "Republicans"
                        6 "Independents"
</pre>

[4] American Institute of Public Opinion, January 1, 15, 17, 1952.

Here, despite the unavoidable imprecisions of American political terminology and the large chance of error through indefiniteness, it seems quite possible to glimpse a wholly familiar reflection of the American political profile, in which certain regional and ideological features superimpose themselves on the fictions of formal identifications. It is remarkable here only insofar as it emerges in this fashion from a random number of people selected primarily for quite other reasons.

Perhaps the most striking and certainly the most unplanned of these correspondences occurs in the matter of distribution by place of birth. In almost all other respects that have been mentioned there was at least some measure of choice present, but the matter of birthplace never in any way entered the process of selection. As already indicated, these 181 individuals were chosen only in terms of who and what they were in relation to communications in our society. All but a few are now located in the northeastern part of the country, where most of the interviews took place. Nevertheless, it developed that these 181 individuals were born—and usually raised and often educated—in 35 of the 48 states and in 12 foreign countries. Those born abroad include 4 Americans born in China and 4 in India, but the remaining 9 countries represent almost all the principal sources of origin of immigrants to this country over the generations.

Plotted against the regional figures for total population and for total number of college graduates, these distributions disclose a quite unexpected measure of correspondence to our national profile, excepting only for the South, which by this count would be underrepresented in the panel. I offer these figures as some kind of testimony to the mobility among these elements of our population, but I trust that it is plain that they do not bear in any significant way on the present study. No attempt was made to group any regional communications patterns as such. Certain geographic factors are of course meaningful but are illustrated in the panel only by individual examples, i.e., a Midwestern Congressman will be likely to reflect some of the characteristics of Midwestern political outlooks; Midwesterners also seem to have had more early contact with missionary enterprise; Californians in certain age brackets may have some distinctive patterns of early experience relating to Chinese, some Southerners may be conditioned a bit differently on matters relating to race. These will all be mentioned in their place, but as individual cases, not as statistics.

So much, then, for the premises of selection, the main groupings, the vital statistics, and the emergent profile. They add up to about all I can tell about the interviewees without disclosing names or identities. It is good if this information helps to make the panel of informants more recognizable as a group, and even better if it reinforces in some measure the sense of validity of the findings based upon what they have said But I must stress once more and finally that these numbers will not be used, as such, to support distributions in any larger universe. In their respective groupings these individuals are presented as examples, not as a stratified sample, of their kinds. I repeat, this does not mean that I will not try to draw larger sense from their assembled uniquenesses. It simply means that in doing so I will be governed by my own appreciation of the material before me, not by the showing of the digits.

### THE INTERVIEWS

All but 19 of the 181 individuals in the panel were subjected to approximately the same interview.

The 19 include the 12 with whom I had the first exploratory conversations and 7 others whom, for various reasons, I had to interview in a similarly informal manner. The material from these interviews covers much, though not all, of the important ground covered by the more systematic schedule used in the great bulk of the interviews. It has been collated with all the rest and, as far as it goes, has been included in the results.

In the other 162 cases, it is necessary to say that "approximately" the same interview was held, because it was impossible to complete precisely the same number of questions with every person Inevitably, there were some informants with too little to say on some matters and some with too much to say on others. In some instances, there were unavoidable restrictions on time, so that choices had to be made, some questions covered and the rest foregone Finally, some groups of questions were used for short periods, like mobile batteries, aimed at temporary targets when they appeared and withdrawn according to circumstances, e.g, questions relating to the Dienbienphu crisis in 1954 or, early in 1955, to the Quemoy-Matsu island issue. These remained quite incidental to the main attack, which was sustained and constant throughout and produced a great majority of substantially completed interviews. The various occasional omissions mean, however, that the tabulations and groupings of answers do not always neatly add up to the total of 181.

The interview itself was designed not merely to extract opinions and information but to give the fullest possible freedom to the play of association, memory, idea, for the retrieval of the forgotten bits and pieces of experience from which we all draw so much of what we think. It attempted to combine several kinds of interrogation. It tried to draw—of course in varying degree and with varying success—on the ground-covering directness of the serious journalist, the question-wording care of the opinion researcher, the detail-interest of the anthropologist, a few of the probing techniques of the psychiatrist, and some of the built-in measuring tools of the more formal social scientist. Within the limits of the time it took—usually two but sometimes three or four hours—it was moderately thorough, occasionally exhausting, and—to judge from interviewee reaction—seldom dull. As already indicated, it was conducted on the basis of a rigid commitment that there would be no quotation attributed to any identifiable individual. This has offered some problems of presentation, but these are almost all a matter of form and style and are, I trust, solved in these pages without default.

More than half and often two-thirds of the interview time was given over to probing for attitudes and feelings and their sources. It made mild use of the technique of free association through which the informant, rather than the interviewer, introduced the leads that were then followed by persistent questioning. The probing was for associations and impressions, even the most vagrant ideas, notions, or images relating to China and India and to Chinese and Indians. Thus the interview schedule would show questions like: "When you think of China, what comes to your mind?" Or: "When you think of these Indians you have met or known, what comes to your mind about them?" It would not, of course, show the further questions, sometimes dozens of them, which the initial answers provoked and which were never asked to lead but always to pursue. The remainder of the interview was designed to unfold the individual's principal sources of information, his major identifications in public affairs, the quality of his knowledge about current Asian politics and problems, his views of contemporary China and India and of American

INTRODUCTION

policy problems relating to them, his opinions of what was being done and what ought to be done, his expectations for the future. Most of this information could be recorded in short answers to various batteries of rapid-fire questions.

With notably few exceptions, the individuals interviewed proved responsive, communicative, candid, and often quite stimulated by the unfamiliar experience of self-examination in these particular matters. Despite preliminary explanations, the interview was usually not at all what they expected. The surprise and novelty of the opening questions tended to loosen any initial inhibitions. Recall was quick and easy for some, quite difficult for others, but once the juices began to flow, the process of remembering and thinking *about* one's thoughts continued for the rest of the interview. I noticed few departures from the fact, well known to any reporter, that there is no more fascinating subject to a person than what he himself thinks or feels. A serious inquiry into this subject is an honest kind of flattery, and there are few so utterly self-contained as not to respond to it. This would be especially true when, as was usually the case, the subject matter did not appear to draw too close to the more sensitive areas of the self. When, as sometimes happened, it unexpectedly did so, the effects were as a rule quite instructive, for by that time the mood for candor generally had been established.

Much of what was asked had to do with impressions that were often vaguely held and rarely, if ever, put in words before. The interviewee found himself called upon to remember, to express, to explain, and, so to speak, to document a whole collection of his own hitherto unexamined ideas or notions. This was frequently a salutary and sobering experience, as many ultimately remarked. Such an inquiry may be easier to make in the present American cultural setting in which people have grown used to the idea of having doorbells rung by a question-asker and in which people of the kind involved in this study have become especially aware of the importance and validity of social science research. In most other cultures of which I know anything, communication at the level achieved in the present interviews occurs only after a much more explicit personal identification and relationship has been established. To be sure, I was personally acquainted with many of those whom I sought out, but to many more I was a total stranger. I was met by fewer than half a dozen refusals, whereas scores of stereotypically rushed and busy Americans, often in high places, stopped to give a stranger two hours or more of their time to answer questions that entered quite deep areas of their life histories, experience, and states of mind. I had the repeated experience of entering such a man's office—or in many cases, his home—with no other introduction than my previous letter, and of plunging him, in a matter of minutes, into a process of self-examination which was often new, arousing, and even disturbing to him There was, in all cases, the knowledge of the legitimacy of the auspices of the study, but there was also an implicit understanding of the usefulness and importance of participating in research, an automatic acceptance of the good faith of the pledge of confidence, a notable degree of candor, a free and interesting yielding to the spirit of the inquiry. This was most impressive in itself, quite apart from the merits of these individuals or the quality or content of the ideas they turned out to hold. In more ways than one, these 181 men and women have been my teachers.

What I learned I took down verbatim in all essentials. No use was made of convenient synonyms. The actual language of the interviewee was recorded, ultimately transcribed onto cards, and shuffled with all the others for analysis by a variety of methods in a variety of combinations. The yes-or-no or otherwise short answers were, of course, easily recorded, and later also transferred to cards. These records are the primary materials from which this report has been written.

But these are by no means all Besides these 181 interviews, there were innumerable other conversations in a great assortment of places. I naturally formed the habit of throwing some of my questions at any target of opportunity, and must have often made an odd kind of occupant of the next seat on a plane or chance sharer of a dining car table, not to say a rather odd kind of host in my own home. Much that was salient in these brief encounters found its way into the diary notes which were kept mainly to record impressions and ideas gleaned from the interviews as they accumulated The interviews themselves opened up many other paths of investigation, and some of these were traveled for a fair distance. References to movies as sources led to the commissioning of a separate study in Hollywood, to which further reference will be made. Cullings were taken from the press, the *Congressional Record,* and a number of other sources to check the appearance and recurrence of many of the most common images indicated by the interviewees. Frequent mention of comics and cartoons led to a collection of samples from news-

INTRODUCTION 31

papers and magazines over many years. Recurring mentions of certain books and authors sent me back for an extended rereading of a shelfful of novels, stories, and other works, newly seen this time for the images they created and the influence they exerted. The search for historical sources led to many other shelves and stacks, including some in my own mind long unvisited, producing re-examination and reappraisal of material first encountered long ago All this too is woven into the fabric of this report and forms an essential part of its design.

### THE INTERVIEWER

As may be evident by now, it is a basic proposition here that an inquiry cannot be divorced from the inquirer. Another inquirer might have asked different questions or asked the same questions differently The reader therefore has the right and the need to know the relevant things not only about the question-answerers and the questions put, but also about the question-asker. Some of these have doubtless already emerged in these pages, but before I can finally banish the more obvious presence of the first person singular, I will have to set forth as directly as I can something about my own credentials, ideas, biases, and approach, and their possible influence on this inquiry.

If I had been on the answering instead of the asking end of this study, I would have had to be identified as a writer in motion between the spheres of journalism and scholarship, emigrant or commuter—I am not sure which—between the mass media and the academic world. My professional training has been that of a reporter. I would also have to be placed among those described as having primary involvement in matters pertaining to Asia This would be based on about eight years' residence and travel, before, during, and after World War II, the bulk of it in China, with only occasional visitor status in India, as part of a much longer period of almost exclusive preoccupation with Asian politics and international relations. My personal contacts would be extensive with Chinese of all sorts in China, though mostly with the kind of people most likely to be interested in politics and ideas, and much more limited with Indians, who would be exclusively of the latter sort

This history suggests the possible presence, or danger, of certain biases There are certainly limits to my ability to identify or discount them all, but this exercise in explicitness requires me to try.

My own greater interest in China in past years might have led me, for example, to gravitate, especially among the specialists, to China people. In fact, the panel, as already indicated, ended up with 25 identified as primarily involved with India and 16 with China. Since there are so few India specialists and relatively so many more for China, this is clearly disproportionate, at least in the numerical sense. But the reasons for this go beyond any attempt merely to compensate for possible error through natural gravitation. China people are not only more numerous but in certain respects better known, not only to me personally but because of the high visibility of the China problem during the last decade or so of sharp public controversy. It was comparatively easy to make a selection that would include not only types in different fields but also known protagonists for different points of view. The India specialists were not only fewer in number but tended also to be scholars, missionaries, or businessmen whose views, say, on current Indian politics, would not usually be available to me until I sought them out and asked them. In the matter of underlying images and personal reactions, this was always a matter of fresh discovery, even in the case of China specialists well known to me I found, however, much greater relative uniformity on this score among the China people than among the India specialists and had to reach out for larger numbers of the latter to get a clearer and fairer picture of the range of attitudes.

I have already mentioned that I was personally acquainted with many whom I interviewed. Since my whole personal history has been in the news field and, more broadly, in the field of communications relating to Asia, it would have been impossible for me to seek out so many people in important roles in precisely this field without reaching many whom I would know. As I check the list of interviewees I note, as a matter of fact, that of the total of 181, I had previously known 82. In addition there were 10 whom I did not know personally who indicated during the interview that they were acquainted with me through having read something I had written Of the 82 there are 30 individuals whom I could say I knew quite well and 52 with whom my acquaintance was primarily professional. I am bound to say that I have taken a long look at these 82 names to try to determine whether in fact any biased selection did take place. I come up with the following observations.

INTRODUCTION                                                                  33

- They are all individuals more or less prominently but in every case legitimately identifiable either as Asian specialists of some kind or as leading figures in mass communications, government, politics, or the academic world. Anybody setting out to assemble such a panel would of course have a wide range of possible selection, but I would venture to say that a good half of these names would recur on any such list no matter by whom assembled.
- These selections were in many cases made precisely to ensure an adequate distribution or balance of known identifications, opinions, and views on relevant public issues. There might be mutual acquaintance, but by no means always mutual agreement. There was as a rule some measure of mutual respect, but by no means always mutual admiration. In any case, the primary interest of this inquiry has been not in political opinions but in the underlying structure of ideas, images, reactions. These were areas seldom, if ever, purposefully explored before Even with close friends of many years, the interview was almost always an experience of revelation.
- Insofar as "rapport" is an important element in interviewing, it is possible that personal acquaintance might affect it either way. in such an encounter speech might be freer or it might, in matters touching upon the individual's ego and his sight of himself in the other's eye, be more inhibited. I can only report that in my notes on the subject of candor, I find only a few cases where I noted some reservations, and these involve both people I knew and people to whom I was a complete stranger before the interview.

Another possible source of bias could conceivably be the injection of my own opinions, images, or prejudices into the interview situation. An interviewer, as is known, can often extract the answers he wants from a sufficiently pliable interviewee, or else the answers can be more indirectly influenced by what the interviewee *thinks* the interviewer wants to hear. Strenuously disciplined effort was made to exclude these risks from the present interviews The nonleading character of the questioning was rigidly preserved. Interviewees of course sometimes would wind up answers by asking· "Don't you think so?" Or: "Do you agree?" Or simply· "What do *you* think?" These efforts to open a discussion were invariably turned aside. I tried—I believe, successfully—to remain an unreacting question-asker, taking it as my task to accept all views or remarks with interest, to be surprised—at least visibly—by none, and certainly never to offer challenge, debate, or provocation. I can report, diffidently but with satisfaction, that a number of interviewees offered unsolicited testimonials on this account. One of them, himself a highly reputed investigator, told a private seminar that he had *tried* during our interview to figure out what the interviewer wanted or expected to hear but had been unable to do so.

Naturally, I have my own views on most of the major political issues in Asian-American relations and have generally been able to put them into print in various places over the years. An examination of these would show, again by the modes in which the interviewees have been grouped, that my political label would now probably be "left-of-center independent," and on the scale of identifications included in the interview, I would probably turn up "liberal," meaning only that I find more sense in Chester Bowles' views about Asia than in Senator Knowland's.

The question of other kinds of bias is somewhat more complicated. My own experience enabled me to recognize many of the impressions volunteered by panelists After all, I had met all the same kinds of people they had, read almost all the books they mentioned, shared in many of the same kinds of experience to which they referred, and formed from them my own attitudes. These undoubtedly shape the observations I make of the ideas and images that have emerged from the interviews. Like everyone else, I prefer to think of my attitudes as judgments and my reasons for them as reasonable. If I still have any undisciplined prejudices, they no doubt show up in the substance of this book whether I will it or not. I can only hope that if they do, they do not too grossly mar or obscure the pages on which they appear.

This inquiry shaped itself out of the elements that have here been described I have functioned primarily as a reporter who has borrowed some of the systematizing tools of social science while at the same time retaining a flexible appreciation of the term "objectivity" as it is applied to the study of human behavior Social scientists have only just begun to examine the nature of intercultural experience as it affects individuals. They have only begun to explore the links between culture and personality. They have barely glimpsed from the threshold the great complexities of this matter It does not lend itself easily to predictable order or simple measurement. Whether he learned it long ago from the philosophers or the poets, or more recently from the nuclear physicists, the student of human behavior must know that the observer, his location, and his method

INTRODUCTION 35

are all undetachable parts of every observation, and that every observation remains subject to the awareness that the aspect of knowledge is constantly changing.

There is more than one kind of relevance for this study in the following passage from Robert Oppenheimer

> To what appear to be the simplest questions, we will tend to give either no answer or an answer which will at first sight be reminiscent more of a strange catechism than of the straightforward affirmatives of physical science If we ask, for instance, whether the position of the electron remains the same, we must say 'no", if we ask whether the electron's position changes with time, we must say "no"; if we ask whether the electron is at rest, we must say "no", if we ask whether it is in motion, we must say "no" The Buddha has given such answers when interrogated as to the conditions of man's self after his death; but they are not familiar answers for the tradition of seventeenth- and eighteenth-century science.[5]

It is to be hoped that the study presented here offers not quite so strange a catechism It reports a series of interlocking observations affected in many ways by what this particular observer is sensitized to, the selections he makes, the frame in which he finds it possible to fit them. They form a compound, like Oppenheimer's physics, "of complementary views, each supplementing the other, neither telling the whole story."

[5] *Science and the Common Understanding*, New York, 1954, p. 40

PART ONE

———————— ✤ ————————

"ASIA"

IN 1942, four months after Pearl Harbor, an opinion poll found that 60 per cent of a national sample of Americans could not locate either China or India on an outline map of the world. By the war's end there were more Americans who could identify and approximately locate such places as Chungking, Manila, and Vladivostok. A smaller number could identify Okinawa, Osaka, Kyushu, and Java, although a majority, even of college-educated people, were still unable to locate Singapore, and it had not yet occurred to the pollsters in 1945 even to ask about place names in India.[1]

Vagueness about Asia has been until now the natural condition even of the educated American. There has been little in his total setting to equip him with much knowledge or information—not to speak of affinities—relating to Asia or things Asian. There is certainly nothing to compare with the intricate web of bonds that tie him in so many different ways to Europe and things European—his near or remote origins, cultural roots, language, religion, history, picture of the world. America was born and grew up in the generations of Europe's world paramountcy, it outgrew Europe's power without ever severing the European parental tie. This makes it diffi-

---

[1] Polls dated March 26, 1942 and May 2, 1945, in *Public Opinion, 1935-1946*, edited by Hadley Cantril, prepared by Mildred Strunk, Princeton, 1951, p 265.

cult for many to realize even now that the European age has ended, that the center of gravity in world affairs has shifted, that Western Europe has to be seen once more as a peninsula at one end of the great Eurasian continent.

On the other hand, consider a paradox: the history of America's emergence as a major world power has been peculiarly linked to Asia and its rise as a primary setting for decisive world events. The first foreign war fought by this country in its maturing period made it a Pacific power. The first major stroke of American diplomacy with a prime impact on world affairs outside this hemisphere was the Open Door initiative of 1899 relating to China. It was an American act that "opened" Japan to the world a century ago, helping to initiate the history that moved on to Tsushima Straits and to Portsmouth in 1905, to Washington in 1921, to Mukden in 1931, and to Pearl Harbor in 1941. It was the explosion of the struggle for the Pacific rather than any culminating event in Europe which finally pushed this country into the Second World War. In the new and even greater power conflicts ushered in by the end of that war, Asia quickly became a major theater, scene of some of the most fateful outcomes and decisions of our current history. America could not conceivably have gone to war over Poland in 1939. It did not even go to war when Britain stood so mortally threatened in 1940. But it did go to war in Korea in 1950 and has almost gone to war more than once since in the Formosa Strait.

In a manner unthinkable even to most thoughtful Americans hardly more than a dozen years ago, China has become a major factor in domestic American politics, seating and unseating men in high office, building or wrecking public reputations, filling the press and the air for months and years on end with concern, alarm, controversy, hand-wringing, recrimination, and contumely. China has become a central and often even a dominating factor in the host of decisions forced on the United States by its new place in world affairs; it affects in some degree our relations with every other nation, friend or foe, on the globe.

China, it can be said, has long been with us. But consider the wholly "new" fact of India. India has had almost no existence at all either in our history or in the minds of most living Americans up to a few years ago. If the marks made upon us in the past by China are visible scratches, those made by India are faint lines which have to be searched out to be seen. Yet in the ten years since the emergence of the independent state of India, it has forced itself upon our awareness, required us to deal with it as a major factor in world affairs, both for its own sake and for its relation to China in the unfolding complex of the new intercontinental shape of things. Smaller in size and weight but scarcely less insistent in their claim upon our attention, the other "new" countries of Asia—Pakistan, Ceylon, Malaya, Indonesia, Burma, Viet Nam, the Philippines—also seek their places in the great new rearrangements with which we must somehow cope

Despite all this, despite the important role of Japan and China in our history before 1941, and of China and India since then, all but a very few Americans—including most of those in high places—have continued through almost all this time to view the rest of the world as though all of it lay across and beyond the Atlantic. Captive to their own cultural bonds and to the picture of the world conveyed by history as they learned it and by the old maps still so largely used in our schools, they have kept their eyes focused on the closer and more recognizable landscapes of Europe. They have seen Asia only beyond it dimly, as "far" and "east" when, just over the northwesterly curve of the globe, much nearer than they realized, the countries and peoples of whom Americans knew so little were shaping so much of the American destiny. Even now we still refer to parts of Asia as "Far" and "Near" and "Middle" as if the most important thing about them were still their distance looking eastward from London. In fact this "east" is in many crucial ways still too "far" to have any real place in our national consciousness. Hardly anything marks more clearly the limits of the American world outlook than the official and popular acceptance of the term "East-West struggle" to describe our conflict with Russia. It suggests how unthinkingly we can still accept the notion that "East" means Eastern Europe, how truly dim and undefined the farther "East" really is, how unblinkingly we give currency to a term that cuts us off psychologically from that "East" and allows Russia so much more easily to identify with it. There is virtually no room in our minds for a sense of the meaning the term "East-West struggle" has or can be made to have for the peoples of Asia. An American Secretary of State, John Foster Dulles, betrayed the limits of his grasp of reality and of what he includes in "the world" when he insisted, in February, 1956, that *"all the world* regards [Goa] as a Portuguese province."

Yet not even all this implies a total lack of awareness. Knowledge is a highly relative matter, our minds are occupied by much more than orderly thought. It is true that most of us "learn" very little about Asia; yet it is also true that we "learn" a great deal. It became a familiar experience during these interviews to hear an individual describe Asia as a cipher in his thinking and then to spend an hour or more uncovering, often to his astonishment, the surprisingly varied array of things he actually carried somewhere in his head on the subject. There are in fact all sorts of scratches on American minds about Asia—associations, images, notions, ideas, information, attitudes, gleaned and acquired in fragments over time from childhood or under the more recent pressures of contemporary events To our appreciations of these events we bring, many of us, the wispy products of the classroom, church, Sunday school, remembered bits out of storybooks and magazines, cartoons and photographs, motion pictures, newspaper headlines and columns, impressions gleaned from friends or acquaintances Many of these deposits left in American minds have in common a quality of remoteness, of the exotic, the bizarre, the strange and unfamiliar, and —until the day before yesterday—a lack of connection with the more visibly important affairs of life. There is, of course, no obvious logic or consistency or order in the way these semiectoplasmic notions inhabit corners of our thinking. They recur in different individuals spasmodically and in dismembered pieces They are sparse in substance yet capable of long life and prodigious multiplication These, like a set of hieroglyphics or cave drawings, became the starting points of our inquiry.

*When you think of Asia, what comes to your mind?*

To this first question in the interview, the first response was often blank surprise. This sometimes truly mirrored an initial blankness Nothing or almost nothing moved clearly and plainly in the mind's foreground; the summons had to reach some remoter mental cranny to arouse an answer. Sometimes it was not blankness but the bewilderment of having to choose suddenly from a clutter of ready replies. One way or the other, the differences in number and kinds of answers provided their own first measure of the differences in all the people to whom the question was put: those to whom Asia was big and complex and far and those to whom it was big and complex and near; those who saw it in a broad blur and those who

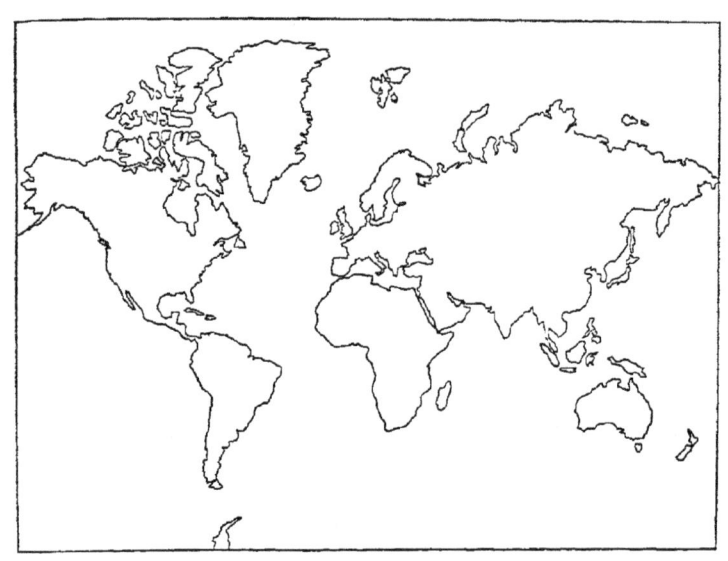

*In the familiar old Mercator world centered on Greenwich, the "East" was far and vast . .*

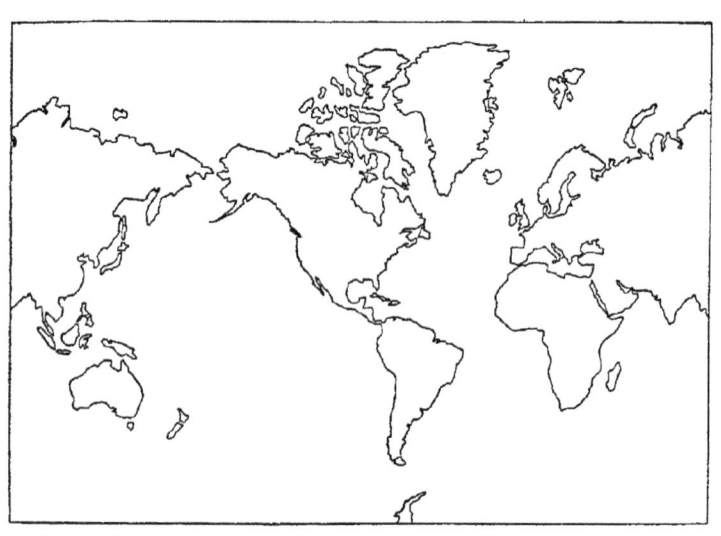

*while in this new American arrangement, centered on Peoria, its shapes and directions are confusingly different*

saw it in some particular, a continent, region, country, or place, people in an undistinguishable mass or individuals with faces and names; those for whom it evoked a misty glamor or else a grim tableau; those who thought of past or present history, societies, politics, problems, and those who thought of themselves in some personal relation to it all

From by far the largest number (139), a first response to a geographic term, Asia, was a geographic image, starting with the map itself, all the great expanse of it carried in outline on some mental screen first exposed in the early grades of school. The location of Asia on this world map which so many of us carry around in our heads is a matter of some importance. A study of geography texts being used in American elementary and secondary schools as late as 1944 showed that all, without a single exception, contained world maps which placed Europe—or more specifically, England—at the center, along the Greenwich meridian. This made it necessary to bisect the Pacific longitudinally just west of the tip of Alaska, with all of Asia thus placed to the east of Europe.[2] It is from this picture of the world that we derive the persistently surviving term "the Far East."

In the last ten years or so, American map makers have begun to take a somewhat more patriotic view of the world, instead of Europe, they place North America in the world's center. The effect—besides moving the center of the world from Greenwich to the longitude of Peoria, Illinois—is to leave Japan and a chunk of eastern Asia visible on the west, with the remainder of a truncated Asia reappearing far, again, in the east. The latest Rand McNally *Cosmopolitan Atlas* (1953), for example, still for most purposes uses the older arrangement with a divided Pacific But it also shows a map on which the dividing line is drawn through Soviet Central Asia, along the borders of Afghanistan and Pakistan, and past the city of Bombay on India's west coast. The literal-minded schoolboy, shown this map and asked to define the "Far East," would look carefully and reply. "Iran, Pakistan, and Afghanistan." He might then, quite logically, call India the "Far West." China would then become, no doubt, the "Middle West" and Japan the "Near West." In the interests of simple consistency one could not stop here with adapting the old

[2] *Treatment of Asia in American Textbooks*, Committee on Asiatic Studies, American Council on Education, and American Council, Institute of Pacific Relations, New York, 1946, p 50.

"ASIA" 43

terms to the new arrangement. If Iran and Pakistan become the "Far East," then surely Athens and Rome must fall within our new "Middle East," and this, of course, places the "Near East" smack down on the Place de la Concorde and Piccadilly Circus. There is plainly no end to the possible absurdities of map making and geographic terminology.

Air-age maps centered on the North Pole and showing the continents in somewhat more realistic relationships are increasingly available, but it is doubtful whether any but a few intercontinental airmen as yet carry the air-age image of the world in their heads It is certain that for anyone over ten years old today, the mental picture of the world map is still the good old Mercator, with the Pacific cut in two, as though it ended indeed on the sharp edge of nothingness, and with the vast expanse of Asia way over there where it belongs, in the far, far east.

It is precisely this vast expanse which emerges as the next most powerful image, a first, single, and overwhelming sense of

> size, great size, huge, vast size, a huge land mass, the continent, the great vast continent . . .

All the vagueness of the way in which we are schooled about the geography of Asia, or all the accidental varieties of reading, travel, or personal experience, can then find reflection in the way this outline is filled in or in some way particularized. The boundaries of Asia, for example, are visualized not as a matter of precise fact but of individual fancy or fantasy, certainly of individual preoccupation, focus, or circumstance. Thus the mind's eye might go in one direction, taking in "Asia" from Japan east or from Pakistan west, or the mind's light might settle on some single large segment grown more familiar through some accident of special knowledge or interest

> I think of China and Southeast Asia rather than of India, see from Indochina down to Singapore, around the Malay Peninsula; Southeast Asia and India stand clear in the foreground while central and eastern Asia fade off beyond, think of eastern Asia, see Siberia looming large, see the coastline clearly but don't get very far inland. . . .

The focus begins to fall on

> the islands, the curve of the coast, the different parts, the great subdivisions . . .

and finally comes to rest on particular countries, either on China alone (24) or India alone (15), or, in the large total of 93 cases, on China and India both.

As we move on with some of our panelists into these continental areas, countries, and places, they quickly cease to be empty spaces on an outline map of land and water. Features of the landscape begin to appear:

> the Himalayas; low-lying Indian villages towns, and cities, wide dusty plains of North China, the flooded valley of the Yangtze . .

and the most visible of the great architectural monuments.

> the Taj Mahal at Agra, the Temple of Heaven and Forbidden City in Peking, the Great Wall of China. .

The differences between the images seen through the frames of the imagination and those of the memory, the parting of romance from reality, begin to show up in clusters like these:

> so far away and so different, all the mystery, all the picturesque elements, a sense of exotic adventure, teak, ivory, elephants, incense peacocks, sarongs, postage stamps, spices, cymbals, gongs, camel trains . .

compared to

> open spaces, mountains, river valleys, villages, primitive farming, bright hot deserts, wet paddy fields, smells .

These scenes begin to fill, with people and pictures, with figures and figments, with fragments of history, personal and political, dim, early, late, and current, and with impressions, prejudices, and opinions. Brought all together, these compose the total stuff of which this study is made, seen here first as through a kaleidoscope

The places of Asia are first of all and overwhelmingly filled with people—

> a lot of people, masses, teeming masses, a plague of people, of one and a half billion people, vast numbers, hordes of people, the largest populations in the world. . . .

This is, moreover, for almost everybody, an image of

> a barefoot, hungry, starving mass, masses of families eking out a bare existence in villages, in overcrowded cities, beggars, peasants, coolies, suffering all the hardships of an extremely low standard of living. . . .

This overwhelming image of an undifferentiated crush of humanity was summoned up instantly by a large number (80) and for many this is the "Asia" that carries with it a dread blur of mystery and fearfulness, associated with vast numbers, with barbarism, and with disease.[8] In many other minds, however, there is also a strong sense of great diversity, of many kinds, nations, classes, castes. For some it becomes peculiarly important to mention that people in Asia are

> dark people, brown people, people of dark skin, yellow to brown; the whole Oriental race, dark-skinned people in tremendous numbers spread out everywhere, with deep-seated prejudices against whites. . .

For other, larger numbers of individuals certain other distinctions are important

> they are heathen, people with other gods, different religious concepts, religiosity: cultural, religious, language differences, customs strange to an American, the idea of the Eastern soul, mind, mentality, morals, different from ours, they are difficult to understand, they are different. . .

The more remote the association evoked by "Asia," the more likely it is to be an image that is broad, or vague, or at least static When we come to the association of "Asia" with oneself, the blurred largeness of it is more often reduced to some single but clear and meaningful personal experience or point of contact brought plainly into view It could still be a distant memory, something out of childhood, like

> the Chinese students who used to come to my father's house, the souvenirs my uncle brought back, the missionaries who visited my home . . .

or the quick unshuttering of

> my own years in China; in India, my first view of Asia from a Liberty ship going up the Hooghly River into Calcutta . .

or emotional reactions in endlessly different combinations·

---

[8] On the subject of "Asian flu," the *Boston Globe*, Sept 7, 1957, reported "To relieve worried Bay Staters, the state director [of health] stressed that there is nothing serious or mysterious about the disease because the descriptive term 'Asian is attached to it That name was applied simply because the first outbreak occurred in the Far East, explained Dr Fecmster 'I would have preferred calling it 'Boston flu' because no one is ever afraid of anything coming from Boston.'"

a warm feeling, of friendships and personal associations, a shrinking feeling; my sense of satisfaction over a job well done, my sense of frustration; I liked India, felt happy and at home there, India repelled me, depressed me; warm, kindly, friendly people; semiaboriginal humanity, spiritual people, superstitious people, my affection for the Chinese, loved it in China, felt at home there from the start; China a great mystery to me, China never intrigued me, have no emotions about it; I like the surface unemotionalism, I never knew where I was with the Chinese, what is it about Asia that gets under the skin of Westerners exposed to it?

Even from these first few glimpses of the range and variety of responses, it may be possible to feel the range and variety of reactions to *difference*. For some it has been a romantic attraction ("all the picturesque mystery, exotic adventure") or repulsion ("a shrinking feeling"). For some it evokes a positive response ("warm feeling of friendships") and for others quite the opposite ("India repelled me") It can imply or plainly become a feeling of contemptuous hostility ("heathen") or fearful hostility ("a plague of people') or a more complicated combination of both ("dark-skinned people in tremendous numbers spread out everywhere"). All of these and many others will appear and reappear many times as the inquiry unfolds. They will vary widely in form, acuteness, and effect, developing out of different measures and combinations of particular personality traits, outlook, knowledge, or an aggravated condition of ignorance.

We do not expect to be able to say much about the place of individual personality traits in these patterns of response We shall try to deal with the more graspable elements of outlook, knowledge, and ignorance. But even these, it seems necessary to note here, are embraced by the less tangible issue of personality. For some individuals the common denominator of simple humanity is apparently enough to enable them to sustain and absorb the shock of almost every kind of human encounter and experience. Most others seem to need the support of some familiarity, some knowledge, some basis for rationalizing the differences they discover. On the other hand, we have observed that empathy is not always necessarily related to knowledge. There are members of our present panel who have lived whole lifetimes in Asia and still react to the sense of difference with something close to acute hostility. There are others who have never been nearer to Asia than a Chinese restaurant in their home city whose reaction to difference remains mild, curious, friendly, or at least open-pored We shall eventually have to wrestle as best we can with the reasons why any two of our people have reacted differently to the same thing. But meanwhile let the reader never be wholly unaware of the specter of personality that hovers over these pages.

Whatever their distinctive individual traits may be, a great many of our panelists share, from way back, an aggravated condition of ignorance about Asia. This is the normal condition Any greater state of knowledge is unusual and derives invariably from special individual circumstances.

Consider first what most of the members of this panel learned about Asia in school No one is likely to claim that the American school child emerges from the classroom with an adequate picture of the world he lives in, even of his own nearby world, or of its history. But ignorance is a highly relative matter There is some quality of knowledge and identification even in the simplest awareness of England-Magna Carta-Shakespeare-Drake-Queen Elizabeth-King George-1776, or of France-Lafayette-Revolution, or Greece-gods, Rome-Caesar But when we come to consider Asia, the identifications are either of quite a different order or nonexistent. These are countries, cultures, and peoples that lie almost entirely outside the world that was discovered to most of our interviewees in their time at school. Later accidents of bent, circumstance, experience, and education turned some of them into individuals with some specialized knowledge of Asia But for all except a rare few, the world as they learned of it at school included Asia only marginally or not at all. Their scattered recall of classroom gleanings conforms almost exactly in all important particulars to the picture we have of the way Asia figured in American schooling from a number of studies of American textbooks commonly in use in American schools during the last fifty years.

In the study *Treatment of Asia in American Textbooks*, it was found that in 1944 an average of about 7 per cent of all the space in elementary and secondary school geography texts was devoted to Asia Of this the bulk was usually given over to China, with something about pigtails, bound feet, rice, invention of gunpowder, and a picture of a primitive irrigation wheel in a rice field or of the Great Wall, a pagoda, or a shrine With the few paragraphs normally devoted to India, the photograph would normally be of the Taj Mahal, or of a scene on the Ganges, usually showing a great mass of pilgrims. An average of 9 per cent was given over to Asia in the world history textbooks, and this space normally mentioned the travels of Marco Polo, Genghiz Khan and the Mongol invasions, the first Western contacts in the age of exploration, and the remaining bulk to Western trade, colonization, evangelization, and wars in Asia. Without exception, the "history of civilization" is presented exclusively in terms of the civilization that arose in the eastern Mediterranean, took form in Greece, and passed on via Rome to Europe. "Not more than one per cent of the content of any of them," the authors note, "is devoted to the rise and current development of the national cultures of this part of the world where half the world's population lives."[4] In an earlier survey covering 26 world history books and 18 geography texts published between 1902 and 1917—the schoolgoing years of many of our older interviewees—Dr. Timothy Lew found from 1 to 15 per cent of the contents devoted to China, with many omitting it altogether. In 1939, Dr. Alfred Church found a total of 3 per cent in world history texts devoted to China and Japan. A more recent study (1954) by an Indian scholar found 15 per cent of the space in 28 world history texts published between 1921 and 1947 devoted to India, and 2.5 to 3 per cent in 27 geography texts.[5] The quality of these classroom exposures was generally commensurate with quantity. Most of the principal details mentioned in these studies are faithfully reproduced in the school memories of our panel. Some examples:

> China had an ancient culture, gunpowder, astronomy, Confucius, Marco Polo, Genghiz Khan and the Mongol hordes, Vasco da Gama, Magellan; Chinese with pigtails, China trade, Perry, silk, spices, Columbus, fabulous India, Chinese silks, semitropical overcrowded British India, snakes and poverty in India, Hastings, Clive, Black Hole of Calcutta, China a place on the map, 400 million people, inverted dishpans for hats, rickshas, ate rice with chopsticks . . .

And from high school hours devoted to current events some mentions of

[4] *Treatment of Asia* . . , pp. 12, 38–39, 43
[5] Cf. Timothy T. Lew, *China in American School Textbooks*, special supplement to *Social and Political Science Review*, Peking, July 1923; Alfred M. Church, *The Study of China and Japan in American Secondary Schools*, unpublished Dr. Ed. thesis, Harvard, 1939; Shyama Deodhar, *The Treatment of India in American Social Studies Textbooks*, unpublished Ph.D. thesis, University of Michigan, 1954

Sun Yat-sen, Gandhi, Chiang Kai-shek Chinese revolutions, militarists, wars, famines, Indians held down by their religious practices.

At the college and university level, we have no curriculum studies to use as a basis for comparison, but to judge from our panelists' recall, the range here is only a little wider and hardly any less scattered, accidental, and incidental In history, Asia would appear largely as the scene of certain episodes in modern Western history Here again a major stress on China:

> the Op um wars, John Hay and the Open Door, Boxer Rebellion, 1911 Revolution, Sun Yat-sen . . .

and on Japan:

> Perry, the Meiji Restoration of 1868, Russo-Japanese war, Portsmouth Conference, the Shantung problem at Versailles . . .

and a much rarer splatter of references to India as an incident in the spread of British empire.

In a very few instances, some core of some more substantial knowledge would turn up among these undergraduate gleanings, and these would almost invariably turn out to be the result of exposure to the varying Asian interests of some particular Asian scholar Frederick Wells Williams at Yale, Paul Reinsch at Wisconsin, Harold Quigley at Minnesota, Kenneth Latourette at Denison University. Asia tended to figure a bit more largely, though still marginally, in the studies of those interested in diplomatic history. It was rare to come upon Asia at all in the study of philosophy, which still starts for most people with the Greeks, moves westward in space and up through the classical European tradition in time. It would be rather in courses on comparative religions, mentioned by 25 of our panel, that the first discoveries would occur of Chinese and Indian thought. Here the names of Confucius, Lao Tze, Buddha, the concepts of Hinduism, come to light, well or barely remembered as the case might be. For a small number of individuals, these first discoveries were not enough As their bents took them on to become missionaries, journalists, scholars, businessmen, government officials, and as circumstances took them—by accident or by choice—to Asia, they broadened or deepened, or at least acquired more knowledge But for the great majority, Asia remained as distant and dreamlike as these bits and pieces retrieved from among their school-day memories For a great many, even these faint scratches had long since faded; 50 interviewees said they could remember nothing specific at all that had ever touched on Asia at any time in all the years of their schooling.

But the classroom is only one place where young minds get scratched. Impressions sharp enough to be retained somewhere in the mind for a lifetime are acquired elsewhere.[6] We shall come upon such impressions, vividly or vaguely remembered, out of the pages of the *National Geographic*, which used to come into so many homes and appears in our interviews as a prime source for the first sight of pictures of strange religious rites and processions, Hindu holy men, Chinese river scenes, or the *Book of Knowledge*, to which some were able to trace their first encounters with Asian history, ancient Chinese inventiveness, Genghiz Khan and the Mongol hordes, the values and moods of Chinese and Indian folk tales. We shall also encounter before long the lasting traces of the reading of later years, over the wide range from Bret Harte to Sax Rohmer to Pearl Buck and the not-so-wide range from Kipling to Katherine Mayo, and of the images caught from the movie screens over the years, and from cartoon strips like "Terry and the Pirates." There are also the sharp images of the Chinese who are part of American community life itself: dozens of people quickly remembered the laundryman in the many home towns, the colorful or fearsome mythologies of the Chinatowns in so many American cities, the restaurant keepers and waiters who belong with the familiar and pleasurable experience of eating Chinese food. Much less often and of quite a different order would be encounters with Asian fellow students at college, mostly Chinese but sometimes Japanese or Indian. But perhaps the most vivid and salient of all early sources was the discovery of Asia through contact with missionaries or talk about mission work at Sunday school and in church. This missionary impact will have a large place among the particulars to come; let it be noted here simply that of 181 interviewees, 123 had some recollection about missionaries, that of these 48 associated the contact with India and 75 with China, that most of these memories were attached to some

[6] Alfred Church cites a study of 289 high school seniors on the West Coast in 1923, in which 55 to 71 per cent mentioned newspapers, conversations, and other sources, and only 13 per cent mentioned the school as a source of information about the Japanese He also cites a later report from Chicago in which school children said they had learned about China from "the funny paper, the radio, and the movies." *Op cit*, pp. 11, 80

"ASIA"

kind of particular images, notions, or feelings about the Chinese and the Indians, deposits left in young minds which had borne interest of a kind over the many years.

Besides school, home, reading, the movies, church, there was, finally, the discovery of Asia through the impact of events as reported in the press, in the newsreels, and by radio. Some awareness, impressions, and knowledge of these events accumulated over time. But the interviewees were not asked simply what events they remembered, they were asked what events had first forced Asia upon their attention as something *important*, something they had to be concerned with as citizens and, perhaps, even as individuals whose own lives might be affected.

Now recall of events is obviously relative in the first place, and in high degree to the simple matter of age. Several individuals at one end of our age scale mentioned the Spanish-American War, and the Russo-Japanese War, while three of our youngest panelists said they had not become seriously aware of Asia until the Korean War broke upon them. It may help to keep the age factor in place if we note here that about three-fourths of the interviewees were already twenty or older at the time Japan's attacks began on China in 1931. It is much less easy to correct mentally for the deforming effect of refraction today's heightened awareness, say, of China, can give new shape to recollections of the way in which news from China was received twenty or twenty-five years ago. With these qualifications in mind, consider these answers from 135 interviewees, which grouped themselves as follows:

```
Events prior to 1930 relating to China  . . .  21
Events prior to 1930 relating to India  . . .   4
Events prior to 1930 relating to other[7] . .   9
                                 TOTAL  34  .        34

Manchurian invasion, Sino-Japanese War (1931–37)  .  48
Japanese attack on Pearl Harbor (1941) . . . . .     41
Indian independence (1947) . . . . . . . .            1
Chinese Communist victory (1949)  . . . .  . .        2
Korean War (1950–53) . . . . . . . . . . . .          3
"After 1951"  .    . . . . . . . . . .                1
Indochina War (1954) . . . . . . . . .   . .          1
"Never"  .  . . . . . . . . . . . . . . .  . . .      3
"Can't recall" . . . . . . . . . . . . . .            1
                                      TOTAL 135
```

[7] Spanish-American War, Russo-Japanese War Philippines insurrection, Versailles Conference, London Naval Conference, etc

A first relevant fact to be noted is that here again, as in all the gleanings from school, home, and other sources, the brightest light falls on China. In this case there are 71 individuals remembering events relating to China and only 5 whose recall had to do with India

A second noticeable fact is that of the 34 who said they had felt the impact of Asian events before 1930, no fewer than 14 were journalists Only 5 of these were men who had reported events from Asia itself. 4 in China and 1 in the Philippines. The other 9 had felt Asian tremors at various other points around the globe, at Versailles in 1919. Moscow in the 1920's, London, Geneva, Washington, New York. They were all individuals whose primary interest had become international politics, and all were able to specify their recollections in fairly precise detail, e.g., the crisis over Shantung at Versailles, the interplay at the Washington Conference in 1921–22, the effect of the Chinese revolutionary upheavals of 1924–27 This precision characterized only 3 among the 5 government officials included in the group. It was present in much less marked degree among the 6 missionaries, 4 scholars, 4 businessmen, and 1 publicist who made up the remainder.

These are all, however, persons with specialized interests and experience. We do not begin to meet other sorts of people in significant numbers until we come to the largest single cluster of 48 who located their first serious awareness of events in Asia in the period of Japan's invasions of China, beginning in Manchuria in September, 1931. Here the specialists join with larger numbers of others spread among all the categories, occupations, spheres of life One reason for this is, again, the matter of age By the 1930's a great many more of our panelists were reading the newspapers. It is also true that in those years events in China acquired, from time to time, a spectacularly high degree of visibility. No matter how peripheral or incidental their interest in Asia might be, serious people interested enough in affairs to read the press with earnest care could hardly help being reached by the news, passions, controversies, and fears aroused by Japan's invasions of China, especially after 1937 when the Chinese government finally began to offer resistance and the pattern of armed Japanese encroachment and successive Chinese surrenders became a war. For the remaining large group of 41 panelists, a new awareness of Asia did not develop until this war became also an American war, their acknowledged marking-off point was the attack on Pearl Harbor There were only a few later comers to the realization of Asia's new importance: a women's organization executive who said it did not dawn upon her until the Communists took power in China, the youths who discovered it in the Korean War, a missionary thrust suddenly in 1951 from another part of the world into an Asian job; a senator's aide who had never personally come to grips with any Asian issue until the Indochina war crisis of 1954. But sooner or later to all, in the years since Pearl Harbor, Asia has come to assume wholly new proportions and significance For some this meant not only the sudden discovery of the hitherto unknown half of the world, but being plunged personally into its midst, into new jobs in strange settings, changing their careers, their preoccupations, their picture of themselves and of their world. For the rest, the swift rush of events in this decade has brought with it confusion, bewilderment, and anger, new and inescapable problems and dangers in a vast part of the globe they could no longer ignore, as much as they might wish to do so There are in the present panel at least 9 individuals who might be described as still isolationist in impulse, outlook, background, or surviving views. Some of them might dearly like to see this country able to ignore Asia, but not one of them thought or said it could afford to do so.

There was certainly no simple isolationist explanation for the three unreconstructed individuals in the panel who said in oddly apologetic, half-joking, or defensively abashed tones that no event in Asia had even yet persuaded them of its commanding importance. They were not really denying the Asian impact; they were trying to evade or resist it. One was a college president for whom the fate of humanity is still exclusively the fate of Western humanity, one was an engineer who had never accepted the seriousness of politics; the last was a businessman who was expressing a deeply personal rejection of the non-European world, who really wished everything beyond his own little universe would fade away and leave him alone. None of these could really modify the unanimous acceptance of the obvious fact that Asia was in all our lives now to stay. It no longer leaves scratches on our minds, but deep gashes

These are deeply wounding, not only with the pain of sudden blows, but sometimes with the anguish of cleavage, the near-severing of vital bonds that link a man to his world. The cry can be one of dogged anger.

I know Asia has acquired a position more important than I have cared to admit, because I am so profoundly European at the bottom of my soul. I don't want to admit that it might acquire top priority I recognize the trend I know it cannot be stopped I have tried to live with it. I know these changes are irreparable. But I also think them undesirable I cannot applaud the setting of the sun I can only take it as a fact of life that has to be faced somehow.

It can also be dogged desperation:

About this whole question of Western relations with Asia, I keep remembering a phrase of R H. Tawney's in which he said the Western world was heading for a situation in which it would be like "an island off Kamchatka, with the rest of the world indifferent or hostile to us." If you want to know how I really feel about it, I feel as though I have been shipwrecked in the middle of the Atlantic, no life rafts, no radio, nobody around, nothing to hang onto, but still feebly trying to stroke through the water to survive I try to understand this, but don't feel there is much I can do. I have too much sense to think that in a short trip to Asia I could learn enough to fill in all the gaps in my knowledge, and I cannot undertake a long one. But every time I sit down to write anything that pertains to Asia, I am haunted by the knowledge of my ignorance of it

This Asia, its existence and importance universally conceded, bristles with problems, tasks, controversies—and, above all, with dangers. In this setting the first and controlling images are still

poverty, misery, disease, hunger, famine, ignorance . . .

multiplied by the unimaginably huge numbers of people caught in this condition. But these people are now in motion in

ferment, unrest, throwing off old ways and groping for new ones; impact of the idea of a better standard of living; the struggle between communism and democracy, a renascent Asia . . .

The problems pinpointed recur:

overcoming backwardness; economic development problems, problems of food, health, irrigation, education, the problem of too many people. . .

Some see these as huge but challenging and graspable problems for Asia Others see them as

insoluble, fantastic, almost insuperable problems, difficulties, an immensity of tasks amid confusion, disorder, chaos, weakness. . . .

Translated into terms of American needs and tasks, they become

> overwhelming United States policy problems, troubles, difficulties; the problem of India, irritation with Nehru and Menon; of Communist China, the emergence of China as a major power; the balance of power, facing Asians whom we took for granted but who now drive for self-determination with rising expectations; facing so many people detached from the democratic world, dark peoples determined to assert themselves; the challenge is to see how we can help, what we can do to meet the dangers of a Chinese-Russian alliance. . .

This sense of worried urgency dominates much of this new awareness of Asia as a problem for the United States. Asia has become important above all because it has become dangerous For most of those to whom Asia is newly discovered, a strong feeling of uneasiness, apprehension, or imminent peril overhangs all the immensity, complexity, unintelligibility of it. Others of longer experience feel much the same emotions. For them too, with only a few exceptions, this is a change, for however they viewed the Asia they knew in the past, they rarely saw it, even potentially, as threatening to the United States. There were of course the old and prescient predictions about what would happen when the sleeping giant awoke. But these always had the quality of biblical prophecy; nobody would really believe until it happened Here again only a very few—maverick diplomats and journalists—saw this shadow when it was a streak in the sky. Now it is optimism that has to be stubborn.

In the present panel, 129 individuals said they feel that Asia has become a source of future danger for the United States, only 16 that it has not. There were 83 who felt that Asia has become a greater source of danger than Europe (i.e., the Russian threat to Europe), 22 who thought that both Asia and Europe presented dangerous aspects for this country, and only 2 who saw no danger, especially military danger, in either place. These strong apprehensions were felt by majorities of all kinds of people represented on the panel. They were shared in ascending proportions by three-fifths of our Asian specialists, two-thirds of those having some secondary involvement in Asian affairs, and three-fourths of those with incidental or no direct involvement of any kind. They were expressed with a great variety of accents and stresses.

There was a first group (of 25) whose primary focus is inward, on the United States itself, its role in these affairs, its measure of responsibility for the dangers perceived, and the consequences it may suffer either from its own acts or from the pressures that fold in upon it from the outside. Some of these individuals were fearful of bad judgment by American leaders faced with critical decisions:

> there is terrible danger if we mishandle the Indochina situation and get into hostilities; the danger (over Quemoy and Matsu) is a U.S.-made danger, what stupidity!; danger can come quickly through ill-conceived action leading to a war that can't be localized, that might spark a big war; we might get embroiled over Formosa and if we do get into war, we will carry a heavy responsibility for it. . . .

Some made this particular responsibility explicit:

> the danger is that our reaction to events, rather than Asian aggression, might lead us into war; the U.S. might feel obliged to fight; the threatening situation might lead to a war initiated by us; the war danger depends on us. . . .

More frequently, the worry was not over decisions made in the face of crisis situations but over failure in the long run to be wise enough to cope.

> we can stumble very badly through lack of adjustment to areas, peoples, problems; it may not necessarily be a great evil sweeping up out of Asia, but our own failure to understand and to act wisely that may isolate us from the world and lead us into war; we can behave so badly that over time we can find ourselves without any friends at all in Asia and thereby run into all sorts of dangers, including war. . . .

Finally there were other inward-lookers still more probingly sober

> war threats may strengthen reactionary and fascist trends in the United States; it may prove difficult for the U.S. to survive in the framework of its present institutions; the gap between Asian aspirations and capabilities may lead to totalitarianism there, making us a garrisoned democratic island off totalitarian Asia and forcing us to become less and less democratic. . . .

A second larger group (42) tended to accent the long-run character of the danger, to see events in the framework of a prolonged, painful, and difficult effort to attain or maintain a favorable balance of power:

> I see extensive political, economic conflict over the long range; Asia as a wide arena for cold-war type hostilities as distinct from any military

"ASIA" 57

threat to us directly; Asia not likely to have in next 10, 25, 50, 100 years an independent resource base capable of making it a direct menace to the United States, see it as a menace as an instrument of Russian policy, a tool of the Russians, dangerous only in combination with Russian power, if those vast untapped material and human resources develop on terms hostile to us, they will be a real danger, but that is many years off, it will be a long time, 10 years, another generation, before we are ever attacked by Asia, but the balance of power may change meanwhile, they will seek to eliminate U.S influence from Asia. but a direct military danger to us seems less likely, we will experience more of what we are experiencing now, turmoil, uncertainty, will have trouble, friction, difficulty, hostility, but they won't have the power to attack us, the danger is in Chinese-Russian leadership of world revolution, spreading social and political unrest in Asia, the Arab states, Africa, danger lies in economic desperation, with Asians becoming

Will history repeat itself?
—*Lewiston Tribune, Idaho*

"Stepping stones"

1937                1955

pawns of Russian power, U.S. is not threatened by Communist ideology but it is threatened by Kremlin expansionism. . . .

A further large group (48) had a much more foreshortened time perspective. They tended to see the danger as closer, sometimes as imminent. Their accent was more on the explicit danger of aggression from the other side, arising out of

> Soviet and Chinese imperialism, Chinese Communist aggressiveness and expansionism, the great aggressive force of a Russian-Chinese combination, China's armies, threat of Communist victories in Southeast Asia; Chinese expansionism is our major danger, just as Japan was fifteen years ago, second now only to Russia. . . .

The danger is often pinpointed in time and place:

> clear and present danger of war at any time; could happen right now; the Indochina problem; danger of attack on Quemoy and Matsu, on Formosa . . .

or linked to some particular contingency or breaking point:

> if collapse occurs in South Viet Nam or Indonesia, if Communists attack the Philippines; if China industrializes and there is no reconciliation; if India goes Communist, if all Asia goes Communist, if a Communist Asia combines with the Soviet Union. . .

The vision of the growth of an intercontinental combination hostile to the United States begins at this point in our spectrum to assume overwhelming proportions in the minds of a certain number (13) of our people. They too see only the external foe, but they see him large, in great, lurid, deep shadows thrown against the screens of the imagination. Here all the entities are huge and all are fearful:

> a greater long-run threat than Russia itself, a solid Communist bloc from Germany to the Pacific, molded by Communism, a threat to the world, a vast continental power, vast resources, a Communist Eurasia spreading its influence to the Western Hemisphere, vast populations spilling over into the less densely populated parts of the world, look ahead 25, 50, or 100 years to an industrialized China, an industrialized Asia, hating the West, Soviet imperialism plus Chinese imperialism, overwhelming combinations of Asian populations; Western civilization is outnumbered, white civilization is outnumbered, and could go under; we have 30 years in which to face up to a bloc of 900 million Com-

munists with a great land empire, vast impact, interior communications, modern weapons. . .

Even in a kaleidoscope, it is no simple matter to pass from the apocalyptic dimensions of the last of these images to other narrower, sharper particulars. In search of a transition, we stopped to look more closely at the 13 apocalyptics. They turned out to be a varied and in fact quite distinguished group. a noted historian and an internationally famous novelist, 3 well-known journalists, one of the country's top publishers, 3 government officials of middle rank and an ex-official of considerably higher place, an executive of a large women's organization, a politician, and a churchman. One thing they visibly had in common was a lack. none had ever had substantial contact with Asia or Asians Four of them had touched down fleetingly in a few Asian cities, 9 had never traveled that way at all Three of the group have latterly had some professional concern with Asian affairs, but peripherally and at a distance, in an editor's chair, at the United Nations in New York, at a desk in Washington. The other 10 were totally uninvolved Unencumbered by any experience with Asians or contact with Asia, they stood far enough away to be able to see it *only* in its continental dimensions. Like most people, they carried these dimensions in their minds on a scale of vast immensity both of space and of numbers of people. They likewise all had an acute appreciation of the Communist danger. Since there were many others who combined the same or similar elements and came out with somewhat different results, it follows that a further quantity, some ingredient of outlook or personality, must be included in the equation: Lack of contact plus Images of undifferentiated vastness plus Fear equals An apocalyptic view Whatever the specific weight of each element, it is at least clear that it is a good deal easier to achieve a vision of the apocalypse if the view remains unimpeded by too many of the complicating particulars of the Asian scene, its infinity of divisions, places, and contending realities.

From this look at the ultrapessimists, we turned with sharpened interest to the other end of the spectrum, to the small band of stubborn optimists, the 16 members of the panel who said that they did not feel that Asia was a source of future danger for the United States. Here again it was clear that more than a view of the world separates the optimist from the pessimist On the nature of the personality differences that distinguish them, we must pass. But other more visible facts about these individuals quickly emerge.

First, this group of 16, in contrast to the much larger group of 129 more worried individuals and even more so to the ultrapessimists, produced a much larger proportion of individuals with Asian experience. It included 6 specialists, 6 with secondary involvement, and only 4 of the uninvolveds.

Second, the uninvolveds were "optimistic" about Asia only because they felt Asia was not a danger to the United States because the real or greater danger lay elsewhere:

> the real danger is outside Asia, i e, in Russia, Asia is only a tool; I see technical advances as the essential aspect, don't even think of Russia by itself as such a tremendous threat, but of Russia combined with Germany; Asia's problems are at the bread and water level, it could provide only large masses of people for Russia to use against us; considering our power [no purely Asian threat] could really be serious if we acted right . . .

The optimism of the 12 Asia-experienced individuals was of quite a different order:

> the peoples I knew in Asia are not aggressive; their own problems and their own progress will remain central, I am optimistic, I think we will be more sensible about Asia and get along better, people are attracted to the West, by and large, in the long run it will work out, Asians don't want to dominate the world, they want to live with it, they don't want Communism. . .

These individuals may be optimists by nature; on this we can offer no finding. But it is also decisively relevant that the Asian experience of all 12 of them is connected with India and in 2 cases also with Southeast Asia. This makes it clear that the peoples they know who, they say, are not aggressive, who are attracted to the West, who want to live with the world, are in no case the Chinese. China, where the great majority of our panelists see a future threat, has in the minds of these individuals remained largely a blank.

We can discern here, if we will, the beginning of an outline of the effect of *kind of experience* on a broad issue of opinion and feeling. A scale has been drawn in these pages on the issue of future danger in Asia, and a range has appeared from stubborn optimists, through a large middle group of mixed views sharing a basically pessimistic or worried outlook, to the ultrapessimists. When we relate location on this scale to kind of contact and experience with Asia, this pattern comes into view:

- Individuals with minimal or no contact with Asia or Asians distribute themselves over the entire range, occupying all of the ultrapessimistic ground and a small corner among the optimists;
- Individuals with Asian experience are wholly absent from the ultrapessimistic extreme, but only people with India or Southeast Asia experience appear among the optimists;
- Individuals with China background are absent from both extremes and all cluster in the large middle group which shares a fear of future danger for the United States in Asia, differing only in the ways they define it.

Here, as throughout this initial kaleidoscopic view of the impact of "Asia" on these American minds, the scene is dominated by China, whether it be among the fainter marks left in a remoter past, the plainer scratches made by events through the years, or the deeper gashes cut by the fears of the present.

PART TWO

---- ✿ ----

# THE CHINESE

LIKE CHINA'S GREAT RIVERS, flooding and receding and shifting their courses to the sea, American images of the Chinese have traveled a long and changing way, from Marco Polo to Pearl Buck, from Genghiz Khan to Mao Tse-tung.

The name of Marco Polo is scratched onto the mind of almost every American school child. Attached to it are powerful images of China's ancient greatness, civilization, art, hoary wisdom. With it in time comes a heavy cluster of admirable qualities widely attributed to the Chinese as people: high intelligence, persistent industry, filial piety, peaceableness, stoicism. These were attributes identified in our own generation with the people of Pearl Buck's novels, solid, simple, courageous folk staunchly coping with the blows of fate and adverse circumstances.

Genghiz Khan and his Mongol hordes are the non-Chinese ancestors of quite another set of images also strongly associated with the Chinese: cruelty, barbarism, inhumanity; a faceless, impenetrable, overwhelming mass, irresistible if once loosed. Along this way we discover the devious and difficult heathen, the killers of girl infants, the binders of women's feet, the torturers of a thousand cuts, the headsmen, the Boxer Rebellion and the Yellow Peril, the nerveless indifference to pain, death, or to human disaster, the whole set of lurid, strange, and fearful images clustered around the notion of the awakening giant and brought vividly to life again by Mao Tse-tung's "human sea" seen flooding down across the Yalu, massed barbarians now armed not with broadswords but with artillery, tanks, and jet planes.

In the long history of our associations with China, these two sets of images rise and fall, move in and out of the center of people's minds over time, never wholly displacing each other, always coexisting, each ready to emerge at the fresh call of circumstance, always new, yet instantly garbed in all the words and pictures of a much-written literature, made substantial and unique in each historic instance by the reality of recurring experience. This interchange might vary lineally from epoch to epoch according to its particular history, or collaterally from person to person, according to his particular experience or personality. Thus, advancing or receding but somewhere always in view, our concepts of China have included both a sense of almost timeless stability and almost unlimited chaos. Our notions of Chinese traits have included sage wisdom and superstitious ignorance, great strength and contemptible weakness, immovable conservatism and unpredictable extremism, philosophic calm and explosive violence. Our emotions about the Chinese have ranged between sympathy and rejection, parental benevolence and parental exasperation, affection and hostility, love and a fear close to hate.

Today these contending views and emotions jostle each other at close quarters, for we are in the midst of a great passage from one set to the other. The dominant impressions of the 181 Americans interviewed for this study were acquired in the past on which the gates clanged so abruptly in 1949. Direct communication was severed almost at a single blow. Since then, live American contact with China itself has been cut until it is virtually nonexistent, dropping to the presence of a handful of Americans held in Chinese Communist prisons and links on Formosa to survivors of the debacle. What went before has already acquired the patina of nostalgia, the quality of sadly retrieving a receding past was almost palpable in many of the interviews. What has happened since 1949 has quickly acquired all the distortions of the unknown, dimly seen and greatly feared across a great distance.

The images of the Chinese that still so largely govern in the minds of most of these Americans are for the most part the product of the experience of the first four decades of this century. This experience is framed in a characteristic and meaningful paradox The beginning of this experience included the powerful prejudice and contempt and violent rejection which had marked American attitudes and behavior toward the Chinese who had come to the United States. Out of this came the exclusion laws and all the mythology and synthetic villainy attached in popular folklore to the Chinatowns and the Chinese laundries right across the country, a pattern which persists in some measure right down to the present time. But these also became the years of the full flowering of the most sympathetic images of the great qualities and great virtues of the Chinese who had sensibly remained in China Whether directly or vicariously, through event, book, or pervading climate, these images were widely spread and absorbed and became part of the mental baggage of almost everyone who could read or went to church. It was common to find in our interviews that even the scantiest notions about China and the Chinese acquired in this time were likely to be in some way, however slight, favorably disposed, kindly, or admiring of the Chinese, or at least vaguely sympathetic to their needs and travails The Chinese—on their own ground—were a people Americans had always helped, a nation that somehow evoked a special and unique benevolence and even a sense of obligation, a people of sterling qualities who deservedly held our high regard

These impressions are not likely to be reproduced in any similar form in the minds of today's children or to reappear in their thinking when they grow into maturity. Their images of the Chinese are being shaped by the new circumstances and their multitudinous reflections in the classroom, in print and film, picture and cartoon, in the voices carrying the news by radio, in the faces on the television screens.[1] The members of our present panel, on the other hand, are creatures of their longer past. They are caught in the melee of the images of China on which they were raised and the new images of hostility, cruelty, of easily imposed and easily maintained tyranny, and even of mortal danger. If Americans do again go to China in coming years in any numbers, they are much less likely to come back, as they did so often in the past, with warm feelings produced

---

[1] Of 380 Connecticut high school students tested in January, 1957, 87 per cent saw China as a nation "to watch out for" Asked to estimate American foreign relations over the next ten years, 59 per cent of the same group predicted that China would be "unfriendly" and 26 per cent said it would be "hostile." Victor E Pitkin, *An Adventure in Educational Television*, Conn State Dept. of Education, Hartford, 1957, pp. 40–41.

by the good life they could lead there, or with the same impressions of Chinese wisdom, approachability, humor, polite deference, friendly hospitality, pragmatic intelligence.

To be sure, the rapidly fading images retrieved in these pages will not disappear entirely. But whenever and however they re-emerge, they will be different or recur in some new combination of circumstances and emotion. The process of reincarnation is not the same thing as the story of the sleeping beauty. In this sense, the passing of these images and attitudes is really a death and this report is an obituary.

China occupies a special place in a great many American minds It is remote, strange, dim, little known. But it is also in many ways and for many people oddly familiar, full of sharp images and associations, and uniquely capable of arousing intense emotion. Some kind of American acquaintance with China and the Chinese goes back to the beginning of our national history. In its quality of vague and long-standing familiarity, this historic connection is matched in the lives of many individuals by a smiling memory evoked from earliest childhood: they knew almost as early as they knew anything that if you dug that hole on down right through the earth you would come out the other side in China. This fixed in many a young mind the idea that China was about as far away as you could get without dropping off into space, but at least it firmly situated China on this planet and gave it a certain unique identity.

Whatever little these Americans went on to learn in school about Asia, most of it generally had to do with China, even if it was nothing more than the bare outlines of the Marco Polo story. Whatever reached them about Asia in their years of growing up from moving pictures, newspapers and magazines, books, or other sources, the bulk again ordinarily dealt with something about China or the Chinese.[2]

[2] The preponderance of China material in the slim Asia content of American school texts has already been indicated. Other indices: Of 8,677 articles about Asian countries in American magazines listed in the *Reader's Guide to Periodical Literature* between 1919 and 1939, 3,833, or nearly half, dealt with China. Of a roughly approximated total of about 3,600 books of American imprint about Asia listed in the *United States Catalog* (1902–27) and the *Cumulative Book Index* (1928–55), about one-third dealt with China. Of 325 films dealing with Asian subjects listed by Dorothy Jones for the period 1896–1955, 246, or more than two-thirds, dealt with the China scene or Chinese characters Cf. her *The Portrayal of China and India on the American Screen, 1896–1955*, Center for International Studies, M.I.T., October, 1955, Appendix III.

If the only image of an "Oriental" in their minds was the image of that well-known "inscrutable Oriental," the chances are that he was dressed and looked like a Chinese. Until the events of only the last fifteen years, which brought so much more of the trans-Pacific world so abruptly into view, China was for many Americans the most identifiable particular associated with Asia as a whole

Chinese motifs have in fact long been woven into parts of the American fabric. Along with the many other ideas they absorbed from the writers and thinkers of Europe's Age of Enlightenment, some of America's first and most important leaders acquired a highly respectful view indeed of the merits of Chinese civilization and even thought it worthy of emulation in their own new world. The tea that was dumped into Boston harbor on the day of that famous party came off a British ship that had just arrived from Amoy, China. The first American clipper ship sailed from New England to the China coast in 1784, the year after the Republic was founded. It was sent out by Robert Morris, the financier of the American Revolution. It bore the name *Empress of China*, and it opened one of the most romantic and glamorized chapters in American maritime history, celebrated to this day in moving pictures, storybooks, and history primers. Ships with names like *Asia* and *Canton* plied this trade for decades. The merchant mariners who sailed in them brought back tea and silk and ideas about China and the Chinese, and even brought back some Chinese as visitors. They added the Chinese touches to the décor of New England homes that are still visible today, they built Chinese pavilions in their suburban gardens and contributed a thin layer of awareness of the Chinese to their countrymen, a blend of romance, excitement, obscurity, beauty, distance, oddity, quaintness, and danger which has continued to exert its influence on American thinking about China down to our time. It was from one of these merchant families, named Delano, that a President of the United States acquired his own active sense of a personal link to knowledge of China.

The merchants were followed quickly to the China coast by some of the first American missionaries. The movement of these missionaries to China, first in twos and threes in the 1830's, then in tens, eventually in hundreds, and ultimately in thousands, made it the largest single theater of American missionary enterprise. This enterprise and the men and women who took part in it placed a permanent and decisive impress on the emotional underpinning of American thinking about China. The scratches they left on American minds over the generations, through the nineteenth century and into our own time, are often the most clearly marked, the longest-enduring, and the most powerfully influential of all. More than any other single thing, the American missionary effort in China is responsible for the unique place China occupies in the American cosmos, for the special claim it has on the American conscience.

Shortly after these Americans began to go to China as evangelists, Chinese emigrants began, for quite different reasons, to come in large numbers to the United States Between 1854 and 1882, some 300,000 Chinese laborers entered this country, most of them for the original purpose of working on the building of the western railroads Those who stayed for more than a short time created the beginnings of a permanent Chinese segment in American life itself. They found a place in the country's increasingly polyglot population and in its prejudice patterns, becoming the first people to be excluded by law from entering the land of the free They produced a whole set of figures, stereotypes, and notions now as firmly fixed in American folklore and literature as the residual Chinese-American population itself (120,000 in 1950) is in American society The experience with Chinese in the United States is second only to the missionary experience as a source of some of the principal images and emotions about the Chinese to be found in contemporary American minds. In addition to the immigrant laborers, some 22,000 other Chinese, usually of a quite different class, also came to this country from China, between 1854 and 1949, to study at American colleges and universities, creating still another major source of image-forming contact and experiences for the Americans, typified by many in our panel, whom they knew as friends, fellow students, and teachers over these several generations.

Other major links have been numerous and long-lasting. American trade with China has been more or less continuous since 1784. Although it never assumed large relative proportions, the lure of what it might be, the dream of 400,000,000 customers, has provided one of the major drives for American interest in China and behavior toward it. This has been particularly true of American political relations with China, which go back in the formal treaty-making sense to the first pact signed by Caleb Cushing in 1844, with major American participation and involvement in Chinese affairs continuous ever since. American armed forces have fought in small wars and

THE CHINESE 69

big in China. They participated in the quelling of the Boxer Rebellion in 1900. They figured repeatedly in subsequent decades in treaty port upheavals and river skirmishes. There were, finally, the great flow of nearly a quarter of a million Americans to China during World War II, and the military teams of the few postwar years that closed one epoch, and the armed collision in Korea, which opened another.

These Chinese pieces in the American mosaic are not large when viewed against the whole of the American pattern of experience, but neither are they small. They are certainly visible to the naked eye. They involved the lives of many thousands of Americans—missionaries, traders, diplomats, soldiers and sailors, scholars, teachers, journalists, among them a small but highly influential number of people who grew deeply committed to their China interests. Their influence spread to an extraordinary number of odd corners in our public and private lives.[3]

Our major cities have their Chinatowns. Our museums are full of examples of Chinese art, our libraries stacked with books by Americans who have written extensively about Chinese life, history, politics, society, art, poetry, gardens, and even cooking, and a familiar literature of another kind, tales of crime and adventure in which Chinese heroes and villains abound.

Our everyday existence is dotted with Chinese flecks familiar to adults and children alike. The vogue for Chinese décor in home decoration, introduced by the New England mariners more than a century ago, is still with us and has extended in more recent years to Chinese themes in women's fashions and even in facial makeup. The national craze for mah-jongg came and went in the 1920's, but Chinese restaurants have become a familiar part of the urban American landscape and "chop suey" and "chow mein" and many more

[3] A directory compiled in 1941 by Wilma Fairbank showed a total of 107 organizations in the United States that were concerned with China. These included 24 mission organizations, 17 interested in medical work in China, 17 concerned with educational activities, a dozen information, news, and propaganda groups, 11 American colleges and universities with China affiliates, and a scattering of others engaged in relief, industrial and agricultural training and exchanges, etc. The directory listed 15 university centers of Chinese studies, 12 major library collections of Chinese books, 5 major Chinese art collections, 9 periodicals concerned with China. This list did not, of course, include business firms with China interests. See Wilma Fairbank, *Directory of Organizations in America Concerned with China*, American Council of Learned Societies, Washington, D C., 1942.

sophisticated dishes have been naturalized in this land of many cuisines. Because of their familiarity with these restaurants, or from the wrappings torn from packets of firecrackers in times past, or from the colorful signs on Chinatown streets, millions of Americans, certainly, are able to identify Chinese writing From a host of common sources, we are able from an early age to recognize with instant familiarity the comical straw hat of the Chinese peasant or the upturned corners of a Chinese-style roof. We know Chinese puzzles, Chinese checkers, Chinese lanterns, Chinese red, Chinese yellow—indeed, *Webster's New International Dictionary* has almost three crowded columns of words prefixed by "Chinese," including some of the best-loved of our flowers, brought in from China and naturalized long ago, azalea, hibiscus, peony, wisteria [4]

There is almost no end to the familiarity of Chinese strangeness, no counting the many bits and pieces of knowledge that add up to our national ignorance about China. Taken all together, they have established an immensely varied array of ideas, images, notions, attitudes, and real or vicarious awareness of China and the Chinese shared in some degree and to some extent by millions of Americans for many generations.

As we consider this array, especially as it appeared in the minds of the people interviewed, it is difficult not to recall that Americans are often stereotypically viewed as people prone to deal in blacks and whites, in contending absolutes, and that the Chinese are often said to have built much of their culture on their sense of the duality of the human spirit and experience. For these American images of the Chinese tend largely to come in jostling pairs The Chinese are seen as a superior people and an inferior people, devilishly exasperating heathens and wonderfully attractive humanists, wise sages and

---

[4] The term "Chinese homer" popped back into public notice in 1954 when Dusty Rhodes of the New York Giants won a World Series game with a 270-foot fly that dropped into a nearby grandstand for a home run A "drooping wallop" like this, the sports writers explained next day, was "a cheap homer" and had come to be called a "Chinese homer" in the last generation because of the popular association with "cheap Chinese labor." It expressed both a sense of Chinese puniness or weakness and the idea of "getting something for nothing." The revival of the term brought a protest from a leading New York Chinatown figure The *New York Times* account felt it necessary to say that the coiner of the phrase "had no thought of disparaging the Chinese people," while the *Boston Globe* devoted its major editorial of the day to a warning that "these times require of Americans the greatest tact," so that "hits like Dusty's must find a new name" (October 1, 1954.)

sadistic executioners; thrifty and honorable men and sly and devious villains, comic opera soldiers and dangerous fighters These and many other pairs occur and recur, with stresses and sources varying widely in time and place. As many of our interviews have shown, they are often jumbled all together, with particular facets coming more clearly into view when struck by the moving lights of changing circumstances.

We have made it our task not only to try to retrieve and describe these images but to try to see them as the lights struck them, in their many historical settings and the emotional climates they created. We have tried to see the reflectors that cast these many pictures into the forefronts of our panelists' minds, and, somewhat like Alice, we have stepped through them to discover what lay behind. Sometimes this has taken us back for a long excursion into history, sometimes back only to yesterday's experience or encounter, a book read or somebody's words remembered. But always, the changing experiences of many decades mingled. As we move among them, a certain chronology establishes itself, and if we were to list it crudely, like an exercise in a history text, it would look something like this:

1. The Age of Respect (Eighteenth Century)
2. The Age of Contempt (1840–1905)
3. The Age of Benevolence (1905–1937)
4. The Age of Admiration (1937–1944)
5. The Age of Disenchantment (1944–1949)
6. The Age of Hostility (1949–    )

But let no one think each of these ages stamps itself uniformly on its time. Each lives on into and through the other, and in all their many expressions they coexist, even now. For these ages are not measured merely by the calendar or the conditions but by all the kinds of people there are. They can suggest only where, in this time or that, the lights shone brightest, and which images therefore were the most clearly seen and which emotions most commonly held. In our own most recent years, these lights have moved with such rapidity that almost every man's view takes on the quality of a kaleidoscope in which all the images blur and in which no single image ever quite comes to rest.

## 1. *A PANEL-EYE VIEW*

A FIRST PANEL-EYE VIEW of a composite of all the bits and pieces in our interviews makes it appear at once that, all politics and problems aside, most of our Americans regarded the Chinese as a most attractive people indeed. Whether this shows up on the kaleidoscope screen in great stereotyped globs or in sharp individualized vignettes, the main effect is much the same. Sweepingly admiring generalizations about the Chinese people as a whole appear in great profusion. They were described as

> down-to-earth, pragmatic, practical, good, kind, highly civilized, vigorous, industrious, persevering, courageous, loyal, wise, independent, pleasant, sensitive, canny, thrifty, rugged, competent, subtly humorous, jolly, dynamic, dignified, cheerful, astute, the finest people; a gifted race; quite wonderful people, the most adult and mature people in the world, the outstanding inhabitants of Asia. . . .

Individual Chinese were described as

> intelligent, high-caliber, attractive, likable, decent, nice, fine, upstanding, topnotch, worthy, lovable, extraordinary, individually just tops . .

And describing their own feelings about the Chinese, panelists said they

> liked them, were fond of them; had great respect for them all, admired them; had deep attachments; warm, friendly feelings; liked being among Chinese, love the Chinese. . . .

Views of this general tenor were held lightly or warmly, mildly or strongly. They were based on much or little experience with Chinese or on none at all, on knowledge, rumor, or on impressions acquired from print, picture, or person. In all their varieties, these predominantly admiring attitudes about the Chinese were shared by 123 members of our panel.

It takes a second, sharper look at the kaleidoscope screen to see the more shadowy places where the less attractive images of the Chinese lurk, and where attitudes of dislike, antipathy, and hostility are to be found. Here too sweeping characterizations of the Chinese were made. By these tokens they were

THE CHINESE 73

unreliable, devious, untrustworthy, cruel, callous, materialistic, inefficient, socially irresponsible, excitable, repulsive in mobs; xenophobic, not highly intellectual, inscrutable, confused, overcivilized, strange, queer, different . . .

and those for whom these characterizations were decisive said:

I don't like the Chinese; can't ever tell what they think; they never show whether they like me, have no high opinion of them; feel funny about the Chinese; felt a certain animosity. . . .

These images and attitudes, as part of a predominantly negative view, were held by 31 members of our panel. In between there were 6 individuals whose views were either too detached or too differentiated to fit any dominant bias.[5]

From a different vantage point, we get a panel-eye view of another kind: a composite of the qualities most frequently attributed to the Chinese. Here, in their most recurrent forms and by the numbers of panelists who mentioned them, is what we see:

*Favorable*

| | |
|---|---|
| Generalized remarks [6] | 114 |
| High intellectual quality | 106 |
| Warm, polite, friendly, charming | 95 |
| Favorable stereotypes ("down-to-earth," etc.) | 91 |
| Vital, good sense of humor | 61 |
| Competent, able | 53 |
| Strong family ties, institutions | 48 |
| Easy to communicate with | 47 |
| Quiet, restrained, reticent | 45 |
| Ancient civilization, etc. | 43 |
| Reliable, honest | 34 |
| Physically attractive | 29 |

*Unfavorable*

| | |
|---|---|
| Unreliable, shrewd, opportunistic, dishonest, devious | 64 |
| Generalized remarks [6] | 53 |
| Military menace | 46 |
| Inscrutable, difficult to communicate with | 41 |
| Cruel | 32 |
| Lack social consciousness | 32 |

[5] The total is 160. There were nine interviewees whose views of the Chinese were too scanty to be included, and 12 whose interviews were incomplete in this respect.

[6] E.g., on the positive side "The Chinese are wonderful people," "I like the Chinese"; or, on the negative· "Strange, xenophobic people," "dislike the Chinese."

Unvital . . . . . . . . . . . . . . . . . . . 14
Incompetent, inefficient . . . . . . . . . . . . . 12
Low intellectual capacity . . . . . . . . . . . . 9
Physically unattractive . . . . . . . . . . . . 8

These assorted views of the Chinese appeared in the interviews in many individual mixes and combinations It is obvious that one could respect the intellectual capacity or competence of a Chinese without necessarily liking him, or, liking him, still find him a menacing figure in the present world scene. Some individuals might have suggested that "the Chinese" are honest or dishonest, others noted more carefully that they had met some Chinese who were honest and some who were crooks This discrimination, I might add, was by no means always the product of greater experience. Some of our oldest "old China hands" were among the most profligate generalizers, others with no experience whatsoever were sometimes more particular. And experience itself varies: some saw Chinese as "quiet, reticent, restrained" where others saw them as violent and excitable, and might have liked or disliked them for either quality The fact is, in any case, that these orderly ranks of contending attributes do not cluster in any such orderly fashion around those who respectively admire or do not admire the Chinese In varying measures, they are all mentioned by all, pro and con What differs from person to person is the weight each gives to these attributes in fixing his own ultimate bias.

Thus you will note that in the heaviest count against the Chinese, 64 individuals mentioned some item along the scale of *dishonest, devious, unreliable, opportunistic, shrewd.* Indeed, almost no person with any substantial experience with Chinese failed to mention it as one of his images or impressions of at least some Chinese. Some even did so admiringly: "You knew he was doing you in the eye, but you didn't resent it." For others, it was simply outweighed, at least until yesterday, by other kindlier characteristics. "They could steal all I had," said a Catholic ex-missionary, "but I would still like them . . . I am prejudiced about the Chinese " Only for 14 of our panelists was it a decisive part of an attitude that was on the whole negative. Again, the sense that Chinese are or can be *cruel* was mentioned by 32 individuals, but for 24 of these it was only a shadowed corner in an otherwise brighter picture; only for 8 did it darken much of what they saw.

## *The Admiring Views*

The remarkably preponderant admiration for the Chinese displayed by this group of Americans is going to take a good deal of scrutiny. As we go along, we shall try to discover its details, its limits, its undersides, its many complications. We shall explore the history and circumstances that produced it. We shall also have to examine the ways in which it is changing, for while these images and attitudes are still too strong, too fresh, too strongly surviving to have passed into history, they have already in large measure become reminiscence. All who hold them must look back to keep them in view

It is plain, to begin with, that a liking for the Chinese, or at least the notion that they are an attractive or an impressive people, could develop in members of our panel out of all sorts and shadings of experience. As we look more closely at the groups that form among these many admirers, we find that those who knew the Chinese best—or at least had the longest and closest contact with them—were the most enthusiastic of all. Of the 19 individuals holding the strongest views on the subject, 12 would qualify as what are known nowadays as "old China hands" and at least 4 others are in the same class at least by association. Said a well-known journalist, whose view is insistently the large one:

> The Chinese have the greatest and most unique history in the world, the only nation on earth with a continuous history since Neolithic times. They are dynamic, resilient, powerful, with a great capacity to survive and come back and a remorseless power of expansion over time. A great practical people. You don't often find a Chinese who is a fool.

An army officer.

> I think of their warmth, friendliness, curiosity, interest, ingenuity, humor They would do you in the eye, but as a game, not to do you harm. Their idea was never to grind a man so far that you take away his rice bowl Even if he is an enemy, leave him something. Terrific energy, resilience to disaster and misfortune. I have a sound and profound respect for them as people. I feel sympathy because I like them I think I understand them It was never difficult to learn to think as a Chinese Like any old people, of course, there is a certain cynicism, too much civilization I think they deserve a better fate than they have had, not only today but under the Kuomintang regime as well.

A China-born notable:

> The Chinese are pretty human. This is an indefinite word. But I mean they have quick instant recognition of the concrete fact of a particular individual. This goes between two Chinese or between a Chinese and an American. What each wants is instantly understood. The Chinese have an intense realism, yet are suffused with a certain poetry and gaiety. No matter how poor he is, the Chinese has his pleasures, in a bird, or in games, or in gambling, in the play of wits, pageantry, festivals, weddings, funerals. Life is hard, but he gets all the enjoyment he can out of it.

A government official·

> I have known too many Chinese to generalize about them. But I tend to like them. They are energetic, vigorous. The educated have subtle minds, a nice sense of humor. I've had a good deal of personal respect even for those on the opposite side of the fence. They are shrewd and dishonest in an institutionalized sort of way, but it doesn't bother you because it is recognized.

These examples could be multiplied several times from within our present panel and many times outside of it, for it is nearly axiomatic that Americans who lived in China during the several decades before Pearl Harbor became admirers of the country and its people. Their experience aroused in them a certain radiating enthusiasm, and since most of these individuals were communicators by profession, they did much to create the mood, air, and feeling attached to many ideas about the Chinese Great hosts of their countrymen were brushed by this Sinophilic fall-out over the years The evidence of its effect is overwhelming in our panel. We shall have occasion later to meet not only more of these Sinophiles but all kinds of Sinophiles-by-association and Sinophiles-by-osmosis. Here are but a few examples:

> My favorable impressions come from people who had been in China. It was a fairly common experience to meet such people They always saw the Chinese as friends, knew China as a friendly country. . . .

> I got my first impression of the Chinese from my "girl" in high school, who belonged to a missionary family They all loved the Chinese. I really don't know why I don't know why I love the Chinese, but I do.

> I have a closer, warmer feeling about the Chinese.  . Maybe it was

the novels of Pearl Buck and Nora Waln. I did have much contact with China-lovers and was filled with China lore before I went out there. . . .

Brief firsthand experience of China popped up quite unexpectedly in the lives of a number of individuals whose careers have had nothing primarily to do with China at all. Thus a former college president and foundation executive:

I went to China with my father on a business trip when I was ten. Later I knew Chinese graduate students at Harvard and since then have met all sorts of officials and visitors here I like them all, almost without exception. The fact is there is almost no Chinese I dislike. I like everything about the Chinese. Somehow "China" and the "Chinese" do not make me think at all of the present political scene and personalities, but of the Chinese silks and embroideries in my home as a child, that steamboat ride up the Yangtze. That trip when I was a kid of ten is the most vivid of all my memories.

Another, now a noted scholar in his own right, visited China with his father when he was sixteen:

Chinese students used to come to our house. In China on that trip many of his ex-students gave tremendous receptions in his honor. Chinese visitors at my father's house were sophisticated, intelligent people. I think of them as Western types, perhaps because of their facility with the language. I think of Chinese in the mass as infinitely primitive, but with dignity, like in the movie of *The Good Earth*, patient, cheerful, industrious, hardy.

A congressman, brought up in a family with strong missionary traditions, spent one year, thirty-five years ago, as a non-missionary teacher in a mission school in China·

My contact with Chinese, students and faculty, was always friendly and cheerful. I think of the Chinese in general as not so religious or spiritual-minded, but with common sense, therefore easy to understand. Relationships were very easy. Even if materialism is less admirable as a quality, it is easier to understand Frailties make you like people sometimes

A similar early teaching experience in China played a part in the development of some of the basic attitudes of an economics specialist who eventually rose to high posts in the government:

> With the Chinese you could get to know their ways of living and thinking. On the philosophic level, felt they were closer to the Western ethic, a more pragmatic philosophy I personally made a great shift in recognizing truth outside of Christian thought and faith Was brought up to think "good" people were Christians But I found many who weren't Christian who were good and many Christians who were skunks I no longer equated right and wrong to Christian belief

One of the country's senior journalists made a brief trip to China in 1927 and remembers it now this way.

> I got to like the Chinese, felt closer, a warm relationship. Chinese are down to earth, more like us in their thinking, practical Always felt comfortable with the Chinese. As a youngster I had thought of "Oriental" and "barbarian" as the same things, but this quickly disappeared in China, where I found the refinements of Chinese civilization, courteous behavior, food. . . The Chinese, I gradually learned, felt just as superior to me as I had once felt toward them

Finally, another distinguished journalist who toured briefly in China in 1929:

> I think of the Chinese as very friendly, affable people, though in official dealings slow, intricate, baffling I think of the food mostly. The Chinese is about the best cuisine in the world outside of the French One feels that a people who have evolved such food must have high qualities and a high civilization.

But by far the majority of these panelists, 81 out of the 123, had never visited China, even fleetingly. China and the Chinese remained, for most of them, at least until recently, at the outermost margins of their preoccupations Most had incidentally encountered only a few Chinese in their whole lives, a few could not remember meeting a single one Yet in every case there had been something to scratch their minds, limited notions, scanty, even wispy, yet sufficient to establish some kind of attitude or bias, sometimes a vague sort of feeling which they were hard put to explain. The sources to which some of them could trace these feelings were highly varied, appearing often in some obscure corner of the individual's own personal life or absorbed, almost by osmosis, from somewhere in his environment.

For some this association was highly personal indeed and only accidentally productive of notions about the Chinese. A newspaper editor said.

> I do have a feeling of sympathy and liking for the Chinese André Siegfried in one of his books compared the Chinese and the French. Both grow old gracefully Both have good food. My wife is French, I like the French very much and this comparison struck me My liking for the Chinese is more like a reaction to a work of art, that is for their whole history and culture, and not for individuals, of whom I have met very few

Chinese works of art figured somewhat more literally in another case, which was by far the most piquant of its kind A scholar of high repute said he thought of the Chinese as

> delicate, subtle, restrained, keeping individuality at a minimum, not too expressive, more formal They have a much higher aesthetic sense than Americans, about the textures of things, imagistic poetry . .

He was not certain, he said, where these highly graphic impressions came from, but as he talked on, it developed that as a student at Harvard, he had found the Chinese art collection at the Boston museum "all strange and unintelligible and not beautiful to me," until he began to court a young woman who happened to be immersed in a study of Chinese art He went back to the museum with his future wife and "she pointed out things" he had not seen before To all Chinese ever since he has lent the qualities he first discovered in Chinese works of art seen through the eyes of love so many years ago

Others, with perhaps a somewhat more impersonal and intellectual bent, often came away deeply impressed even by a scraping acquaintance with Chinese philosophy. An example:

> Confucian rationalism, moderation, disrespect for magic, freedom from intense sentiment, anything goes so long as it's kept within bounds and without too much disturbance—I admire a culture that houses this

Quite often the sources are readily traced to books read out of some general or related interest in peoples and their affairs. Here is one, a writer himself of considerable note, who was quite explicit in these identifications

> I have pictures in my mind of rice fields, temples, pagodas, padded clothing, women with children on their backs From Pearl Buck the idea that Chinese are *good* people. From Lin Yu-tang the idea of their finesse and subtlety. From Malraux deep conspiracies, shadows, vice

dens, opium, and concubines From Anna Louise Strong, Agnes Smedley, and Jack Belden, adulation for the Chinese. From poetry and painting, fine lines I feel the Chinese are hardier, more industrious, good craftsmen, good businessmen—I get this impression from the Chinese I've seen in other countries, all the overseas Chinese laborers who rose to the middle class—think of 600 million of these efficient, able people!

Others recall some single past encounter that helped shape a whole mold of thinking and attitude:

A speech I heard a Chinese diplomat make when I was twenty, made a great impression on me Urbane, humane. Took his remarks at face value, especially his insistence that the Chinese are not unfathomable. He set up my initial stereotypes of the Chinese, that they were practical, relaxed, could laugh at themselves.

Another academician and sometime high government official:

The best restaurant in my home town was Ah Hey's, I used to sell him pigeons which I raised. He was kind and generous to kids. Warm, kind, wonderful people. Later in Washington I found Chinese officials shrewd and persuasive and in Honolulu the Chinese I dealt with were the slickest swindlers, but such wonderful, pleasant, cheerful people!

A vaguely favorable feeling, at first unsupported by any remembered detail, made a frequent appearance in some of these interviews. An engineer, for example, volunteered: "I have never known any Chinese, but I have a generally favorable idea about them." Ideas about what, he was asked. "Nothing special I can think of," he replied. But then he began to think of things, one by one, and here is what came to light·

Well, I think of carved ivory, good workmanship, neatness and care, Pearl Buck, the movie *Good Earth*, newsreels, trains full of people, Japanese bombings Read Snow's book Had a Sunday school teacher whose brother or sister was a missionary in China. Suppose some of my ideas got some start there. Terry and the Pirates. Saw a Charlie Chan movie on TV the other night.

In another case, involving an impressively conscientious Washington correspondent, the colloquy went like this:

I can't recall anything specific
Anything in general?
No, it is more that I have no recollection of anything about China that isn't favorable or friendly to the Chinese. It's a mood, I can't

specify, but I do know I've always had this feeling persisting through the years.

What about——

Wait, come to think of it, some of my fraternity brothers went to China as medical missionaries Also Pearl Buck's *Good Earth*, gentle, simple, hardworking peasants She was probably uncritical Then the idea that the Chinese are individualistic. What about this idea? It's been drilled into us all the time that they are individualistic

Who's drilling?

I can't say who's doing the drilling, but this generalization is always being made You hear it, read it, and never get any counterview.

Anything else?

Well, all the Americans I've met who've been in China. I get a feeling of tremendous affection for the Chinese people.

A publicist pursued his initial blankness this way·

Well, you always seemed to hear a lot about the Chinese without ever knowing very much Back in high school and college, the Chinese were always the symbols of Asia. A great people, placid, unaggressive, solidly rooted in its culture, how China remained unaltered through the centuries, always enduring A people had to have backbone and some greatness for this. And then Pearl Buck and the idea of the Chinese as a great human people, fine, patient, ingenious, generous, long-suffering, hard-working, smart, philosophical. . . .

One of the youngest of our panelists, finally, a student still in college, said. "I've always had a liking for China for some reason." The "reason" turned out to include:

In high school in 1944 we had something about China in current events about the war Even before that when the Chinese were fighting Japan, I was fighting for the Chinese in our kid games. At the summer mission the nuns told us about children in China, how poor they were. We had clothing drives for them and at home we had a little bank to drop pennies in for the missionaries in China . .

By the time, in the pages to come, we have placed such remembered items and associations in relation to the circumstances that produced them, the reader may be better able to appreciate why these have been the patterns of image, attitude, and feeling that from the beginning of this century until quite recently dominated so much American thinking about the Chinese.

## The Unadmiring Views

Of the 31 members of our panel who did not admire, like, or think well of the Chinese, only 3 have ever been to China.

Two of these are businessmen, and the views of both are governed by recent events. The first is a banker who spent the troubled interlude of 1946–48 in Shanghai. During those months between the takeover from the Japanese and the approach of the new Communist conquerors, he found his bank a small islet of relative order where "we dealt with credit-worthy people" while outside brutality and chaos reigned.

> When Chiang Kai-shek's son came into Shanghai, he shot down a lot of people. Almost everyone was saying that nothing could be worse than the Nationalists.

The second businessman, an oil company executive, visited China only briefly a few times long before the war. He said:

> I am now pretty confused. I had always considered Chinese businessmen to be high-class, honorable people. But I could now easily see every Chinaman drawn and quartered over their unwarranted interference in Korea. I was sympathetic to the Chinese when Japan attacked them, but now I have changed quite a bit. I'm still prepared to be friendly with the Chinese I know, but I am not sure now that I can trust even them. Events have changed my attitudes.

The third is a Catholic priest whose focus is a rather different one. He visited China for several months in 1931 and said he found "the simple people in the countryside" to be "charming, attractive, hardworking," but he also decided:

> The Chinese is not spiritual in outlook. In the interior drive of the spirit, China is at the lowest level in all Asia. They are more materialist-minded, have no yen for religion, just for empty forms.

The two businessmen had both spent long years of their careers in India and in several respects compared the Chinese unfavorably to the Indians. The priest, likewise, had visited India, and his remarks about the Chinese were bracketed with more favorable views of the greater "religion-mindedness" of the people he had met in India. These are not accidental juxtapositions, for among the 31 members of our panel with a more or less negative bias toward the Chinese, 11 are individuals identified in some degree with India.

## THE CHINESE

We shall discover later that the converse is equally true. Americans who identify strongly with the Chinese are almost all distinctly unattracted to Indians. This is a highly suggestive fact, but it will have to wait for us at the far end of the long galleries of images of the Chinese and the Indians which we have now only just entered.

The remaining 27 members of this group of Unadmirers share a marked sparseness of personal contact with Chinese. They include individuals from every quarter of our panel. Aside from those whose contacts in Asia have been with India, other identifying clusters are few and not necessarily significant. There are several individuals whose links abroad are quite exclusively European; several are products of Southern birth and upbringing; several are Negroes There is a certain uniformity in all their views. For example, allowing for wide differences in degree, most of them have images of the Chinese dominated by notions of deviousness and inscrutability. In its mildest form this appears as a mistrust of formal Chinese politeness:

> I've known a few students, met a few Chinese officials They are very polite, I can almost say careful. They don't want to say or do the wrong thing They make much more of an effort to be like you than like themselves. I value frankness highly The ceremonial approach does not appeal to me This formality means that I don't know where I stand with Chinese I meet I think this is why Americans are often suspicious of the Chinese, think they are dishonest, can't be trusted.

The strong sense of *mistrust* of the Chinese among these individuals rises much more strongly out of their use of words like

> shrewd, wily, crafty, slick, opportunistic, cunning, sly, calculating, scheming, unscrupulous, devious . . .

Some or all of these qualities are associated by some with the Chinese businessman, especially the overseas trader, and with the oft-used phrase, picked up by one Midwestern congressman, 'the Jews of the Asiatics" This does not always mean outright dishonesty, but something fairly close to it. It is interesting to note that no American businessman in our panel described his Chinese counterparts in this way. One of them did say that the Chinese "would double-cross and triple-cross you if he could," but he made this observation self-admiringly, it only proved how smart an American businessman had to be to come out on top In some cases the notion of Chinese dishonesty was linked with the institution of so-called "squeeze"—the unofficial pocketing of suitable commissions for those concerned in almost any transaction. But by far the strongest basis for this impression was the solidly entrenched idea of large-scale corruption in high Chinese places derived from the widely current accounts of misuse of aid and relief funds by Chinese officials during and just after the Second World War, the notion popularly summed up in the phrase "operation rathole." Even individuals not generally inclined to think too ill of the Chinese remarked on this— "Chinese officials have set new standards of chicanery," said one "I always think of them as having ill-gotten gains stashed away somewhere," said another.

The idea of crafty deviousness carries with it the notions of guile and hidden motives, and these go with bland impenetrability The Chinese are, in a word, inscrutable A congressman said:

> I think of Chinese pretending ignorance but understanding perfectly well. Pretended passivity and resistance, apt at concealing what they think. This does not necessarily mean they are undesirable characters

Another congressman who said he had gotten an idea of the Chinese as a "savage people" from the comic strip "The Gumps," said:

> Remember one fellow, bright and courteous, but uncommunicative Didn't know what he thought. He spoke good English, had no difficulty communicating, but he didn't communicate very much. The Chinese officials here in Washington are pretty unfathomable. I have never met a Chinaman that I felt I could know, always a barrier

A foundation official:

> I have always found the Chinese difficult, never felt that I really understood them. Maybe it is a stereotype I've had since childhood of the Chinese as mysterious people. I couldn't have got it in my home, where we almost made a fetish of tolerance of other people. Maybe it was the Fu Manchu stories. Has the idea of "inscrutable" attached to it The fact is I did have the experience of dealing with Chinese and never knowing what they really had in mind.

There were only 14 individuals for whom this difficulty in communication formed part of a generally unadmiring view of the Chinese. There were others who cited the same difficulty, though usually in less dramatic form—for some it was a matter of language, for others a feeling that Chinese liked to keep communication on the surface or to confine it to the amenities. The striking thing is that among the 41 in all who felt this lack of effective contact, there was no one who had ever known any Chinese well. On no other characteristic attributed to the Chinese, good or bad, is this correlation so clear and so complete.

There is a final group among these non-admirers of the Chinese whose feelings about the Chinese have only the most tenuous connection of all to the Chinese themselves, relating far more to some personality trait, outlook, or particular tangent of experience of their own.

One of these is an editor and writer who is so totally immersed as a political and cultural being in Europe that he has largely cut all non-European people and cultures out of his line of vision He could not remember ever meeting any Chinese or forming any personal impression. He acknowledged only some "left-over clichés from Pearl Buck" and some notion of China as a land of "ancestral cults." He thought of the Chinese either as "enormous masses of people" or as non-Western people he had seen in Western settings, wearing Western clothes, talking Western languages, and displaying Western manners. For all "non-Westerners with a Western veneer," he proclaimed his profound aversion, and this was a prejudice held almost without regard to race, creed, or color. He applied it to virtually all the people occupying all the world's space from the Alps to the Pacific Ocean. Indeed, Americans got inside his barrier only as the heirs and products of Western European culture and traditions.

Another in this category was a government official, born, raised, and educated in the Deep South He said.

> Despite all I've heard about Oriental cultures, I do not get the impression of any of them as fine, cultivated people. I don't find myself liking the Chinese. I don't know why exactly.

Two top correspondents for major journals are in this group. One of them is a Southerner who remembered that in the city where he lived "a lot of Chinese intermarried with Negroes. They were not looked on too favorably, a separate people." From what he heard during the war about corruption in high Chinese places, from the episode of a Chinese official who used his diplomatic status "to change wives rather easily," and even from Pearl Buck's novels, he acquired the strong notion that the Chinese have "a concept of behavior quite alien to the Westerner." The second journalist is a religiously inclined individual who remarked that Confucianism seemed to be little more than "a code of manners." The Chinese "never produced great ideas, that is, emotional religious works."

> From what I've read about them, they seem capable of great ruthlessness and brutality They have no grasp of the Christian concept of humanitarianism. The speed and ease with which they butcher large numbers of people! Beheadings! I remember pictures of rows of heads ready for the ax, some old and some more recent. . . The great confusion in American interpretations of Chinese affairs makes me think it cannot be easy for a Westerner to communicate with the Chinese. . . .

Since we have already quoted one panelist who admired the Chinese because they were somehow like the French, it is of some interest that these two newsmen both made the same comparison for quite the opposite purpose. Said one

> I draw a parallel between the Chinese and the French. Overripe civilizations left both peoples unsuited to hold their own against more vigorous, less civilized peoples Both have an overdeveloped sense of individual interest, and the national interest suffers.

Said the other:

> The Chinese are in a way the French of the Far East; a people self-satisfied with their own culture

This group also included a well-known public figure who came out of a New England background positively cluttered with all the classic American links to the Chinese which have ordinarily produced a glowingly sentimental feeling about them Members of his family had been in the "China trade" and his grandmother's home was "full of all kinds of art objects" they had brought back with them from their adventurous voyages. His uncle had been a "great admirer of the Chinese," and he himself had been fascinated as a lad "by the things in the stores in Boston's Chinatown." But for some reason which remained locked away in his past, he had come to think of China as "a country that seemed asleep" and of all Chinese as "passive" and "undynamic."

There was nothing obscure about the uniquely particular bias toward the Chinese which appeared in the reactions of several Negro panelists. A first example:

> I came to regard the Chinese as international Uncle Toms, bootlickers of the white men Because Chinese restaurants would refuse to serve a Negro The Chinese aping the whites. . . . The same sort of reaction to Mme Chiang Kai-shek's refusal to see a Negro reporter when she was over here Still feel funny about the Chinese They try so damned hard to be accepted by whites I have never discussed this with any Chinese, never knew any well enough. I think of the Chinese in general as slick, "damned clever, these Chinese" . . Never read any of Pearl Buck's novels out of lack of interest in her subject Don't think I ever read any book about China as such.

A second:

> One night in San Francisco during the UN conference in 1945, we were turned away from a Chinese place. I said to the Chinese headwaiter: "I hope the Japanese kill every goddam Chinaman in China!" Of course then we got a table, because they wanted no rumpus In Washington we never went to Chinese restaurants because we knew we would be barred. Chinese have followed the patterns of the dominant group Our feelings against nonwhites who do this sort of thing are stronger than our feelings against the white man From childhood folklore, movies, the Chinese is wily, astute But the Chinese were historically outsmarted in power politics Couldn't defend their country against the white man or the Japanese. Haven't been so clever as these childish notions made them out. . . . I didn't put much stock in the heroic Chinese fight against the Japanese. Chinese seemed to me to be incapable of asserting themselves What was important to me was that in areas under Japanese control, the white men would be unable to practice discrimination I thought at the time that people who allow strangers to come in and put up signs saying "No Chinese or dogs allowed" deserved to have the hell beat out of them. . . . The Communists have now asserted the equality of the darker with the white race and from this point of view, leaving other matters aside, it's a wholesome thing

These were, in tone and feeling, the strongest and most hostile of all the views of the Chinese to emerge among members of our panel

## *"Old" and "New"*

The onset of "new" images of the Chinese arising out of China's new setting as a Communist power, an efficient tyranny, and a dangerous foe, is a later part of our story Even from this first panel-eye view, however, it may be clear that these "new" images are not "new" at all, but for the most part old and long-established conceptions of the Chinese which are only now, again, after a long time in the backstage shadows, being brought out into the bright—and sometimes lurid—light of changing circumstances To fit the new images of the brainwashers, the brutal masters, the devilishly clever totalitarians, there are all the older impressions of Chinese cruelty, callousness, deviousness, untrustworthiness, and inscrutability. These do not in the least contradict the many other attributes of high intelligence, perseverance, adaptability, and a great capacity to endure hardship which aroused so much admiration. It is only the combination of arrangement of all these traits in the total image that has begun to change.

For the minority in our panel who never did admire, like, or think well of the Chinese, the rise of the new circumstances provides a certain reinforcement. In many of these cases this is an association rather dimly made, from afar, by individuals who for the most part have known very few Chinese personally and often none at all. But also for many who knew the Chinese well, the shift in roles is not always a shocking surprise Only the most sentimental Sinophiles saw the Chinese in single dimensions, and these are the ones who now often tend to characterize the "new" manifestations of Chinese behavior as not "Chinese" at all, but rather "Communist" or even "Russian." The more knowing Sinophile has a more complicated view than this, he not only has more knowledge but he also has a whole past of intimate associations to reconcile with present experience in which no individual Chinese figure at all. Sometimes he sits in his American exile from his old home and, in the Chinese phrase, eats bitterness:

> It is the bad time of the last years that is now uppermost in my mind . . I think Sinophiles were attracted not so much by Chinese character as by Chinese culture, art, history, language. Though it was disillusioning to get too close to the Chinese, I do like them fundamentally. They have great vitality, humor, individualism, adaptability, no spiritual pretenses, definitely materialistic, a capacity to work things out. I rather like this. But their shrewd opportunism is more obtrusive now in my thinking I hear from Chinese now when they want something They always look out for Number 1. I'm getting older and I tend to be impatient these days, but my impatience is like that of a member of a large family in trouble . . .

or else suffers his nostalgia sadly:

> It is hard to answer in general, there were so many different individuals. But I liked the Chinese in sum, admired many of them, enjoyed being among them. I was at ease among them except in times of political stress, like now, because their personal attitudes and actions would be affected by the general political situation But I think of their sense of humor persisting under difficult circumstances, of personal relations based on a whole system of life and the art of survival, of resilience in situations like the Chungking bombings, of the ability to enjoy life in the most unpromising circumstances, of gusto, of a tendency to dramatize and to live by the rules of the game, especially the game of life in public. On the other hand, I think of callousness and brutality about human life and suffering of the ease with which principles can be compromised, of the lack of inner guiding motivations or ideals. . . . My young son now hears and reads about the "terrible Chinese." We try to tell him . .

After these testimonials, coming from two individuals who had each spent decades of his life in China, it would almost seem that a third, a journalist, was not far wrong when, as a result of brief tours in China during and just after the Second World War, he concluded: "All the clichés I'd ever heard about the Chinese seemed to be true."

Let us look more closely now at some of these "clichés" and try to see how and when they came to be held.

## 2. *THE SUPERIOR PEOPLE*

THE IDEA THAT the Chinese are a superior people is connected in many minds with the powerful image of China's ancient civilization, its great age and its aged greatness. From 102 of the 181 members of our panel came recurring mention of

> China's ancient and great culture; a beautiful, wonderful, cohesive culture, its great civilization; a bond of ancient traditions, a culture devoted to the arts and sciences; an aesthetic, artistic style of life, unaltered through the centuries, exquisite, stylized poetry, paintings; have great respect for Chinese art, for Chinese thought, Chinese architecture, customs, mores. . . .

These historic attributes rub off frequently onto the people themselves. Thus the Chinese are

> an artistic, highly cultured people; they have a deep attachment to an old ethical system, the wise old Chinese; a great and noble race; a people highly cultured for many centuries, the outstanding inhabitants of Asia, the Chinese equal and exceed Americans in culture and education; their civilization is more humanistic than ours, they are ahead of us in many ways . .

The transfer from culture to people is strikingly often accompanied by a shift in tense: China *was* a land of great culture, the Chinese *are* a highly cultured people Because in so many visible forms the "old" China persisted so long into modern times, because so many Chinese are viewed as the heirs and carriers of this great past, or often simply because the Chinese are in any case the products of such an impressively long history, the feeling of respectful admiration is maintained, frequently without any clear placement in time.

This image of China's admirable antiquity gained currency quite early in the history of our own civilization, and it is acquired, in no matter how fragmentary a form, quite early in each of our own lives even now The impression is widely held. It is shared by many who can go on to specify it in great and learned detail and by many more who may have little more than the bare notion itself, reinforced only by the schoolbook versions of the Marco Polo story [7] and the information that the Chinese had invented such things as paper, movable type, the compass, porcelain, gunpowder, and had great sages, poets, and artists long before Western man had civilized himself The stream of this impression is fed by many rivulets. Some individuals recalled, always with a glow of pleasure, reading Chinese folk tales, like those to be found in the *Book of Knowledge* or in many anthologies and storybooks still widely read by children. It is from these storybooks, and sometimes from school geographies, that most people learn to recognize the shapes of Chinese architecture or the conventional figure of a Chinese sage. The words *fine* and *exquisite* are almost invariably associated with the examples of

---

[7] An NBC-TV "spectacular" based on the Marco Polo story (May 15, 1956) had a sequence in which Marco Polo spends a year in exhaustive and exhausting study of the most abstruse subjects At the end of the year he says that he has now acquired the knowledge normally possessed in China "by any nine-year-old boy."

Chinese art that abound around us in so many museum collections, the bronzes, jades, ivories, porcelains, paintings, scrolls, rich silks, and tapestries, all marvelously old. The feeling of consummate *delicacy* is attached to fine *chinaware,* and the same words and values recur constantly where Chinese motifs in decoration and fashions occur

These impressions live side by side with a host of others, a good deal less respectful, a good deal more rejecting, suspicious, even contemptuous and hostile. But they are hardly ever wholly absent from any single person's mind when he thinks of China. They manage somehow to color or qualify every view. They add a certain dimension to every outlook on China and a certain stature to every observed individual Chinese. Thus when some people remarked that the Chinese they had met gave them an impression of

> a proud sense of superiority, pride of race, great self-respect . . .

they did so approvingly, or at least with acceptance. As far as they were concerned, the Chinese who had this attitude were quite entitled to it.

> I see the Chinese as having a certain nonassimilable stability, and this comes from their sense of superiority. I used to think the British and the Chinese were the two peoples most sure of the integrity of their own conditioning and their own society. Not arrogant, just a strong sense of superiority.

Only one individual in the whole panel saw it differently:

> They are arrogant They have the biggest superiority complex I know

The qualities that are admired or respected in the Chinese are often most directly related to the impression of China's antique wisdom, its powerfully surviving traditions, a system of ideas that were old long before the Christian era began. This is the setting in which we often find

> Confucius, Lao Tze, the scholar-philosophers and philosopher-statesmen, bearded sages, patriarchs, scholars, a scholar-run nation, traditional reverence for the scholar; the idea of wise old scholars, that scholars come first, soldiers last . . .

"Confucius" may be for some a scratch left on the mind by Earl Derr Biggers' magazine and movie character, the detective Charlie Chan, and what he said Confucius said. But there are many individuals in our panel whose scholarly or religious interests have led them to some acquaintance with Chinese thought or who have ideas about the way Chinese think The extent of their knowledge and the depth of their interest varies widely, but almost invariably they describe Chinese thought or the Chinese way of thinking as

> pragmatic, rationalist, orderly, serene, sophisticated, empirical, non-doctrinaire, nonabstract, sagacious, humanistic, sharp, inquisitive, clear, commonsensical. . . .

These are all qualities of intellect, mind, and outlook which generally enjoy a high value in American culture. When they are perceived in Chinese encountered by Americans interested in such things, they establish at least one strong basis for quick affinity. This holds equally for certain other features of the Chinese tradition and its required patterns of behavior. The strength and cohesiveness of the Chinese family was admiringly mentioned by 49 people, along with scattered salutes to Chinese filial piety, respect for the aged, admiration for learning, and the talent for art and good workmanship.

One of the strongest ideas also attached to the notions of age and durability is the idea that China is

> unconquerable, more likely to absorb foreign influence than be taken over by it; often conquered but always retained the identity of their civilization, always absorbed their conquerors; have a unique capacity to survive and come back. . .

Those who think of recent events in China in terms of a Russian conquest appear to derive solace from this idea. Those who think the current changes in China arise out of a resurrected Chinese dynamism are a good deal less comforted by the conviction that China goes on forever. The "newer" or more "modern" China becomes, the greater the nostalgia that attaches itself for some to the "old" order of things. This has happened before, when foreigners faced with changes they regarded as inimical to their interests have become ardent defenders of the traditionalism which, at other times, they have deplored as a brake on Chinese progress.

Among our panelists there were, to be sure, significant dissents from this general admiration for China's heritage. Several persons remarked in effect that the authoritarian character of Chinese society and its institutions established the basis for the passive acceptance of Communist totalitarianism by great masses of the Chinese people.

THE CHINESE 93

Others felt a critical lack of spirituality in Chinese philosophy, religion, and behavior. Another observed that while the Chinese traditionally and theoretically despised the military man, every Chinese dynasty was in fact founded by a soldier or at least by force of arms, and that the greatest curse of modern China, before the Communists, was the war lord. Only a small number (9) said they saw Chinese traditionalism as a vast burden which Chinese in modern times have had to bear to their great detriment, but a larger number (32) observed that Chinese tradition was responsible for

> lack of national, civic responsibility in Chinese; lack of social consciousness, lack of ability to organize themselves politically, they don't give a damn who runs the country as long as their own affairs are intact or they have enough to eat; family obligations displaced obligations to the community . . .

Both the enthusiasm for Chinese civilization and the dissent from it have a long history in the West, going back well beyond the beginnings of the American republic. For more than a century before the first American clipper ships sailed to China, Europe had been delighting itself with the *chinoiseries* introduced by the merchant-adventurers who had followed in the path of Marco Polo. Chinese silks, dyes, porcelains, paints, and pigments had a high vogue. Chinese costumes appeared at masqued balls, Chinese themes in dramatic spectacles, Chinese magical tricks and jugglers in the common entertainments. Chinese pavilions appeared in the gardens of the rich and the royal, at Versailles, Potsdam, and elsewhere, Chinese décor in the mansions of the mighty, a mode adopted in this country a little later and persisting into our own time.[8] The extremes of sinophilic faddism and sentimentalism in that day as well as in a much later one drew the light of scorn of more sophisticated minds. Goethe in 1796 wrote a poem called "The Chinaman in Rome" in which he scoffed:

> Behold the type of many a moon-struck bard,
> Who vaunts his tissue, woven of a dream,

[8] Looking into the "pleasure gardens" of old New York for the *New Yorker* (November 10, 1956), Robert Shaplen discovered that "one of the earliest, dating from 1793, was a vauxhall decorated in Chinese style . . ." With a report of a charity-fund-raising tour of palatial homes in and near New York, the *New York Times*, May 13, 1956, published photos of the "Chinese dining room" in one of them and of one pleased hostess sitting "before a Chinese panel in her library."

'Gainst nature's tapestry, that lasts for aye,
Proclaims as sick the truly sound, and this,
That he, the truly sick, may pass for sound.[9]

The youthful Ralph Waldo Emerson wrote in 1824:

I laugh at those who while they gape and gaze
The bald antiquity of China praise [10]

But *chinoiseries* apart, both Goethe and Emerson, like a great number of leading thinkers and writers of the Enlightenment during the whole preceding century, took China very seriously indeed. The impact of ideas from and about China on the intellectual environment of Europe from the late seventeenth through the eighteenth century was considerable. It was also characteristically controversial. Herrlee Creel has briefly reviewed this history [11] and its many confusions, the first glowing reports of the early Jesuit missions to China on Confucian ideas and the Chinese art of government, the immense enthusiasm they aroused in people like Voltaire, the Physiocrat François Quesnay, the constant use of the Chinese example in the great discussions, pro and con, on the nature of absolutism and freedom, the controversies that arose over the more critical views brought back from China by traders concerning the despotic and limited character of the Chinese regime. Indeed, the discussion was so wide and constant and prolonged that Creel finds it "probable that literate Occidentals knew more about China in the eighteenth century than they do in the twentieth." But his own account illustrates how much the knowledge of China in that time resembled that of our own in the violence and hyperbole of controversy in a situation in which the facts were dim and long in coming into clearer view. In that time, as again more recently, disenchantment crushed the enchanted The very emperor whom Voltaire had praised so extravagantly as an "example of tolerance" turned out to be in fact "one of the greatest destroyers of literature (in the name of suppression of 'dangerous thought') in all history." Creel summarizes.

[9] Quoted by Thomas E Ennis, "The Influence of China and Japan upon German Culture," *Eastern World* (London), May, 1956 For other details see also his "Contributions of China to French Civilization," *Eastern World*, May, 1955
[10] Quoted by Arthur Christy, *The Orient in American Transcendentalism*, New York, 1932 p 125
[11] *Confucius, The Man and the Myth*, New York, 1949, Chapter XV.

THE CHINESE 95

> Chinese philosophy was introduced to Europe by the Jesuits. They reported chiefly on what they considered best, the ideas of Confucius... Being rationalist in temper and tending in a democratic direction, this philosophy was hailed as a revolutionary gospel from another world. A little later, however, Europeans learned more about the later forms of Confucianism which . were in part a perversion of that philosophy designed to make it serve the purposes of monarchic authority. Simultaneously it was emphasized that in fact the government of China, which had been so highly praised, had at least many of the characteristics of a despotism; indeed some of its very champions hailed it as such. It was concluded that the virtues of Confucius and of Chinese government had alike been inventions of the Jesuits, perpetrated for purposes of propaganda At this time the Jesuit order became so thoroughly discredited that in 1773 . . . it was dissolved by the Pope. Disillusionment became complete, the "Chinese dream" was over. Never again in the West, since the end of the 18th century, has interest in China and esteem for that country risen so high [12]

Never again was disillusionment so complete and interest so high, that is, until recently, for almost anyone can make in this passage his own substitutions to make it read like a summary of the way in which this history repeated itself after 1950.

But during that earlier, longer, less volcanic time, some very important American minds indeed were scratched with ideas relating to China, including that awe and envy of Chinese civilization which so widely permeated the writings of the period. In the salutatory introduction to the first volume of the American Philosophical Society founded by Benjamin Franklin in 1768, this passage occurs:

> Could we be so fortunate as to introduce the industry of the Chinese, their arts of living and improvements in husbandry, . America might become in time as populous as China. . . .[13]

Franklin and Jefferson, it is suggested, were strongly influenced by the Physiocratic ideas which Quesnay himself had declared to be nothing but "a systematic account of the Chinese doctrine, which deserves to be taken as a model for all states." Jefferson, says Creel, was especially interested in that feature of Quesnay's thought which bore on the need of the state to promote agriculture. Later, whether by direct borrowing from China or not, Jefferson became the leading

---

[12] Creel, *op cit.*, p 263.
[13] Quoted by Kenneth Latourette, *The History of Early Relations Between the United States and China*, New Haven, 1917, p. 124.

advocate of the selection of a "natural" aristocracy to hold government office. When the British civil service system was established—with some evidence of the direct influence of the model of the Chinese examination system—and the American government eventually followed suit, Emerson was there to point out how long China had been in preceding us in this matter. Emerson read with delight in the Chinese classics as they became available in European translations and drew upon them to illustrate his own ideas about the gentlemanly proprieties, the ethics of individual and social behavior, morality in politics, and the mutual responsibility of men in the manner of the interacting parts of the mechanism of a watch.[14]

But these first glowing images cast abroad by China's arts and ideas were kept only fitfully alive in Emerson's pages and in the continuing interests of a few scholars. For the Age of Respect was passing. The whole basis of intercourse between the West and China was changing. The century of Western assault had begun. Having failed to breach Chinese isolation by respectful propitiation, the Europeans came now as men of force intent upon breaking it down In 1839, Great Britain began the first of a series of wars in China in the course of which China's power and integrity began to be stripped from her, by 1860, the foreigner was imposing himself almost at will. In the same years a small band of Christian evangelists from Britain and the United States undertook to storm the ancient bastions of Chinese religion and morality, the missionary movement followed the traders and the flag. These circumstances drastically altered relationships and images. There was no respect in the men of power for the weaklings who buckled before them, and none in the men who saw themselves as men of God for those whom they saw as utterly godless. The conception of China's ancient greatness did not die, it was simply submerged The Chinese of the nineteenth century came to be viewed in the main by Westerners as inferior people, as victims and subjects, sources of profit, objects of scorn and pity, and ultimately, by the Americans, as wards.

[14] Christy, *passim*, especially pp. 6, 125, 138 ff, 159.

## 3. THE INFERIOR PEOPLE

IN THEIR CURRENT feelings about the Chinese, most of our panelists are moving uncertainly somewhere between admiration and fear, trying to preserve the distinction between the objects of these two emotions. At neither end of the scale is there much room for ideas of the Chinese as inferior people, for they are dominated alike by a strong sense of Chinese vitality and capacity. Yet notions of the Chinese as lesser men lie not too far below the surface. The Chinese were submerged too long, the habit of patronizing them was too old and too strong—whether in kindly fashion or contemptuous—for these ideas to have disappeared entirely. And woven oddly close to all the strands in this pattern that have made for contempt are those that make for fear. They all still form part of the patchwork of images that fill our minds.

WEAKLINGS: In a few cases (14)—all of them individuals with little or no actual contact with the Chinese—the idea of Chinese weakness clearly survives. They saw the Chinese as

> nonaggressive; inert; submissive, servile; passively accept things, slow; cannot solve their own problems, couldn't defend their country against the white man or the Japanese, never used their resources to become a modern nation like Japan; don't have any fighting spirit, being "yellow" means being afraid . . .[15]

The image of the Chinese as weaklings does not get much support from recent events It tends to be held by people whose contact is too slight to budge impressions deeply anchored in the past, or by some who see reinforcement for their notion in the weak submission of the Chinese masses to the Russian-provided—and therefore "un-Chinese"—strength of the Communists. The notion of Chinese weakness is also the idea at the root of the belief that a "show of force" will suffice to deal with any problem the Chinese raise for us or, put another way, that force is the only thing the Chinese will

---

[15] "Yellow" as a symbol for fear or cowardice does not appear to be derived from connection with the Chinese or any other Asian source According to the dictionaries, this use of the word goes back about 100 years in this country, but its origin dates back to older European medical folklore about a disease, perhaps jaundice, which turned the skin yellow and produced weakness and debilitation.

respect. This is of course doctrine that is by no means peculiarly applied to the Chinese; it still governs in almost all important international affairs. It has been a central tenet in the creed of empire from the beginning, has been applied in many times and places, and was, along with the weapons provided by a more advanced technology, the pillar on which Western power rested for so long in Asia and Africa. It required only the presence of a small and self-confident force of Westerners well tooled for war, and a large, docile, and unself-confident non-Western population without comparable means of retaliation. Out of the many successes of this nineteenth century formula rose the strongly stereotyped notion, so current in the Western world until only yesterday, that the European was uniquely endowed to rule and the non-European to submit.

The Chinese became part of this pattern from the time that small British and allied European forces successfully humbled the great Celestial Empire beginning just about a century ago. With the first victory by a small British expedition in the Opium War of 1839–40, the great prestige of the Chinese came tumbling down

> A sudden revulsion of feeling took place [writes a major American historian of the period] and from being respected and admired, China's utter collapse before the British arms and her unwillingness to receive Western intercourse and ideals led to a feeling of contempt. . . Contrasting their old ideas of her greatness with their sudden discovery of her weakness, the impression spread through America and Europe that China was decadent, dying, fallen greatly from her glorious past.[16]

The Age of Respect ended then and there and the Age of Contempt began. Thereafter Chinese recalcitrance was punished by military force. this was the beginning of the "gunboat era" and the "unequal treaties." By helping to crush the most serious of the rebellions that rose against the Manchu Dynasty in the next two decades, the Powers reduced the Chinese regime to helpless dependence upon them. China itself was torn at like a prostrate carcass, and by the end of the nineteenth century, under great predatory swoops upon its territory and its governmental authority, it appeared to be on the verge of total dismemberment. The Chinese who figured in this history were, in the eyes of most Westerners, supine, helpless, and almost beyond pity.

This was history that Americans especially had need to rationalize.

[16] Latourette, *The History of Early Relations Between China and the United States*, pp 124–125.

They eventually accomplished this, as we shall see, by the elaborate structure of guardianship, benevolent purpose, sympathetic good will, and high moral intent that still surrounds the American self-picture in relation to China and the Chinese. But it was also achieved more obscurely by many people in quite another way, by the belief that the people who thus allowed themselves to be imposed upon hardly deserved any better fate, that they were, indeed, hardly people at all. One of the principal mechanisms of this process was the concept of the faceless mass.

THE FACELESS MASS: The one thing everybody knows about the Chinese is that there is a fantastically large number of them. In the interviews the key phrases, recurring again and again, were:

> teeming masses, seething, tremendous, huge, great, vast masses, enormous, dense, tremendous population; people living in droves, too many of them, an awful lot of them; thousands per square mile; so numerous nobody can swallow them; amorphous mass of humanity; a mass of jelly, a large, faceless mass. . . .

Of the 55 panelists who summoned up these images, only 5 were people who had lived in China. The impression seemed to be primarily one of an undifferentiated mass in which the individual is completely obliterated, a vast agglomeration of beings without identities. This blurred image is plainly and commonly expressed in the cliché: "You can't tell one Chinese [or one "Oriental"] from another." When it is endowed with hostile vigor and motion, this great indistinguishable mass becomes one of the most fearful of all the projected images, the barbarian hordes sweeping all before them by sheer numbers and rapacity, an image never wholly absent from the minds of Western men since the time of Genghiz Khan and fearfully re-evoked for a great many in the time of Mao Tse-tung. But for most of the time with which we are concerned, and for most of our panelists, the image of this mass is marked by its passivity and by its poverty, its incredible, unbelievable, incomprehensible poverty. Thus in our interviews the Chinese were seen (by 67) as

> a vast, hungry people; millions dying, misery, disease, beggars, skinny kids, destitution, wretched squalor, scrambling for garbage thrown from the ship, hunger, starvation, illiteracy, ignorance, superstition. . . .

The Americans of our panel are with few exceptions people aware of poverty only at the seldom-seen margins of their own society. But even this poverty bears small resemblance to the conditions that pervade most of Chinese life, either as they have observed it, heard about it, or seen it pictured. The reaction of such Americans to such poverty can and does vary widely, but it almost always includes something of shame and even more of revulsion. The American visitor to the rural or urban slums of China (or, for that matter, of India, of Egypt, or of any grossly crowded, grossly poor land) has the air and the feeling of a visitor to some other planet many light years away from his own, with inhabitants plainly belonging to a

THE MARCHING CHINESE

IF ALL THE CHINESE IN THE WORLD WERE TO MARCH- 4 ABREAST-PAST A GIVEN POINT THEY WOULD NEVER FINISH PASSING THOUGH THEY MARCHED FOREVER AND EVER

(Based on U S Army marching regulations)

Ripley's *Believe It Or Not*, Simon & Schuster, 1929-31-34

race of beings quite other than his own. If he remained in this setting by need or by choice, he usually adapted himself to it by accepting the vast difference between his conditions of life and those of the people around him as part of some natural order. He might find in the mode and manner of Chinese acceptance of these circumstances the basis for a guilty kind of admiration, for no ordinary people could adapt so cheerfully to such conditions. But more commonly, the constant confronting of his own well-being by this massive deprivation would lead him in some measure to downgrade or even to deny the humanity of the amorphous, jellylike mass among whom he passed his privileged way. For those who held this image of crowded Asian poverty from afar, there was hardly any problem. The sheer elements of size, numbers, and distance were almost enough in themselves to spur the dehumanizing process.

"THE ABSENCE OF NERVES": To endure inhuman conditions requires inhuman powers of endurance. There is a vast lore about the Chinese in this respect. They are pervasively and almost uniquely held to be capable of putting up with any hardship, enduring any pain, and living on less than any ordinary human being.

An early systematic statement of this special Chinese attribute occurs in the observations of Arthur H. Smith, the missionary author of the famous work, *Chinese Characteristics*, published in 1894. Smith titled one of his chapters "The Absence of Nerves," in which he declared that if the Chinese do have nerves like any other human being, "nothing is plainer than that they are nerves of a very different sort from those with which we are familiar." Chinese can stand in one position all day, sleep anywhere in any posture, need no air. Overcrowding is their "normal condition" and "they do not appear to be inconvenienced by it all." They have a remarkable ability "to bear without flinching a degree of pain from which the stoutest of us would shrink in terror." After citing numerous examples of this, Smith concluded: "The Chinese are and must continue to be to us more or less a puzzle, but we shall make no approach to comprehending them until we have settled firmly in our minds that, as compared with us, they are gifted with the 'absence of nerves.'" [17]

Following Smith, the American sociologist E. A. Ross, traveling in China in 1911, took the evidence of missionary doctors about the

[17] *Chinese Characteristics*, pp. 90–94.

remarkable recuperative powers of the Chinese in situations which, they averred, would have indubitably ended in death for any European. Ross concluded that the Chinese had "a special race vitality" owing to "longer and severer elimination of the less fit," acquiring thereby a special "resistance to infection and tolerance of unwholesome conditions of living."[18] Ross' effort to explain these circumstances by the natural process of selection was a good deal less exciting to the imagination than the idea of "nervelessness" which seeped into a great many capillaries of the American system for the circulation of ideas. In *Race Attitudes in Children*, published in 1929, Bruno Lasker quoted from a contemporary detective story magazine a passage which described the unbelievable capacity of a certain midget to take in alcohol and which then explained:

In the case of a white man, such indulgence might have caused sensational results. The midget, though, was Chinese, which means that his nerves were not highly organized—that he was virtually immune to stimulants.

Lasker also quoted from a popular camping manual for boys, dated 1921, in which the author discussed nature's power to adapt animal life to the environment, and after speaking of "certain vertebrates, such as the mud turtle and hellbender," goes on, in direct though unacknowledged borrowing from Arthur Smith

And there is the Chinaman, who being of a breed that has been crowded and coerced for thousands of years, seems to have done away with nerves He will stand all day in one place without seeming in the least distressed, he thrives amidst the most unsanitary surroundings, overcrowding and bad air are as nothing to him, he does not demand quiet when he would sleep nor even when he is sick, he can starve to death with supreme complacency.[19]

Such notions seemed to be needed to explain away the capacity of the Chinese to adapt himself to incredibly adverse circumstance. This capacity, which became for some the basis for great admiration of the Chinese, was seen by others as a quality akin to that of the dumb animal who knows no better, for they could not relate it to what seemed to them more comprehending and more comprehensible behavior of human beings. Something like this was required over the years to exorcise the reality of hardship in China, to make

[18] *The Changing Chinese*, New York, 1920, p 42
[19] *Race Attitudes in Children*, pp 205, 207

it possible over many decades for American (and other Western) newspapers to report the deaths of thousands and sometimes millions of people in Chinese famines, floods, and droughts, and to do so in obscure paragraphs seldom exceeding a few lines in length. These ordinarily commanded little reaction or attention; a few million Chinese more or less in that great faceless mass could not seem humanly important, or could not be allowed to seem so.

Experienced from afar, as it was by most people, this process of downgrading the humanity of the Chinese could take place casually and indifferently and could pass from person to person as invisibly as a virus Certain retarded infants, for example, are called "Mongoloids," a term said to have been adopted by a doctor in 1866 because he thought he saw "Oriental" characteristics in their faces.[20] Another example is imbedded in the joke, current in the 1930's, in which a Chinese receives successive battle reports 1,000 Japanese and 5,000 Chinese killed, 5,000 Japanese and 20,000 Chinese killed; 10,000 Japanese and 100,000 Chinese. The Chinese smiles gleefully at each new tiding The surprised foreigner asks him why he is pleased, and the Chinese chortles· "Is fine! Pretty soon no more Japanese!"

At closer quarters, the emotional effect of dehumanizing the Chinese is stronger and uglier. Essentially the same denial of human identity applied earlier to the American Indian and the Negro slave was made in relation to the Chinese in the mob violence against them in the 1870's in California and elsewhere. It provided a rationalization for the foreigners who perpetrated wanton atrocities on the Chinese in China on repeated occasions during the nineteenth century and later. During World War II, an army of young Americans abruptly transplanted to China was brought face to face, so to speak, with the faceless mass, with all the surrounding circumstances of

[20] *Collier's Encyclopedia*, New York, 1950, Vol 14, p 93 An interesting note on the subject appears in *Science Digest*, April, 1952, p 64. "In facial appearance they are strangely Oriental, an effect resulting from the broad, flat, passive features . . . The eyes are small and almond-shaped It was this appearance that inspired the word 'Mongoloid' although many doctors now refer to such cases as 'ill-finished' or 'unfinished.'" This might have been a retarded reaction among medical men to the wartime changes in popular images which made "mongoloid" sound inappropriate A medical report on the subject summarized in the *New York Times*, September 15, 1956, uses the terms "mongolism" and "mongoloid" quite unself-consciously On December 13, 1954, a liberal radio news commentator, John Vandercook, spoke in a broadcast of "Russia's monstrous Mongoloid baby, Communist China"

poverty and harshness and cruelty in Chinese life. Of the young soldier in this experience, I wrote:

His initial reaction of shock, pity, perhaps even indignation, usually soon dissolved He got used to it, as you get used to the smell of a stockyard He had to live with it, adapt himself to it. He found it increasingly difficult to look upon these Asiatics as men and women Only some subhuman species could live as they did, submit as they did. You could not apply normal standards to your thinking about them. Pity usually gave way to indifference, impatience, contempt, even hatred [21]

It is necessary to leave this point barely stated and not at all explored. I would suggest here only the thought that Western man— and especially American man—is haunted by the largely unheeded injunction to be his brother's keeper. Confronted by a stranger whom he perceives as a threat or as a victim, or faced with the human hardship of others about which he could or would do nothing, his only tolerable way out is to deny or at least to diminish the human quality of the enemy or of the suffering in view, to make the victim something less than his brother. This can be done by distinguishing no individual victim at all in the great faceless mass, or transmuting him into a different kind of being with a different set of nerves, or no nerves at all, a person, in fact, who can "starve to death with supreme complacency," a person who places so much lower a value on this life than we do that we cannot—or dare not— equate his life with one of our own In short, to make him subhuman

THE CRUEL CHINESE The inhuman powers of endurance attributed to the Chinese are closely related to the idea that they are also inhumanly cruel This association of cruelty with the Chinese is very literal, is often quite specific, and is not at all mythological or

[21] Harold R Isaacs, *No Peace For Asia*, New York, 1947, p. 8 In this same setting, to a remark about the courage of Chinese soldiers in an obscure battle action, an American officer replied: "Courage? Do you say a mule has courage because he keeps on going until he drops?" Or again "One American was describing with some passion the course of operations across the river 'They threw away 3,000 men,' he said, '3,000 men!' One of the others looked at him contemptuously 'So what?' he said, 'since when are you bleeding for 3,000 slopeys? They don't bleed about it, do they?'" (*Ibid*, p 30–31 ) Ordered not to use the term "Chinks," the American GI's in China quickly termed the Chinese "slopeys," from "slope-eyed" or, some say, from "slope-headed " This word took its place with "wogs" (Indians and Arabs) and "gooks" (any nonwhite "native") in the lexicon of the time

imaginary. It is an image that goes all the way back as an attribute of "Oriental character" to the barbarism of Genghiz Khan and his hordes. It is almost continuously present on the underside of all the more admiring images of China, ancient, old, or new. Dormant in years when more favorable views of the Chinese were dominant, it has more recently been brought into the foreground again by events both in China itself and in Korea during the Korean War. In our panel, 32 individuals mentioned it, including 7 who know China and the Chinese very well indeed. In varying contexts, they remarked that the Chinese are or could be

> cruel, savage, ruthless, barbaric, ferocious, violent, brutal; have no regard for human life or suffering; life is cheap; they butcher large numbers of people; beheadings, tortures; would save a hat in a river but not a man, are insensible to soldiers' lives; are cruel and brutal to animals. . . .

The way in which fresh events could activate old images was illustrated by the remark of an editor:

> I remember that when we heard of Japanese cruelties in China [at the time of the Sino-Japanese war] a friend of mine who had lived in China told me that when it comes to cruelty, the Chinese don't have to take lessons from anybody We are seeing some of this now in the Communist regime .

The emergence at the Hong Kong barrier of a missionary lady whose mind and body had been all but destroyed by five years in Chinese Communist prisons brought this comment in a broadcast by Eric Sevareid:

> Mrs. Bradshaw's blank, white face no longer bears any recognizable sign, save the seal of Communism, and perhaps the seal of the Orient as well. What the proportions of the two may be, no one can tell for sure The Chinese Reds did not invent official Chinese indifference to human life; several thousand years of teeming misery and official tyrannies in various forms, under various names, is the deeper reason No American who saw China before the Reds came in can have many illusions He cannot forget the total official indifference to the famines and the floods, he cannot forget the sight of Chinese soldiers dying of sickness and starvation in the ditches as their officers dined in the nearest tea house [22]

The term "Chinese torture" has a place in our language signifying

[22] Reprinted in *The Reporter*, January 12, 1956

devilishly ingenious methods of inflicting pain and death. While Chinese tortures may not actually be more devilish than those even more familiarly associated with medieval Europe, they appear to have had attached to them a quality of terrifying exquisiteness never quite achieved on the racks of the Inquisition. Images of the Chinese torturer and executioner had often been evoked in numerous early reports and scholarly works.[23] But they made their most vivid impact on a wider public during the events of the Boxer Rebellion in 1900. In the popular press and along the more intimate channels of missionary-church communications passed vivid accounts and pictures of the descent of Boxer fanatics on foreign and Chinese Christians, of brutal killings and tortures, among them the celebrated "torture of a thousand cuts." Images of consummate and fearful evil were joined to those of the merely wicked or misled heathen, an evil not only ungodly but inhuman. On all who lived through these events or were touched by them, the scratches made were cut deep and were never afterward wholly effaced, although they were usually smoothed down over time by more benign experience. One member of our panel, a man who devoted his whole career to China and rose to prominent place in his field of work, called up almost at once the sensation of terror aroused by accounts of the Boxer time which he had read as a boy The impression was so sharp that much later when as a young man he unexpectedly received word that he was to be sent to China, the vivid pictures he had seen in a *Youth's Companion* story rose to haunt his dreams and rose again, hardly any less vivid, in our interview thirty years after that.[24]

Many Americans, who in the following decades made China their second home and held a generally sympathetic view of the Chinese, tried often to "understand" the deep and broad streak of cruelty in Chinese life by relating it to the extreme harshness of the struggle for existence or by offering religious explanations for some of its manifestations.[25] For one or another of these reasons, they accepted

[23] Cf. S Wells Williams, *The Middle Kingdom*, New York, 1883, Vol I, p 507

[24] When we tracked it down, the story turned out to be "The Cross and the Dragon," the date 1911 A passage "His captors proceeded to extract information by means of such ingenious threats of torture that Jack begged 'Don't say anything more, Wang Chou! . This talk of slicing him to death by inches gives me the cold shivers!"

[25] In her autobiography, *My Several Worlds* (New York, 1954), Pearl Buck deals with the oft-observed and oft-mentioned indifference of Chinese to the

the fact that humanitarianism as Westerners understand it (i.e., Good Samaritanism) is largely absent from Chinese social relations outside the boundaries of the family, and even to a considerable extent within it. But whatever the force of the rationalization, few could wholly "accept" the many evidences of common and sadistic violence, infanticide practiced on girl babies, the existence of slavery and the maltreatment of slaves and other dependents, the callous indifference to the fate of almost all human beings outside one's own most immediate circle. Nor could friendly understanding mitigate the indisputable existence of torture in the Chinese penal system and the subjection to it of those who ran afoul of power, whether under the Communist regime, its Kuomintang predecessor, or the many other regimes which went before

Here again, however, the facets shine only when the lights hit them The theme of cruelty in Chinese life is prominent in nineteenth-century accounts and vivid at the Boxer time and for a few years thereafter. It then fades into the more disregarded shadows, rises only intermittently during the war-lord period, and all but disappears during the years 1937–45 when the images of "Oriental cruelty" in most American minds were transferred from the Chinese to the Japanese In a July, 1942, opinion poll [26] only 3 per cent of the sample chose the adjective "cruel" to describe the Chinese, while 56 per cent applied it to the Japanese. Other characteristics were similarly transferred. only 4 per cent saw the Chinese as "treacherous" compared to 73 per cent for the Japanese, and only 8 per cent called them "sly" compared to 63 per cent for the Japanese. It is certain that such a poll taken ten years later, at the height of the Korean War or at the time of the liberation of American prisoners after the truce, would have disclosed the return of these images to their ancestral Chinese home.[27] The onset of Communist

---

suffering or disaster that befalls others and explains that "the pervading atmosphere of Buddhism through the centuries had persuaded the people generally to believe that fate pursued the sufferer, that his hour had come for death If one saved him, thus defying fate, the rescuer must assume the responsibilities for the one saved " Again "The cruelty to animals which shocks so many foreigners when they visit China" is explained by the belief that animals are reincarnated humans being punished for their wickedness in a previous life and therefore deserving only of contempt

[26] Office of Public Opinion Research, July, 1942, in Cantril, *Public Opinion*, pp 499, 501.

[27] The end of Japanese custody of the most evil and hateful of the "Oriental" images held by Americans was sanctioned from on high by Douglas Mac-

108                    SCRATCHES ON OUR MINDS

terror and "persuasion" in China has clearly revived in full and growing measure all the deeply latent images of cruelty and disregard for human life associated with the Chinese in many American minds, suggesting a power of evil that is not merely inhumane but bestial, not human at all, but subhuman

Holland, *Chicago Tribune*, 1955

*New Images for Old*

---

Arthur in his speech to Congress, April 19, 1951, in which he spoke of the Japanese return to "individual liberty and personal dignity      political morality . . and social justice" and their "profoundly beneficial influence over the course of events in Asia " Japanese thrift, enterprise, and acumen have been restored to high American regard, Japanese art exhibits draw admiring American audiences, and a visiting company of Kabuki dancers has scored a critical and popular triumph

In a Hollywood publicity interview the actor Marlon Brando, back from making a picture in Japan, enthused "I was terribly impressed with Japan The people are the nicest I've ever met in my life They unquestionably are the most courteous, honorable, well-meaning, and self-respecting people   . . hypersensitively attuned to other people in their relationships "—*Boston Traveler*, June 29, 1956.

## 4. "CHINK, CHINK, CHINAMAN"

IMAGES rooted in the American experience with Chinese in the United States itself are almost all images of the Chinese as an inferior people On the Americans' own ground, the Chinese was different, sometimes harmlessly but for long periods dangerously so He was able sometimes to appear in American eyes to be only quaintly odd, but for a much longer time he was menacingly mysterious Even the industry and thrift so often attributed to him were qualities that became threatening, and the honesty with which he was also widely credited was largely canceled out by the more powerful notions of his deviousness and inscrutability. Only for the briefest intervals in his century-long history in this land has the Chinese in America enjoyed anything resembling the friendly approval of his American neighbors or the admiration aroused in some Americans by his countrymen at home in China.

Here are one man's boyhood recollections of the Chinese who lived in a small New Jersey town early in the century:

The Chinese, of course, were by far the most foreign and outlandish. They ran laundries, no work for a man anyway, they had no families or children, they were neither Democrats nor Republicans. They wrote backwards and upside down, with a brush, they worked incessantly night and day, Saturdays and Sundays, all of which stamped them as the most alien heathen . . . We knew that they lived entirely on a horrible dish called chopsooey which was composed of rats, mice, cats, and puppydogs. We knew that the long pigtail that they wore at the time was their most cherished possession and . . if any foolish little white boy were to lay profane hands on one and give it a yank, the Chink would reach under the counter, draw out a razor-sharp cleaver which he kept there in readiness, and cut off your head as quick as a wink . . .

[Some older boys] were reputed to have flung open the doors of various laundries and tossed in dead cats, rats, or mice, escaping the dreaded cleavers by only a hair's breadth. . . .

These do not happen to be the words of any member of our present panel, but when Robert Lawson, the writer and illustrator, set them down in his autobiography,[28] he was reproducing notions that recur often in some part in the memories of many of our inter-

[28] *At That Time*, New York, 1947, pp. 43–45

viewees. Lawson added that when he thought now of "the years of devoted service" and the "sweet and childish friendship" of the Chinese cooks he has had in his own home, it made him feel "very shamefaced and apologetic for that noisy little brat who used to taunt their countrymen." Since very few of our panelists ever had Chinese cooks in their homes, they could not quite match his amends, though they could often reflect the same unconsciously patronizing air. The mention of "Chinese" brought up in the minds of 82 of them a variety of associations with the Chinese in the United States. Many of these were quite simply *laundrymen* or *restaurant men*, familiar fixtures in so many American communities, and in some minds these figures appeared attached to the same bits of childhood folklore reported by Lawson. They were, in these young eyes,

> evil, dangerous, they kidnapped children, engaged in white slave traffic; were always the villains in movies, strange, dreaded; they might cut you up, sinister, they ate rats, smoked opium. . . .

A few remembered the rhyme they chanted:

> Chink, Chink, Chinaman, sitting on a rail,
> Along comes a white man and cuts off his tail . . .

They are perhaps too few in number to make a case out of, but it is still rather striking to note that the sharpest and most highly colored recollections of the most childishly cruel nonsense aimed at the Chinese appeared in the minds of half a dozen panelists who were themselves members of other minority groups, Jews, Negroes, Irishmen, who grew up in slums or near-slums close to those in which the Chinese ordinarily lived. These experiences and attitudes are, however, by no means confined to such settings. They occur in Midwestern backgrounds and in Western origins, where clear traces appear of the sinister and hated Chinese of the "Yellow Peril" period and even of the owlishly devious "heathen Chinee" of the Bret Harte epoch a generation earlier.

Actually the Chinese in the United States has remained largely—indeed, almost wholly—a creature of stereotypes. He has rarely been anything else because intimacy or even close acquaintance between him and Americans has been rare. Only one panelist spoke of close Chinatown friendships and one other of an acquaintance with a restaurant proprietor in his city. Another mentioned Chinese schoolmates with whom he had played in the schoolyard but rarely ever saw after school hours Changes in this pattern have begun to take place, with the spread of Chinese-Americans into more varied spheres of American life, but these are quite recent and still uncommon. Only one panelist referred to a close professional colleague who happened to be Chinese-American

From the beginning of Chinese immigration a century ago down to the present, the Chinese has essentially remained a sort of oddity His high visibility has never permitted him to disappear into the stream of the population. His only escape from prejudice and hostility was until recently to try to disappear by withdrawing as far as he could into his tiny little communities and into himself He became, in the eyes of most of the Americans around him, a familiar curiosity, in turn welcomed, patronized, mocked, feared, hated, lynched, excluded, ignored, tolerated, liked—oddly feared or oddly admired, but scarcely ever known, understood, or simply accepted. Something of many or all of these reactions or the knowledge of them stirs in many an American's mind even today when out of the long history of associations, from the mining camps of California a hundred years ago to his own last visit to a Chinese restaurant, he plucks some fragment of information or of feeling.

The story of the Chinese in this country is largely the story of the brutal bigotry of Americans. It has been much written, and there is neither need nor space to review its details here It is our task, rather, to trace an outline through all this history of how the Chinese were viewed by the Americans among whom they came and especially of how these images have shifted with time and circumstance

In the initial period, through the 1850's and into the 1860's, when the gold-hunters and empire-builders had no time for ordinary labor, the Chinese immigrants—brought over by a contract system that amounted to helotry—were soon being welcomed in California into every craft and service where the drudgery was greatest and the gain the least. They were greeted not only without hostility or race prejudice but occasionally even with warmth. "Scarcely a ship arrives that does not bring an increase to this worthy integer of our population," said the *Daily Alta California* on May 12, 1852. "The China boys will yet vote at the same polls, study at the same schools and bow at the same altar as our countrymen " [29] In this time of their great

[29] Quoted by Foster Rhea Dulles, *China and America*, New York, 1946, p 79.

usefulness, reports one study, the newcomers were generally described as

> the most worthy of our newly-adopted citizens, ... the best immigrants in California; . thrifty, sober, tractable, inoffensive, law-abiding, with all-around ability and adaptability...

But as white men kept swarming into the state and the prospects of quick wealth dimmed, and especially when the end of railroad building threw masses of both races into unemployment, the value of plain work rose. The Chinese had been quickly driven away from the mining of gold, but now the white man began to shoulder him out of the way in the service trades, manufacturing, and agriculture. Amid rising hostility, agitation, and mob violence, reaching peaks of arson, pillage, and murder during the depression years of the 1870's, the Chinese became

> "a distinct people," "unassimilable," "keeping to their own customs and laws" They "lowered the plane of living" ... "shut out white labor" They were "clannish," "dangerous," "criminal," "secretive in their actions," "debased and servile," "deceitful and vicious," "inferior from a mental and moral point of view," "filthy and loathsome in their habits" .. Every aspect of the invaders became unpleasant; their slant eyes bespoke slyness, their conversation among themselves frightful jabbering....[30]

In 1868, Anson Burlingame, the American minister in Peking, had negotiated the nearest thing to a friendly treaty signed by any Power with the Chinese up to that time and in this pact had especially provided for encouragement of Chinese immigration into the United States This was done at the spur of American employers who still wanted cheap Chinese labor But the treaty was already being overtaken by events by the time it was signed. A wild clamor arose in California and elsewhere for exclusion of the Chinese. By 1876 both major political parties, anxious for California's votes, had adopted Chinese exclusion planks in their platforms. In 1879 a California vote on the exclusion issue ran 154,638 for and 883 against. Even as the rights of Americans in China were being enforced by arms when necessary and by the exercise of extraterritorial rights which placed foreigners in China above Chinese law, the American government moved to discriminate legally against the Chinese within its

[30] B Schneke, *Alien Americans*, New York, 1936, pp 11–12

own borders. A new treaty exacting Chinese consent and correcting Burlingame's "mistake" was signed in 1880 In 1882, the Congress passed the Chinese Exclusion Act, the first of its kind in the country's history, and hardened and extended it by subsequent legislation during the next several decades.[31] In all the fine blur of benevolence which shrouds so much of the American self-image in relation to China, it is seldom remembered that the first antiforeign boycott ever mounted in China arose, in 1905, in protest against American exclusion and the brutal treatment of Chinese in America.

The images and the shame and some of the anger and the irony of these events can be found in the pages of both Bret Harte and Mark Twain. Among our panelists the best-remembered and the most often quoted lines from Harte were, of course:

> That for ways that are dark
> And tricks that are vain,
> The heathen Chinee is peculiar. . . .

Harte's portrait of the Chinese was usually of an incomprehensible, pidgin-English-speaking character whose apparent silly stupidity cloaked a devious and wily and guileful shrewdness. But no member of our panel appeared to remember the sharper edge of Harte's vignettes. "Dead, my reverend friends, dead," he wrote in his obituary of Wan Lee, "stoned to death in the streets of San Francisco, in the year of grace 1869, by a mob of half-grown boys and Christian school children." Or, again, of a Chinese making a journey in California.

On the road to Sacramento, he was twice playfully thrown from the top of the stagecoach by an intelligent but deeply intoxicated Caucasian, whose moral nature was shocked at riding with one addicted to opium-smoking At Hangtown he was beaten by a passing stranger—purely an act of Christian supererogation. At Dutch Flat he was robbed by well-known hands from unknown motives. At Sacramento he was arrested on suspicion of being something or other and discharged with a severe reprimand—possibly for not being it, and so delaying the course of justice. At San Francisco he was freely stoned by children of the public schools, but by carefully avoiding the monuments of enlightened progress, he at

---

[31] There is a large literature on this subject One work especially rich in contemporary source materials and with an extensive bibliography is Elmer C. Sandmeyer, *The Anti-Chinese Movement in California*, Illinois Studies in the Social Sciences, Vol. XXIV, No 3, 1939.

last reached, in comparative safety, the Chinese quarter where his abuse was confined to the police and limited by the strong arm of the law.[82]

In an essay called "John Chinaman," Harte wrote that he thought he saw

an abiding consciousness of degradation—a secret pain of self-humiliation in the lines of the mouth and eye. . . . They seldom smile, and their laughter is of such an extraordinary and sardonic nature—so purely a mechanical spasm, quite independent of any mirthful attribute—that to this day I am doubtful whether I ever saw a Chinaman laugh.

And he concluded.

From the persecutions of the young and old of a certain class, his life was a torment I don't know what was the exact philosophy that Confucius taught, but it is to be hoped that poor John in his persecution is still able to detect the conscious hate and fear with which inferiority always regards the possibility of even-handed justice, and which is the key note to the vulgar clamor about servile and degraded races.[83]

Among his newspaper pieces in 1870, Mark Twain included a series of imaginary letters in which a Chinese immigrant bitingly describes his expectations and his experiences in "that noble realm where all are free and all are equal" and where he was robbed, beaten, set upon by dogs, reviled, arrested, and when he could not produce money for a bribe was thrown by his captor into a cell with the words: "Rot there, ye furrin spawn, till ye lairn that there's no room in America for the likes of ye or your nation."[34] In *Roughing It*, he gave his views both of the Chinese and of their persecutors.

They are a harmless race when white men either let them alone or treat them no worse than dogs, in fact, they are almost entirely harmless anyhow, for they seldom think of resenting the vilest insults or the cruelest injuries. They are quiet, peaceable, tractable, free from drunkenness, and they are as industrious as the day is long. A disorderly Chinaman is rare and a lazy one does not exist. . . He is a great convenience to everybody—even to the worst class of white men, for he bears most of their sins, suffering fines for their petty thefts, imprisonment for their

[82] *Selected Stories of Bret Harte*, New York, 1946, pp 148–151
[83] Bret Harte, *The Luck of Roaring Camp and Other Sketches*, Boston, n d., pp 242, 246–247.
[34] F L. Patee, *Mark Twain, Selections with Bibliography*, New York, 1935, pp. 98–104.

THE CHINESE 115

robberies, and death for their murders. Any white man can swear a
Chinaman's life away in the courts, but no Chinaman can testify against
a white man. Ours is the "land of the free"—nobody denies that—nobody challenges it. (Maybe it is because we won't let other people
testify ) As I write, news comes that in broad daylight in San Francisco,
some boys have stoned an inoffensive Chinaman to death, and that
although a large crowd witnessed the shameful deed, no one interfered.... No Californian *gentleman or lady* ever abuses or oppresses a
Chinaman under any circumstances, an explanation that seems to be
much needed in the East. Only the scum of the population do it—they
and their children, they, and naturally and consistently, the policemen
and politicians, likewise, for these are the dust-licking pimps and slaves
of the scum, there as well as elsewhere in America. .[35]

This was the era and these the events which introduced into our
language the phrase "a Chinaman's chance"—meaning no chance at
all [36]

Fleeing from this violence and, after the turn of the century, from
the cry of "Yellow Peril" (aimed at the newly arriving Japanese and
the Chinese both, lumped together as "Orientals"), many Chinese
quit the Western states, settled elsewhere, and gradually established
new refuges in the Chinatowns that sprang up in various cities
around the country.[37] They sought safety in the trades where they
might remain undisturbed—laundries, restaurants, curio shops—and
in domestic service. They withdrew into the isolation of their own
communities and, even more, into the supercaution of what the
American saw as an unreacting expressionlessness. It was actually a

[35] *Roughing It*, New York, 1913, (originally published 1872), Chapter XIII
[36] "Chinaman" is one of those terms whose derogatory quality rose out of the
manner of its usage, for it was a product of the contemptuous attitudes of the
nineteenth century. It was used by many quite explicitly in this spirit and echoed
by many others quite unaware of its feeling-tone As early as the 1890's, Arthur
Smith, author of *Chinese Characteristics*, was deploring the universal use of the
term by writers about China "John Chinaman," generically applied to all
Chinese, was an expression of the idea that all Chinese were "alike" and had no
individual identities It was widely used in this way in the United States, although
"Chink" was the more direct and more violent epithet. In our panel of 181, no
one used "Chink" and only 10 used "Chinaman " Of these 10, seven had never
been to China, two had visited briefly, and one had somewhat more experience
there as a businessman Four of the 10 had generally negative views about the
Chinese and came by the prejudiced term naturally. The other 6 simply did not
know better
[37] Cf Rose Hum Lee, "The Decline of the Chinatowns in the United States,"
*American Journal of Sociology*, LIV, 5, March, 1949

great care not to become involved in matters that might draw the white man's attention to them. Hence the impressions noted by some 10 panelists, that Chinese-Americans "know their place," and are "less venturesome intellectually," that they tended to "live in a closed society, to stay by themselves, to stand apart," and in a situation of controversy on a college campus "avoided taking positions." Here too, in its own special place, belongs the observation of several Negro panelists that the Chinese docilely followed the white man's patterns in imposing Jim Crow restrictions on their restaurant clientele.

The Chinese defense against a hostile environment strongly reinforced the illusion of Chinese 'inscrutability." The crowded, honeycombed Chinatowns themselves quickly also became dark places of mystery, sin, and crime in the popular magazines and, before long, in the films. No evil was too devilish to be attributed to the Chinese villains who stalked their victims in dark alleys and through secret passages, who lolled with their opium pipes, smuggled drugs, slaves, prostitutes, or other Chinese, or hacked away at each other in the tong war versions of the crime-and-gangster themes that filled American screens during the 1920's. These films appear again and again in the recollections of our panel. Dorothy Jones lists a long series of them, all using common devices:

> The mystery of Chinatown was suggested by a whole series of visual cliches—the ominous shadow of an Oriental figure thrown against a wall, secret panels which slide back to reveal an inscrutable Oriental face, the huge shadow of a hand with tapering fingers and long pointed fingernails poised menacingly, the raised dagger appearing suddenly and unexpectedly from between closed curtains.[38]

The dominant and by far the best-remembered figure from this genre of film and story was that most sinister and most evil of all men, Dr. Fu Manchu. The creature of an English writer using the pseudonym Sax Rohmer, Fu Manchu was quickly established as a public character in this country and enjoyed a great vogue, especially after he began appearing in a series of films starting in 1929. In the language of the Hollywood studio publicity material, Fu Manchu had "menace in every twitch of his finger, a threat in every twitch of his eyebrow, terror in each split-second of his slanted eyes." He was revengeful, merciless, adept at obscure forms of slow torture, a master

---

[38] Dorothy Jones, *op cit*, p 24.

THE CHINESE 117

of unknown drugs, and the lord of a vast army of thugs and slaves ready to do his worst bidding. He was so evil that he periodically had to be killed off, and was so mysteriously superpowerful that he always miraculously reappeared in time for the next episode Fu Manchu ultimately did die what seemed like a natural death in the years when the Chinese, as heroic fighters and allies in the war against Japan, commanded general sympathy. He has recently made another of his miraculous reappearances, trailing with all his absurdities in the wake of the more recently reviving and infinitely more somber images of dangerousness attached to the Chinese.

The wry paradox is that the more wicked the Chinatown locale was made to appear in the movies and pulps of the 1920's, the less wicked it became in fact. There was some real gang warfare in the Chinatowns but it was brought quickly to an end, continuing for years afterward only in the neighborhood movie houses. The Chinatowns became generally quiet places where the aura of evil and lurid melodrama was preserved for the vicarious titillation of visiting tourists who came out of curiosity and, more and more, to enjoy Chinese food. In the crowded world beyond the Chinatowns, hostility toward the Chinese was also dying away. In 1924 immigration bars, hitherto held only against "Orientals," had been raised against a good part of the world, including much of Europe. The bigot impulse had other targets—Negroes, Jews, Italians, Eastern Europeans— and for "Orientals" had the more newly-arriving Japanese to vent itself upon. The Chinese were so unresisting and so few in number that the image of them as evil and dangerous could be propped up only by the crude efforts of the Hollywood writers. The air of evil mystery remained, but it became pure mythology not even the small boys really believed the laundryman kept a cleaver under his counter. The attribute of fearsome strangeness was beginning to give way and to be replaced by one of unfearful oddity. Social rejection continued, but it was beginning, if not to give place, at least to share place with a certain friendly sympathy.

A wide array of circumstances, not always by any means interrelated or tidily arrangeable into a pattern, fueled this process. One was the larger picture relating to China itself. China was in revolutionary upheaval in the 1920's, foreign privileges there were threatened by new nationalist forces stronger than any known before. Along with anxiety over the new developments, there was also a new respect and even a certain sympathy for Chinese reassertion. In the

United States this seemed to be reflected, in part at least, in a certain mitigation of the prejudice and hostility felt toward the local Chinese In a paper she wrote as a graduate student at the University of Chicago in 1944, Dr. Rose Hum Lee traced the changing tone of the periodical press of this country, which began in this period to move away from the highly colored stories of slave and drug traffic and "tong" wars to friendlier efforts to describe Chinatown life. Dr Lee, looking at home rather than abroad for the reasons, noted one turning point in the sympathy for the Chinese aroused by police excesses in going after the "tongs." Rough handling of Chinese by police and courts touched off protests among liberals and in the press It aroused that feeling for the underdog which can always make itself most effectively felt in our society when no important group or interest feels threatened. The first serious sociological study of the Chinese communities was made at this time, undertaken by Dr. Robert E. Park of Chicago and its findings summarized in a special issue of *Survey Graphic* in May, 1926 Dr. Lee found that "even the *Literary Digest,* noted for its anti-Chinese sentiments, toned down." She quoted from it part of a Chinese student's sardonic little list of American beliefs about the Chinese:

The favorite delicacies of the Chinese are rats and snakes.
The Chinese say yes for no and vice versa ...
They eat soup with chopsticks.
Chop suey and chow mein are their national dishes and that besides these dishes they eat nothing but rice
Chinese men wear skirts and women pants.
A Chinaman never gets drunk.
A Chinese is properly a Chinaman and that the word "Chinee" is singular for "Chinese."
The Chinese are a nation of laundrymen yet have a highly developed civilization. ..
All Chinese are cunning and crafty.
All Chinese are honest and absolutely trustworthy
The Chinese never lose their tempers.
The United States is the friend and protector of China.
All Chinese look alike.
The Chinese have no nerves and can sleep anywhere. ...
They have no souls because they are not Christians.
They never say what they mean and abhor straight lines.
The Chinese invented pretty nearly everything that was ever invented.
The Chinese all hate water and never bathe.

They are a mysterious and inscrutable race and that they do everything backwards.[39]

Certainly one of the principal instruments and the most popular symbol of the shift from wily evil to wily virtue in the Chinese in America in this period was the fictional character of Charlie Chan, the famous Chinese detective. Inspired, it is said, by the exploits of a Chinese sleuth in Honolulu, Charlie Chan was introduced to the public by Earl Derr Biggers in 1925. He moved through the columns of the *Saturday Evening Post*, a raft of books, and no fewer than 48 feature films, to the status of a national institution. Chan was the epitome of the "damned clever Chinese," blandly humble in the face of Occidental contempt and invariably confounding all concerned by his shrewd solution of the crime. His aphorisms, always prefaced by "Confucius say——", passed into the national vernacular. His approximations of Confucius were swelled by every man's wit into approximations of Charlie Chan. The formula required only some homely or humorous bit of real or alleged wisdom put into pidgin English, e.g., "Hasty conclusion easy to make, like hole in water," or, "Theory, like mist on eyeglasses, obscures fact." As Mrs. Jones points out in her film study, Charlie Chan was still "the inscrutable Chinese of the mystery film," the man of few words, popping up unexpectedly and unseen, with a great power for slithering through complex situations, and unfathomable cleverness in plumbing motives and coping with his foes. Only unlike Fu Manchu and his ilk, Charlie Chan was on the side of the law and virtue and was constantly winning friends and influencing people to take a new view of the Chinese. He was, in part, consciously intended to serve this end. The stock treatment of Chinese in American films had begun to draw protests from China, and Mrs. Jones quotes John Stone, the producer of the original Chan films at Fox Studios, as saying that the Chan characterization "was deliberately decided upon as a refuta-

[39] *Literary Digest*, March 12, 1927, quoted by Rose Hum Lee in "Social Attitudes Toward Chinese in the United States, Expressed in Periodical Literature from 1919 to 1944," Unpublished mss., 1944. Miss Lee interestingly did not note in her paper that this list of characteristics was published as one feature in a lengthy special section devoted to the events in China, opening with a photograph of Chinese nationalist soldiers with the caption "Troops that have made the whole world wake up to New China." It also included a feature on the Chinese in the United States which observes that "these picturesque and enigmatic visitors acquire a new interest in our eyes because of the titanic and transforming forces that are astir in their native land."

tion of the unfortunate Fu Manchu characterization of the Chinese, and partly as a demonstration of his [Stone's] own idea that any minority group could be sympathetically portrayed on the screen with the right story and the right approach." [40]

When pendulums of this kind swing among Americans they generally swing high and wide. The circumstances of the late 1930's and early 1940's ticked out a highly favorable time for the Chinese as viewed through American eyes. The reasons lay mostly in China—these were the years of the Sino-Japanese War, Pearl Harbor, and the emergence of the Chinese as our heroic allies. One result, for China, was the abrogation of the previous "unequal treaties" and the surrender of extraterritoriality in a new treaty in 1943. In the same year the United States Congress repealed the Chinese Exclusion Act of 1882. A quota of 105 was established for "persons of Chinese ancestry," the only surviving discrimination on entry based on race, as such. (All others are based on country of origin.) In the wartime atmosphere the Chinese in America began to bask, not to say blink, in a new kindliness. Just as the Chinese in China had found immensely popular interpreters in Pearl Buck and Lin Yutang, the American Chinatowns and their inhabitants achieved a new and unaccustomed glorification at the hands of a considerable body of eager writers headed by Carl Glick, author of *Shake Hands with the Dragon* (1941). Instead of the "tongs" whose members killed each other off with hatchets, the large Chinese community organizations were examined with interest as benevolent mutual help societies which kept Chinese off the relief rolls during the depression. Chinatown life became more than ever quaint, fascinating, and sentimentally attractive, and the Chinese themselves an incomparable people of unsurpassed virtue, so much so that Dr. Lee, writing in 1944, had to point out that this literature managed "to adorn the Chinese with a pair of wings and a halo!" And she added, acutely

> As violently as the Chinese were once attacked, they are now glorified and mounted on a pedestal. It is impossible to predict how lasting this change will be.... Largely grounded on the sandy loam of sentimentality, one is left conjecturing what the tone of literature toward the Chinese will be in 1954.

There is little direct evidence to show how far these more sympathetic images and attitudes were translated into more sympathetic individual or social behavior. The pioneering studies made by Emory

[40] Jones, *op. cit.*, p. 34.

THE CHINESE                                                                                                                121

Bogardus between 1924 and 1927 had shown that the Chinese were at the bottom of his social distance scales, sharing place there with other "non-white" peoples and with the Turks.[41] Several studies using a version of the Bogardus scale were conducted by Elmo Roper in 1942 and 1948. While the results cannot be compared directly or in detail to the Bogardus findings, they do strongly suggest that the social acceptability of the Chinese had been considerably enhanced in the intervening years. They shared in the general breaking down of bars in employment and occupation which resulted from the pressures of the war period. Roper's findings suggested that within a continuing pattern of considerable prejudice and discrimination, the Chinese in the war years became somewhat less unacceptable than Jews except as kin by marriage where the color factor was decisive. A national cross section of high school students questioned in the 1942 Roper survey showed large indifference to what kinds of people they would share employment with, but 38 per cent said that a Chinese would be their last choice as a roommate (compared to 45 per cent for Jews and 78 per cent for Negroes) and 78 per cent said they would not marry a Chinese (compared to 51 per cent for Jews and 92 per cent for Negroes.) A national cross section of factory workers showed 28 per cent who would have least liked to see Chinese move into their neighborhoods (compared to 42 per cent for Jews and 72 per cent for Negroes).[42] The 1948 study, based on a national cross-section sample of the whole population over twenty-one, suggested that the Chinese occupied a position in the American prejudice pattern roughly comparable to that of the Jews in all matters except marriage. In almost all of Roper's groupings of questions and categories, the Chinese ended up in the middle position among eight groups named, behind Protestants, Catholics, Italians and Jews, and ahead of Filipinos, Mexicans, and Negroes.[43]

[41] Emory S Bogardus, *Immigration and Race Attitudes*, New York, 1928, p 25 and *passim*.
[42] Roper *New York Herald Tribune* and *Fortune* polls, November, 1942, in Cantril, *Public Opinion*, p. 477.
[43] Roper National 21 and over survey, September, 1948, from the Roper files. An excerpt from the gross findings on the total sample

| Prefer NOT to have | Chinese | Jews | Negroes |
|---|---|---|---|
| as fellow-worker | 14 2% | 13 2% | 40.8% |
| as neighbor | 28.0 | 21.3 | 62.0 |
| as guest in home | 23.5 | 14 2 | 56.0 |
| as kin by marriage | 64 6 | 45 8 | 78.9 |

Some interesting details· Prejudice patterns were strongest in the South and Far West, less so in the Midwest, least noticeable in the Northeast. Far Westerners

In our own interviews, relatively little was said in this connection about Chinese in the United States beyond the familiar, and older, stereotypes. In a certain number (21) more detailed observations did appear, most of them when the panelists were asked to give their impressions how other Americans generally regarded the Chinese. Some tried quite conscientiously to imagine what the common views might be; others lapsed back into notions of their own:

> I suppose they think of the laundryman, restauranteur, the heathen Chinee. Conflicts in California, ignorance, dirt, superstition, pounding gongs to drive away dragons and devils, Chinatowns I visited the San Francisco Chinatown (when I was a young man) and heard them banging gongs....

Or again:

> All levels of U S. society find the Chinese inscrutable, that we cannot understand them no matter how hard we try, that their ultimate thinking is untouched and unreached by us. Suppose this comes from Fu Manchu, early movie villains, the devious mysterious Chinese. Am at a loss to judge this myself, though I did get some of their feeling from my contacts with them . . . The Chinese I knew puzzled me the most, always seemed impenetrable to me

From a Midwestern editor:

> The common idea of "how do you tell them apart?" People not given to showing emotion, stoic. Also geniality, from Charlie Chan, the genial sleuth . . .

A professor of economics:

> Wouldn't distinguish my views from others. . . . They include the Chinese laundryman, happy, hardworking, obsequious, overpolite . . . The Fu Manchu image, devious, slant-eyed, Oriental schemer, though I never took this one seriously. . . .

A public opinion specialist

> Have never seen a cross section taken on this Would assume in

---

were about like others in readiness to "work with" Chinese but markedly less willing to have them as neighbors College-educated people were somewhat more willing than less-educated folks to entertain Chinese as guests, but were markedly less willing to have them as neighbors Except in the marriage column, the Chinese remained generally behind the Jews in degree of acceptability with two striking exceptions The "college-educated" and the "professional and executive" groups were more willing to have Chinese than Jews as fellow workers, although Jews were still slightly more acceptable for these groups as neighbors and guests, and by a wide margin, as kin-by-marriage

most a vast ignorance. Of those with some knowledge, would expect casual contacts in restaurants, laundries, movies. Very little else Might think the Chinese untrustworthy in business, capable of living on impossibly low wages. All hearsay and vague ideas. "Never trust a Chink"—I heard this dozens of times in my boyhood. . . .

A social scientist of European background:

I would know little of this. Assume the average thinking is based on more actual contact, laundrymen, waiters, restaurant owners, taxi-drivers, Chinatowns Rather friendly feelings so long as the underdog status remains unchanged. Suspect white Americans feel kindlier toward Negroes. Classify them comparably to Negroes but see no threat of equality or penetration.

Several with Californian backgrounds:

Idea of the "Chinks" in California in the 1930's. Yellow peril, sea of immigration, keep them out, deviousness. . . .

Most Americans think of Chinese unfavorably, especially on the West coast. They would "rather not discuss it," pretty much like polite people talking about Jews. A strong feeling that the Chinese are OK so long as they are in Chinatown, but not anywhere else. . . .

My father thinks of the Chinese as honest and industrious .. I did have the San Francisco stereotype of the Chinese who knows his menial place and sticks to it. But I think the old anti-Chinese prejudice is pretty dead.

Californians think of the Chinese largely as coolies because that is what they were here, hardworking, frugal, cheaper, undersell anybody, "undesirables," especially as purchasers of land. Don't hear this much anymore Passage of time has changed this Up to time of war, heard more about Japanese. The Chinese were seen as pathetic—"poor bastards." But now Chinese here are Americans and are accepted as such. Tension point now very low, with some exceptions It could be aroused again.

In 1952, a Chinese, a former Nationalist army officer named Sing Sheng, moved with his family into a San Francisco suburb called Southwood. His new neighbors protested and demanded that he and his family leave. Believing that majority opinion would be with him, Sing Sheng proposed a vote and said he would abide by the result The community voted 174 against him, 28 for, and 14 were without opinion When this news appeared, offers of new homes reached the family from all over the country and they finally moved to Sonoma, California, where they were assured they would be welcome. In May, 1955, a *New York Times* survey of racial bias in the country reported optimistically: "Since World War II, people of Japanese and Chinese lineage, who in the West coast states used to be the targets of the most systematic discrimination, have moved into a status close to first-class citizenship." In a paper presented at the meeting of the Far Eastern Association in 1956, Dr. Rose Hum Lee pointed out that native-born Chinese-Americans now comprise about half the total Chinese population in this country, that in large numbers they have moved up the educational and occupational ladders, have left behind them much of their identification with the ancestral homeland, a process of alienation hastened for many by the Communist conquest of power in China For these Chinese-Americans, Dr Lee hopefully foresaw a bright prospect of increasingly rapid integration into American society.[44]

On the other hand, in October, 1956, not on the West Coast but at Evanston, Illinois, a Northwestern University fraternity embarrassedly withdrew a pledge it had offered to a Chinese freshman, Sherman Wu, son of a former high official of the Chinese Nationalist government. "At least seven freshmen declined to be pledged because of Mr. Wu," the president of the fraternity was quoted as saying "Later," the news account went on, "Mr. Wu said two other fraternities had offered him membership. 'If they are sincere enough, I may join one. I don't know yet,' he said."[45]

## 5. *THE WARDS*

"ALL MY LIFE," said a United States Senator, a member of our panel, "I'd looked upon the Chinese as wards. We always tried to protect them, always resisted attacks on them."

In these words, including their tense and their tone, the Senator stated succinctly one of the most commanding of all the themes that emerge from this natural history of American images of the Chinese

---

[44] Dr Rose Hum Lee, "The Integration of the Chinese in the United States," presented before the Far Eastern Association, Philadelphia, March 29, 1956.
[45] *New York Times*, November 1, 1956.

From the conception of the Chinese as inferior people to the image of the Chinese as wards is really but a small step. There were 400 million subhumans who, with appropriate protection and enterprise, could become 400 million customers and open endless vistas for American trade and industry. There were 400 million benighted souls which, with appropriate guidance and instruction, could be saved from damnation and add a vast realm to God's kingdom on earth. These twin dreams inspired the role of benevolent guardian in which the American saw himself in relation to the Chinese and which is so heavily stamped on the American view of all this history.

Because of the nature of his own recent past and the moral commitments it imposed upon him, the nineteenth century American, by and large, had to suppress the impulse to proceed abroad in the empire-building manner of the times. The pull of these influences was strong enough to give a peculiar cast of ineptitude and inconsistency to American imperial temptations and to burden them with a weight of conscience and a sense of wrongdoing unfelt as a rule by the European participants in these affairs Hence Americans chose the other alternative, which was to keep other foreigners from turning China into an exclusive preserve for themselves. This was done by insisting upon the American right to enjoy the same perquisites and privileges exacted from China by force or threats by any other Power. Thus in 1844, as already noted, Caleb Cushing negotiated for the United States the concessions won by the British in the war of 1839–41. The same intent led, in 1858, to the spectacle of an American minister waiting at the river's mouth while English and French cannon battered the forts, then sailing in to negotiate the American share of the fruits of Anglo-French victory.[46]

[46] Foster Rhea Dulles, *China and America*, Princeton, 1946, p 58 "The English barbarians," the Imperial Commissioner wrote the Emperor about this time, "are full of insidious schemes, uncontrollably fierce and imperious The American nation does no more than follow in their direction." Quoted by Dulles, *ibid.*, p 62.

Tyler Dennett, detailing expansionist maneuvers and strong-arm tactics used by William H Seward as secretary of state (1861–69)—one of the earliest and strongest believers in an American Pacific destiny—records apologetically that Seward had been guilty of "a list of very un-American actions."—"Seward's Far Eastern Policy," *American Historical Review*, XXVIII, 1923, p 61

The imperialists of the Roosevelt-McKinley era had to buck the strong opposition and revulsion of a large number of prominent Americans who "did not oppose colonial expansion for commercial, religious, constitutional or humanitarian reasons [but] because they thought that an imperialist policy ran counter to the political doctrines of the Declaration of Independence, Washington's

This was the open door, insisted upon from the beginning, which was eventually enthroned as the Open Door by John Hay's notes to the Powers in 1899-1900 Gradually enlarged in interpretation if not intent and draped over with all sorts of real and synthetic appurtenances of high moral purpose, this policy established the American role as protector not only of access to China, but necessarily of China's accessibility, or in more suitable language, its freedom, independence, and integrity From this came the special sense of a benevolent American guardianship over China's well-being.

But traders, especially in that past day, seldom had to idealize their purposes. For politicians and diplomats it was a somewhat more stringent though not an imperative requirement. It was the missionary, his brother's keeper by vocation, who gave this experience its unique cast, who played a special and sometimes decisive role in matters of policy in war and peace affecting China, and who was more responsible by far than either the trader or the diplomat for the images of the Chinese created in American minds over these many decades.

Some of the earliest Catholic missionaries, quite unlike Francis of Assisi, or the famous traveler, Father Matteo Ricci, had come to China actually buckled in armor and in command of armed expeditions Protestant missionaries, arriving some two hundred years later, came more sedately a step behind the adventurers and the traders. One of the first New England merchants to make a fortune in the China trade was a pious Yankee named D. W. C. Olyphant. He provided the funds in 1830 to bring over and establish in Canton the first American mission to the Chinese During the next 119 years— to its effective liquidation in 1949—this enterprise ultimately came to involve thousands of missionaries and their families and the investment and annual expenditure of many millions of dollars.[47] Both in

---

Farewell Address, and Lincoln's Gettysburg Address—the doctrines which asserted that a government could not rule peoples without their consent . ."— "The Anti-Imperialist Movement in the United States, 1898-1900,' by Fred H Harrington, *The Mississippi Historical Review*, XXII, No 2, 1935, p 211 For a gruff and cantless summary of some of these events as viewed by an economic determinist, see Charles A Beard, *The Rise of American Civilization*, New York, 1930, Vol I, pp 717-724

[47] Precise and inclusive figures are lacking. Some estimates have placed capital investment in mission institutions in China at $50,000,000, which would have made it one-fourth of the total American investment in China in 1930 An indication of the annual outlay by U S contributors in the peak decades is the figure for 1935, given as an incomplete total for China of $3,817,307 The total

people and in dollars, China became the largest single field of American missionary effort.

The missionary movement grew out of evangelical Christianity with its deepest roots in rural America. It created a special place for China in the minds of millions of churchgoing Americans over some five generations China was, moreover, the only field of mission effort which was also, from the very beginning, a sphere of important American political and economic interests, the only place where these interests and missionary enterprise were so inextricably entwined over so long a time. It took a newspaper to send Stanley into Africa to find the lonely Livingstone, but the United States government, together with a group of European nations, sent an army into China to quell a rebellion of which missionaries were the principal foreign victims, and kept on sending gunboats up China's rivers for decades to punish molesters of mission stations. The direct stake so many Americans acquired in China through their churches made it an almost unique exception to the rule whereby most Americans considered the rest of the world no part of their business This is at least one key to the remarkable role played by China in American national life in the last decade and even more a key to the role played in these matters by leaders deeply rooted in the isolationist tradition. It also begins to identify the peculiarly parental emotions that are threaded through the whole mesh of American-Chinese affairs.

The nature of missionary feeling about China and the Chinese, past and present, is a largely unstudied subject. A vast body of literature awaits scrutiny, a rich and almost wholly unexplored territory where great prizes await the perspicacious prospector. We can do hardly more here than try to glimpse the peaks and the valleys and to pick up a few samples selected for assay at different distances from our present location in time.

## *The Wonderful Heathen*

Let us move first only a short way from where we stand now, back to the growing-up years of the majority of the members of our panel To judge from what we know of them, there must be relatively few

---

given for American missionaries in China that year, also incomplete, is 2,785 Both totals are for Protestants only. Cf. *Interpretative Statistical Survey of the World Mission of the Christian Church*, International Missionary Council New York, 1938, pp. 87, 127

people of mature age in this country today who, if they belong to one of the great Protestant denominations and have been brought up in churchgoing families, have not in some way been touched by the missionary experience. Close kin or family connections, or friends, fellow townsfolk, or fellow students went to China as missionaries Visiting missionaries back from China appeared quite frequently to tell about their Work, ministers and Sunday school teachers spurred their flocks week after week to help in the cause. Pennies, nickels, dimes, and dollars, heaping into millions, were folded carefully into envelopes or dropped into collection plates or baskets by children and adults week in and week out, year after year. Here is where young minds were often scratched most meaningfully and most permanently.

There was impressive evidence of this among the panel's 137 Protestants and 13 Catholics. When they were asked to recall their earliest associations connected with Asia, 123 of these individuals quickly mentioned "missionaries"—missionaries seen or heard or heard about, mission committees that would meet in their homes, mission publications on the table in the parlor, mission activity at denominational colleges, an essential part of the good Christian life in support of which, from their earliest years, they yielded up weekly their cherished coins.

Of these 123, 78 associated the memory with China. Of these 78, 26 produced no more than the single connecting strand: Asia-missionaries-China. But the majority brought this association up out of musty corners of memory trailing wisps of feeling-impression, things they could remember hearing about China or the Chinese in the missionary setting.

In 4 of these cases, the tone was neuter. The Chinese were *backward, unusual, different,* and—without passion—*heathen*

In 8 others, some of these same notions reappear, but now strongly flavored with the scent of sin and damnation.

> an idea of heathenish, strange, slant-eyed, devious people, different, heathenish, wicked because they were not Christian, poverty, filth, disease; wretched, wicked, hungry; backward people who bound women's feet, chaotic conditions, lawlessness, banditry, cruelty, corruption ..

But in all the rest (40), the recall associated with missionaries carried with it a note of kind or benevolent sympathy, e g.·

a poor downtrodden people, great human misery, suffering, how poor the children were; felt sorry for them; backward people in need of our help; suffering poverty, famine, starvation. . . .

or a note of high regard, even affection for the Chinese·

their charming ways, goodness, kindness, sympathy, friendliness, poor, gentle, peaceful, kindly people; good, simple, hardworking, worthy people; nice, poor, intelligent people who arouse friendly feelings, honest, needy people; generous, humane, appreciative of things done for them; responding to efforts of missionaries; a fine, sympathetic feeling; humans like we are, with an ancient culture in some ways superior to ours; had great love and respect for the Chinese. . . .

Within the limits set by their particular emotional needs and involvements, missionaries often—although not always—develop a special bias for the people among whom they work. This can run sometimes to strong partisanship where political or other conflicts arise; e.g., India missionaries and Pakistan missionaries may argue over the disputed issue of Kashmir just like Indians and Pakistanis. This could be just good mission politics. It could also be a matter of plain local loyalties not very different from those attached to the old alma mater or the local ball team In one of our interviews a Catholic prelate described with amused relish a scene he witnessed in a Hong Kong hostel in which missionaries from a number of Asian countries reached the point of angrily pulling each others' beards across the table in an argument over the relative merits of "their" various peoples. But even within this general pattern, China missionaries have won a particular reputation for highly emotional attachments to "their" country and its people. Some typical examples from missionaries in our panel:

Like all who have lived there, I have warm, friendly feelings, great admiration for the Chinese Personal relations, feeling for the ability, culture, character of the Chinese, more outgoing and easier to know, for example, than the Japanese Despite all the difficulties, our experience there was pleasant. I would like to go back. No one can read Chinese history without acquiring great respect for Chinese thought and philosophy I think of the Chinese, the beauty spots, the carved feeling of the past of China, its great attraction, its unusual atmosphere . Of course corruption and conflicts and squeeze, in many of the churches too . . .

I think of all those I knew, baptized, ordained, trained. All so devoted and loyal. I think of a cinerama of things, mostly that I should really be back there now. . . . People who love China really go over the edge about it. . . . But I think this feeling has some basis in fact Of course there are lots of negative things about the Chinese too. They lie for politeness' sake, are often dishonest about money matters, smoke opium. But I like all the Chinese . . .

The Chinese are one of the finest peoples I have known, generous, have a sense of humor, are loyal to their families, devoted to the arts and sciences. I think of the loyal amahs who cared for missionary children, friends loyal over long years . . .

It should be easy from these samples to see how other members of our panel collected from firsthand or secondhand missionary sources impressions like the following.

A special feeling about China, highly sympathetic notions out of the missionary tradition. . . .

I have an impression from the writings of John Caldwell and the whole Protestant missionary world, about which I hardly know anything, of a sort of great basic sympathy for China rooted in missionary activity. . . .

At Yale there was quite a bit of tradition about China, Yale-in-China, Henry Luce, John Hersey. . . China certainly does shatter people, affects their lives so greatly. I always recognize this in people I meet who have been connected with China and make lifelong commitments to it. . . .

My ideas come from missionaries, of how wonderful the Chinese are, how much they needed to be helped, and how receptive they were to help. . . .

I have an impression of tremendous affection for the Chinese people. I remember it in a missionary I met in Tientsin. . . .

I have a feeling of sympathetic attitudes about the Chinese, from missionaries, ladies and societies doing things for them, missionary books telling of their experiences. . .

They love the Chinese. They never get over it Several on my staff have been daughters of China missionaries But anybody who ever was in China is like this . . .

Emanations of this kind from China missionaries have been strong enough, often, to arouse the nettled and envious irritation of missionaries who have served in other countries. One, who worked in

Japan, said: "The Chinese missionaries were so critical of the Japanese that it made me defensive about the Japanese and negative about the Chinese." Another missionary official who had the task of picking up the pieces after the 1949 exodus from China:

> When I came to this job I had many meetings with ex-China people available for the jobs open. They made me feel shut out because I knew nothing about China. They felt resentful because they thought the only significant mission work had been done in China. So I came to feel—the heck with them I resisted learning about it, never became interested in it, and never tried to acquire any interest in the Chinese.

One of our panelists remembered that a certain retired member of a China missionary family in his Midwestern home town used to speak disparagingly of the Chinese and was therefore regarded by the neighbors as queer. "She was a chowderhead anyway," he said, "and if she wasn't in a mental hospital, she should have been." He could easily summon up, after nearly thirty years and almost with anger, this ghost of a memory so long laid away. But let us live now with that ghost for a while. For the dissident old lady who did not share the general enthusiasm for the Chinese was simply persisting in views that had been the common ones of her own time, when most of these admiring enthusiasts were not quite born or were still small children. We catch a glimpse of this in the difference between what most of our panelists who were born between about 1905 and 1915 remember about missionary views of the Chinese and these recollections from one of our older panelists, born in 1898:

> I was named after a China missionary My mother was active in the Christian Missionary Alliance When I was between about six and ten, we had a summer place where the Alliance had annual camp meetings. Missionaries from China . . . the Chinese were pretty heathen Benighted. Perverse for being heathen, a poor benighted mass, a people to be pitied and helped. . . . Also in some other connection wily and untrustworthy. . . .

It is not necessary to go too far back or to look too deeply into the written record to discover that all was not always so glowing, China not always so admired, the Chinese not always so beloved by missionaries as they became in recent decades. As late as 1938, Carl Crow, a journalist-turned-businessman whose own experience in China went back to 1911, had this to say about missionaries:

Having come to China to conquer sin, they have a keen and wary eye out for the ancient enemy. Anyone who looks for sin in any part of the world will have no difficulty about finding it, and the search for evidence of sin has never been prosecuted in any country with more perseverance and skill than by the missionaries whose work brought them to China, where sin is not only prevalent but exists unconcealed in many a picturesque guise. It is only of recent years that some missionaries have come to take a more tolerant and sympathetic view of the Chinese people [48]

This "more tolerant and sympathetic view" which was beginning to appear more commonly in the 1930's was rather less common in the troubled 1920's and had become only intermittently visible in the decade or so before that. The farther back we retrace the record, the more astringent becomes the feeling-tone of it. Indeed, as we move toward the far side of the marker 1900, we soon become aware that the dominant view of that day was the view held in our present panel by only a tiny majority. In this older, more tarnished mirror we catch images of the Chinese as a heathenish, wickedly mendacious, obstinate, and on the whole quite difficult people. The tone then, as now, was benevolent, but before it became kindly it was often strained, angry, and even contemptuous.

## The Exasperating Heathen

The pioneering generations of missionaries were stern men of God, fixed in their notions of eternal righteousness and with little patience for the sinful vagaries of the benighted ones not yet bathed in grace. For many of them Satan was triumphant even in Christian denominations other than their own—and this among their own kind. How much more surely did he rule, then, over the iniquities of Oriental heathenism, especially Chinese heathenism which so stubbornly resisted salvation, which not only did not accept or acknowledge Christian and Western superiority, but insisted that its own was the only superior civilization in a world of barbarians? A writer in the first volume of the first missionary publication in China gives us this glimpse of what seemed to be the common early-impression view of 1832:

Everything that has been published respecting the Chinese only serves to show, more and more forcibly, that they are a very peculiar people, of

[48] Carl Crow, *The Chinese Are Like That*, New York, 1938, Tower Edition, 1943, p. 144.

whose character, dispositions, and prejudices, it is extremely difficult to obtain a correct knowledge—even by long residence among them ... One of the predominating characteristics of the Chinese is that love of specious falsehood which stamps almost all their words and actions, which must be mainly attributed to their long subjection under a despotic sway, and the almost universal tyranny of their corrupt and unprincipled rulers. Another characteristic is their exclusive selfishness, which, coupled with their pride and arrogance, leads them to regard their own country as the crown of nations, and the centre of civilization, and to look on all foreigners as an inferior race of beings, deserving ought but their hatred and contempt [49]

Shortly, the Europeans, led by the British, began to use brute force to break down this prideful and arrogant Chinese notion of superiority and, by the only means they had, to correct the Chinese idea that all foreigners were an inferior race of beings. It is impossible to separate the missionaries from this assault, they were too much a part of it. Over the next sixty years missionaries and mission interests were wound in with the commercial and diplomatic interests of the Powers, with the early wars, and—after a certain early hesitant confusion owing to its neo-Christian character—with the foreign role in helping the Manchu Dynasty suppress the Taiping Rebellion, and with innumerable smaller punitive actions climaxed by the suppression of the Boxer Rebellion in 1900. In all these events the missionaries were intimately concerned, as victims of Chinese hostility and mob violence, as beneficiaries of special clauses inserted in the treaties of conquest—which they helped draft and negotiate—and as recipients of indemnities for damage to property and persons—which they helped to exact and then to collect and administer. Missionaries served their governments as interpreters and emissaries and utilized to the full the support of their governments and armed forces for their effort to propagate their Gospel. By virtue of all this, writes Kenneth Latourette, himself a product of the missionary movement and one of its principal American historians, "the Church had become a partner in Western imperialism and could not well disavow some responsibility for the consequences." [50]

The early wars which opened China to the mission effort were fought primarily to force entry for European traders and, most immediately, to force Chinese acceptance of the highly profitable trade

[49] *The Chinese Repository*, Canton, Vol 1, October, 1832, pp. 213–214.
[50] *A History of Christian Missions in China*, New York, 1929, p 280.

in opium, which was brought to the China coast from India. As one English historian wryly put it, the Gospel and the drug "came together, have been fought for together, and were finally legalized together." [51] If there were any moral qualms among the missionaries over any of these proceedings, they do not show very plainly in the record. S. Wells Williams, one of the first American missionaries, a participant in these events, and later the first major American sinologue, tells us how the very secular Lord Elgin, the British plenipotentiary, standing off Canton in his warship ready to bombard the town, felt ashamed and sad "I feel," he told the ship's captain, "that I am earning for myself a place in the Litany immediately after 'plague, pestilence, and famine.'" He knew himself unable to act otherwise than he did, but he still "thought bitterly of those who, for the most selfish objects, are trampling under foot this ancient civilization." [52] But Williams himself suggests that the role of opium in these wars caused only a moment's "melancholy reflection" to the Christian missionary of the day He gave it as his judgment that the war, "though eminently unjust in its cause as an opium war .. was still, as far as human sagacity can perceive, a wholesome infliction upon a government which haughtily refused all equal intercourse with other nations." [53] A writer in the *Chinese Repository* saw it all as another of God's mysterious wonders. "The events of this year [1842] .. show in a wonderful manner the working of His providence, who often mercifully brings good out of evil, making human wrath productive alike of man's happiness and God's glory." [54] Latourette records that there was a certain indignation over the obvious iniquities of the opium trade. "Yet in this indignation," he goes on, "there was mixed a curiously inconsistent enthusiasm over the prospect of an open China and the opportunities it would offer. While deploring the means, Americans exulted in the end " [55]

[51] Joshua Rowntree, *The Imperial Drug Trade*, London, 1908, p 242
[52] *The Middle Kingdom*, Vol II, p. 644
[53] Ibid , Vol. II, p 572
[54] "Retrospection, or a Review of Public Occurrences in China during the Year 1842," *Chinese Repository*, Vol. 2, December, 1842, p 673.
[55] *History of Early Relations* , p 126. In his later larger and more definitive work, Latourette touches lightly again on this delicate matter "It may be open to debate whether representatives of Jesus ought to have accepted privileges wrung from a nation by force of arms It is probably even more a question whether they ought to have given their countenance to the negotiations which obtained these privileges for them Missionaries and their advocates in America, however, appear to have been troubled little if any by these doubts The opium

During the subsequent decades, missionaries generally exercised to the full the powers of extraterritoriality and the privilege of special protection provided by the treaties for their Chinese converts. Exceptions were rare On one occasion the great James Legge, an Englishman and translator of the Chinese classics, advised his friends: "If news comes that I have been murdered, go at once to the English consul and tell him that it is my wish that no English gunboat should be sent up the river to punish the people for my death" But this was eccentric conduct Missionaries generally, the record shows, exercised their "rights" to the full and sometimes beyond it, and felt quite righteously just in doing so.

It is plain that the Chinese had to be great sinners indeed and the need for their salvation commanding beyond ordinary measure to justify this behavior. There was certainly much in China life to support this view, at least in the mind of the sin-seeking Christian evangelist Whatever the virtues so widely celebrated at a distance by the men of the Enlightenment a century before, these men of the Evangelical Awakening, observing China close up, found the most noxious and sinful vices. When in addition to being wicked, the Chinese turned out to be weak, the common feeling for them among these foreigners was certainly bound to be something a good deal short of admiration

Wells Williams, who worked harder than most in his forty-three years in China "to obtain a correct knowledge" of the country and its people, published in 1848 the first edition of his classic work, *The Middle Kingdom,* and in 1883 a revised edition carrying events up to that time, so that his volumes cover the knowledge and experience of China and the attitudes acquired during the first half-century of the missionary enterprise. His principal object, he wrote, was "to divest the Chinese people and civilisation of that peculiar and indefinable impression of ridicule which has been so generally given them by foreign authors." He "endeavored to show the better traits of their national character" and considered that "the time is speedily passing when the people of the Flowery Land can fairly be classified

---

traffic was vigorously criticized . No one, however, seems seriously to have challenged the propriety of missionaries accepting the opportunities thus obtained Missionaries or former missionaries served as interpreters and secretaries in negotiating each of the main treaties . In both Protestant and Catholic circles, the treaties were welcomed as marking a new era in missions and advantage was at once taken of them "—*A History of Christian Missions in China,* pp. 231–232

among the uncivilised nations." He was hopeful of the forthcoming "descent of the Holy Spirit" and was confident that with the growing success of the mission cause, the Chinese people would "become fitted for taking up the work themselves," for only in "the success of this cause lies the salvation of China as a people, both in its moral and political aspects." [56]

It is certain from his account that few peoples on earth needed this regeneration more sorely than the Chinese. Chinese civilization might appear to have a unique character, he observed, but "a slight acquaintance with their morals proves their similarities to their fellow men in the lineaments of a fallen and depraved nature." He found admirable the peace and order of Chinese life, the security of life and property, the homogeneity of their education, and the examination system which "removes the main incentive to violence in order to obtain posts of power and dignity." Their antiquity had also left them "fully settled in a great regard for the family compact and deep reverence for parents and superiors." Then he continued.

When, however, these traits have been mentioned, the Chinese are still more left without excuse for their wickedness. . . . With a general regard for outward decency, they are vile and polluted in a shocked degree; their conversation is full of filthy expressions and their lives of impure acts. . . More uneradicable than the sins of the flesh is the falsity of the Chinese and its attendant sin of base ingratitude . . There is nothing which tires one so much when living among them as their disregard of truth, and renders him so indifferent as to what calamities may befall so mendacious a race, an abiding impression of suspicion toward everybody rests upon the mind, which chills the warmest wishes for their welfare and thwarts many a plan to benefit them. Their better traits diminish in the distance and patience is exhausted in its daily proximity and friction with this ancestor of all sins. . . Thieving is exceedingly common. . . . The politeness which they exhibit seldom has its motive in goodwill and consequently, when the varnish is off, the rudeness, brutality, and coarseness of the material is seen . . . Female infanticide in some parts openly confessed and divested of all disgrace and penalties . . the universal practice of lying and dishonest dealings, the unblushing lewdness of old and young, harsh cruelty toward prisoners by officers and tyranny over slaves by masters—all form a full unchecked torrent of human depravity, and prove the existence of a kind and degree of moral degradation of which an excessive statement can scarcely be made or an adequate conception hardly be formed.

[56] *Middle Kingdom*, Vol I, pp. xiv–xv.

On the whole [he concludes] the Chinese present a singular mixture: if there is something to commend, there is more to blame, if they have some glaring vices, they have more virtues than most pagan nations. Ostentatious kindness and inbred suspicion, ceremonious civility and real rudeness, partial invention and servile imitation, industry and waste, sycophancy and self-dependence, are, with other dark and bright qualities, strangely blended.[57]

Essentially the same image of the Chinese, and the same suggestion of exhausted patience, appears somewhat later in much more systematic form in Arthur Smith's *Chinese Characteristics*. Smith, a missionary of twenty-one years' experience in China, was at least a partial product of the age of Darwin and Lewis Morgan He undertook to write of the Chinese in the scholarly manner, complete with prefatory warnings against generalizations and a text dotted with sweeping statements But he did bring together the sum of the experience and feeling of his contemporaries as well as his own, and his book stood for many years as a standard work, not only as an essential item in the preparation of new workers about to enter the vineyards, but as the source for some of the most widely held notions of the nature of the Chinese people

There is an occasional touch of rueful humor in Smith's portrayal of Chinese vagaries which is almost entirely lacking in Williams. The Chinese, he noted, were often accurately likened to the bamboo. "It is graceful, it is everywhere useful, it is supple, and it is hollow. When the east wind blows, it bends to the west. When the west wind blows, it bends to the east. When no wind blows, it does not bend at all." Concerning Chinese attitudes toward foreigners: "Many Chinese unconsciously adopt toward foreigners an air of amused interest combined with depreciation, like that with which Mr. Littimer regarded David Copperfield, as if mentally saying perpetually, 'So young, sir, so young!' " In a time when foreigners in China were rarely able to view themselves critically, Smith could acknowledge that there was "very little in the conduct of any Western nation in its dealings with the Chinese of which we have any reason to be proud." He even thought Westerners, and especially Americans, might benefit from borrowing some of the less excessive and less insincere forms of Chinese politeness, filial piety, and most of all, the "innate cheerfulness" and "staying powers" of the Chi-

[57] *Middle Kingdom*, Vol I, pp 833-836

nese and their "unlimited capacity for patient endurance." From these qualities—which ultimately became the basis for much more unqualified admiration of the Chinese by many Americans—Smith derived, like Williams and others, a strong sense of the "great future" that lay before this "sensitive, obstinate, conservative people."

But these gleams of humor and respect are all but totally submerged in Smith's pages in a pervasive tone of irritation and anger over the inconceivably devious and wicked puzzles of Chinese ways and Chinese character, a feeling which, as in Williams, seemed held in check at times only by the most heroic kind of Christian forbearance. Some chapter heads suggest the mood: The Disregard of Time, The Disregard of Accuracy, The Talent for Misunderstanding, The Talent for Indirection, Flexible Inflexibility, Intellectual Turbidity, The Absence of Nerves, Contempt for Foreigners, The Absence of Public Spirit, The Absence of Sympathy, Mutual Suspicion, The Absence of Sincerity, and so on.

"All Chinese are gifted," wrote Smith, "with an instinct for taking advantage of misunderstandings." Or: "The Chinese marry at a very early age and the desire for posterity is the one ruling passion in which, next to the love of money, the Chinese race is most agreed." Much of the code of politeness is "bewildering and a little maddening to the foreigner," and "no extended experience of the Chinese is required to enable a foreigner to arrive at the conclusion that it is impossible, from merely hearing what a Chinese says, to tell what he means." These texts are often illustrated, like so many foreigners' stories about the Chinese, with anecdotes about servants. A special acerbity is reserved for the way in which the Chinese waste the Westerner's valuable time· "No Chinese has ever yet learned that when he kills time it is well to make certain that it is time which belongs to him, and not that of someone else." He is distinctly bothered by the "jealous contempt" of the Chinese literati for all foreigners and by the "intellectual turbidity" which produced "conformity for conformity's sake." As for religion, the millions of China were "as destitute of anything which ought to be called faith as they are of an acquaintance with Chinese hieroglyphics." [58]

The tone of Smith's observations is wry or rueful, sad or angry, but never affectionate It is above all exasperated. These were wayward, delinquent, difficult people, whose good qualities would never

[58] *Chinese Characteristics, passim.*

prevail until they had fully and finally adopted for their own the Gospel these foreigners brought. For what China needed was "a new life in every individual soul, in the family, and in society," and these manifold needs would be met "permanently, completely, only by Christian civilization " Smith and his contemporaries believed this passionately and with all their hearts and were devoting their lives to it The hostility they met was bad enough; the most intolerably exasperating of all was the fact that in their overwhelming numbers, the Chinese simply could not care less.

The Chinese are not the only ones to whom the whole mission enterprise could seem odd or outrageous. But this only accents the pathos of the earlier history of the undertaking. Hardship, suffering, hostility, and mortal danger filled the lives of these remarkably circumscribed people who went, unsought and uninvited but with such utter conviction, to minister to the reluctant heathen so far away. Their families were often decimated by disease; many an infant sacrifice to the cause was laid in a grave in this inhospitable land. They frequently had to flee from violence. There was little peace or comfort in their lives at best, and even at best, they still had to cope with all the exasperatingly sinful qualities of the Chinese— mendacity, gross self-interest, godlessness, love of money, superstition, cruelty. There was not much here, as they must have seen it, to become sentimental about, little time for love, even among themselves. They were *foreign devils* unwanted in a strange land, and their need to sustain their own faith was too pressing to allow them to find too much virtue in the great mass of hostile or indifferent sinners by whom they were surrounded.

Indeed the accumulated hostility of the Chinese toward these foreigners exploded once more half a dozen years after Arthur Smith's book appeared. Those final years of the century were marked by unrestrained foreign depredations in China, the humiliating defeat inflicted upon China by Japan in 1895, and the tearing away of concession after concession by the European Powers in the scramble that followed Chinese helplessness and frustration produced the convulsive gesture of the Boxer Rebellion Before the bloodletting of 1900 was over, more than 200 *foreign devils* and a reputed total of some 30,000 *secondary devils* (Chinese Christians) had been killed, and an Allied punitive expedition that marched from Tientsin to Peking, and later fanned out over northeastern China, took many times more that number in gross retribution. There was Christian martyrdom; then there was looting, rapine, and slaughter by the avenging Christian armies. In the sequel of capitulation, negotiation, collection, and disbursement of punitive indemnities, many missionaries and Chinese Christians appear to have played a distinctly unheroic and uncharitable role.[59]

This was hardly the "descent of the Holy Spirit" which Wells Williams had so prayerfully predicted only a few years earlier. But it was a catharsis and, ironically, it did usher in the nearest thing to a golden age the missionaries—and foreigners generally—ever enjoyed in China. The new relationship between the triumphant foreigner and the thoroughly defeated Chinese produced the kindlier, more sympathetic and enthusiastically admiring images of the Chinese which were carried over into our own time.

## 6. *THE ATTRACTIVE PEOPLE (1905–37)*

IN THE EARLY YEARS of this century, when most of our panelists were being born, new lights began to shine on American images of the Chinese; they began to be differently seen and to arouse new and kindlier emotions. Since there is room in every present for the whole past, there were still a great many who continued to feel an indecipherable strangeness in the Chinese and to react to them with exasperated impatience and contempt. But to a great many others, the subhumans began to appear as people who inspired a certain sympathy and affection. These attitudes and emotions, rising more and more commonly among the increasing numbers of Americans who came to live and work in China in this period, were communicated to a steadily widening audience at home. It was an audience that grew over the years and decades as events of great magnitude linked Chinese and Americans in matters of continuously growing moment. These were precisely the growing-up years of most

[59] "Missionaries were not entirely guiltless of taking advantage of the situation to further their interests."—Latourette, *A History of Christian Missions in China*, pp. 520 ff. For a savage contemporary comment on this matter by Mark Twain, see "To the Person Sitting in Darkness," reprinted in *The Portable Mark Twain*, New York, 1946, pp. 594–613.

of the members of our panel, and the impact of these changing images and attitudes is plainly visible upon them.

A great many events funneled their consequences into this process, some small and meaningful in the lives of particular individuals, some portentous in the lives of nations. To review the details of all this experience in terms of evolving American perceptions of the Chinese is a task that still waits on interested scholarship In all the unending writing of books about China by Americans, very little of this has ever been consciously or systematically done, appearing if at all only implicitly or in sporadic parentheses. All we can hope to do here is to prospect for traces of the nature and location of the great divide between these two half-centuries of contact between Americans and Chinese, to discover the main routes by which the exasperated devotion of the first passed over into the devoted exasperation of the second and, in the form of some ideas and perhaps some token footnotes, to leave markers where there is surely much else to be found They will, I think, at least indicate the environments in which so many of the Americans interviewed in the course of this study came to acquire so many of the notions and attitudes that govern so much of their thinking about the Chinese.

## New Starting Points

It was in Asia at the turn of the century that the United States entered world politics as a principal. In the form given to it by John Hay, the Open Door policy became a pillar of a new American diplomacy. This period is marked by American participation in the Boxer events, the war with Spain and the acquisition in the Philippines of America's first colony; the burgeoning of all sorts of schemes —mostly abortive—for American financial involvement in Chinese development; the American role in settling the Russo-Japanese War; the opening of the power conflict with Japan Just before the First World War, the Department of State began to send junior Foreign Service officers to China and Japan as language students, the first of a cadre that came to include many who played leading roles in the more turbulent diplomacy of a later day This growing American involvement in Asia's affairs underpins the new look which many Americans began to turn on the Chinese during these years.

In China itself, events had brought changes in the mutual status of the Chinese and the foreigner, some obvious, some subtle. The Boxer episode had shifted the locus of self-assertion in Chinese society. The crushing of the rebellion had totally chastened the Manchu court and sent it sliding down toward extinction It had stifled the xenophobic violence among the rural traditionalists from whom the Boxers had sprung. The next antiforeign movement in China was of a totally different kind and rose in a totally different segment of society. an economic boycott promoted by the merchant class, and its target, ironically enough, was the United States. Administration of the exclusion law in America had led to a long series of incidents in which Chinese merchants traveling to that country were grievously humiliated. In retaliation, the merchant guilds in Shanghai and Canton in 1905 launched a boycott of American goods and firms. This was a new kind of weapon and marked the first stirring of new nationalist impulses destined to grow in scope and force in China over the coming years. That it was directed in the first instance against the Americans is apt testimony to the gap that could exist between Chinese images of Americans and the Americans' image of themselves, for they were at this time still full of self-congratulation over having saved China from dismemberment through John Hay's diplomacy. The boycott agitation in China led to a few acts of violence against Americans in 1906. President Theodore Roosevelt—who "did not have that somewhat sentimental though wholly honorable regard for the Chinese with which we have been made familiar in the last few years" [60]—actually moved troops to the Philippines with the thought of retaliating against China by new military action. Oswald Garrison Villard's *Nation* described the government's reaction this way:

> The attitude of our government in brief is one of distrust and contempt, and smacks of the same spirit which makes the average American look upon every Chinaman as an underfed and overworked laundryman, to be kicked and stoned.[61]

But new pressures were already altering the older reactions. In the United States there was a certain revulsion against the maltreatment of the Chinese, and agitation started up to correct the worst abuses in the administration of the exclusion law, although there was no question of the validity of the law itself. In China, while the boycott

---

[60] Tyler Dennett, *Roosevelt and the Russo-Japanese War*, New York, 1925, p 153
[61] *Nation*, February 17, 1906. Quoted by Jessie A. Miller, *China in American Policy and Opinion, 1906–1909*, Ph D thesis, Clark University, 1940

only slightly pinched the businessmen, it found the missionaries more sensitive. They had begun to feel the opening of golden new opportunities, and they began to press hard—and successfully—for a more conciliatory course of conduct.

Actually, the boycott movement of 1905–06 had come as a surprise, a student of the period has noted, because, as a New York newspaper put it: "Kicking back in that quarter was the last thing any white man had expected." [62] For with the Boxer blood bath, the foreigner in China had emerged from the decades of difficult, harried, and often dangerous life he had led and had begun a new era of sunny security. For the next two decades or so, from the Boxer events to the nationalist upheavals of 1925–27, the foreigner was physically safer in China than he had ever been before. The breakdown of Chinese institutions, the fall of the dynasty, the aborted republic, the rise of war-lordism, all brought immense travail upon the Chinese themselves. But except for rare lapses, not upon the foreigner. His person was sacrosanct, his concessions, settlements, and special privileges unchallenged, and even his mission compounds in the hinterlands all but inviolate. Only isolated acts of banditry marred the perfect order of his comings and goings amid the vast disorder of Chinese life. The foreigner was lord in the land, a member of the master race ascendant, and he enjoyed every day the great satisfactions of high individual visibility, deference, and accepted superior status. He could now afford, if he would, to look with kindlier tolerance on the people and the life around him.

For the Chinese, the Boxer Rebellion had been the last feeble challenge of traditionalism to the inevitability of change. The crushing of the rebellion, the drastic punishments and penalties heaped upon China by the Powers, all but broke the back of the dying Manchu Dynasty. Its heavenly mandate was clearly running out. Moreover, the adhesives in Chinese society itself were flaking away. The proud and obtuse recalcitrance of the Chinese based on their belief in their own real superiority over the rapacious foreign barbarian could no longer be so generally maintained, even as a face-saving fiction. In the broadest sense, the old Chinese social order was finally giving way after more than half a century of Western assault. Survival demanded change. Those classes of Chinese most directly affected turned from blind resistance to accommodation, and this shift

[62] *Commercial and Financial Chronicle*, August 12, 1905. Quoted by Miller, *op. cit.*, p. 57.

became perceptible after 1900 through all the levels of Chinese society that were in contact with the foreigner.

## *The Missionary's Golden Age*

The collapse of Chinese resistance to foreign influence opened the way for foreign education. The great flow abroad was to Japan; after 1895, but especially after 1905 when Japan electrifyingly inflicted the first modern Asian defeat on a Western power, upper-class Chinese sent their sons in large numbers to discover the secrets of Japanese success. Chiang Kai-shek himself was one of these He was in military school in Tokyo when the Manchu Dynasty fell in 1911.

It was in fact the fear that Americans would lose out in grasping this new opportunity that led, among other things, to the famous remission of the Boxer indemnity for educational purposes The anti-American boycott agitation had led to some "dismissal of American teachers and the banning of American books from Chinese schools" As this happened just at the time when Japan was gaining enormously in prestige because of her victory over Russia, a cry of alarm went up, from American educators and even from some businessmen. There was a public demand for steps to attract Chinese students to the United States so that they might "act as commercial missionaries," lest Japan, Germany, and Britain benefit alone from China's "awakening." The most eloquent and widely publicized appeal of this kind came from a college president, who argued that had the United States acted differently over the preceding years, she would "have been controlling the development of China in that most satisfactory and subtle of all ways—through the intellectual and spiritual domination of its leaders " [63] The matter was pressed convincingly upon a reluctant Theodore Roosevelt, and he finally agreed to a project for remission of the unused balance of the Boxer indemnity, which was duly voted by Congress in 1908 and took effect in 1909. It provided the sum of about $11,000,000, which, it was tacitly understood, would be used to finance education for Chinese students both in China and in the United States. This act is still invariably cited as a peculiarly symbolic example of American benevolence toward China. It is hardly ever mentioned, or indeed seemingly even recalled, that the money was Chinese money in the first place, exacted as a punitive indemnity, and that the sum remitted was the

[63] Quoted by Miller, *op cit*, p 132

balance remaining only after all American damage claims and costs had been amply—and perhaps more than amply—covered. Here the United States strikes the far more accurately symbolic posture of the stern guardian relenting, without cost to himself, toward a previously rebellious but now wholly chastened ward.

Besides this governmental largesse, private American funds poured out to support expansion of mission work in China The weekly offerings of millions of Americans—many of our panelists among them—began mounting to totals ranging from about two to about four million dollars a year to save, elevate, and educate the Chinese. In addition, the Rockefeller and other great fortunes moved more millions of dollars via various foundations into the endowment of hospitals and colleges These were the years in which Americans kept hearing —as was so frequently mentioned in the interviews—that the Chinese were deeply grateful and strongly responsive to the aid they were receiving They poured by the thousands into mission schools, and the good work spread throughout the land. The post-Boxer decades became the golden age of missionary enterprise in China, the high point of Chinese acceptance of foreign, and especially American, benevolence.

Dozens of new mission societies entered the China field in this period. By 1925 there were 27 mission colleges and universities in China, of which 21 had been founded since 1900. In the year 1925, when events were already signaling the end of the golden age, these mission institutions had about 3,700 students and had graduated some 4,300 Below college level, there were 300,000 Chinese students in Protestant mission schools and 260,000 in Catholic schools, these including missions of all nationalities. Protestant communicants were said to number about 700,000 and Catholics about twice that many [64]

These were droplets in the great sea of 400 million, still for American missionaries they represented great accomplishment. The hostility and indifference of the pre-1900 days had not exactly been succeeded by the wholesale descent of the Holy Spirit on the great masses of the Chinese. But the missionary effort was no longer an obscure failure. The country was covered by its institutions, a small but important segment of the population had come under its influence. More widely and more potently, perhaps, than many missionaries realized, the mission schools flung open the doors to a new era

[64] *China Year Book*, Shanghai, 1925, 1926

for the emerging generation of China's leaders Christian and Western education produced notable recruits for almost every kind of leadership in the subsequent development of Chinese politics except one capable of creating a democratic movement based on Christian liberal-humanitarian principles This is another one of the many facets of this history awaiting critical re-examination. What concerns us here is that the flocking of Chinese into the schools set up by foreign missionaries during the first twenty-odd years of this century helped to create a whole new set of relationships between foreigners and Chinese and to create a whole new set of attitudes, at least on the part of the foreigners.

The new and rapid growth of their enterprise, placed a great many missionaries in direct superior-subordinate relationship to a considerable number of Chinese. This produced its frictions in matters of staffing, handling money, carrying through prescribed programs, for Chinese ways of doing things seldom resembled American notions of efficiency. This produced much exasperation, borne as far as possible with fortitude and patience.[65] On the other hand, the great expansion of mission education brought a much larger number of missionaries than ever before into much more benignly sympathetic relations with a great many Chinese. They could enjoy not only the privileges of their status as foreigners, but the far more richly satisfying honor and deference which the Chinese traditionally accorded to their teachers. It took a thickly crusted individual indeed to do less than deeply appreciate this experience. To illustrate the warmly expansive effect of being both a foreigner and a teacher in China, here is a passage written in 1919 by a prominent missionary educator:

> During his furlough at home the missionary more than once feels the lack of courtesy for which the Far East is famed. He is accustomed in the Orient to seeing students rise and bow at the beginning of the recitation, and he feels ill at ease when no one at the occidental university takes note of the entrance of the professor, and the opening sentence of the lecture cuts across a buzz of conversation.[66]

[65] Cf Orville A Petty, ed, *Laymen's Foreign Missions Inquiry*, Fact-Finders' Reports, China, Vol V, Supplementary Series, New York, 1933, p 47

[66] Earl Herbert Cressy, "Converting the Missionary," *Asia*, June, 1919. Cressy also described how when visiting friends in America he would be shown on parting simply to the apartment door and be left to find his own way out of the building. "The first time this happens, he cannot help feeling a little queer as he recalls how some official had the great doors of the yamen opened and bowed him out with all ceremony" No American yamen opened its great doors

Two members of our panel whose own first experiences in China date from this same period summoned up the same pleasant memories as part of their explanation for their warm feelings about the Chinese. A noted scholar who first went to teach in China in 1910 had his mind scratched for life by "the courtesy of the boys and students," and a retired public servant with a lifetime China career behind him thought almost first of all of the students who were "so pleasant and respectful in class" when he taught them at a mission school between 1909 and 1914.

The Chinese students of this era were often much more than merely polite. They respected not only the teacher but also what he had to teach, and for the right teacher this could be a richly stimulating experience. Of the students he encountered as a visiting lecturer in Peking at this time, John Dewey wrote:

> There is a maturity of interest far beyond that which marks American students of the same years. . . . [They] would listen soberly and intelligently to lectures on subjects that would create nothing but bored restlessness in an American school There is an eager thirst for ideas—beyond anything existing, I am convinced, in the youth of any other country on earth.[67]

Many of the missionaries who came to China in this period had a new concept of their calling. Many came not as evangelists but rather as teachers, doctors, social workers. Old-fashioned brimstone fundamentalism was still very present, but the "higher criticism" had its products too, and it was no longer always necessary for a missionary to regard any non-Christian culture as unrelievedly sinful and its heathenism as totally without virtue. A more inquiring and respectful attitude toward Chinese society became more common. This was more than an intellectual pose; it came to some out of living experience. In the more relaxed and friendly circumstances, many a missionary was almost insensibly acclimatized. He began not only to learn more about the life of the people around him, but also to savor it and once in a while even to become part of it. For some missionaries, at least, the First World War contributed much to this onset of greater humility. It made Western civilization look a good deal less superior, it made some Christians less supremely confident

---

for the headmaster of an obscure school. The Chinese way of doing things was obviously more satisfactory.

[67] "New Culture in China," *Asia*, July 1921, p 586.

of their own virtue and rightness. It severely shook the conviction of invincible progress always held up hitherto as a contrast to the dying stagnation of China and Chinese outlooks. The war, indeed, and especially its Russian aftermath, stirred Chinese youth to accept ideas that few missionaries could appreciate or follow. But it did move some of the latter to a more charitable view of the civilization they had always previously wished to make over in their own image. Thus Earl Cressy, again, on the conversion of a missionary·

> He had come to the Far East with a message that he was on fire to give, but in the process of transmission the East had spoken its message to him He had gone out to change the East and was returning, himself a changed man.... The conversion of the missionary by the Far East results in his being not only a missionary but an internationalist, an intermediary between the two great civilizations that inherit the earth. Abroad he represents a universal religion, and is himself an embodiment of the strivings of the West to attain its ideals of social justice and world brotherhood; at home he is constantly changing the attitude of the millions of his constituency ... bringing to them something of his new breadth of vision, and helping them to a larger appreciation of the greatness and worth of the civilization of the Far East

## The Sinophiles

Not only missionaries were engaged in the business of "changing the attitude of the millions" of Americans at home about the Chinese. In the two decades following the First World War, many Americans went to China in a great variety of roles—as businessmen, diplomats and officials, newspapermen, scholars, educators, or simply curious wanderers. They were numerous enough—there were about 13,000 Americans in China in the peak years of the 1930's—and varied enough in calling to make their influence felt at home in all the circles where the members of our present panel grew up, were educated, and spent their working years—and this includes almost everywhere in the world of affairs. In our panel a great majority (138 out of 181) had never been to China, but almost all at one time or another had met someone who had. The impressions of the Chinese they gleaned from these encounters are almost uniform in tenor. Some examples out of many:

> I know some officials who worked in China All have great sympathy for the Chinese people, their feeling almost one of brotherly affection, understanding, and sympathy. ..

There was Dr. S——— who did public health work in Chinese villages, always spoke of Chinese as "my fellow peasants."

One of my associates made a business trip there a long time ago. Came back quite impressed. . . . Others who have been there always seem to like the people.

Newspaper people who have been there have great admiration for the Chinese people, sensitive sort of wonderful people to deal with in all except official dealings. . .

Know a lot of Americans from China They love the Chinese, think they're wonderful. I really don't know why. Remember a friend telling me how the Chinese said "can do" and did impossible things, made something out of nothing, practical, ingenious kind of people. . . .

Businessmen like China and the Chinese very much. Can't recall anybody I've met who I could say didn't like the Chinese as people, not the government or the progress they made, but as people. . . .

In academic life, I'm always running into people who had to do with China, uniformly sympathetic to the Chinese people. . . .

Never met an American who's been in China who didn't have affection for China . . . they seem to fall in love with China. . . .

Always highly emotional about China, great devotion, love the Chinese, admired Chinese qualities, engaged their affections. Everybody has pet Chinese students Remember this when I was at school Always protective to the Chinese. . . .

All China Americans seem to have liked or been fascinated by the Chinese. The Old China Hand phenomenon. All ages. Just really love the country and the people. . . .

Once they've been to China they become China hands and stay that way I've asked them why and they say they like the energy and attitude toward life and living of the Chinese, vigorous people. . . .

The K———s lived there in 1936, lived a charmed life, brought back beautiful things Unlimited delight and appreciation of China, especially re the upper-crust Chinese world . . .

American scholars would take for granted the pleasant fruitful nature of their relationship with their Chinese opposite numbers, jovial understanding. General warm friendly feeling, almost as an abstraction. A great mystery to me.

They would see Chinese as constructive, solid, sensible, agreeable, mixed up with pleasurable life of foreigners in China. This is quite important. The aura of extraordinary pleasure of foreign life in China in the age of concessions is very heavy. . . . I never really understood this passionate devotion to China. . . .

The Americans who appear as the carriers of such marked Sinophilia are actually of many kinds, and they speak of their experience with different accents. Aside from the missionaries, with whom we have already dealt, we can discern among them several major groups.

THE "OLD CHINA HANDS": To those who shared in the China experience in the years before the Second World War, the term "old China hand" had a quite specific meaning. It signified the old-time treaty port resident who had never outgrown the outlooks and attitudes of the previous century. It was usually used to describe the veteran British businessman, whose mode of life and manners many American later-comers tended to ape. Latterly in the United States the term has come to be applied to anyone who lived in China in the good old days before Mao Tse-tung, but anybody who did not share the treaty port outlook and is aware of the older meaning of the phrase still winces when it is misused at his expense.

Many a missionary, to be sure, was all but indistinguishable from the "old China hand," especially if he was of the older generation. But the treaty port businessman, for his part, normally did not share or highly respect the missionary's do-gooding impulse, had no interest at all in soul-saving, and was even often quite suspicious of the unsettling effects of too much education of the kind the mission schools offered to the Chinese According to the typical possessor of what was called "the Shanghai mind," the Chinese did "not want to deal with us on a basis of equality, which they are not equipped by nature or historical experience to appreciate," and the effort of the missionary to "cultivate a sentimental regard for China" was nothing short of "dangerous" and "demoralizing." [68]

The nostalgia for China expressed by the "old China hand" was most likely to be for his own life there, his clubs, his comforts, his profits, his easy ascendancy. He generally would value the Chinese chiefly as adjuncts to his own well-being. The upper-bracket businessman could lead a kingly existence indeed, but even to the lowlier members of the master race came all the appurtenances of high caste

---

[68] Rodney Gilbert, *What's Wrong With China*, New York, 1932, p 303

and high creature comfort at low cost. Unlike their more directly colonial counterparts elsewhere in Asia, these foreigners bore no responsibility to the place or people; they were unsubject to its laws and unburdened by concern for any welfare but their own. Thus situated, they could often develop a certain air of expansive tolerance toward the people around them, accepting the rascality of their servants and even of their business counterparts with a kind of patronizing affection. The late Carl Crow's books, *400 Million Customers* and *The Chinese Are Like That*, were the products of a more detachedly inquiring mind and a great appreciation of the humors of Chinese ways. But Carl Crow, it has to be said, was a newspaperman in China long before he became a businessman, and even his light and affectionate accounts are not quite free of the underlying patronage of the Chinese common to his milieu

A businessman member of our panel, whose own years in China were in the 1920's, suggested the quality of this nostalgia perhaps most succinctly

> In my time everybody loved China The white man was respected to a high degree. We loved the way of life. Business was good The white man was master It was a cheap place to live There were varying views of the Chinese, but generally people were pretty fond of them.

THE PEKING MEN: A nostalgia of quite another kind is identified mainly with the nonmissionary, noncommercial expatriate colony that grew in China during these years, with its primary interest in one or another aspect of Chinese culture, and with its heart and center in the ancient and beautiful city of Peking.

As the official seat of the government until 1928, Peking had become the playground for a typical legation "set" which lived a largely insulated life of its own, in but not of China. But even before the First World War, some retired missionaries and ex-officials of various nationalities had begun to settle in that unique city, among them some who had developed over their years in China a commanding intellectual or aesthetic interest in some aspect of Chinese life or history During and after that first war, Peking became a greater university center, the principal site of the great shift from the classical tradition to modern, Western-style education. Here flocked the cream of China's student youth, and growing numbers of foreign scholars and educators, some to stay for long terms, others, like the philosopher John Dewey, for brief but impactful visits. Here neophyte Sinologues, missionaries, and diplomats went to the Peking Language School, where at least some of them found the keys to an immense range of new and eagerly explored interests. Their respect was won and their minds stirred by the great past, the impressiveness of the literature and the annals of the dynasties, the history, the art, or the visible relics and legacies of it all—the temples, the walls, the palaces, the countrysides encrusted with the many layers of the millennia. All time seemed spread out there on the Peking plain, and the searcher could penetrate it at almost any point and find rich satisfaction of almost any interest, however narrow, however near or distant in history.

In this flourishing academic and intellectual community, a great many Americans and other foreigners lived in an atmosphere planets away from that of the treaty ports. They met with their students as honored teachers, with their Chinese colleagues and friends as equals with common interests, and with people generally on a basis of mutually friendly curiosity. Here too came art collectors, wandering writers and journalists, and all sorts of disaffected people moved from their customary places by the urges of the restless 1920's and 1930's. All together they shared the spacious, placid life of the old capital, most of them indifferent to the comings and goings of the successive war lords and rulers who moved in and out of Peking during these years. They lived graciously in and around ancient stone courtyards, poking around libraries, temples, palaces, market places, in the surrounding fields and villages and up into the nearby blue hills. All sorts, all kinds found niches for themselves, enjoying in their many different ways all the humors and beauty of Peking life. Part of each year great winds blew dust storms down upon them from the Gobi. But the rest of the year, under its wide, clear skies and its rich color, Peking exercised upon them its indescribable quality of timelessness and charm. Still largely untouched by the deforming ugliness of modern commerce, undefaced by factories, it was still the home of great artisans and handicraftsmen. It was filled with the magnificent monuments and artifacts of a past so long since gone and yet somehow, in that city, so extraordinarily alive.

It is this Peking man, and his similars unfortunate enough to have lived elsewhere in China, who gives to this nostalgia about China its most poignantly affectionate quality. He is scattered now in many different places following many pursuits. But wherever he is, he is the true exile from what was probably the most satisfying interlude of his life. It was sometimes genuinely intellectual or aesthetic, perhaps sometimes arty or even precious, but it was almost always hedonistic in the most complete sense of that word. These individuals were comparatively few in number, but they were in their time the authors of many books, the writers of much correspondence, lecturers on innumerable platforms, highly articulate communicators, all of them, of the special quality of their special emotion about things Chinese.[69]

THE CHINA-BORN: Most of these expatriates became Sinophiles by chance. But among them in these years also appeared a considerable number committed to China by birth. These were in most cases the sons and daughters of missionary families, typically raised in mission compounds, sent back to the United States at high school or more commonly at college age. Many remained there, but quite a few—no one knows how many—returned to China as missionaries, teachers, administrators, doctors, specialists and technicians of various kinds. Some entered academic careers outside the missionary orbit, some went into business or into other professions, and a good number into the American Foreign Service, forming an early cadre among the language officers in Peking and going on to diplomatic careers spent largely, in several notable cases, in China itself.

The nature and role of these China-born Americans, as persons and as figures in American-Chinese affairs, still awaits someone's closer look. At present we have little more than fragmentary single impressions. We know that many of them spent their Chinese childhoods peculiarly isolated from the Chinese among whom they lived. Their whole position as superior foreigners, and as superior foreigners whose parents were trying to bring to the Chinese a superior creed, set up barriers between them and their Chinese environment which few indeed were really able to breach. Their parents, moreover, natu-

---

[69] In what could be its most extreme form, this experience is described by George Kates in *The Years That Were Fat*, Peking, 1933-40, New York, 1952. For some of the titles of books written out of this setting on subjects ranging from Manchu court life to the Chinese theater and Chinese gardens, see Dulles, *China and America*, p 178. Many a foreign writer's novel has tried to recapture the magic of Peking, but for some suggestion of its atmosphere, the reader is referred to the descriptive passages in Lin Yutang's novel, *Moment in Peking*, New York, 1939, and the interlarded essays on the changing Peking seasons in Lau Shaw's *The Yellow Storm*, New York, 1951.

rally intent upon preserving their Americanness, often consciously or unconsciously kept the bars as high as they could The schools established for missionary children in China were generally segregated schools. They were sent home in adolescence, before any deeper relationships with Chinese of the same or the opposite sex could develop [70] Back home in the United States, these young people often had to cope with being "different" from their fellows because of their unusual backgrounds, and our interview notes include from one of them a description of how painfully he tried to efface all vestiges of his China birth from his mind in order to qualify for more natural acceptance in the American environment.

But whatever the nature of their childhood or youthful experiences, it is certain that the China-born were people whose lives and personalities were decisively shaped not only by emotional involvements with their parents as people—like everyone else—but with their parents as missionaries, and with their parents as missionaries in China Every one of them had to order these three dimensions in some pattern in coming to terms with himself Some, we know, never succeeded in doing so Among those who made their own careers in China, a number have exerted a visibly strong influence on the pattern of American thinking about the Chinese. In our interviews, the China-born appear with remarkable frequency, remembered as classmates, as kin or fellow townsmen, as colleagues or associates in university, government, or business. With rare exceptions they appear as carriers and communicators of a deep or at least a noticeable attachment to the faraway land of their birth.

Some of these individuals made their impression on a scale wider than that of the individual encounter, a few have played nationally prominent roles: John Leighton Stuart, former missionary educator who became United States Ambassador to China in the critical postwar years; Henry Luce, publisher of *Time* and *Life*, John Paton Davies, late of the Department of State, and finally one who, strictly speaking, was not China-born at all, but who is perhaps the most China-identified American of this generation: the novelist Pearl Buck.

[70] There seems to have been hardly any history of intermarriage with the Chinese among members of the missionary community and only the rarest instances of extramarital lapses involving Chinese The system was quite heavily bulwarked, both institutionally and psychologically, against any kind of love aside from the pastoral, the parental, the avuncular, or the platonic, at least as far as relations with the Chinese were concerned

## Pearl Buck's Chinese

Of all the Sinophiles who have tried to depict and interpret the Chinese for Americans, none has done so with more effect than Pearl Buck. No single book about China has had a greater impact than her famous novel, *The Good Earth*. It can almost be said that for a whole generation of Americans she "created' the Chinese, in the same sense that Dickens "created" for so many of us the people who lived in the slums of Victorian England. The extent of her influence is illustrated in our own panel by the fact that 69 individuals spontaneously mentioned Pearl Buck as a major source of their own impressions of the Chinese [71] and these were almost uniformly impressions of a wonderfully attractive people.

Pearl Buck happened "quite accidentally" to be born in the United States while her missionary mother was home recuperating from an illness. She was carried back to China when she was three months old and lived there most of her next forty years. Of her childhood in a missionary compound she has written these illuminating lines:

> I had a few dolls, but my "children" were the small folk of the servants quarters and the neighbors and we had wonderful hours of play. . . . I remember going to bed at night replete with satisfaction because the day had been so packed with pleasurable play. . . .[72]

She early abandoned the missionary claims and creed, seeking her satisfactions in both private and public life in a more encompassing emotional attachment. In her relations with Chinese, in particular and in general, and indeed, with the whole world and all the people in it, Pearl Buck has tried to be warmly, competently, and for the most part undemandingly, maternal. There is more than this, to be sure, in the books she has written, but it *is* the thread that links her to the whole pattern of American-Chinese relationships.

Her single most successful book, *The Good Earth*, a novel about a Chinese peasant and his wife and their struggle against adversity, against the cruelties of men and the angers of nature, appeared in 1931. It had an instant and immense popular success. According to

---

[71] Many more would undoubtedly have done so if directly asked. As it was, the total of 69 mentions was by far the largest for any book or author connected with China. Next largest was 21, for Edgar Snow's *Red Star Over China*, and the next 13 for Lin Yutang, mostly for *My Country and My People*.
[72] *My Several Worlds*, p. 17.

its publishers, the John Day Company, its many editions and reprintings ran up to an eventual total of more than 2,000,000 copies.[73] In 1937, it appeared as a remarkably powerful and successful film that was seen over the ensuing years, according to its makers, by some 23,000,000 Americans and by an estimated 42,000,000 other people all over the world.[74]

Book and film together, *The Good Earth* almost singlehandedly replaced the fantasy images of China and the Chinese held by most Americans with a somewhat more realistic picture of what China was like and a new, more intimate, and more appealing picture of the Chinese themselves. Indeed, *The Good Earth* accomplished the great feat of providing faces for the faceless mass.

One of our panelists—a journalist who later in his life spent several years in China—described the Buck influence this way:

> My first exposure to Asia came through Pearl Buck. China was a place on the map to me, with 400 million people who wore inverted dishpans for hats, rode rickshas and ate rice with chopsticks. This much I got in high school. Then I read *The Good Earth*. Pearl Buck made people out of the Chinese for me....

This seemed to have been an experience shared by many. In the hours that it took to read or to watch, it transformed the blurred subhumans into particular human beings for whom a great and moving sympathy was evoked by a momentary sharing in the universal experiences of mating, parenthood, suffering, devotion, weakness, aspiration. The Chinese girl in the story, O-lan, bride, mother, and grandmother, and the man, Wang, dogged, strong, weak, and sometimes sinning, are certainly the first such individuals in all literature about China with whom literally millions of Americans were able to identify warmly.

This achievement was something new in American writing about China. Pearl Buck did not, for one thing, write about Chinese in relation to foreigners, but about Chinese in relation to one another. Nor, like Lin Yutang in *My Country and My People*, which enjoyed its own much smaller vogue in this same period,[75] did she concen-

---

[73] Pearl Buck's other novels with a China background have had over the years a total trade edition sale of 640,000. Figures on reprints could not be obtained.

[74] Dorothy Jones, *op. cit.*, p. 47

[75] Published in 1935, *My Country and My People* sold a total of 55,705 copies in its trade editions and 26,000 in a reprint edition.

THE CHINESE 157

trate on the charm of Chinese ways and wisdom. Pearl Buck chose instead to write about the lowliest of all Chinese, the peasant, and to deal with the harshness of his struggle for existence. Some Chinese critics complained of this, often out of envy and discomfort, suggesting that the book was no adequate picture of Chinese life because neither they nor their prototypes appeared in its pages. But what Pearl Buck was really after was to humanize the Chinese peasant and to cast him in the universally understood role of the man rooted in the soil, and this she succeeded in doing for most of her large audience. For some of her missionary readers, indeed, the book was a bit too earthy, but this had no adverse effect on its popularity.

The times were ready with a welcome for *The Good Earth* It appeared coincidentally with Japan's attacks on China. In a way that never could have been accomplished by event or propaganda, it humanized the people who became Japan's principal victims. The film based on the book appeared when Japan's piecemeal attacks had broadened into a full-scale war and American sympathy for the Chinese had become a powerful national emotion. Although it did not deal with the war itself, it gave the quality of individual recognition to the figure of the heroic Chinese peasant or peasant-soldier who offered battle to the Japanese against such great odds in the years just before Pearl Harbor. This film, indeed, set the molds for a long series of imitative sequels that followed during the war years, dramatizing the war itself and China's stand One of these was a filming of one of Miss Buck's own later books, *Dragon Seed* In all of them, however, Dorothy Jones observes, "the character of the Chinese peasant in general follows that dramatized in *The Good Earth*—he is hardworking, strong, persevering, and able to withstand the most severe adversities, kind toward children, respectful toward elders, all in all an admirable [and] warmly lovable character." [76]

The impressions left on the minds of our panelists, re-evoked after the passage of nearly twenty years, suggest that they retained from Pearl Buck not the memory of any individual Chinese, but a broad notion of what Chinese in general were like. By creating the first Chinese individuals capable of impressing themselves on American minds, Pearl Buck in effect created a new stereotype. Nobody remembered the evil and wickedness and cruelty also portrayed in her book, what they had retained was an image of the Noble Chinese Peasant, solid, wonderful, virtuous, admirable.

[76] *Op. cit.*, p 36.

It is no accident that the reader of Pearl Buck's novels about China acquires an impression of the Chinese in general which is sharper and more memorable than any individual character she has created. For Pearl Buck herself, when asked directly, willingly generalizes, and it is interesting to note that, so often charged herself with sentimentality, the Chinese virtue she values above all else is unsentimentality:

When I think of the Chinese, I think of a kind of person I like. He is not poetic, but extremely realistic, practical rather than artistic. The Chinese artist is never an artist for art's sake. Art is always a means or a philosophy with the Chinese China could not produce a Matisse or a Gaugin, certainly not a Picasso There are no Chinese cubists. The Chinese is a loyal father and friend. But this has its limits. He is not fantastically loyal This loyalty will come to an end if occasion demands it. He is common-sensible about everything. . . The Chinese can be terribly cruel. He never loves an animal He will never die of love. He is not egocentric He is remote from the maudlin in everything. He is a man of principle, but not to the point of folly, for his goal is larger than any one principle or any one situation I see these as features of the basic character of the Chinese, the basis of all the characters I have created, the variety occurring as I discover deviations and combinations of so many different kinds. There is some mixture of some or all of these qualities in every Chinese I have ever known. Americans seem to me to differ more in individual personalities than Chinese do I feel a greater uniformity among them Their corners are much more smoothed off than ours have been. I don't know if under a Communist-controlled society the Chinese is becoming a different kind of man I find it difficult to think so. I continue to think of the Chinese who sees everything against the background of eternity....

The chances are that even now, for those who read and are influenced by the books of Pearl Buck, it is the image of the Chinese peasant that she created that rises to the forefront of their minds whenever they think of the Chinese people marshaled under the demanding leadership of the Communist zealots [77]

[77] The only other China-born American writer of major popular repute is John Hersey Hersey has been back to China only occasionally since his youth, however, and only recently published the first book he has written that has a China background, *A Single Pebble*, New York, 1956 In this little parable-like story of a Yangtze tracker, Hersey evokes through the blurred vision of an American stranger all the familiar images of the perplexingly wonderful Chinese, the vigor and deep unlettered learning of the simple riverfolk, their timeless traditions, and the values they have that remain impenetrable to the inquiring foreigner. Hersey gives no hint that his own China birth makes them any less impenetrable to him

## *The Partisans*

Next to Pearl Buck, the Sinophile who has left the deepest marks on the largest number of Americans in the last twenty years has been the political partisan. In this figure we find something more than the individual admirer of the Chinese who communicates his admiration to all whom he meets. He is the admirer turned advocate who has sought in every possible public forum to urge or attack some particular American policy concerning China, to make himself heard as the defender or the opponent of some particular Chinese regime or even some individual Chinese leader.

This partisanship has a certain tradition in American-Chinese history, in the American self-conception as champion of China's interests vis-à-vis other foreign powers. In the last century there was the unique case of a former American minister to China, Anson Burlingame, accepting appointment as emissary of the Peking court to foreign capitals. Several generations later, the journalist Thomas Millard devoted a notable career to advising the Chinese government and writing many eloquent books and papers pleading the Chinese cause against foreign encroachment during and after the First World War.

But generally speaking, interest in Chinese politics within China came late among the Sinophiles In the first decades of what we have called the Age of Benevolence, only a few professionals—mostly journalists and diplomats—concerned themselves at all with the comings and goings of obscure and impotent Chinese premiers, ministers, and officials, the marching up and down of the rival armies, the rising and falling of more or less eccentric and picturesque war lords. Businessmen and missionaries often had to deal with the militarists and officials in their day-to-day affairs, but they did so from protected positions and never really had to take Chinese politics very seriously. To most foreigners, indeed, the war lords and their acolytes were for the most part rather comic figures whose activities were odd, curious, or laughable but impinged only incidentally and marginally on foreign lives and interests. They were taken seriously only as proof that the Chinese were incapable of effective or orderly self-rule. The chaotic disorder of Chinese political life suited the foreigner very well indeed so long as his own privileged position remained untouched. Only when this position was again directly threatened—as eventually it had to be—did Chinese politics cease to seem amusing or unimportant.

China's "awakening"—so long foreseen—was actually beginning in the years that followed the First World War, and for many of these foreigners it was bound to be a rude one In the oncoming revolution, many a Chinese father was bound to lose his authority The more or less fondly paternal foreigner could hardly retain his; the idyll had to end. The way it ended is the sum of all that has happened in China in the last forty years, a history far too full and complex to be crowded into any adequate summary in this space. What concerns us here is that in these enormously crowded and eventful years, the contending forces that rose in China came to be mirrored by contending sets of American partisans. These advocates presented to the American public wholly conflicting views of what was going on in China and ultimately offered wholly different though equally ineffectual prescriptions for American policy. These controversies, winning greater or lesser audiences from time to time, went on across many years, coming to a confused climax in the great and stormy national post-mortem held in this country in 1950–51 over what had happened in China. By that time, these many partisan influences had left deep scratches on a great many American minds; we came upon them repeatedly during our interviews.

In the decade or so preceding Pearl Harbor, at least three distinct sets of partisans pressed their particular views of China on the American public.

The first and feeblest were the surviving defenders of the old treaty port system, the possessors of what used to be called "the Shanghai mind " To these businessmen and their journalistic spokesmen, the emergence of Chiang Kai-shek and his government at Nanking in 1927–28 only proved again the noxious effects of the "coddling" of the Chinese by misguided missionary zeal The recurrence of costly civil wars, war-lord satrapies, inefficient and corrupt administration, confirmed for them their belief in the futility of counting on the Chinese to put their house in order. What they wanted was reassertion of foreign rule in China by open force, and they wrote more or less passionate books and articles advocating their cause.[78] Unfortunately for them, their appeal was heeded not by their own government, but by the Japanese, who in 1931 began

[78] Cf Rodney Gilbert, op cit , Hallett Abend, *Tortured China*, New York, 1930

their new effort to conquer China. Indeed, at the outset, not a few of these partisans welcomed Japan's move as a salutary development. They deplored only its singlehandedness and their own government's unwillingness to make it a united venture. The full significance of Japan's action did not dawn on some of them until Japanese troops were in occupation of their cherished concessions and they themselves sat in Japanese prisons, with time, before being repatriated, to ruminate over the unkindliness of the times and the unwisdom of those at home who had failed to take their timely advice. Many of them, now scattered in many places, will still tell you that a "strong hand" by the Western powers in China in those early days would have saved a good deal of later trouble But their voices, echoes of an irretrievably dead past, have long since ceased being heard, swallowed in the tumult of great events The field of American partisanship concerning China passed meanwhile to two other principal groups: those who profoundly admired Chiang Kai-shek and those who profoundly admired his Communist opponents.

The pro-Chiang partisans arose in the beginning almost exclusively from among the missionaries. During the events that had brought Chiang to power in 1925–27, the missionaries had become again the most visible symbols of hated foreign imperialism Several thousand of them had been compelled to flee before the Nationalist advance Many joined the businessmen behind the reinforced treaty port garrisons bristling at the concession borders, demanding more troops, more warships, stronger action by the Powers, watching the fruits of their past benevolence drop from their hands and feeling once more in full tide the angry exasperation and hostility inherited from the pre-Boxer era. But now there were other missionaries, many quite influential, who spoke up for the validity of Chinese nationalist claims. Together with a few maverick American journalists who took a similar view, they won considerable backing in the mission-supporting sections of the American public. At the same time that he was establishing his bona fides as the proper recipient of foreign and especially American support, Chiang Kai-shek became a Christian. He married the American-educated Soong Mai-ling, whose family formed part of the new power elite, and he embraced the Methodist creed in which she had been raised. In this new regime, now headed by a Christian couple and staffed largely by the products of mission schools and American universities, influential sections of the missionary movement saw their first hope for full official sanction and support for their endeavors In return for this bright promise they gave Chiang and his wife and the Kuomintang regime their full, uncritical, and passionate support From about 1930 on, the entire missionary network of communications in the United States became the carrier of the most deeply self-persuaded partisanship, favoring not merely China or the Chinese, their character, their society, or their civilization, but a particular Chinese government and its particular leaders When Japan s full-scale attack on China in 1937 raised the whole issue of China's fate to a new level of visibility and interest among Americans, Chiang's American missionary partisans played a cardinal role in shaping public views and influencing official policy.

The admiring supporters of Chiang Kai-shek had to accept on faith his pledge that the "one-party tutelage" of the Kuomintang would eventually be replaced by a freer and more democratic regime. The actual functioning of the regime made this act of faith a peculiarly demanding one There was no democratic opposition to Chiang because none was allowed to exist. Almost in the nature of things, one had to be invented, and the credit for the first working model must unquestionably go to Edgar Snow's famous book, *Red Star Over China*, which appeared early in 1938.

In the first years of Chiang's rule, a favorable view of the Chinese Communist armies, far from sight deep in the hinterland, was provided only by the Communists themselves and their more or less open sympathizers. They found one of their first and more romantic chroniclers in the late Agnes Smedley, whose highly colored, strongly partisan, but secondhand early accounts enjoyed a certain vogue among the party faithful but not very far beyond. Her books [79] were mentioned by only two of our present panelists But the times were providing a widening audience for the Communist case. the depression, the rise of Hitler, the outbreak of civil war in Spain, the Comintern shift from ultraradicalism to the total inclusiveness of the "People's Front." In China, this turn took the dramatic form of Communist offers to drop their more harshly radical program to join hands with Chiang Kai-shek, their mortal foe, if he would only drop his policy of nonresistance and take up arms against Japan. This was

[79] E g , *Chinese Destinies,* New York, 1933, *China's Red Army Marches,* New York, 1934.

where matters stood in mid-1936 when Snow, a journalist of some years' experience in China, made his enterprising trip into the Communist areas in China's northwest. Six months after that, the Japanese began their all-out war. They again attacked Shanghai, where Chinese forces resisted spectacularly for nearly four months before falling back. In December, 1937, they bombed an American gunboat, the *Panay*, on the Yangtze, killing three Americans, and occupied Nanking in an orgy of rapine and slaughter. These events had aroused popular American concern, interest, and sympathy for the Chinese to an unprecedented pitch, and this was the setting in which Snow's image-forming book appeared.

*Red Star Over China* gave a highly laudatory account of the Chinese Communists, their program, their methods, and their practices. Like many much less politically susceptible Americans who followed him into direct contact with the Chinese Communists, Snow was greatly struck by the contrast between the Communists in their hinterland refuge and the Kuomintang When Snow came upon them, the Communists were still wholly confined to rural areas, were engaged in a major shift to milder and reformist policies, and had developed to a fine point their great skill in enlisting the mass of peasants in their cause. Snow described this Communist regime as "rural equalitarianism." [80] Snow faithfully presented the full party line and made it quite plain that the aim remained full conquest of Communist power, but it is still probably fair to locate in his ardent pages the birthplace of the eventful idea that the Chinese Communists, unlike any other Communists anywhere else, were nothing but "agrarian reformers." In any case, *Red Star Over China* was well and widely received and had an impact hardly measured by its relatively small sale (it went through seven editions with a total of 23,500 copies [81]) or by the fact that 21 panelists mentioned it. The book made its deepest impression on increasingly worried and world-conscious liberal intellectuals It began the creation in a great many American minds of the impression of the Chinese Communists as austere, dedicated patriots as contrasted to the heavy-handed, corrupt, and unreliable leaders of Chiang Kai-shek's Kuomintang

But the "united front" so tenuously formed and held by the

[80] *Red Star Over China*, New York, 1938, p 211.

[81] According to its publishers, Random House, in September of 1944 it reappeared in the Modern Library series and had six printings of just over 27,000 copies

Kuomintang and the Communists in China in 1937 was for the next few years dutifully reproduced in a "united front" of their respective partisans in the United States. The Japanese were invading the land, the Chinese were resisting. Strife was muted. There was glory to be shed on all. In the large pictures that flashed on American screens, there was room now, at least for a while, only for anger and awe and admiration. Americans watched from afar as the Chinese stood up to the Japanese attack as best they could. Slowly—very slowly indeed from the Chinese point of view—they came to see that China's foe was also their own, but they had barely come to the point of acting on what they saw when Pearl Harbor made Americans and Chinese allies in a common struggle for survival. It was a space of a few years when truth and propaganda, fears, hopes, and fuzzy illusions blurred together in a hazy drama distantly seen. The many different realities of these years will face each other in the contending pages of the historians for a long time, but viewed in its place in our present history of American perceptions of the Chinese, its character is plain. This brief interval is the only one in which wholly sympathetic images of the Chinese dominated the entire area of American-Chinese relations. Of all the ages through which these images have passed, this one alone could be called the Age of Admiration.

## 7. *THE HEROES RISEN*

WE HAVE COME by now to the years of the adulthood of almost all the members of our panel. By 1931 most of them were of college age or older. Whatever had reached them earlier about China had in most cases glanced off their youthful minds at odd tangents, leaving scratches to be sure, but leaving them more or less faintly on the outer edges of their awareness. They had acquired thereby a variety of images and attitudes which governed some of their thinking and behavior but which, except for a few, had touched no central interest in their lives. All this and much more changed in the decade that began with Japan's renewed attack on China in 1931 and ended with its attack on Pearl Harbor in 1941. These were the years when events involving China made their own most direct impact on the individuals whose minds we are presently exploring. It has already been noted that when they were asked what events had first forced upon them a sense of the importance of Asia in American affairs, 48 mentioned the Sino-Japanese conflict of the 1930's, 41 mentioned Pearl Harbor. Taken together with 21 others who mentioned earlier events in China and who were of course affected deeply by these climactic developments, we have a total of 110 individuals out of 181 for whom this was a peculiarly decisive mind-shaping time.

The recall of "the Sino-Japanese War" or "the invasion of Manchuria" or "the attack on Pearl Harbor" actually telescopes a decade of experience during which total outlooks were drastically changed and every man's own individual life profoundly affected. These events marked a great turning in American-Asian history, but they were also part of a turning of all history, part of the great and stormy passage which carried a great mass of Americans to new conceptions of the world and their place in it, wrenching them from their cherished insulation to reluctant involvement in the world's affairs. Japan's initial move in China was only the beginning, and most Americans, still held in the traditional grooves of isolation and deeply engrossed by the depression, paid it small heed But explosion followed explosion: Hitler's rise, the Ethiopian war, the Spanish civil war, Munich, the Stalin-Hitler pact, the Nazi march into Poland—the war in China had become part of the onset of the new holocaust. This was a time when history shook every man's life apart, and though he might piece it together again, it was never again the same. This is what happened to our panelists, in common with all their countrymen and great masses of people elsewhere, in the ten years that began with an obscure episode in far-off Manchuria sometimes called "the Mukden incident" and ended with the engulfment of the whole world in total war. This nearly universal experience of education through catastrophe has already been chronicled in many ways and will doubtless be scrutinized and reinterpreted for generations hereafter. We are concerned here only with that particular piece of the process that had to do with American images of China and the Chinese and how they fared amid all the changes.

In their great bulk Americans did not by any means react at once to Japan's attack on China like the aroused parents of beleaguered offspring. There were certain traditional American attitudes—relating to China and to any underdog-bully situation—which dictated an automatic editorial sympathy for the Chinese in the American press But there was certainly not enough of this sympathy to offset or upset the governing conceptions of American self-interest, which were still strongly isolationist. This was at least one reason for the failure of Henry L Stimson's effort, as Secretary of State, to organize a strong line of international diplomatic resistance to Japan

Stimson has given us the picture he had in his mind of "the great sluggish population" of China undergoing a vast transformation. He was persuaded that "the eventual trans-Pacific relations of the United States would be enormously, if not predominantly, affected by the future development of the 450 millions of China," especially if these "hundreds of millions of hitherto industrious and peace-loving people should in their awakening to modern life be transformed into an aggressive power, fired by the memories of the wrongs done to them by other nations. . ."[82] Stimson ran into obstacles, not only among "the other nations," i e., the British and the French, who believed at that time that Japan's moves served their interests, but equally at home, where the conviction governed that Japan's moves had nothing to do with any vital American interest at all. This was the conviction represented at the policy-making summit by the President himself. Herbert Hoover was, indeed, an "old China hand" himself, a veteran of the Boxer siege and a sufficient authority on the subject of Chinese civilization to marshal his images of China in support of his isolationist views In a memorandum he presented to his Cabinet, Mr. Hoover wrote

> We must remember some essentials of Asiatic life. . . Time moves more slowly there, political movements are measured in decades or centuries, not in days or months, that while Japan has the military ascendancy today and no doubt could take over parts or all of China, yet the Chinese people possess transcendent cultural resistance, that the mores of the race have carried through a dozen foreign dynasties over 3,000 years, . No matter what Japan does . . . they will not Japanify China and if they stay long enough they will be absorbed or expelled by the Chinese. For America to undertake this on behalf of China might expedite it, but would not make it more inevitable.

Mr. Hoover went on to say that "there is something on the side of Japan . . . and we should in friendship consider her side also," and after making a persuasive case for Japan's side, he concluded

[82] *The Far Eastern Crisis*, New York, 1936, pp 10–13

THE CHINESE 167

Neither our obligations to China, nor our own interest, nor our dignity require us to go to war over these questions. These acts do not imperil the freedom of the American people, the economic or moral future of our people. I do not propose ever to sacrifice American life for anything short of this [83]

American passivity toward events in China was encouraged over the next five years not only by preoccupation with affairs at home but by the fact that Japanese aggression in China took the form of small nibbling while official Chinese policy remained one of "non-resistance" to Japanese encroachments. There were episodic acts of resistance, but these occurred in defiance of the official leadership The most spectacular of these was the thirty-four-day struggle of the Nineteenth Route Army at Shanghai in January-February 1932. The Shanghai battle was in particular widely reported, since it took place at the edge of a protected foreign settlement before the eyes of astounded foreign observers and a large corps of hastily assembled foreign correspondents from all over the world It has a special place in our present history because it began the transformation of the image of an ineffectual Chinese soldiery and a passive population into a picture of hardy and brave soldiers and devoted civilians capable of great feats when decently led and motivated. Here really began the ripples of fear and sympathy which would eventually swell into a great tide.

This did not begin to happen, however, until after July, 1937, when the Japanese took to arms for keeps and Chiang Kai-shek finally began fighting back Now the China war was heavily splashed across the front pages of the American press day after day, and newsreel films, entering upon their heyday as an independent medium of communication, made their vivid impact week after week on a movie-going public A new and more prolonged Chinese defense at Shanghai in the fall months of 1937 sharpened and enlarged the new image of Chinese staunchness [84] It began the process by which

[83] R L Wilbur and A. M Hyde, *The Hoover Policies*, New York, 1937, p 600.

[84] One of the most successful "propaganda" pieces of all time was a product of this battle It was a photo, taken by a Chinese newsreel photographer, of an abandoned Chinese child, injured, bleeding, bawling on its haunches in the midst of the smoking destruction of Shanghai's railway station *Life* (October 4, 1937, p. 102) estimated that 136,000,000 people all over the world saw this photo in newspapers or the newsreel of which it was a part *Life* readers selected it as one of ten Pictures of the Year 1937

a popular picture of the Chinese heroically defending their homeland against an infinitely more powerful invader gradually grew to much more than life-size proportions In December, 1937, came the Japanese sack of Nanking, "a saturnalia of butchery" which revolted, angered, and aroused a large American public.[85] Of all the incidents in this now dimly remembered time, the *"Panay* incident" was recalled by members of our panel more frequently than any other, and the reason is undoubtedly that it marked for many of them not only the awakening of sympathy for the Chinese and indignation at the Japanese, but of vital American interest in these distant events. The sinking of the *Panay* raised abruptly for a great many Americans the specter of their own involvement in the war.

The war in China was, of course, only one in a kaleidoscope of events that were beginning to force Americans to take a new view of the world and their place in it. Hitler's shadow was high over Europe by now, and many of the complexities of the time were enigmatically wrapped up in the civil war in Spain. As the much-written record of the time shows, the great majority of Americans still powerfully believed that they were uninvolved, that strict neutrality and a curb on nefarious bankers and munitions makers would suffice to keep them from being beguiled again as they believed they had been in 1917. When President Franklin D. Roosevelt made his famous "quarantine-the-aggressor" speech on October 5, 1937, he found himself unaccustomedly alone and had to beat a hasty retreat. "It's a terrible thing," he told an aide, "to look over your shoulder when you are trying to lead—and to find no one there." [86]

Franklin Roosevelt's associations with China were not, like Theodore Roosevelt's, shaped by feelings of racial chauvinism, nor based, like Herbert Hoover's, on the experience of overlordship. F. D. Roosevelt had the romantic view of China, drawn mainly from the fact that his mother's family, the Delanos, were merchants in the China trade and the Roosevelt family lore was full of the familiar glamor of that calling, as apparently he never tired of telling callers whenever the subject of China was apropos and often when it was not.

[85] For examples see "The Sack of Nanking," *Reader's Digest*, July, 1938, and correspondence exchanged under the title "We Were in Nanking," *Reader's Digest*, October, 1938

[86] Quoted by L. A. Sussman, "FDR and the White House Mail," *Public Opinion Quarterly*, XX, 1, Spring 1956, p 11, cf Henry L Stimson, *On Active Service*, New York, 1948, p 312, Sumner Welles, *Seven Decisions That Shaped History*, New York, 1951, pp. 73–74

The other ingredient in his outlook on China, suggests Sumner Welles, was supplied by his term as Assistant Secretary of the Navy in the Wilson Administration, when he had "become imbued with the Navy's conviction that Japan was America's Number 1 antagonist." Welles says:

> It is quite true that during Hitler's first years in power, the President, like most of us, underestimated the extent of the Nazi menace. But he never underestimated the danger to the United States in the course of aggression on which Japan had embarked in 1931.[87]

Thus it was possibly not without blessings from the highest places that small but powerful groups still at the outer edges of American public opinion went strenuously to work at about this time to assist events in changing the massive convictions that most Americans still held During 1938 an intensive campaign, inspired and heavily staffed by missionaries or mission-connected individuals, was mounted to command a more active interest in China's plight, to demand a halt to shipment of war materials to Japan, and to combat the widely accepted view that to avoid conflict, the United States should withdraw all its citizens and armed forces from China. By wide circulation of missionary and other eyewitness reports of Japanese crimes and Chinese heroism, by the organization of committees of many different kinds—to promote a boycott of Japanese goods, to seek "non-participation in Japanese aggression," to send medical aid to China—and by strong pressure on Congress and through direct personal contact with influential leaders, these groups made a powerful impact both on public opinion and on government policy.[88]

The course of the war in China provided ample materials for the drive to awaken and activate American sympathies and fears It was during the great retreat inland from the coast of China in 1938 that the phrase "scorched earth" entered our language. A picture of the valor and sacrifices of Chinese soldiers and civilians was exposed, via the public prints and the newsreels, to the view of almost every adult American. To newsreel films of relentless Japanese bombings, Joris

---

[87] *Seven Decisions*, p 66
[88] For a detailed description of this activity see John W Masland, "Missionary Influence Upon American Far Eastern Policy," *Pacific Historical Review*, X, 3, September, 1941, pp. 279–296, cf also William E Daugherty, "China's Official Publicity in the United States," *Public Opinion Quarterly*, Spring 1942, pp 70–86.

Ivens and John Ferno added in 1938 their famous documentary *The Four Hundred Million* From these sources dozens of our panelists vividly recalled of this period the pictures that showed the long lines of Chinese burden-bearers carrying whole factories in bits and pieces, each bearing his load and trudging on in endless winding columns over the hills leading to China's inner hinterland. Chinese universities were moved inland by the same means, and Chinese laborers began building by hand, rock by rock and one basket of dirt after another, the "Burma Road" that was going to restore their connection with the outside world.[89] Cartoonists pictured China as the slowly waking giant facing the puny Japanese attacker A Fitzpatrick cartoon in the *St Louis Post-Dispatch* showed a Chinese peasant in the struggle with the caption: "Father Time Is on His Side." Combat dispatches from the obscure central China fronts rang with the phrases: "fighting against fantastic odds with high courage" or "they stood firm through long weeks while the superbly equipped Japanese forces shelled and bombed them without cessation." Advertisements appealed to sympathy and to conscience:

> Men, women and children are being killed by the thousands, the Chinese people whose only crime has been to defend their homes from the vicious attacks of the Japanese warlords . . . Help to halt the most horrible crime of modern times. Will you knowingly share in the crime of invading China?" [90]

There was enough reality here to bolster unlimited exaggeration and an endless mythology. Ideas about the defenders of China became common currency among millions of Americans at this time. They were heavily personalized in the figures of Chiang Kai-shek and his wife Missionary propaganda concentrated heavily, says Masland, on:

> highly favorable accounts of the Chinese government and high Chinese officials . . . They have never failed to point with pride to the fact that a high percentage of the officials of the government have been educated in Christian institutions, and that many of them are themselves Christians, including Generalissimo Chiang Kai-shek Madame Chiang has practically become a saint to them [91]

[89] Cf "China Moves Inland" a condensation of a collection of articles, *Reader's Digest*, May, 1939
[90] Cf. *Asia*, March, 1938, p 267
[91] Masland, loc cit , p 287

*Time,* edited by China-born, missionary's son Henry Luce, named Chiang Kai-shek and Madame Chiang Man and Wife of the Year 1938.

The abandonment—or more accurately, the rejection—of isolationist outlooks by a substantial majority of the American public under the pressure of events between 1937 and the end of 1941 was one of the major occurrences of contemporary American history. Already much chronicled, the study of this massive shift will remain unfinished business for a long time to come; one of its many facets still awaiting scrutiny is the relative weight and importance in the whole process of events in Asia and events in Europe. We offer here neither a summary nor any judgment on this complicated matter; only some remarks.

Most of the members of our present panel—aside from those already preoccupied with Asia—remember themselves at this time as being concerned chiefly with domestic American affairs or—if they looked abroad at all—with Europe. This was the normal and quite predictable pattern among almost all the educated professionals in our society, for whom the non-American world was, until quite recently, the transatlantic world. Yet, by another one of those paradoxes so common in this history, there is much to suggest a greater American sensitivity to the threat of Japan than to the threat of Hitler's Reich. Hitler had actually been on the march for only a slightly shorter time than Japan, but nobody was forming high-level American committees to combat Nazi aggression until Britain and France stood directly under its shadow At the outbreak of war in Europe there was, away from the North Atlantic seaboard, almost no disposition to see America as directly threatened. To a commanding segment of the population, it was 1914 all over again, and the thing for Americans to do was to avoid repeating what they saw as the Wall-Street-inspired mistake of 1917. On the issues which led to war, there was never any serious current of pro-Japanese sentiment, while there were not a few Americans, of both high and low repute, on whom Hitler's Germany was able to count in the propaganda warfare that preceded actual hostilities. Actually there was no European counterpart for the impression of Japan as a sort of traditional foe-to-be, an idea which we have seen attributed to Franklin Roosevelt and which goes back, among our important public men, to the time of the aging Admiral Mahan and to the first Roosevelt's second thoughts after Portsmouth. No European power stood in any similar position in the world view of Americans, none, at least, since Britain had ceased to do so sometime late in the last century.

Just how the American "public" saw this matter over time is a good deal more difficult to say. "Public opinion" has always been a more elusive quarry for the historian than the views of individual public men. It has usually been deduced from these views, from the press, from overt public behavior—as in riots or elections—and perhaps most often taken from the impressions of more or less observant contemporaries. For the period we now have under view, the historian will have available for the first time a body of somewhat more precise evidence in the form of the accumulated results of opinion polls which began to appear in 1936 These inquiries, based on various kinds of cross-section samples of the national population, were crude and were framed by a host of limitations and shortcomings, but even at their crudest, they added a new dimension to the exploration of the public mind The future student of American attitudes in the pre-Pearl Harbor decade will find a marshaler of facts like Herbert Feis saying that in the face of Japanese depredations in China, "America became angered" and that "the picture of Japan before American eyes grew more sinister" [92] In the opinion polls of the time he will be able to pass from impressionistic generalizations to impressionistic percentages, which he may often find to be more graphic and more informative. In the tracings of the public mind made by the polls, he may find suggestions for locating the high starting points and steady recession of the great American belief that safety lay in total insulation from the world, and the low beginnings and the steady rise of the conviction that this was not so. The polls suggest that what the American acquired in this time was not necessarily an interventionist or internationalist outlook, but the knowledge that the United States itself was threatened and would have to act in its own behalf. What began as a fairly minor and detached reaction of sympathy for the Chinese became a much more active emotion as the conviction grew that Japan was a dangerous foe, not only of China, but of the United States itself Coming along a little more slowly, approximately the same process occurred with regard to England and Germany It was when the two threats coalesced that the American isolationist illusion disappeared, at least for then.

We can take the space here only to sample some of these sam-

[92] *The Road to Pearl Harbor*, Princeton, 1950, p 18.

THE CHINESE                                                             173

plings Here, for example, is the way George Gallup's American Institute of Public Opinion polls registered the course of American sympathies in the Sino-Japanese War.[93]

|                | "Neutral" | "Pro-China" | "Pro-Japan" |
|----------------|-----------|-------------|-------------|
| August, 1937   | 55%       | 43%         | 2%          |
| October, 1937  | 40        | 59          | 1           |
| May, 1939      | 24        | 74          | 2           |

An Elmo Roper poll in July, 1938, asked a national sample: "Which of the recent foreign military aggressions disturbed you most?" The answers:[94]

| | |
|---|---|
| Japan's invasion of China | 29.4% |
| Germany's seizure of Austria | 22.8 |
| Outside intervention in Spain | 10.3 |
| Russian treason trials | 2.7 |
| All | 6 |
| None | 21.3 |
| Don't know | 12.9 |

This suggests that there was still at this time at least a third of a national sample unmoved by any events abroad, while among the rest there was somewhat more of an eye for what Japan was doing in China than for what Hitler was doing in Europe. Within two years, Hitler's activities in Europe had become cataclysmic enough to shake the most deeply imbedded American illusions of security and non-involvement. It seems all the more striking, therefore, to note that at least in the polls the Nazi conquest of Europe in the summer of 1940 did not by itself puncture the anti-interventionist majorities. Hitler stood at the Channel and tried to reduce Britain from the air, and Britain, quite alone, fought back. On the other side of the world Japan was bombing Chungking almost as mercilessly and had begun its moves southward to new jumping-off places in Indochina and Thailand. In September, Japan formally joined the Axis in a pact clearly aimed at the United States. It was only after this merging of the transpacific and transatlantic threats to American safety that the opinion poll majorities shifted ground. For the first time, in answers to questions put by the pollsters, majorities began to say that

[93] *Public Opinion*, pp. 1081-1082
[94] *Public Opinion*, p. 1074.

Japan had to be halted "even at the risk of war" and that it had become more important to the United States to "help Britain" than it was to "stay out of the war."[95]

To the very end, the poll majorities clung to the hope that the national safety could be maintained by steps "short of war," but the polls clearly trace through the whole course of 1941 the steady growth of the conviction that events would decree otherwise. The active instinct for self-preservation passed from those who still believed it was possible to remain aloof and attached itself to the reluctant acceptance of the inevitability of involvement. The manner of the climax, Pearl Harbor, was in itself a stunning surprise. But there were few thoughtful people for whom the plunge into hostilities was, late in 1941, still unexpected.

The already considerable figure of the heroic Chinese defender of his land gained even larger dimensions when he became also our heroic ally. The warmth with which he was now hailed and his virtues extolled increased just about in inverse ratio to the actual American ability to come, at last, to his assistance. The first great American and Allied strategic decision was to fight the European war first. This left only a trickle of men and means to cope with Japan, which swept on from victory to victory through Southeast Asia. For the next two years, the great double mirrors of wartime news, information, and propaganda had little to reflect from China except the story of its heroic glamor. Documentary films raced their vivid and moving accounts across American screens (*The Battle of China*, 1942; *Inside Fighting China*, 1942, *Ravaged Earth*, 1943) and a stream of feature films (*Burma Convoy, A Yank on the Burma Road, China Girl, The Flying Tigers, God Is My Co-Pilot*, etc.) began to provide Chinese backgrounds for American heroes as well. In 1943, when Mme Chiang Kai-shek came to the United States to plead for more substantial American aid to China, she had an im-

---

[95] *Public Opinion*, pp. 973–974, 1076–1077. Feis reports that on October 14, 1940, President Roosevelt received a "report on the turn of American opinion after the Tripartite Pact" as shown by polls made through the Gallup facilities by Hadley Cantril's Office of Public Opinion Research at Princeton. One of these polls asked: "Should the United States take steps to keep Japan from becoming more powerful even if this means risking war?" The answers reported 57 per cent as saying "Yes." This change, Feis suggests, was reflected directly in the hardening of American policy during the ensuing months —*Road to Pearl Harbor*, p 122n, 123

THE CHINESE                                                              175

mense public success. Members of the United States Senate "rose and thundered" an ovation for her, and after she had spoken to the House of Representatives, reported *Time*, "tough guys melted 'Goddam it,' said one grizzled Congressman, 'I never saw anything like it. Madame Chiang had me on the verge of bursting into tears.' "[96]

"*BURDEN OF THE YEARS*"

*1944*

But however it was seen, in fact or half-fact, truth or half-myth, well symbolized or poorly, a sympathetic image of the Chinese rose now to a unique pinnacle in a mass of American minds He was no doubt grotesquely draped, but there the Chinese figure briefly stood,

[96] *Time*, March 1, 1943.

rich with all the medals won by his ceaseless coping with an adverse fate, his devotion to family and ancient past and his land, his adaptability, his quenchless devotion to what he valued. After all the long ages of contempt and benevolence through which he had lived in American minds, the Chinese, largely unbeknownst to him, now enjoyed there his finest hour. This was strictly an American, not a Chinese experience, and the marks of it are plainly visible still on American minds—they were still there on the minds of almost every member of our present panel—despite its brevity and despite all that has happened since to the Chinese, their images, and to us.

## 8. *THE HEROES FALLEN*

The brief hours of enchantment ticked swiftly away and then, as if at the last stroke of midnight, they ended and disenchantment set in. Americans who came to China on war missions carried with them the shining slipper left by the propaganda of the heroic period before Pearl Harbor But there was no happy ending to this story, because they found no Chinese on whom it really fit. This does not mean that the heroic defenders of China were pure chimera; too much real blood had been shed, too many heavy burdens carried, too many sacrifices made. These could not be waved away now, as though they had been characters and episodes in a fairy tale all along. The difficulty was that this had all been seen by too many Americans as though it had been a fantasy, seen in a setting divested of all its reality. The image-makers in their simple-minded enthusiasm had turned China at war into a movie set and had made the Chinese into plaster saints, including Generalissimo and Madame Chiang Kai-shek. But the China war was not a movie and the Chinese were not saints, plaster or any other kind, least of all the Chiangs. This mythology could hardly survive any live experience, and its passing, for many, was quite painful.

The Americans who turned up in China after Pearl Harbor discovered there a stalemated absence of peace rather than a war They came up against the stricken weariness of the Chinese nation, its size and backwardness, its vast array of unsettled problems and unresolved conflicts, the corruption and ineptitude in its high and low places, and its lack of a leadership capable of arousing and maintaining popular support and sustained effort. Because of all this, these Americans found it impossible between 1942 and 1945 to overcome what appeared to them to be China's utter incapacity to marshal and use an effective military force. There was great toil and great effort, but the result, in the end, was abandonment of all Allied military plans that called for any important culminating effort against Japan on mainland China.

The American experience in China during the war with Japan has remained obscure and little known except to the narrowest kind of a public. The literature it has produced is remarkably small. Two volumes of a military history have been issued by the Department of the Army.[97] Several volumes of documents have been released by the Department of State.[98] In addition to these pieces of the official record, we have had some excerpts from General Stilwell's diaries, a personal account from the China air force commander, General Claire Chennault, and a scanty handful of titles by journalists and a few others.[99]

The war had turned places on every continent and in every ocean into godforsaken holes for young Americans. Wherever they went, they were involuntary transplants, unwilling exiles. The claim could no doubt be disputed from many another corner, but those who went to the China-Burma-India theater unquestionably felt that they, of all the men in the war, had been relegated to the most dis-

[97] *The United States Army in World War II, China-Burma-India Theater, Stilwell's Mission to China*, 1953, and *Stilwell's Command Problems*, 1956, by Charles F Romanus and Riley Sunderland, Office of the Chief of Military History, Department of the Army, Washington, D C

[98] Especially the so-called "White Paper," *United States Relations with China, with Special Reference to the Period 1944-1949*, Washington, D.C., 1949; and *Foreign Relations of the United States, Diplomatic Papers, China, 1942*, Department of State Publication 6353, Washington, D C, 1956.

[99] *The Stilwell Papers*, edited by T H White, New York, 1948; Claire Chennault, *Way of a Fighter*, New York, 1949 The only attempt at a detailed summary based on official records and papers has been Herbert Feis, *The China Tangle*, Princeton, 1953. The *Cumulative Book Index* under the heading "World War, 1939-1946" discloses, for the years up through 1956, not a single title of a book by an American dealing primarily with the CBI wartime experience in India, only three or four such books on Burma, and barely two dozen titles on China Of the latter the only one to achieve best-seller status was White and Jacoby's *Thunder out of China*, New York, 1947 Perhaps the fullest account, the angriest, and the most intensely personal, will be found in Graham Peck's *Two Kinds of Time*, Boston, 1950.

tant, the most forsaken, the filthiest, most tiresome, backward, ridiculous, and least-regarded byway of the war. "CBI" did, indeed, enjoy the lowest priority and make the least imperative demands on the attentions of the war planners and the press. Only Claire Chennault's small band of volunteer fliers at the beginning, the jungle battles in Burma, and, later, the extraordinary aerial conquest of the Himalayan "Hump" caught at any edges of the popular imagination. The nearest thing to a major public personality the China experience produced for the American public, aside from Madame Chiang Kai-shek, was that crusty old general, Joe Stilwell, who won his moment as a minor legend chiefly because he disdained to make excuses when he got beaten. No less extraordinary and far more decisive events were happening elsewhere across the world. A picture of what was going on in the distant dimness of Chiang Kai-shek's China could hardly be squeezed onto the screen that had to take in MacArthur's Pacific, Roosevelt's America, Churchill's England, Hitler's Europe, Stalin's Russia, Montgomery's and Rommel's Africa, and the shaping of Eisenhower's massive counterattack, by air and by land, on the conquered continent Millions of Americans were very personally involved in these larger events. Amongst all these, the 200-odd thousand Americans who shared in the obscure experience of the China-Burma-India theater of the war formed a small and nearly unnoticed number.

About half of these served their time at bases in India, which they found to be a hideously crowded country, or pushing a road across North Burma, which they found to be a hot and hideously unpopulated jungle. The rest crossed the great mountains into China, to fly or service planes, to man supply lines, to help train Chinese troops On both sides of the "Hump," the great bulk of these men reacted to the people they encountered with feelings that ranged, in most cases, from contemptuous disregard to virulent hatred. Forbearing only with the greatest difficulty from citing at length my own observations on this score,[100] I find among the sparse books on the CBI experience a few of the even sparser allusions to this particular subject

> The one abiding sentiment that almost all American enlisted personnel and most of the officers shared was contempt and dislike for China. . . . They believed that all Chinese were corrupt, inefficient, unreliable. . . .

[100] *No Peace For Asia*, pp. 7–34

THE CHINESE 179

They saw the squalor, filth, and ignorance . . . with loathing and revulsion....[101]

Graham Peck, who tells a thousand stories of the corruption and chicanery to which Americans were exposed during their effort to wage war from Chiang's China, speaks of the "bitter personal hatred" that "was very common among military men." He found that "many Americans let race prejudice lead them to condemn all Chinese" but reported most of their reaction as a legitimate anger and disgust at the behavior of the Chinese with whom they had to deal

> I think every American who came to Kuomintang territory on war duty has bitter memories of do-nothing attitudes, and of profiteering which ranged from the prices the U.S. Army had to pay for airfields to the prices GI's were charged in restaurants.[102]

The pattern of reaction to the Chinese among these young Americans was in almost all respects quite different from that arising out of the previous experience of Americans in China These were different Americans—they were not missionaries, nor students, nor businessmen, and certainly not curious tourists—in a different part of China, come to the country under quite different conditions, and having almost daily experiences which seldom fell to the lot of the prewar Sinophile. Indeed, the occasional Sinophile-in-uniform was a lonely and unhappy man in those dark, tired war years in West China. One of them was the theater commander, General Joe Stilwell. Stilwell had a sentimentally strong regard for the ordinary Chinese soldier, whom he regarded as "the best in the world" if properly trained, fed, and led. He had with him a handful of China veterans and a small cadre of officers who had received some Chinese language instruction before coming out to the theater. Among these one occasionally encountered individuals who made some of the necessary distinctions about the people and the situation in China. But by far most commonly, the American soldier acquired a power-

---

[101] White and Jacoby, *Thunder Out of China*, p 164 White also refers (p. 165) to an incident described in *No Peace For Asia* (p. 21) in which a group of correspondents spent an afternoon trying to explain China and the Chinese to an audience of American soldiers At the end of the session one of them walked up, looked the correspondents over, and said "I been out twenty-four months and you know, you're the first guys I ever met that had a good word for the Chinese"

[102] *Two Kinds of Time*, p. 387 and *passim*

fully violent prejudice about the Chinese and could feel that it came to him out of his own indelible experience.

Part of this was the American's arrogant or self-protective reaction to the poverty, backwardness, and squalor, the features of Chinese life which, as we have already noted, led him to see the people involved as somehow subhuman But it also came out of the venality, corruption, and brutality these Americans encountered on all sides among the Chinese with whom they principally came into contact. These were largely the civil and military officials, brutalized policemen, and bureaucrats living off a pauperized population. They saw ragged soldiers for whom they only rarely had any respect and scarcely any pity, even, sometimes, when they saw them die They saw peasants in the fields or passers-by with whom they could establish neither a common tongue nor barely a common thought or impulse. For the rest, they saw brothelkeepers and black market thieves. The young American soldier came away from his China experience most typically attributing to the whole Chinese people the characteristics he found so common in the mass of male and female camp followers of both high and low estate who inevitably attached themselves to the American military establishment in China like sucklings to the teats of a sow. Any Chinese who differed from this norm was exceptional and highly uncommon. Any American who held a different view of the Chinese was a maverick, a "slopey-lover," like General Stilwell Stilwell, as the published portions of his diaries show, did not extend his admiration for the Chinese people in general to Chiang Kai-shek and his generals in particular The "slopey-lover" conducted at the summit his losing battle against the same venality which provided the principal ingredient of the common GI view below. For whether out of some small personal experience or out of the common gossip (usually exaggerated but rarely wholly false) about the fate of supplies being brought into China at such heavy cost, the great mass of these young Americans acquired above all else the strong and nearly universal conviction that the "slopeys" were a bunch of congenital crooks

The interaction between these Americans and the people among whom they so strangely and so briefly came has left almost no literary trace Only a few journalists—those outriders for the historians—have thought it worth mentioning. From among the GI's who spent their war in CBI, no novelist has emerged to take this interaction as his theme, none, at least, that I have been able to discover.[103] Considering the relative meagerness of the literary returns from the war as a whole and the persisting indigestibility of the times that have followed it, this small, hardly noticeable gap may never be filled at all. Historians will doubtless be able to reassemble the pieces of skeleton as they are gradually unearthed—and enjoy their quarrels over the rights and the wrongs of the assembly—but the flesh and substance of the experience may very well fade completely from memory for lack of timely recapture in preservable prose by someone who shared it.

Scattered in their small number through the population now, these CBI veterans have presumably scratched their share of nearby minds. In our panel we ran on a few faint traces of this, as when a publisher said:

> Some Hump fliers I met during the war told me China was a hopeless, bogged-down mess.

A Washington consultant:

> From people who were there during the war, I got the idea that the Chinese were not cooperating as they should, all sorts of black marketing, diversion of materiel. . . .

A university professor:

> We have had about fifteen or twenty ex-GI's around here who were in China, and to judge from them, the Chinese are a bunch of crooks, can't be trusted. . . They seem to feel this pretty strongly. . . .

At least 20 members of our panel were in China or India at some time during that war, most of them in their various capacities as specialists. One of them, however, had been a GI enlisted man himself, and he said:

> The GI's hated it The stealing! Who wouldn't?

[103] Indeed, the only novel I have been able to find that deals with this aspect of the wartime American experience in China is Preston Schoyer's *The Indefinite River*, New York, 1947 In this book there are some glimpses of the GI in China and some of his characteristic reactions to the Chinese, but Schoyer himself is hardly classifiable as an ex-GI novelist. His China experience antedated the war—he was a teacher at Yale-In-China—and his wartime experience took place, as does his novel, in a setting that was quite remote from the more typical GI experience

The idea of individual chicanery and public corruption was hardly a new one in connection with China. It had long been familiar as "squeeze" or "graft," institutionalized at almost all levels of Chinese life. Among our panelists who knew China, it was knowingly and tolerantly accepted as part of the Chinese scheme of things, or cited as basis for the well-established image of the Chinese as somewhat less than "honest" by ordinary Western or American standards, or, more strongly, as the reason why Chinese, in particular or in general, were untrustworthy, devious, and downright dishonest This Chinese who could never be trusted in money matters occupied a place in some minds right next to "Honest John Chinaman" whose word was invariably as good as his bond and was likely to commit suicide if he did not pay up his proper debts on settlement day, both images coexisting and coequal and both enjoying a reasonable share of substance in the Chinese actuality.

Certainly with regard to Chinese public affairs, and most particularly in the period immediately preceding the war, the prevalence of official corruption was part of the common knowledge of all who were associated in any way with China. It was, indeed, so well known that many of those most familiar with it failed to recognize it as part of the rot that was eating away the regime and would ultimately cause it to collapse. But then China entered upon its "heroic" period, the brief phase of active resistance to Japan It became unkind, unfashionable, and even injudicious for anyone to call attention to the seedier garments hidden by the shining armor. In the great romantic mythology about China through which so many Americans first discovered the country after 1937, there was not much room for the notion that a great many Chinese might not be totally virtuous. Even the Communists and their sympathizers, vigilant always to exalt their Communist heroes and deprecate their Kuomintang foes, joined in the common litany and were silent in this time on those subjects whose airing might have shaken the harmony of the "united front." The typically liberal and well-disposed individual whose whole image of China and the Chinese was shaped by the fuzzy and romantically colored information and emotions of this period was, much like Candide, in for a rude shock when confronted with more naked truths.

For a detailed description of precisely this experience of shocked discovery we are indebted to Leland Stowe, a correspondent of liberal and crusading impulses, who went into China via the Burma

Road late in 1941, just before Pearl Harbor. Stowe's experience was fairly typical of many who came after him with approximately the same mental and intellectual equipment. In an account published while the war was still on,[104] Stowe said that he "came to China with a typically American romantic attitude, without any faint conception of the oppressive poverty and squalor . . . and with only a vague idea of the complexity of the Orient's problems." He begins by complaining, only half-humorously, that nobody had ever told him about the smells. Indicating that he had the same romantic notions about thirteenth century Europe as he did about twentieth century China, Stowe archly chided that famous ancestor of all romantic Sinophilism:

> Old Marco Polo was a remarkably talented reporter but he . . . apparently had no sense of smell whatever. In all his famous pages . . he fails to make the slightest mention of the unbelievable and fantastic olfactory diversity. . . .

But the smells Stowe encountered assailed more than his nose. He also made the "jarring and unpleasant" and deeply depressing discovery that "the splendid picture of China's great war for independence has its black blotches and its darker side":

> I discovered also that my vision, like that of almost all Americans, had been seriously blurred by my enthusiasm for the Chinese people's magnificent and incredible resistance to Japan. Somehow you did not pause to reflect that people who fought on and on so marvelously could still be handicapped or betrayed by corruption, selfishness, or indifference among a considerable portion of their governing class. . . .

Stowe's 1941-vintage liberal romanticism remained thoroughly proof against the discovery of any blotches either among the heroic and deserving masses at the base of China, or its heroic and deserving leaders at the summit, Generalissimo and Madame Chiang Kai-shek, whom he portrayed for his readers in almost totally undisenchanted hyperbole. He did find that "Free China" was something less than free in such matters as the press and political opposition, but this could be rationalized without too much wrenching. Many liberals of that day were rationalizing much greater discrepancies in the case of the Soviet Union. What Stowe could not blink away, however, was the "orgy of racketeering" which he was immeas-

[104] Leland Stowe, *They Shall Not Sleep*, New York, 1944, pp 4-85

urably shocked to find rife along the Burma Road, China's vital lifeline, its jugular vein, its only link with the world, its only source for the intake of the goods of survival. "Few disillusionments of mine had ever been greater or more acid than this which I had suffered behind China's front," Stowe wrote. He finally decided with a certain anguish of spirit—and a characteristically exaggerated notion of the effect of a single news story—to try to report what he had found although he "knew it would come as a tremendous shock to an American public which had come to look upon all Chinese as Sir Galahads and patriots."

It is extraordinary testimony to the power of the China mythology of these years that a presumably sophisticated foreign correspondent —a member of a craft in which a certain minimum skepticism is a professional requirement—could be this "shocked" and expect his public to be bowled over by the news that there were crooked things going on in China. The extreme gullibility that made such deception possible was common to a large American public at that time with respect to China, and especially to a large segment of what was called "liberal opinion." These were mostly people of great goodwill who were being wakened by rude events to the fearful dangers abroad in the world They readily—even anxiously—grasped as their own the shining images of distant decency and bravery offered to them by highly interested parties as a substitute for the harsher facts with which decency and bravery were so inextricably mixed. In the name of a formless and largely mindless "anti-Fascism" many of them accepted in the 1930's a whole body of factitious images relating to Spain, Russia, and China. These have been at least in part responsible for the great disarray and the almost chronic sense of shock, betrayal, and disenchantment with which many of these individuals reacted to events thereafter.

But not everyone was so remote from the actualities nor so naïve about them. There was from the very beginning of this particular situation in China a wide gap between the popular picture of the Chinese at war and the private and more somber appreciations of some of the people in positions of actual responsibility. This difference existed, at least in some measure, at the policy-making summit. Writing for publication during the war, Sumner Welles, then Undersecretary of State, referred to the Chinese government and its major leaders with all the fervid admiration so current at the time, e.g., Madame Chiang Kai-shek's "amazing knowledge ... quiet dignity ... clarity of perception," and T. V. Soong, "a constructive influence, brilliant, tough, resilient."[105] It was not until after the war that Welles, speaking of the same period of time—September, 1943—quoted President Roosevelt as telling him of "the innumerable difficulties ... with Chiang Kai-shek ... [speaking] in no measured terms of the corruption and inefficiency which characterized his administration, he [FDR] had no patience with the regime's apparent lack of sympathy for the abject misery of the masses of the Chinese people."[106]

This difference between public and private views was especially marked in statements about what was being reported of the war in China, especially at the time of Pearl Harbor and thereafter. Some unusually striking examples of this appear in the diplomatic papers of 1942, published late in 1956.[107] The head of the first American military mission in Chungking was Brigadier General John A. Magruder, who had served in China as an assistant military attaché and was thus able to preface one of his early post-Pearl Harbor reports (February, 1942) with an elaborate statement of his own images of the Chinese:

It is a known fact that the Chinese are great believers in the world of make-believe, and that they frequently shut their eyes to hard and unpleasant actualities, preferring rather to indulge their fancy in flattering but fictitious symbols, which they regard as more real than cold facts. Manifestations of this national escape-psychology have been clearly discernible in China's international relations. She has consciously given free rein to her native penchant for alluring fiction in Chinese propaganda abroad. People in other countries swallow such glib untruths whole without realizing that they are being deceived. As instances of this deceptive symbolism, I may adduce many reports emanating from Chinese diplomatic sources abroad, referring to the marvelous achievements and abilities of the Chinese Army. Such reports are absolutely without foundation. They are largely due to the above-mentioned Chinese love of symbolism, or else can be attributed to nothing other than a downright desire to achieve certain specific objectives by clever deception

[105] *The Time For Decision*, New York, 1944, pp 282–285.
[106] *Seven Decisions that Shaped History*, New York, 1951, p 151
[107] All quotations on following pages are from *Foreign Relations of the United States, Diplomatic Papers, China*, 1942, pp. 13–16, 19, 24–25, 31, 112, 208, 246, etc.

Magruder went on to say that "because of the sponsorship accorded such propaganda on the part of many outstanding individuals, including missionaries as well as adherents to radical and liberal viewpoints, this propaganda has influenced public opinion in the United States, usually so sane and well-informed, to a surprising extent."

Some radio broadcasts heard from San Francisco's KGEI give me great cause for alarm. If they are at all typical, the true state of affairs in China is being seriously distorted, and China's military successes are being highly exaggerated, by what is being given out in American newspapers . . . There is grave danger that such continued distortions of fact as to the prowess of China's military forces are spreading about a false sense of security . . . in the United States, and even [among] Chinese officials themselves. . . . Such propaganda could lead to grave defects in American war plans, if our own officials should be influenced by it even to the slightest extent Perhaps all this is designed to raise popular morale in the United States and to flatter the Chinese, if so, it is going a bit too far.

At the State Department in Washington, Magruder's sour report was received with a certain irritation. A commenting memorandum said that while "some" of his facts were "accurate," his statements reflected "an attitude of a person who is too close to unpleasant detail and who has forgotten or overlooked broader aspects." This conflict between "unpleasant detail" from the scene itself and the emphasis on 'broader aspects" in Washington characterizes a great deal of the tangled difficulties into which the Chinese-American relationship now moved. It is striking to note, reading these documents fifteen years after the event, how "right" both treatments of the situation could often be. Thus Magruder and others after him were only telling the simple truth when they declared that Chinese military communiqués were almost pure fantasy. On the other hand, Stanley Hornbeck, a generally hardheaded State Department adviser on China (who, however, had not actually been to China for many years) was also "right," at least in essence, when he retorted. "The Chinese at least have a record of having 'taken it' for four and one-half years. . . ." Or. "Chiang Kai-shek has for four and one-half years successfully carried on defensive operations which most of the military experts of practically all of the other powers (including Japan) thought and said at the outset . . . could not be continued beyond a few weeks or at the utmost a few months." Or, finally: "Chiang is just as much entitled and just as well qualified to play national interest politics in connection with allied strategy as are responsible leaders of any other of the allied nations."

But it was easier to deprecate or ignore the "unpleasant detail" from 10,000 miles away than it was on the ground. Asked to comment on the Magruder telegram, the American ambassador in Chungking, Clarence Gauss, replied:

> I have repeatedly pointed out that China is not prepared physically or psychologically to participate on a major scale in this war, that the Chinese armies do not possess the supplies, equipment, or aggressive spirit for any major military offensives or expeditions, and that we should not expect from them more. . . . whatever assurances or offers of greater cooperation may be forthcoming. . . It is also true that China is not now making any all-out war effort on the military front. . . . I agree that the American press has unwisely accepted and exaggerated Chinese propaganda reports of alleged military successes which . . . have little foundation in fact. . . . I agree that all this fulsome praise of China's war effort may have the effect not only of intoxicating the Chinese with ideas of their own prowess . . . but also of inducing a greater complacency. . . .

In July, 1942, on the fifth anniversary of the all-out Japanese invasion of China, Secretary of State Cordell Hull issued a public message to Chiang Kai-shek in which he said: "The American people have watched with deep sympathy and admiration the heroic fortitude and tenacity with which for five long and bitter years the Chinese people have fought on against heavy odds." And President Roosevelt said: "All the world knows how well you have carried on that fight which is the fight of all mankind." In a memorandum written at Chungking a few days later Ambassador Gauss said:

> It is unfortunate that Chiang and the Chinese have been "built up" in the United States to a point where Americans have been made to believe that China has been "fighting" the Japanese for five years, and that the Generalissimo, a great leader, has been directing the energetic resistance of China to Japan and is a world hero. Looking the cold facts in the face, one could only dismiss this as "rot."

There is too heavy a burden of historic consequence in this matter to dismiss this "rot" as merely another sample of the routine hypocrisy common in the public and private lives of nations, especially in wartime. The fact is that the "rot" in China was eating away a regime and a social order.

Chinese-American wartime relations finally exploded in public with the recall of General Stilwell, in October, 1944. The rash of "revelations" of conditions in China which filled the press on this occasion began the process by which the Chiang Kai-shek regime in China became powerfully identified with the single theme and single idea of *corruption*. This was used both in the more limited sense of plain thievery and in the profounder sense of the inner decay of a regime that seemed incapable of overcoming its own inherent weaknesses, much less coping with the staggering problems of the people over whom it ruled. This became the dominant impression created by almost all the news reported from China in the war's aftermath.

The Nationalist regime was brought closer to view by its return to the seaboard provinces and cities. To the shocked dismay of both the people and foreign well-wishers, the return of Kuomintang officials appeared more like a descent of locusts than a liberation Conditions in Shanghai were such that even the foreign businessmen who had returned generally felt—as was commonly reported at the time and described again by one of our panelists who shared in this experience—that Communist conquest was preferable to Kuomintang anarchy. The attempt to organize relief in postwar China brought in a whole new contingent of international public servants working for UNRRA (the United Nations Relief and Rehabilitation Administration). The wholesale abuses in the handling of relief supplies by the cooperating Chinese agencies during the next two years brought on a series of public denunciations and resignations among UNRRA officials, causing small explosions in the news which were nevertheless heard quite loudly around the world and added to the general impression of Kuomintang decay.

In almost every account, in newspaper, magazine, or book, that appeared about China between 1946 and 1949, the ineptitude, paralysis, and outright corruption of the officialdom remained the dominant themes and created the main lines of foreign—and particularly American—impressions as the Kuomintang-Communist civil war ran its course and the American mission headed by General George C. Marshall failed hopelessly to stem the onrush of doom. The swift crumbling of the Nationalist armies before the advancing Communists in 1949 completed the picture of a Chinese leadership not heroic but hopeless, rendered impotent largely by its own internal weakness, and of a Chinese mass too crushed by events to want anything but the order the victors promised to bring. By the end of 1949, barely four years after Japan's surrender, the Communists were

THE CHINESE                                                      189

masters of all of China. Chiang Kai-shek and the remnants of his government and army had taken refuge on the island of Formosa. Great and turbulent and conclusive events had brought about this massive change in China, and a great and turbulent and inconclusive debate about them has been going on more or less continuously ever since in the United States. In this process, the plaster-saint images of the Chinese, and much more, came tumbling down.

### The Great Oriental Disappearing Act

## 9. THE UNGRATEFUL WRETCHES

These events are of recent date, the issues raised by them are still very much alive. Yet they are also already disappearing from view, washing away under the high and strong and often even more turbulent tides that have since come in. All sorts of lumps and crevices have been filled or covered, the thinner tracings left so recently are already all gone. New issues and new dilemmas have pressed upon us while all the old ones were still unresolved. The debate produced no decision. As it receded, people were left clinging either to surviving bits and pieces of what they had thought before, or clinging to nothing at all Some of these would say frankly, as members of our panel did say, that they were not sure now what they thought about what had happened in China.

At least one idea found firm lodging. Despite valiant rear-guard action by Chiang Kai-shek's partisans, the idea of corruption became almost automatically identified with the regime he had failed to maintain in China. Despite all the frenzied finger-pointing and scapegoat-hunting, the notion of *failure-through-corruption* was still the principal reason assigned by the largest single group in our panel for the collapse of the Nationalist regime and the victory of the Communists. The question was "What do you think was the main reason for the Communist conquest of power in China?" and the answers grouped themselves as follows:

| | |
|---|---|
| Kuomintang corruption, failure to cope with the people's problems | 80 |
| Shrewd Communist tactics | 46 |
| American errors of policy or judgment | 32 |
| Russian help to the Communists | 10 |
| Treason in the U S. government | 7 [108] |

[108] A Gallup poll on August 13, 1954, showed a somewhat different set of emphases in the responses of a national cross-section sample to the question. "Judging from what you have heard and read, what would you say are the main reasons China went Communist?" The replies

| | |
|---|---|
| Poverty, living conditions, ignorance of masses | 33% |
| Russian pressure, propaganda | 33 |
| U.S. policy, failure to support Chiang | 7 |
| Corruption of Nationalist regime | 7 |
| Fifth column, traitors | 3 |
| Miscellaneous | 17 |
| Don't know | 23 |

(The table adds to more than 100 per cent because some persons gave more than one reason)

The task of placing these events under reasonably dispassionate scrutiny has hardly been begun. There is no such thing as a non-controversial account of the collapse of Kuomintang China, or a coherent account of the impact of this event in the United States. A chronicler of the decade 1945-55 has noted, wonderingly, that the Chinese Communist victory had violated some "law of history" which gave Americans "a special mission" in Asia, that Americans had found the China outcome "peculiarly intolerable.'[109] But the detailed essences of the matter still lie, in all their contemporary freshness, in the great unsorted masses of all that was written on the subject, spoken, argued, charged, and countercharged in all the many overheated public forums of the land during the early 1950's.

The China theme was, to be sure, only one in a time of many complicated discords. The "loss" of China was part of a larger loss so many Americans suffered at this time, a loss of self-confidence, a loss of assurance about security and power, especially atom power, a loss of certainty about the shape of the world and America's place in it—most of all, perhaps, the loss of the hope and expectation that they could return to their private American world, the best of all possible worlds, and be free without fear or concern to enjoy it. The China "loss" was all these losses. It was magnified and its impact multiplied many times by the outbreak of the Korean War, which late in 1950 produced the staggeringly new spectacle of Americans suffering defeats at Chinese hands. This added new elements of anger and humiliation to the confused disarray and made it even easier for unscrupulous politicians to use the "loss" of China as the handiest and biggest available stick with which to beat political foes. There was much more than China in these affairs, yet China's peculiar prominence in the spasms of the time is striking and meaningful. The famous "pumpkin papers" of Chambers-Hiss had largely to do with China—albeit of the late 1930's—the Yalta "sellout" was, above all, a "sellout" of our Chinese ally. The most relentlessly pursued and highly publicized victims of the time were almost all China-identified officials of the State Department who were accused of having helped "sell China down the river to the Communists." The remorseless vendetta conducted against Secretary of State Dean Acheson was based primarily on his connection with American China policy. Because of his part in the affair, George C. Marshall, one of

[109] Eric Goldman, *The Crucial Decade*, New York, 1956, pp. 116-117.

the more austere patriots of his generation, was publicly called "traitor." Even President Harry Truman was publicly accused, after he left office, of having knowingly protected a spy in a high administration post who was charged with having done much to undermine the American position in China. With the Korean truce and the tardy squelching of the McCarthyist hysteria midway through the first Eisenhower administration, these issues lost some of their heat but none of their underlying confusion. The argument was not ended; it simply came to an exhausted halt.

On the China issue itself, the essential positions confronting each other can perhaps be represented by two reasonably picturesque and forthright passages, both by men who saw much of the China events at first hand, this one by Joseph Alsop:

If you have kicked a drowning friend briskly in the face as he sank for the second and third times, you cannot later explain that he was doomed anyway because he was such a bad swimmer. The question that must be answered is not whether the Chinese did their best to save themselves, which they most certainly did not. The question is whether we did our best to save China ... Throughout the fateful years in China, the American representatives there actively favored the Chinese communists They also contributed to the weakness, both political and military, of the Nationalist Government. And in the end they came close to offering China up to the Communists, like a trussed bird on a platter... [110]

And this one by Graham Peck:

To blame the collapse of feudal China on any modern Americans is like claiming that a house which had been decaying for a century and had been fatally undermined by its own inhabitants was really blown down by the sneezing of neighbors... We did not err by trying to stabilize Chiang Kai-shek's relations with the increasingly powerful Communists, or by giving him too little material aid.... We gave him too much, helping him ignore [the fact that] competition with the Communists—offering the Chinese people better conditions of life than the Communists could—was the one way a non-Communist China could survive.[111]

In contending recriminations like these (and there were many much less tempered), there might be no full answers to questions about what happened in China, but there was much to suggest—in their common assumption of the special American responsibility—some

[110] "Why We Lost China," *Saturday Evening Post*, January 7, 1950.
[111] *Two Kinds of Time*, pp. 592, 700.

reasons for the pain and passion aroused by these climactic events. In one way or another, it seems, the Chinese failed us, or we failed them.

A key that unlocks at least one of the inner sanctums of American feeling about China and the Chinese is the phrase occurring and recurring in our interviews: "a country we have always helped, a people to be helped." This came from the oldest of our panelists, who had spent most of his life "helping" China, and from one of the youngest, who had never been there at all but who said: "I have always felt responsible to China somehow, to help her out."

Over more than a century, an extraordinarily large number of Americans came to think of themselves as the benevolent guardians and benefactors of China and the Chinese, as saviors, teachers, healers, protectors, as warm and faithful friends and admirers. Americans assumed responsibility for the minds, bodies, and immortal souls of the Chinese, and the United States assumed responsibility for China's political independence and administrative integrity. This is how they saw what they did and this is how they described it in their churches, wrote about it in their history books, and told their children about it in all the classrooms It was an experience shared by all the millions who put pennies, dimes, and quarters on collection plates for generations, who contributed to relief funds for the Chinese, and whose tax money made up the vast sums, ultimately billions of dollars, paid out to succor and support China and its people in peace and war. After all this, the Chinese massively and decisively rejected American help, hopes, wishes, and precepts. They took the path of hostility toward Americans and opposition to American interests. In effect, they ejected Americans from China through that very Door which Americans had striven so long and so valiantly to keep Open. In doing these things, the Chinese were plainly biting the hands that had fed them these many years. They were repaying good with evil. They were, in short, ungrateful wretches.

A number of our panelists identified this feeling quite explicitly, usually when they were trying to describe what "other Americans" were thinking and feeling about the Chinese. Thus a career official at the State Department said:

Because of what we did while others were treating them badly, we think the Chinese ought to be grateful to us. I run into this idea often, in our way of writing about China policy, our acts in China, back to Boxer days and John Hay. The Chinese should be grateful. That's why we're so riled up about Red China. That they should go and join up with the Russians makes us doubly mad. I hear this among my associates, especially from public members at U.N delegation meetings. . . .

A missionary who spent a long career in China:

I occasionally hear people say. "Look how they've turned against us after all we've done!"

A public opinion analyst:

I have never investigated this myself, but if I guessed I would say that Americans are greatly disappointed Their earlier idea of the Chinese as friendly, honest people was wrong. The Chinese bit the hand that fed them. Now they have to see them as a menace to the United States

A government official who had spent two decades in China:

Have a feeling Americans are hurt, surprised. We've always been friendly, done things for them. This verges on extreme bitterness because of betrayal. Maybe this is just my own feeling, but I get it from missionaries and others who have lived there. Maybe it comes from embarrassment over being identified somehow with the Chinese.

The feeling that the Chinese had somehow failed us arises not only in the reaction to the Communist victory but dominates the pervasive disillusionment of the closing years of the war and its aftermath, when the extent of the erosion within Chiang Kai-shek's Kuomintang regime became visible. The illusions about the Communists (as "agrarian reformers" or as "democrats") were certainly the product of a familiar kind of political euphoria characteristic of certain currents of "liberal" public opinion at the time. Many of the China-identified individuals who seized so avidly upon these notions were really reaching for some way of keeping their expectations about the Chinese alive, of justifying their own beliefs and their own behavior But Kuomintang Chinese and Communist Chinese alike had nothing but painful shocks for hopeful Americans, who were left by it all with little more than a feeling of having been betrayed. In the end, all the proffered salvation was scorned, generations of devoted help nullified, all the schooling, healing, ministering brought to nought, all the advice ignored, all the hundreds of millions of dollars frittered uselessly away, all the hopes of a

China "strong and free and democratic" glimmering and gone, all the dreams of making the Chinese over in some kind of American image—customer, Christian—extinguished, seemingly forever. It was possible for the most dogged American believers in the dream to keep their faith with the "people," but the Chinese "people" in their mass, it had to be acknowledged, had scarcely ever been reached by any American benefactions. It was the leadership that had come within the American purview. It was this generation of leaders that Americans had touched with schools, gifts, loans, ideas, examples, and these were precisely the ones who had failed so utterly to live up to expectations. Whether in Kuomintang exile or in Communist-ruled China, these were the most ungrateful of all the ungrateful wretches of today.

But the idea that *they failed us* is unavoidably edged by its uncomfortable corollary, which is that *we failed them* The guardian is responsible, the ward's failure can never be the ward's alone. The parent, as everyone knows, bears the guilt of his child's delinquency. This, as everyone also knows, is a burden not readily to be borne if it can convincingly be transferred to someone else. Hence the mad scramble for scapegoats who, treasonably or otherwise, "lost China." It was striking evidence of the special place held by China in American thinking that there seemed to be so many people ready to believe—or to find nothing absurd in the belief—that we "had" China to "lose." No such notion, indeed, had ever arisen in American public life about any other country, because toward no other country had Americans ever assumed the same parental responsibility. Only as a flouted parent could the American feel that the Chinese, in their waywardness and delinquency, had strayed or allowed themselves to be led astray, that they had failed to appreciate and be guided by paternal precept and example and had thus brought down upon themselves a wrathful fate. It was also only as a rejected parent that the American could be assailed by so great a sense of guilt, the feeling that he was somehow responsible for what had happened to the Chinese. Only because there were these emotions to exploit could political demagogues make so much of the China issue in American public life in the aftermath of the fall of China to the Communists.

The decisive place of the emotions of parentalism in American-Chinese relations was perceived a long time ago, with unique, acute, and characteristic clarity by John Dewey. For Dewey China was but one among many interests. His writings on the subject are perhaps little noted among the great volume of other works upon which his fame rests as philosopher and educator. Yet it would be difficult to find in any American writing about China a passage more filled with meaningful insight than this one, penned by Dewey in a magazine article written in 1926. At a time when the first great surge of Chinese nationalism was signaling the coming revision of all Chinese-Western relations, here is what Dewey observed:

> We have presented a certain type of culture to China as a model to be imitated As far as we have gone at all, we have gone *in loco parentis*, with advice, with instruction, with example and precept. Like a good parent we would have brought up China in the way in which she should go. There is a genial and generous aspect to all this But nonetheless it has created a situation . . . fraught with danger. . .
>
> We have not done as much positively as we pride ourselves upon; but from the negative side, by absence of aggression, by smoothing things down when we could without great trouble to ourselves, we have played a parental role. Such a part arouses expectations which are not always to be met. Expectations may be unreasonable and yet their not being met may arouse disappointment and resentment. There is something of this sort in the temper of China towards us today, a feeling that we have aroused false hopes only to neglect fulfillment of obligations involved in the arousal. On the other side, parents are rarely able to free themselves from the notion that gratitude is due them; failure to receive it passes readily into anger and dislike. Unless this country has more than the average amount of parental understanding, it may soon be charging China with ingratitude . .
>
> China is rapidly growing up. . . . It will henceforth resent more and more any assumption of parental tutelage even of a professedly benevolent kind. Signs of the resentment are already apparent. Missions and even schools are no longer welcome if they assume an air of superiority either as to what they have to offer or in their administration . . Politically also the Chinese no longer wish for any foreign guardianship. . . .
>
> There is a crisis in most families when those who have been under care and protection grow to the point of asserting their independence. It is the same in the family of nations . . . In the next ten years we shall have . . to alter our traditional parental attitude, colored as it has been by a temper of patronage, conscious or unconscious, into one of respect and esteem for a cultural equal If we cannot successfully make the change, the relationship of this country with the entire Far East will take a decided turn for the worse.[112]

[112] *The Survey*, May 1, 1926, p 188.

In his sensitive translation of both historical and current political conflict into the language of individual human relationships, Dewey anticipated by a good many years what is now a much more familiar approach to the study of human affairs. Although he spoke so plainly, he was quite beyond the hearing of his immediate audience. Neither the movers of the earth nor the heralds of heaven could dream of all that lay in his philosophy. They had to play out their roles to the end before confronting the consequences of their own behavior. Within but one decade after the decade of grace he had allowed, Dewey's foresight was confirmed in the event, and most crushingly in precisely the terms he had described. No father rejected by his son ever suffered more painfully than the United States suffered from the departure of China from its fold.

It may be that only a novelist has sufficient freedom to deal with the possible role of *guilt* in the story of American relations with the Chinese. Guilt is perhaps the most subjective of emotions; societies, like individuals, are ingenious at transforming it into something else. It does not often become explicit in the record. Yet even the most cursory look at the American-Chinese record suggests in many ways how heavy the burden on the American conscience might be.

Consider, for one thing, the differences between American-Chinese relations in China and American-Chinese relations in the United States. Both are filled with violence and all sorts of other affronts to the dignity of Chinese. The peculiar vulnerability of the Chinese—their membership in an "inferior" race and their citizenship in an impotent state—encouraged American impulses to dominate as well as American impulses to protect. But whereas in China the missionary influence and the special conditions of European competition combined to give at least a benevolent cast to American mastery, in America itself there were no such inhibiting influences. Brother's keepers had short shrift at the hands of the expanding master race in the years of the great opening of the American West. All who stood in the way or could not compete on equal terms—first the American Indian and then the Chinese—became prey to unhindered violence. Thus, in the face of all the deeply felt generalized professions about American national life and culture and religion, a great many individual Americans brutally maltreated the Chinese who came among them. The Chinese were lynched, mobbed, deprived of due process of law, and finally excluded from the country by the first legislation of its kind in history. It could be said that the worst persecutors and most brutal assailants of the Chinese were "Americans" of hardly more recent date than the Chinese themselves, immigrants brought from the other side of the world to meet the same needs for which Chinese "coolie labor" had been brought in and who found themselves in direct competition with the Chinese as laboring men. But the fact remains that this pattern of behavior enveloped all segments of the new American society. Most of those who did not join in the violence condoned it, and both state and federal governments enshrined its essence in the law, largely because the society as a whole shared the belief in Chinese racial inferiority. Even after the worst mob violence against Chinese subsided, Americans did not accord Chinese in the United States their full legal equality with all others until it was impossible to avoid doing so—and this did not take place until 1946, when new laws for the first time gave the Chinese the right to become naturalized citizens and provided them with an immigration quota. To this day, moreover, legality aside, we still do not universally acknowledge the rights of Chinese in this country on a completely equal and automatic basis. For all the vast progress Americans have made in these matters, the individual Chinese still never *knows* that he can freely and always enjoy all the rights and privileges enjoyed by members of the dominant groups in the country.

There were, of course, always Americans who protested the injustice and cruelty practiced on Chinese in this country. But these never came to represent an effective majority capable, for example, of changing the exclusion laws. They remained, in fact, a small group of unheeded well-intentioned folk. Yet the same people, in great masses, who would not dream of becoming keepers of their Chinese brothers close to home were quite prepared to help keep, with their pennies and dimes, their Chinese brothers in China far away. I am not in a position even to guess how far this contradiction between American behavior toward Chinese in the United States and American professions and purposes in China ever became an article of guilt in any American minds. But anyone engaged in balancing up the historic record can hardly, looking back, avoid giving this anomaly its place in the scales.

The gap between American profession and American practice in China is a much more complex affair. Americans who went to

China were no doubt different in many ways from the Americans who lynched Chinese in Western cities in the 1870's and 1880's, but not so different, perhaps, from the run of Americans who accepted the premises on which so much of this violence was based. Whether they went to China to make money or to save souls, a great many of these individuals no doubt carried with them the same assumptions of racial superiority, the same attitudes which produced contempt and indifference and a readiness to use or to justify violence when it suited their own needs or interests. They felt all the powerful and self-justifying convictions of the Western white man of the nineteenth century—convictions of the superiority of their own race, civilization, religion—and felt reinforced on all counts when they compared themselves to the puny, starving, ignorant peoples who inhabited so much of the rest of the world, and the plainly sinful and heathenish religions they professed and the backward and barbarous societies they could so ill defend.

But there were at least two other pieces of mental baggage these Americans knowingly or unknowingly carried with them. One was the peculiarly pressing American need to rationalize any behavior inconsistent with the idea that all men were created free and equal. The other was a brother's-keeper impulse which has always been one of the most deeply imbedded characteristics of American Protestantism. Whether consciously or not, I suspect that the American had to relate himself somehow to these ideas and compulsions which formed the core of his secular and religious creed. He could either deny them and brush them aside—in which case he either felt, or would eventually be felt by others to be—guilty of a wrong; or he had to believe and insist that his behavior conformed to their requirements—in which case he skirted constantly the dangers of self-righteousness or hypocrisy. In their many possible combinations, these compulsions and their consequences have had a certain American uniqueness, and the result of it lies heavily marked across all Chinese-American history.

In China a wonderfully expedient convergence of motives, pressures, and circumstances seemed to conspire to give Americans the best of both possible worlds Since the only way to keep China open to American commercial interests was to keep anyone else from closing it, it became basic American policy to try to keep China open to all. The missionary movement, drawn into China by its almost unique accessibility to this kind of American enterprise, gave an almost natural air of sanctity to this role of benevolent guardian. In doing so it produced a certain number of Americans who were convinced that the most meaningful things in their lives were the sacrifices they were making for Chinese well-being. The expediency, hypocrisy, and downright ethnocentric foolishness in all of this—especially as seen from the point of view of a Chinese—nearly defy description. On the other hand, many of these individuals were moved or torn by strong compulsions. The fact is that American belief in freedom, equality, and those inalienable rights was a powerful creed which in the end somehow shaped American political behavior and by which, in the end, Americans expected to judge or be judged. And while history's verdict on the missionary movement may be a harsh one, it is not likely to erase altogether the profound brother-keeping impulse in American society which produced it and which, even now, in new forms and language, remains an essential part of the substance of American world policy. To be sure the American, like the European, had made it a habit to invoke a certain routine divine sanction, even for his most unsanctifiable acts. But only quite recently has the European felt required to invoke for non-European peoples the traditions of freedom which hitherto he had valued only for himself. The American, I think it can be said, has never been free of this necessity. In the end it has imposed itself upon all his acts, and this helps explain, I suspect, the American's numerous failures as a wielder of power in world politics. He has been too much a believer in his own myths. Hence a great many of the contradictions and conflicts and the acute discomfort and guilt feelings suffered by Americans in world affairs. For the American, goaded by these rigorous demands of the spirit—freedom, equality, Good Samaritanism—has been all the more woefully weak in the flesh.

Americans who turned up in China as traders usually had all the characteristic features of the nineteenth-century imperialist urge. Few then saw cause to apologize for money-making and power-seeking. Abroad, as well as at home, many felt the need to use force, often against weak obstacles that stood in the way. There was competition to be met, recalcitrance to be overcome, advantage to be sought and guarded. There were selfish interests to be served and they usually were Hence a long series of expansionist acts by American governments, from William Seward's day through Theodore

Roosevelt's, a succession of compacts of dubious virtue, from the opium-legalizing treaties of Caleb Cushing's day to Franklin Roosevelt's horse trade with Stalin at Yalta. The plain truth is that while the United States wore with a flourish the mantle of China's guardian-protector, in fact it served China's national interests only when it seemed to serve American national interest to do so Americans piously believed in their own good faith as brother's-keepers, but Americans rarely hesitated, when their interests required it, to inflict painful injury on the brother they so fondly felt they were keeping. All of this had to be rationalized and explained. In the nature of things, this took considerable self-deception and no small meed of downright hypocrisy. This can be shown to be the characteristic pattern in much American behavior in China in the nineteenth century. It became patent in Theodore Roosevelt's time, when America was trying to play the power game by Europe's rules. It took on perhaps its most ironic and poignant form in the American capitulation to Japan at Versailles in 1919. In the interest of what he saw as some greater good, Wilson helped inflict a heavy new blow on China, and, quite unwittingly, he thereby ignited the first of the great nationalist explosions which have since transformed that country. The paradox which places a Wilson in this role vis-à-vis China is perhaps the aptest symbol we have for the inner sense of the prime contradictions in Chinese-American history which now rise to haunt us It is not at all hard to summon up a few more of these ghosts out of the history since Wilson's time to suggest the kind of burdens about China that Americans of our own time knowingly or unknowingly may carry on their consciences.

In the events of the 1920's which provoked John Dewey's thoughtful warning about American paternalism in China, there were some Americans, especially among the missionaries, who felt an active sympathy for Chinese nationalism. Some American newspapers of the time assumed an air of avuncular and slightly amused tolerance: the principal Chinese target was Britain, and Americans in the United States who followed the events could feel a certain smug satisfaction in England's discomfiture. But the dominant and effective American reaction was to reach for the rod. American troops and warships moved in, along with those of other nations, to reinforce the treaty ports. A great many refugee missionaries reverted automatically to the pre-Boxer attitudes of exasperation, joined the businessmen and "old China hands" in demanding still larger forces and much stronger action. Soon, as Dewey had predicted, they were denouncing their Chinese wards and pupils for "their apparent lack of appreciation for what is being done for them," in the words of a contemporary report on mission schools, or, again, in the words of another report of the time, by an "irate educationalist":

> I cannot slobber and sentimentalize over young China's aspirations— they aren't aspirations; they are merely the expression of an inherent love of evading honest work, respect for authority of any sort, and a general penchant for kicking up a row If young China could learn reverence and obedience, half China's troubles would be solved.[113]

Lewis Gannett, later the distinguished critic and essayist, but then in China as a roving reporter, watched the American marines policing Shanghai's streets, and among the twenty foreign warships anchored in the Whangpoo off the city's International Settlement he counted thirteen flying the American flag, and he observed:

> Americans are doing all sorts of nice things for China, but they are not doing the one thing the Chinese most want—they are not abandoning the special privileges which make the foreigners a class apart in all the twenty-one provinces of the republic

He went one day in 1926 to the young "Red general" who as friend and ally of the Russians and the Communists had become commander-in-chief of the Chinese nationalist armies, and this general told him:

> "Thinking men in China hate America more than they hate Japan Japan talks to us in ultimatums, she says frankly that she wants special privileges.... We understand that and know how to meet it The Americans come to us with smiling faces and friendly talk, but in the end your government acts just like the Japanese. And we, disarmed by your fair words, do not know how to meet such insincerity.
>
> "That is what is behind the anti-Christian movement in China. Your missionaries write 'charity' over their doors, and I do not deny that many of them are good men who do good work. But in the end they make it easier for American policy to follow that of the other imperialist Powers. So because we have been deceived by your sympathetic talk, we end by hating you most. Why cannot America act independently? Why does she preach fine sermons, but in the end tag along with the others? Why can she not, like Russia, prove her friendliness by acts?" [114]

[113] *China Year Book*, 1928, p 499
[114] *The Survey*, May 1, 1926, p. 181.

This young general's name was Chiang Kai-shek. His attitude toward Russia changed not long thereafter, but it is doubtful whether he has ever had serious cause to change his view of the United States. As the head of a conservative Nationalist government at Nanking, Chiang Kai-shek all but threw himself on the mercies of the United States He won over the dominant missionary constituency by becoming a Christian, but the United States yielded nothing of substance to him It would not validate his claim to nationalist leadership by surrendering any of its special privileges. Moreover, in 1934, the American Congress passed a bill aimed at helping the crisis-hit silver producers of the United States. This Silver Purchase Act had the principal effect of dealing a mortal blow at the staggering Chinese economy by putting a price on silver which drew vital quantities of it out of China at a time when it could least afford any weakening of its currency In 1937, when Chiang Kai-shek could no longer evade the issue of war with Japan, he looked for American help but received, as we have seen, only a mild measure of sympathy, which Madame Chiang Kai-shek herself has described acidly:

> The interest, although sympathetic, was as detached as that of spectators at a college football game, cheering from the safety of the stand while taking no personal risk in the game themselves.[115]

Then followed the issue of the uninterrupted sale of American oil and scrap to Japan. "The odds against which [the Chinese] are fighting," cried Henry L. Stimson, "are being made possible by us. . . ."[116] When he wrote of the fervent admiration among Americans for China's stand against the Japanese, Leland Stowe acutely remarked: "Perhaps . . . our enthusiasm for all things Chinese is fanned higher by a secret guilt for having made their sufferings so much greater through our prolonged shipments of scrap iron, gasoline, and other materials to the Japanese."[117] In the closing stages of the American-Japanese negotiations just before Pearl Harbor, Americans intent upon buying even a little more time to improve American readiness for war considered offering Japan a modus vivendi at China's expense. This was not actually done, but the fact that it was contemplated became known to the Chinese, and Sumner Welles has suggested that this "seriously impaired the confidence of Chiang

---

[115] Quoted by Dulles, *China and America*, p. 207
[116] "Shall We Keep on Helping Japan?," *Reader's Digest*, December, 1937.
[117] *They Shall Not Sleep*, p 37.

Kai-shek and his entourage in the United States . . . [and] was responsible for much of the friction and suspicion that clouded relations between Washington and the Nationalist Chinese government in subsequent years." [118] When the United States was, at last, allied with China in the war against Japan, we find among the mutual recriminations of the first months an angry telegram from Chiang Kai-shek to Washington in which it is easy to hear the echo of the statements he had made to Lewis Gannett in that time long ago when it all began:

> I have to fight continually against demoralizing doubts on the part of my officers, who conclude that American attitude toward China is in essence no different from that held by other nations, that both in the all-important matters of joint staff conferences and war supplies, China is treated not as an equal, like Britain and Russia, but as a ward [119]

Nothing happened during the rest of the war to relieve Chiang of his sense of neglect, not even Franklin Roosevelt's attempt to meet the American sense of the needs of the situation by establishing a "Great Power" status for China in the councils of the nations. This perplexed Winston Churchill but gave no solace whatever to Chiang. In the years since, of course, as many a visitor to Formosa could testify, Chiang Kai-shek has seen himself in large measure as a victim of American baseness and betrayal.[120]

In the controversy over American China policy, there are those who argue that America betrayed the Chinese people by myopically supporting Chiang Kai-shek and his regime, while others argue that the chief victim of American betrayal was Chiang himself. The case can be argued either way, but both versions agree in offering the American not much more than a burden of failure and guilt. This can be made to apply equally to the whole course of American-Chinese affairs. Americans were going to save Chinese souls, but they never saved enough of them to leaven the heathen mass. They were going to educate the Chinese to become the leaders of a "free, strong, democratic China," but leaders they educated proved incapable of making, much less keeping China free, strong, or democratic. They

---

[118] Welles, *Seven Decisions*, pp 67–68

[119] Chiang to T V. Soong, April 19, 1942, *Documents, China*, p 33.

[120] He nearly floored a sympathetic American visitor, Thomas E. Dewey, in 1951, "with a blast of searing emotional bitterness" in which he described his people as "victims of total abandonment by all those on whose side we fought so long." Dewey, *Journey to the Far Pacific*, New York, 1952, p. 132.

were going to protect China from hostile encroachment and help it in its time of need, but this help was denied for too long, and in the end it was the American effort that the Chinese rejected as the least acceptable encroachment of all.

In these matters of guilt and conscience—as indeed in all matters relating to American-Chinese relations—the missionary occupies a central place. It was he, after all, who gave these relations their heavy Samaritan cast. It was the missionary who was able, in China, to influence the shape and tenor of affairs far beyond his normal sphere. It was the missionary, finally, who via his vast constituencies in the churches of the country for so many generations, gave China its unique place in the American consciousness. In relation to no other country, in no other connection, has the missionary played even a remotely comparable role in American affairs.

Today he cuts a poignant or a pathetic figure, according to how you view him and his role in all this history, and where you locate the sinners and the sinned against and how you assign the items of the sowing and the reaping. The missionary had to see himself as the bearer of the superior religion, the higher morality, the greater wisdom, the richer life here or hereafter. He devoted himself to the task of bringing these gifts to the wayward, the straying, and the unknowing of God's children He came quite unbidden to the Chinese *in loco parentis*, and in his case the parent was God. This was, by all odds, a sizable assumption for any man to make and to expect the Chinese to accept, even if we try to speak here only of the best and leave aside those for whom the mission was more a job than a vocation, more an answer to their own personal problems than to the problems of the Chinese, a niche among the money-changers rather than a place in any temple of the spirit.

The essentially parental role of the missionary was the same, whether in the nineteenth century when he found God's Chinese children so exasperating, or during the twentieth when, for a time, he found some of them so much more compliant and more attractive. The difference between these generations may, indeed, be something like the difference between the permissive parent of our own times and the authoritarian model of a few generations ago. In either guise, the missionary-parent grievously failed The stern authoritarians who first came to take the Chinese by the hand and lead them to the light succeeded mainly in arousing acute hostility and provoking decisive rejection. The Chinese had authorities of their own which they largely preferred. The nineteenth-century missionary believed in chastisement, and he did not hesitate to use the secular arm available to him for this purpose. This mixed him up with gunboats, treaties, trade, governments, and power, and if anyone is interested in tracing the sins of missionaries in China, this is one good place to start looking. These procedures did finally bring the Chinese around to a certain posture of docility and, on the part of some of them, to a calculated interest in Western learning and Western ways. Perhaps the missionary movement can be credited, along with the deeper-going elements of political and economic change, with a role in hastening the breakup of Chinese traditional society. But it never brought any really substantial number of Chinese around to a full acceptance of the particular salvation these Westerners brought. To these missionary fathers, the Chinese in their great mass seemed, and indeed were, obstinately committed to their own evil ways. Their more permissive successors in more recent times tried to love the Chinese better. But whereas frustration had led their predecessors to feelings of exasperation, their own more loving and kindlier ways led them inescapably to attitudes that were essentially patronizing. Some missionaries were coming around to thinking that the Chinese could walk toward the light alone, perhaps even in their own way. But even these earnest well-wishers were overtaken by harsh events before they could fully let go. Now, from exile, they have to decide what to think about the outcome of their century-old enterprise.

At the end of 119 years of Protestant missionary work in China, there were said to be somewhere between half a million and a million Chinese Protestants. The much older Catholic missions were said to minister to about two million Catholics. All told, these estimates added up to about one-half of 1 per cent of the population. One recent summary guessed that there were "over 250,000 alumni of Christian colleges and middle schools" in China in 1945,[121] and there must have been at that time certainly more than 5,000 graduates of American universities. Products of Western education formed a major segment of the leadership which had had its chance in China for nearly a generation. At its summit was Chiang Kai-shek, a Christian, though not Western-educated, and a small group of families whose leading men and women all held American college degrees. This

[121] *China Handbook,* 1937–1945, Chinese Ministry of Information, New York, 1947, p 560.

leadership was toppled and ejected from the country.[122] It had failed to leaven the heathen and uneducated mass sufficiently to put China on the path to a future that looked bright and attractive from any American point of view. One can reasonably guess that the great majority of the living graduates and products of Christian schools of the past thirty to forty years—and perhaps even a majority of the graduates of schools in the United States—are now working in or for the Communist party or the Communist government, that the people generally, in their much celebrated practical down-to-earthness, are submitting to the new regime. By every hope and expectation the missionary movement had ever represented, they are all now, leaders and led, educated and uneducated, walking not toward the light but into the darkness. "The children are the ones that scare you," said a Catholic priest who emerged at Hong Kong after a term in a Communist prison. "It breaks your heart to have a child you have known from birth stand at your gate and call you an 'imperialist dog.' What will they be like ten years from now?"[123]

But I fear there is more in this than the earnest missionary or many another ardent Sinophile can quite embrace in his philosophy, more than sorrow, more than error. For what strikes me powerfully about these high American emotions regarding the Chinese is their *one-sidedness*. I certainly cannot document this, but I emerge from this long review of American-Chinese relations with a vivid picture in my own mind of Americans going through all kinds of gyrations of feeling, assuming all the time in the Chinese reciprocal emotions which were simply not there. At most points, I suspect that the Chinese simply did not care at all, that to contempt he returned indifference, to admiration, disdain. The American suffering a sense of rejection is a doubly pathetic figure, because he was never really accepted, merely borne. There was certainly the experience of high good faith, fidelity, and mutual esteem between individuals; a few such are always the saving grace of every human story. But in the characteristic American-Chinese context, one wonders how many individual relationships were not in some way centrally rooted in the American seen as benefactor and the Chinese as beneficiary, and

---

[122] Thomas E. Dewey learned that he had on Formosa sixty fellow-alumni from Columbia and eighty from Michigan, all members of Chiang Kai-shek's government-in-exile. *Journey to the Far Pacific*, p. 111

[123] Henry R. Lieberman, "Inside Mao's China, Clues to a Mystery," *New York Times Magazine*, April 5, 1953

therefore productive not of regard but of hostility. In one of our interviews a former India missionary, recalling that old China missionaries had always talked so glowingly about China and the Chinese, reported with a certain relish a conversation with some younger people who had gone out to China after 1945 and remained until shortly after the Communists took power. "They told me," he said, "that they had never realized how much hostility the Chinese must have really felt towards us until the Communists came along. They were sure that such hostility must have been there all along."

A cruelly pathetic epilogue to this insight has been written since then on the island of Formosa, where all actively surviving American-Chinese relations have been concentrated since 1950. These consist of relations between nearly 10,000 American soldiers and civilians, and the exiled Kuomintang government and army and some 2,000,000 Chinese refugees. Here the classic guardian-ward relationship of the past has been stripped to naked Chinese dependency on Americans for their survival as a political force, for their economic maintenance, their military protection, and their hope of returning to the mainland. These would create sufficient strains even under more favorable conditions, but as it is they are all drawn tightly together in a narrow physical space, and relations between people are subject to all the abnormalities of what amounts to a military occupation and regime, in reality a twin occupation by both Chinese and Americans of a land alien to both. In this setting we would expect to find reproduced most of the conditions created by American-Chinese relations in West China during the war with Japan, only in smaller compass, shorter, tighter, harsher, and without even the catharsis of actual war. Here at the summits of the Chinese Taipeh regime, we have had a gnawing mistrust of the durability of American protection, and the gathering realization that not all the American ships, planes, or men would ever actually help put the Kuomintang back in China again. Here too in the populace at large accumulated all the resentments over the "brash" and "loutish" conduct of American soldiers and civilians [124] in ordinary everyday contacts. In May, 1957, an American soldier who had murdered a Chinese was acquitted, before an applauding American crowd, by an army court-martial. On May 24, in what was described as a spontaneous eruption of mob violence, a crowd of thousands of Chinese

[124] *New York Times*, June 2, 1957.

sacked the American embassy and information agency building, tore down the American flag and ripped it to shreds. Several Americans were injured. An army of 30,000 Chinese soldiers was moved into Taipeh to restore order. More than embassy cars and desks were toppled that day in Taipeh. In the breasts of the staunchest keepers of the dream, citadels were shaken. The Taipeh violence, said Senator William Knowland of California, was "shocking to me and to friends of Free China." The ungrateful wretches on Formosa were the most unbearably ungrateful and the most unbearably wretched of all.

## 10. *THE AWAKENED DRAGON*

EVERY TIME DURING the last half-century or more that the sleeping Chinese dragon flicked his tail, there were American watchers anxiously sure that it was at last coming awake. A quick scanning of a variety of periodical and book indexes turns up the titles of some sixty magazine articles and thirty-odd books, published at various times between 1890 and 1940, in which China, or the giant, or the dragon, has awakened, is waking, or is stirring, rising, changing, or being reborn. Each time, however, the great recumbent figure relapsed into its semicomatose state But the prophets erred only in time, not in their expectations. When the Communists took power in China in 1949, the event so often foretold finally came to pass, and despite all the foretelling, it came as a rude shock. The monster awakened bore only the most coincidental resemblance to the monster asleep. Opening his red eyes, rising into motion, breathing fire, he has completely altered the arrangement of lights and shadows in which he was previously seen. There is nothing delicate or subtle about him now, he is tough and crude. He is not torpid, but driving, not passive or yielding, but aggressive and unmanageable.

Indeed, we may in a way have come around the fullness of the circle. The Middle Kingdom of Mao Tse-tung is by no means celestial, but it is again sealed off, at least from Americans. Its rulers once more require the kowtow or its equivalent; only the obeisant bringing tribute are welcomed to the Forbidden City. It is again a power that arouses hostility. But it also now, after these many genera-

FACE TO FACE.—From the *World* (New York).
1900

*HOW TO LET GO WITH DIGNITY?*

1955

1921

1957

tions, again commands respect. None of the more habitual American postures of past decades—lordly contempt, patronizing affection, sentimental admiration, avuncular kindness, or parental solicitude—could quite meet the new situation. New postures had to be assumed, and the change, after so long a time, was bound to cause much painful dislocation.

## *The Nearly Total Severance*

This dislocation was first of all purely physical. There was no place in the Communists' China for the American as purveyor of the goods of a superior civilization, as soul-saver, teacher, mentor, guardian, protector, nor even as scholar, journalist, or merely curious onlooker The initial pell-mell exodus, the imprisonment of stragglers, the swift liquidation of American enterprises, the military collision in Korea, and the subsequent stalemated hostility, all made the mutual sealing-off process nearly complete. In mid-1957 there were, as far as was definitely known, 23 Americans all told in all of China, compared to 13,300 American residents in 1937, the last "peacetime" year.[125] Thus, within only a few years after Congress had finally repealed the sixty-year-old laws excluding Chinese as immigrants from the United States, the turn of events created a situation which sweepingly excluded Americans of every description from China.

This exclusion, to compound the irony, was discriminatory· it applied to Americans only. Communist China became, after its first few years, a veritable mecca for visiting delegations and individuals from many other countries. Many who came—though not all—tended to be sympathetic votaries of the regime, come to marvel or to gain by the contact, or invited guests on whom the Communists hoped to make a decisive impression. From among these travelers, writers of several nationalities soon produced a small mountain of literature on their observations in China. Most of it was highly partisan and very little of it reached American readers. Among books reflecting firsthand experience by non-Americans, we had two accounts by disillusioned young Chinese (Liu Shao-tang, *Out of Red*

---

[125] The 23 included four missionaries still restrictedly at large, 6 still captive in Communist prisons; and 13 surviving members of the group of 21 American POW's who elected to remain with their Communist captors after the end of the Korean war in 1953. The Department of State has suggested that with others whose presence in China is not so definitely known—including some Americans of Chinese origin who are thought to be concealing their citizenship for personal security reasons—the figure of 23 might be raised to a guessed total of about 100.

*China*, 1953, and Maria Yen, *The Umbrella Garden*, 1954); two by Indian visitors (Frank Moraes' *Report on Mao's China* and G. P. Hutheesing's *The Great Peace*, both in 1953) who were a good deal less uncritically admiring of the Chinese Communists than most of their touring countrymen; and several accounts by Englishmen (e.g., the reportorial *No Flies in China* by George S. Gale and James Cameron's *Mandarin Red*, both in 1955, and the more partisanly sympathetic *Daybreak in China* by Basil Davidson in 1953); and, in 1957, Robert Guillain's deeply worried *600 Million Chinese*. These all appeared in American editions, but none had any wide sale. The *New York Times* occasionally printed Peking dispatches from Reuter's, the British news agency. Even more occasionally, a series of articles by some English or Australian correspondent or noted traveler (like Clement Attlee) was syndicated to American newspapers. Such, almost in sum, was the writing at firsthand about China by non-Americans which reached any American readers.

Writing by Americans about China, such a massive flow only a few years before, had meanwhile dried to the merest trickle. After the initial accounts of the Communist takeover, written by Americans still there at the time, there were a few later books by missionaries and others who brought up the rear of the general exodus,[126] one plainly pro-Communist account,[127] and occasional articles based on the experience of soldiers and prisoners in Korea or of repatriates who came blinking across the Hong Kong barrier at wide intervals. Scholars or others with specialized interests in China had to depend on the careful culling of Chinese Communist publications and to venture description, analysis, and interpretation without chance or hope of verifying their insights by inquiry on the ground.[128] The only more or less regular reports appearing in the American press or heard on the American radio were based almost entirely on cullings from the Chinese press and radio and other indirect accounts secured by observers and correspondents in Hong Kong or in Formosa.[129]

[126] E.g., A. M. Dunlap, *Behind the Bamboo Curtain*, 1956, Sister Mary Victoria, *Nun in Red China*, 1953; Robert W. Greene, *Calvary in China*, 1953, etc.
[127] Julian Schuman, *Assignment China*, New York, 1956
[128] Some examples· W. W. Rostow and others, *Prospects for Communist China*, New York, 1954; Y L Wu, *An Economic Survey of Communist China*, New York, 1956; Richard L. Walker, *China Under Communism The First Five Years*, New York, 1955; Boorman, Eckstein, Mosely, and Schwartz, *Moscow-Peking Axis*, New York, 1957.
[129] For an example of competent marshaling of available material at secondhand, see *New Republic*, "Special Report on Communist China," May 13, 1957.

American contact with mainland China and with any of its people had thus, by the end of 1956, been reduced virtually to zero. Outside of China only the most vagrant encounters were to be had: meetings with refugees or other travelers in Hong Kong, glimpses of Chinese touring abroad on various missions, of Chinese delegations at international conferences—Panmunjom, Geneva, Bandung—or of the peripatetic Chou En-lai during his generally triumphant foreign tours. This was just about all. Printed matter and no doubt an occasional letter still passed in the mails, but that was the whole of it. in trade, travel, news reporting, personal contact, the severance was nearly total, more complete than at any time since the first American traders and missionaries landed at Canton and, in modern comparable circumstances, more complete by far than the degree of separation that existed between Russia and the United States at any time, including the sixteen-year span between the Bolshevik revolution and the resumption of Russian-American diplomatic relations.

During the course of 1957, however, it became obvious that, barring any new outbreak of actual hostilities, this condition of affairs would not be much longer maintained. An accumulation of political, economic, and strategic pressures was forcing changes on both sides. Slow and stiff but direct diplomatic contact had begun in a marathon series of Chinese-American talks at Geneva. The rigid trade embargo imposed on China during the Korean War had begun to break down. Some resumption of travel and press contact appeared to be coming into view.[130] But however and whenever this occurred, it was plain

---

[130] American newsmen were barred from China by the Communists until midsummer, 1956, when Peking suddenly offered 60-day visas to 18 of them. The U.S government refused to sanction the arrangement, thereby taking over from the Communists the responsibility for the news blockade Three men defied the ban, William Worthy of the *Baltimore Afro-American*, and Edmund Stevens and Philip Harrington of *Look*, who entered China in December, 1956, for brief visits Worthy's impressions appeared in the *New York Post* and other papers in January-February, 1957 He found the Chinese Communists "more flexible, more intelligent and . [therefore] more dangerous than the stiff Soviet bureaucracy." Stevens, in *Look*, April 16, 1957, said he found "the people more friendly than we expected and the officials we dealt with far more relaxed and agreeable than the Russians" Of the trio only Worthy was penalized by being refused renewal of his passport, an issue that started up through the courts as a test of Secretary of State John Foster Dulles' assumption of power to abrogate rights of the press and the freedom of travel and inquiry. In August, 1957, Mr Dulles agreed to sanction 7-month visas for China for 24 correspondents, but refused in advance

that renewal of contact would not merely revive or resurrect the patterns of the past but would mark the opening of a new phase producing new relationships and new arrangements of all the old images and attitudes.

But meanwhile this total separation in the conditions of these years had added its own peculiar degree of distortion to the changing American images of China and the Chinese. It is true that every wing in our long gallery of images of the Chinese has been in its way a hall of mirrors in which reflections have often seemed more real than the reality. But in each one of them, at least, many Americans passed in their time, and some lingered long. All the many images that appeared in these mirrors were in some way validated by some intimate knowledge and some living experience. But through this newest wing, no Americans now pass It is not only unfinished and still largely unhoused, it remains quite inaccessible. We see it only from afar, the atmosphere is murky, the light is bad, and the visibility often nil. Our imaginations are left to supply the details of outlines we can barely see: the mirrors here are more like those one used to see at amusement parks, throwing back all kinds of grotesquely elongated or flattened or wriggly pictures. We view them from our distance unbelievingly or with dismay.

## The "New" Images Are Large Images

One effect is that only the larger images—of "China" or "Red China"—are visible at all, and these are almost all images of anathema. They are etched not only in pain but in fear. The peculiar anguish caused to so many Americans by the "loss" of China was not the product only of rejected parentalism. There was more to the matter than damaged egos. China had not merely strayed away. It had become part of the new Soviet power system. In the same season of 1949 that China fell to the Communists, Russia exploded its first atom bomb and had become something new in the American cosmos: a foe to be feared. Less than a year later Americans were fighting in Korea and an American offensive was stunningly and unexpectedly smashed by a Chinese army that had crossed the Yalu River and

---

to grant reciprocal rights to any Chinese Communist correspondents. On this issue the matter remained stalled at the end of 1957 Meanwhile the Dulles ban on travel to China had been breached again by 41 Americans who had gone to Moscow for a Russian-sponsored "youth festival" and had gone on to visit China as guests of the Peking government.

waited for the Americans in perfect concealment. The Chinese were transformed, seemingly almost overnight, from scorned or patronized weaklings into a formidable foe. In this new role, they contributed heavily to the confusion and fright with which some Americans greeted the new shapes, dangers, and tasks imposed upon them by a world they felt they had never made, and of which most of them wanted no part. The China events and their sequel in Korea played a large role in creating the atmosphere hospitable to the spasms of fear and frustration that shook American public life in the early 1950's. "China" and "Red China" became primary symbols in the inquisitorial circuses that dominated all our national affairs with the notion that traitorous conspirators were responsible for all the defeats and alarms of the time.

The popular image of "the Chinese people" inevitably began to be pressed by these circumstances into new shapes. The vague but nearly universal esteem for the Chinese—so largely the product of the missionaries, Pearl Buck, and the war against Japan—could not withstand indefinitely the influence of the new and more hostile environment. There are fragments of opinion poll evidence to suggest how far it has begun to give way. A National Opinion Research Center poll in 1947 indicated, although indirectly, that Chinese were regarded less highly by Americans at that point only than Englishmen, Swedes, and Frenchmen, and more highly than Mexicans, Greeks, Germans, Russians, and Japanese.[131] Much more directly and specifically, in another NORC poll, in March, 1951, 64 per cent of a national sample indicated a "favorable impression" of the Chinese people. By March, 1955, in an identical poll, this had shrunk to 45 per cent. Only 21 per cent said in 1951 that they had an "unfavorable impression" of the Chinese; in 1955, this figure had risen to 40 per cent.[132]

In our panel of interviewees, the new circumstances and their "new" images showed up much less crudely, were less globular and

[131] *UNESCO and Public Opinion Today*, Report No. 35. NORC, Chicago, 1947.
[132] National Opinion Research Center, #300, March 20, 1951, #370, March 11, 1955. The question was "I'd like to ask about the *people* who live in certain countries—*not* their governments but the people themselves. In general do you have a favorable or unfavorable impression of ———?" The results showed that while esteem for the Chinese was dropping, it was rising steeply for the Germans and Japanese.

more filled with particulars. The entire panel shared, to be sure, a common ignorance about what is actually happening to the Chinese in Communist China. Yet from all they had read or heard, they appeared to have no doubt that the Communists had set out to make China over in their own image, to make over the entire fabric of the society and its people, that they were engaged on a sweepingly pervasive campaign of control and conditioning of a whole vast nation that was without parallel, even in the history of modern totalitarianism. In this process the Communists were clearly effacing or displacing or transforming a great many of the images of the Chinese which many Americans had held for a long time—or were threatening to do so. But here too, we found, these were the larger images, of the whole country, the whole people, or some whole political or military entity. The individual Chinese in China had become a much dimmer and often a rather elusive figure.

The panelists who knew and liked this individual Chinese in China could still know him now only as he knew him then; he had become memory, reminiscence, an article of dogged faith. The well-entrenched image of him sat intact in the mind's inner sanctum, assailed but—in most cases—quite unshaken But in the minds of the great majority of our panelists, ideas about the Chinese were not so firmly fixed and were certainly not located in any inner mental sanctum. They floated more freely, rather, in some mental antechamber, where they were much more easily buffeted or crowded into changing shapes by passing circumstances or energetic new arrivals. Examples of this kind were frequent.

> I have been surprised by the Communist ability to unify the country....

> I always thought of lack of political organization, going back to all I'd ever heard about China. . . Now there is greater organizational discipline.... The Communists seem to be working changes ...

> Before the Korean war, I think most Americans thought of the Chinese as a kindly people. Now there is an association of cruelty....

> The public's idea of the Chinese is now all mixed up with the Communists. The man in the street probably feels that the Chinese people are all right, but are in the grip of a Communist government. Therefore his stereotype of the evil and untrustworthy Oriental, which he was beginning to lose, is being renewed

All the qualities attributed to the "evil and untrustworthy Oriental" come into their own in the new circumstances and the new hostile setting. They are drawn upon particularly to reinforce one of the most powerful of all the "new" images emerging, the image of the Chinese as *brainwashers* At the time the interviews were conducted for this study, we still had only the most fragmentary kind of picture of the practices and effectiveness of Chinese Communist thought control, and we were only just beginning to get some of the vivid impressions created by the experience of American war prisoners in Korea. The dilemma of the American subjected to "brainwashing" by an unscrupulous and remorseless foe was only just becoming the subject of governmental, medical, social scientific, and literary inquiry. But it was clear that great power was already attached to the special *mystique* which gave the Chinese such extraordinary skill in the use of these weapons of mental and emotional torture. It obviously was going to outstrip by far anything attributed to the Russians by way of explanation for the "confessions" of the accused in the purge trials of the Stalin era, e.g., as in Arthur Koestler's *Darkness At Noon*, or as projected by George Orwell in 1984 For the Chinese there was a whole battery of relevant qualities to draw upon, qualities which had been long attributed to them in some unique measure in the past their inhuman cruelty, for one thing, and at its service, their inscrutability, their deviousness, their subtlety, and their devilish cleverness.

There are signs that in the shadow of these new images and the somber and rather frightening realities they reflect, the older figure of the "evil and untrustworthy Oriental" has become rather ridiculous. The fictionally evil Fu Manchu could hardly compete with a real-life Chinese Communist commissar. And indeed, attempts to revive the old-style Chinese villain and his old-style villainy appear to have fallen quite flat on our TV screens. Fu Manchu reappeared as a rather preposterous figure in what a Boston critic described as "one of the corniest adventure shows ever seen on TV." [133] This particular show was poor entertainment by any standard, but a similar reaction was provoked by similar fare offered on a much more highly rated program and starring such dignitaries as Sir Cedric Hardwicke and Peter Lorre. "The result," said the *New York Times* critic, "was an insipid Oriental mystery as full of intrigue as a bowl of chow

[133] *Boston Record*, July 5, 1956

mein and a good deal less exhilarating."[134] Nature scoffs at this feeble and obsolete art. The new Chinese realities, as we only just are beginning to perceive them, still far outrace the plodding fantasies of the past. The new cycle has only just opened; our tortoiselike imaginations will no doubt doggedly pursue the harelike events of our time.

Meanwhile, the problem of adjusting minds to the new images goes on in many different ways. One of our panelists, a distinguished historian, said:

> I get a picture of Communist fanaticism winning acceptance. It doesn't fit with my previous theory that the Chinese were pragmatic, nondoctrinaire, nonmessianic.

Actually, for those with deeply entrenched, admiring images of the Chinese, there is a great deal in the new situation which does not "fit." In the images of the Chinese that they see in the Communist mirrors, these Americans see no more deferential politeness, no more gratitude, and distressingly little humor, no more philosophic calm, no more sage wisdom, no more respect for antiquity or tradition, or passive and smiling reliance on timeless verities—almost none, in short, of all the features that made the Chinese so attractive and often so dear. So much so, indeed, that it is frequently impossible for some of these Americans to accept the "new" images as being "Chinese" at all. They are "Communist" or "Russian," in any case alien. "I don't regard the Communist government as Chinese," said one panelist, for example. "There isn't any China," said another, "it is now part of Russia."

This notion of the un-Chineseness of the new regime is a necessary bulwark for those who see Communist China primarily as the product of a new foreign conquest. Their picture is one of a small band of alienated Chinese radicals, aided and abetted by the Russians, taking advantage of the chaos of war and its aftermath to seize the country and to begin lashing the people into new and alien molds. This idea recurs in our panel, and it also often appears, not at all coincidentally, in the public prints, as in this *New York Times* editorial:

> Mainland China has been conquered by still another external group and for the time being by a set of ideas basically foreign to the Chinese concept of good living . . the Confucian ethics that had become part

[134] *New York Times*, July 28, 1956.

of the admirable Chinese character. There is no place in the Communist world for the personal and family loyalty that were the very heart of Chinese society. There is no place for humor and generosity, for patience and kindliness, for honor and warmth of heart....[135]

The advantage in thinking of China as a conquered country lies in the fact that China, as almost everyone knows, is really unconquerable, that it has always absorbed its foreign rulers and reasserted its own culturally sovereign identity. Hence the Communist regime is a temporary phenomenon due sooner or later to give way. Here are four examples of this familiar concept, offering a range of time spans

> It is my feeling that the Chinese are so numerous, nobody can swallow them. China is unconquerable, even by the Communists This is just a phase, maybe it will take twenty years to get rid of it. . .
>
> I cannot believe for the life of me that China can long stay Communist . . I don't think you can put a Chinaman in a mold. You can't do it. It is going to evolve eventually over there in some other way in the longer run. But I don't know what the long run is. . . .
>
> China is gone, but it will come back. These people are not easily conquered It may be slow. . . . I see this evolution as lasting a couple of hundred years. . . .

Our fourth panelist in this group found the long historical view considerably longer than his patience:

> I see the ultimate fate of China as being in our hands, so far as any hope of destroying Communism on the mainland goes. The alternative is to wait for a thousand years of evolution.

While for these individuals it is the "un-Chinese" character of the regime that guarantees its ultimate downfall, others find hope in it precisely because it *is* Chinese

> China is too important to stay subservient to Russia very long. . .
>
> China will evolve away from Russian communism, but it is optimistic to think that it will become a Jeffersonian democracy. . . .
>
> I have a sort of confidence that somehow they will come through with a better government, nearer to democratic government than we expect. I respect their basic good sense

The most common and most pervasive reactions in our panel to Communist China are dominated by the notion of *released energy*.

[135] *New York Times*, October 10, 1955.

THE CHINESE                                                                 221

That special Chinese vitality, mentioned so often as a major trait, has now finally been generalized for the nation as a whole. The solemn predictions of a century and more are coming to pass. The effect is powerful and, for some, quite overwhelming. Most of the individuals in this group are without any important previous contact or experience in China. The situation has newly burst upon most of them, sometimes, indeed, with the impact of a sudden and nearby explosion. It is among these individuals that we come upon some of the newer postures, e.g., of a certain respectful awe:

> A civilization bottled up for a long time, corroded by the West, now bursting forth with tremendous energy. This had to come. The Communists are merely riding the crest. . . .

Ed Fisher © 1956 The New Yorker Magazine Inc

*"Surely, Morton, you're not going to let a little dust on your trousers threaten our entire strategic position in the Far East!"*

A country of 600 million, going to be a tremendous force in the world, with a welded leadership, public health, mass ideas, technology, terrific potential for change There is little we can do to alter it.

Tremendous force on the way to being realized. Great human aggregation, great dynamism, great biological persistence, destined to play a great part in human affairs. . . .

Or a growing apprehension, as in these remarks of a former high government official:

I feel apprehension, a great deal of apprehension, the feeling that the whole pattern of inferiority has disappeared. They've got resources and Communist ideology, and a foreign policy based on their tradition of expansion. It creates a major danger for the United States. . . .

Or, again, from a businessman.

Tremendous potential in unharnessed power. Gives you the creeps to think what happens when it gets harnessed the wrong way, as now. . .

The awakened giant is still only half on his feet, but he already looks a lot bigger than he did on his back. When, in the mind's eyes of some of our panelists, he rises to his full height and starts throwing his great weight around, his new dimensions become, as we have observed before, apocalyptic:

We have to build dikes somehow Chinese power in the next hundred years will absorb all of Southeast Asia There will be no stopping them. . . .

I think of a solid Communist bloc from Germany to the Pacific. Fear is the honest word . .

A prominent politician who was born in the South has this characteristic reaction

Is China going to take the lead in fomenting feeling against the white race? . America is much more afraid of Chinese Communism than of Russian Communism and I think even Russia is beginning to fear that side more than its western borders. . . China is a rising country with tremendous strength, great potential . . . a people with dark skins who have been exploited. . . .

A career diplomat.

In thirty years China will be a tremendous danger to the Orient if other countries do not keep up with Chinese advances. Like the danger of Japan, a physical, imperialist danger, and to the United States too insofar as any expanding imperialistic power blocks the United States in They will try to dominate South Asia and Australia if they can. This is inevitable. I do not say this with bitterness or animosity. Any nation would do this if it could . . .

This great sense of energies released in China is, let it be quite clear, no matter merely of image or imagination. This is a "large" image which is verified by "large" facts that almost everybody can see, even from a great distance, and these facts are, according to your disposition, impressive, overwhelming, or frightening. The new growth of power in China is no myth. There is nothing ephemeral about its rapid industrial progress. There is nothing ephemeral either about the system's intellectual robotism, its police terror, and its critical problems in agriculture. But carrying all these along with them, the Communists, mobilizing great new energies, are rapidly changing the face of their country and opening up vast and incalculable prospects for the future The new facts, already marked on the economic maps by many multiplying symbols, have already become part of a broad public impression. Thus, for example, *Life* magazine —not prone to sympathetic illusions about Communist China—published in January, 1957, a series of pictures made by a New Zealand cameraman in China, shots of Chinese men and women workers laying rails, pumping oil, building bridges, using modern farm machinery, studying in laboratories, taking off on pioneer treks to construction projects along the distant frontiers. This picture report, remarked *Life*, made it clear "that Red China has made some formidable efforts" and added: "If it reaches its set goals, Communist China, by 1962, will rank among the world's ten top industrial powers " [136]

But Communist China, still an industrial pygmy compared to the Soviet Union or the United States, already clearly ranked among the world's top three or four powers in the matter of international influence and importance By its sheer economic and military weight, Russia remained after Stalin the center of power in the Communist world, but the mantle of status and prestige within the Soviet orbit began to pass, almost perceptibly, to the Communist rulers in Peking. The redistribution of effective influence along the Moscow-Peking axis within the Communist orbit is already—even though still nascent

[136] *Life*, January 21, 1957.

and tentative—one of the most significant developments in world affairs.

The special aura of Chinese prestige and unique power and independence within the Soviet orbit was displayed in many ways even before Stalin's death. Peking became the Mecca-like center of the Communist world. There are great ironies and meanings to be explored in the fact that it was the European Communist who gained prestige by traveling to Peking and brushing shoulders there with Mao Tse-tung and his top cohorts.[137] But the new and pivotal position of the Chinese Communists became universally apparent beginning late in 1956, when the Moscow regime was badly shaken by the near breakup of its Eastern European satellite empire with the revolts against Moscow authority in Poland and Hungary. The Polish Communists, pressing for a somewhat more sovereign status, leaned heavily and publicly on the impression that the Chinese Communists looked kindly on their cause. "The new Polish leadership," reported a *Times* correspondent from Warsaw, "attributed the Polish revolution against Stalinism in great part to the strong and continuous support from the Chinese Communist leaders." The report quoted "responsible Polish sources" on China's "ever-increasing impact on the affairs of Communist countries in Europe, including the Soviet Union" and predicted that "Chinese influence will continue to play an even more important role as time passes."[138] The Russians barely managed to hold on in Hungary by brute force and in Poland by temporizing, and the repercussions of these events began to pull Communist parties apart all over the world. Communist capitals buzzed with reports that Khrushchev had even flown secretly to Peking to invoke Mao Tse-tung's support. The sequel was, in any event, a statement from Peking coming powerfully to the Kremlin's aid, while stressing the need for "rectifying errors of the past" in relations between Communist parties. Chou En-lai, the Chinese Communist premier, traveled first to Moscow and then to Warsaw and Budapest expressly as the advocate of preserving the solidarity of the Communist bloc under Russian leadership. He re-established

---

[137] The flavor of this is communicated by a sentence in a Berlin dispatch about a difficult moment in the life of the East German Communist government late in 1955: "In another development, perhaps designed to increase the prestige of the East German regime, it was announced that Premier Otto Grotewohl had accepted an invitation from Communist China to visit Peiping."—*New York Times*, December 5, 1955

[138] *New York Times*, December 25, 1956

in some degree that compliance with Moscow's rule which in the language of the Soviet bloc is called "proletarian internationalism." In this process, as observers all over the world were quick to guess, the key role of arbiter, if not leader, in the Communist power bloc passed in effect from the Kremlin to the men who sit under the golden tiles of Peking's Forbidden City. In Moscow, too, there must be great changes to record in the images leaders have of the Chinese.

## The Chinese as Warrior

Around the sleeping giant a whole conception was woven: philosophic calm and patience, timelessness, immobility, an intelligence too great for combativeness or truculence, a genius for achieving ends not by bruising direct action but by smooth circumlocution, a wisdom too weary with years to accept the angry haste and short-lived violences of Western man. The giant shredded this gossamer web as he rose, full now of his own haste, crudity, violence, impatience, and aggressive self-assertion. Now he is dangerously vital, vigorous, energetic, bursting out at all his seams. Of all the shifts and displacements this requires in our mental picture of the Chinese, none is more radical or sweeping than the changes in our image of China as a military power and of the Chinese as a warrior.

These changes have been in the making for some time. They were already visible in American estimates of the Communist armies during the war with Japan. They were spurred by the events of the Communist take-over in China in 1948–49. But they really came into their own in American minds as a result of what happened after the Chinese intervened in the Korean war in the winter of 1950. Some vivid examples of how individuals experienced this change turned up in several interviews. A Congressman said:

> I could not visualize the Oriental as a terrific, rugged, capable soldier. It was first brought home to me in Korea in 1951. Iron Mike O'Daniel told me the Chinese army was as well staffed and trained as any he knew . . . Seemed strange for Chinamen, went against the whole idea I'd ever had of the Chinese . . . I knew a streak of cruelty was there, but couldn't quite see them as the terrible, tenacious soldiers they turned out to be. . .

One of the country's best-known newsmen:

> They have a limitless manpower and from my experience in Korea, a technical skill far in excess of what Americans ever thought possible

The Chinese were better artillerymen than the Germans ever were. This was quite a shock, considering one's previous picture. I remember a sergeant who said to me: "We thought all we had to do was show them our uniforms, and they would run like hell. Instead they shot the ——— out of us." With some allowance for exaggeration, this was my experience too.

Or this, finally, from a former high official of the Eisenhower administration:

I was brought up to think the Chinese couldn't handle a machine. Now, suddenly, the Chinese are flying jets! The American idea was that Asiatics are nonmechanical, except the Japanese, and the Japanese were freaks, not really mechanical, just copied what others did. In practically everything one ever read . . . the Asiatic is always plowing with his fingernails and the European is handling the machine.

WHEN A FELLER NEEDS A FRIEND

*San Francisco Chronicle*
1922

Now the Chinese is flying a jet! Disturbing, especially since you have several hundred million of them teamed up with the USSR I always thought the Yellow Peril business was nonsense. . . Now I can visualize that Asiatics teamed up with the Slavs could indeed conquer the world!

It required an experience as jolting as that in Korea to introduce these new images of the Chinese as a warrior, for the contrary images of the Chinese as unaggressive, nonmechanical, and unmartial are among the oldest and most deeply imbedded in our entire gallery. Indeed, to find almost any generalized image of the Chinese as dangerous fighting men, one has to go all the way back to their non-Chinese antecedents and onetime conquerors, the Mongol hordes of Genghiz Khan, which overran so much of the known world in the twelfth century. The encounter with the Chinese army in Korea, "human sea" and all, in a way signaled another sort of rounding of the circle: our images of the Chinese as warriors had progressed from fearful hordes to fearful hordes in seven centuries.

Maybe That's Why They're Called 'Reds'!

NEA Service, Inc.

1951

THE MONGOL HORDES: The idea of the Mongol hordes has never lurked very far from the more generalized images of "Asiatic" or "Oriental" barbarism. It might lie dormant for long periods, but it is summoned up at a touch, instantly revived by some evidence of wanton cruelty or by some particularly fearful event. A crowded panoply of images and sensations seemingly waits in almost every Western man's mind, ready to move at the cue A recent and somewhat mordant example of this occurred in the report of a refugee from the Russian repression of the Hungarian revolt in November, 1956. He said that Russian soldiers in Budapest had "refused to fight us" but finally had been "terrorized" into turning their guns against the rebels after the Soviet Union "had sent in new and tougher troops, including two Mongolian divisions." The Mongols had "terrorized" the Russians, and the wanton slaughter began.[139] Here even the onus for Russian Communist barbarism is shifted from white Europeans to twentieth-century descendants of the same Mongol barbarians who had been to Budapest at least once before—in 1241, when the hordes of Batu Khan had destroyed a Hungarian army, put the city of Pesth to the torch, and covered the land with the corpses of its people.

During a time of severe tension in the Formosa Strait in 1955 when the threat of an American war with Communist China was strong in people's minds, I heard a White House official at a Washington dinner suddenly summon up this same ancestral specter. The discussion made him think, he said, of a fantastic story he had once read. It was called "The Red Napoleon," written by the sensationalist Floyd Gibbons for the Hearst press in 1929 Nightmarishly illustrated—mainly with the ravished bodies of white women—it had depicted the rise of a new Genghiz Khan somewhere in Communist Asia At the head of a new Mongol barbarian horde, this new Khan would come close to conquering the world in a war which Gibbons imagined as taking place between 1933 and 1938. This particular series was only one of many in a chain of newspapers that constantly screamed with huge headlines and lurid pictures. Yet it had made a deep and permanent scratch on this one person's mind, who could not have been much more than sixteen at the time and found himself now a member of a President's staff

The Chinese Communists themselves have borrowed something

[139] *New York Times,* November 15, 1956

of the aura of the Genghiz Khan image They built a new mausoleum for the Mongol conqueror in Inner Mongolia and in June, 1956, on the 729th anniversary of his death, staged a great memorial service in his honor.

THE LOW-STATUS WARRIOR. Between our images of the barbarian hordes of the twelfth and thirteenth centuries and the rise of the successor hordes and their successor images in the twentieth, a wholly different set of notions intervened about the Chinese as warriors. These quite contrary ideas have dominated all but the most recent history linking Americans and Chinese. One of the best-known of these was based on the fact that traditional Chinese society put a low value on the soldier He was no pariah—Chinese history is full of its warrior-heroes—but socially he was ranked at the bottom of the ladder. This tradition was, like many others in Chinese life, more formal than real. But it was real enough to form one of the many differences between Chinese ideas and the rougher-and-readier canons of European—or especially of Anglo-Saxon—culture. It was one of the "odd" things about the Chinese, and it helped create the contempt in which, as we have seen, dominant Westerners came to hold the Chinese after they found they could defeat them so easily in war. On the other hand, the nonmartial spirit of the Chinese was sanctioned, in theory at least, by some of the central ideas in professed Western religion, the Christian pacifist could hardly scoff at it with an easy conscience. It also played a part in creating the idealized image of reasonableness—the Chinese were too civilized to think that anything could be accomplished by fighting, something Westerners had yet to learn. In these and other ways, the low value placed by the Chinese on professional soldiering contributed to the high value placed on Chinese wisdom, serenity, and superior culture

THE COMIC OPERA WARRIOR: A corollary and more familiar image associated with more recent times was definitely comic in its impact: the image of the comic opera Chinese soldier of the war-lord era, roughly the decades between 1912 and 1937. This was the Chinese soldier carrying an umbrella and a token rifle, the era of the armies that fought battles across teacups, of victories won by "silver bullets" —i e., through the judicious purchase of treason in the camp of the foe or by compromise arrangements to live and let live. The impression left by most of the voluminous writing by Americans in this period was one of recurring civil wars which managed to disrupt the life of the country without ever quite attaining the bloody dignity of actual conflict. The Chinese soldier and his war-lord master became in this time the butt of a good deal of scornful humor in the foreign press. Of this humor Major (now Brigadier General, retired) Thomas Magruder wrote in 1931:

> Insofar as this humor expresses the essential nonmartial character of the soldiers, it is an accurate reflection of the facts. . . . By nature the Chinese have never been and are not now a warlike people . . . they have developed no scientific military traditions . . At heart the Chinese believe that the continuance of their race . . will not be accomplished by the exercise of military qualities. Their confident faith in their destiny seems to lie in their one-mindedness, patience, and persistence . . in a locust-like mass momentum and propagation. . . .

Magruder said that he had observed that the Chinese soldier would fight for some direct personal interest, mainly his livelihood, but could not be aroused by any matter of pure or abstract principle. He concluded:

> If martial spirit does grow, the development will be a slow process. It will not necessarily be a concomitant of the present rapid social and political change. It will be the result of a fundamental change in national character. Given money, equipment, and training, there is no doubt that a first class fighting machine can be made of, say, 20,000 Bulgars or Turks The same cannot be said of the 20,000 Chinese without numerous qualifications. The difference has nothing to do with physical stamina, courage, or intelligence. It is spiritual, or possibly intellectual, and may be loosely summed up in those racial qualities which create a natural antipathy for joining battle with an enemy instead of a relish for combat. . .
> I have never heard of a Chinese militarist . . . who at heart was not a man of peace.[140]

This analysis has been undergoing the contradiction of events almost since it was written, though much had to happen before Hanson Baldwin, writing in 1951, in a direct commentary on the Magruder article could say.

That the world no longer thinks of the Chinese in terms of pacifism is a measure of the change in China. . The picture we once entertained of the somewhat benign, inscrutable but wise and civilized Chinese, too

---

[140] "The Chinese as a Fighting Man," *Foreign Affairs*, Vol. 9, No 2, January 1931, pp 469–476.

intelligent for war—an oversimplified caricature 20 years ago—has even less validity today For the future China is in the hands of peasant stock, of patient men who have shown on many battlefields that they *will fight*. We have learned this, somewhat to our surprise and at heavy cost, in Korea.[141]

Between the unsoldierly soldier of Major Magruder's day and the fighting men encountered in Korea, several transitional figures passed whom we have already glimpsed. The comic opera Chinese soldier disappeared forever in the bloody abysses of the Japanese war. In his place came the heroic defender of his land, and after him the brave and hardy but hapless victim of the corruption and ineptitude of his leaders Chiang Kai-shek, says the U. S. Army history of the war in China, indicated to General Stilwell "his belief that masses of the latest and best materiel would win the war."

Stilwell retorted that the only way was to reorganize thoroughly the Chinese army. His point then, and later, was that it was fatuous to give a medium tank or a howitzer to a peasant soldier who had never seen anything more complex than his father's wheelbarrow, that the Chinese army had to be trained and reorganized before it could profitably be given new equipment. To this belief the Chinese never subscribed.[142]

The collapse of Chiang Kai-shek's armies before the Communists in 1948–49 confirmed the picture these Americans already had of an amorphous, buttery mass, incapable of functioning effectively, too ridden by backwardness and dishonesty, unable to make good use of modern weapons and techniques. Such was the final military judgment offered from the field by the general commanding the United States Advisory Group in 1948.

No battle has been lost since my arrival due to lack of ammunition or other factors Their military debacles in my opinion can all be attributed to the world's worst leadership and many other morale-destroying factors that lead to a complete loss of the will to fight [and] the complete ineptness throughout the Armed Forces . .[143]

---

[141] "China as a Military Power," *Foreign Affairs*, Vol 30, No 1, October 1951, p. 51
[142] *Stilwell's Mission to China*, p 155. Similar observations dot the whole record For an account based on talks with officers in the field, cf Harold R Isaacs, "Ignorant Men and Modern Weapons," *Newsweek*, November 20, 1944, pp 44–48
[143] Major General David Barr to Department of the Army, November 16, 1948, quoted in *United States Relations With China*, Department of State, Washington, D C, August 1949, p 358

Of the Communist armies, a certain number of Americans had begun to acquire a more respectful picture, both during the war against Japan and the civil war that followed.[144] But the difference did not impress itself deep or far. Most of the Americans concerned apparently continued to believe, as General Barr did, that in the showdown conflicts of the civil war, "only the active participation of United States troops could affect a remedy." The real displacement of American images of the Chinese as warriors did not take place until Americans faced Chinese as foes in Korea.

## The Human Sea

In October, 1950, American Eighth Army intelligence officers in Korea reported the appearance of Chinese units along the North Korean front. The military historian S. L. A. Marshall has written that these reports were regarded with considerable concern by officers on the ground. But we still have no clear picture of how these reports were received and evaluated as they rose along the echelons to the top command. We do not know if they were ignored, or underestimated, or scornfully rejected. We do not know whether the presence of a large Chinese army was doubted or whether the decision-makers, like the sergeant quoted by one of our panelists, thought that "all we had to do was show them our uniforms and they would run like hell." The fact is that General Douglas MacArthur did not regard these reports as a deterrent to his planned action. He went ahead on November 24 with his famous "home-by-Christmas" offensive. When the American troops came staggering back from the impact of the Chinese armies that so unexpectedly struck them, a whole epoch passed and a swift and massive displacement of images had taken place.

Chinese soldiery, hitherto always seen as a pulpy and ineffectual mass, had suddenly become a powerfully threatening foe. The picture was one of a small American and allied force being engulfed by a vast Chinese army which had concealed itself with a skill at deception that was, in Colonel Marshall's words, "suited to the Oriental nature." The effect was a pell-mell retreat in pell-mell disorder. The new realities of that battlefield were grim enough, but

[144] One of the early enthusiastically admiring accounts was given by Evans Carlson, *The Chinese Army*, New York, 1940. A considerably more unromantic view appears in Lt Col Robert Riggs *Red China's Fighting Hordes*, Harrisburg, Pennsylvania, 1951.

they were swiftly compounded by the old, old mythologies that lay so readily to hand, all the nameless fears implied, for example, in Colonel Marshall's description of an engagement in which an American force "was swamped by a *yellow tide* which moved upon it from all sides." [145] The "yellow tide" in Korea swept up all sorts of ancestral memories. The "new" images were built up swiftly, not only out of the reality of the new foe, but out of materials that had lain long in the recesses of time and the mind. The Mongol hordes had reappeared.

The first and principal ingredient of this "new" image of the Chinese was the idea of their numbers, their sheer vast numbers. "The Chinese Communist army . . . combat effectiveness was limited to the tactic of the 'human sea,'" wrote General Mark Clark, "because all it had initially was an overwhelming superiority in numbers of men. . . . The enemy hurled overwhelming numbers of men at us, apparently heedless of how many he lost." [146] This indifference to life and death is a second dominating aspect of the new set of images. ("It is well to remember," wrote Hanson Baldwin, "that the Chinese soldier springs from a land where life is cheap. . . . [He] is fatalistic, with little regard for human life." [147]) Necessarily coupled to this was a special quality of cruel sadism. ("There is a sadism and brutality inherent in many Asiatics," observed Colonel Riggs, "that is not commonly found within men of the better educated areas of the world." This special brutality is being spread, he went on, "to countless masses of uniformed robots." [148]) A third ingredient is described variously as "blind obedience" or "stupid automatism" or "iron discipline"—the quality that made it possible for Chinese soldiers to act with suicidal madness, like marching squarely into the face of murderous fire until ordered to stop. Marshall quotes one officer as saying: "It was like dealing with mass lunacy." [149] Baldwin notes that this behavior led to the popular notion, which he adds he could never verify, that Chinese soldiers were "hopped up with opium" before going into action.[150]

---

[145] *The River and the Gauntlet*, New York, 1953, p 210, italics supplied Col. Riggs, in his study of the Chinese Red forces, usually calls them "ochre hordes"

[146] Mark Clark, *From the Danube to the Yalu*, New York, 1954, pp 87–101

[147] Baldwin, *loc cit*

[148] Riggs, pp 19, 105.

[149] Marshall, *op cit*, p 105.

[150] Baldwin, *loc cit*, p. 55.

The reader will recognize in all of these some older and quite well-established images, assigned in the recent past to the Japanese and restored here once more to the Chinese. Here again, on Korean battlefields, were the *faceless masses*, the *cruel and nerveless subhumans*, the *incomprehensible* and the *inscrutable* Chinese whom

THE EXPENDABLES    *St Louis Post-Dispatch*, 1951

we have met before in other times and places, reappearing out of obscurity to stand again in the foreground of the imagination to help "explain" the main picture to emerge from this phase of the Korean War, a picture of an overwhelming mass overcoming by "human sea assaults" the technically superior but numerically inferior American foe

As fact and as phrase, "the human sea" experience in the Korean war is a subject for an inquiry in itself. As phrase, it became part of the daily jargon of war reporting, e.g.:

Attacking in a "human sea" offensive, the enemy infantry had rolled forward eighteen to twenty miles . . . in the traditional pattern of the Korean war, matched sheer manpower of infantry armed with rifles and machine guns against the mechanized Allied army....[151]

As described in a *Saturday Evening Post* article:

The "human sea assault" is a most wasteful but effective device. . . . In this limitless resource of expendable manpower lies the Chinese Red Army's strength. Squads, platoons, and companies are organized into the much publicized assault units. Each unit flings itself into battle at the command "Charge!" The men in these rushes keep going until they are cut down by the enemy or gain their objective.[152]

What was the "human sea" as fact? This appears to be more difficult to answer Even a cursory reading of the battle reporting and commentary of the time suggests a number of questions which we can hardly expect to answer here. In the literal sense of onrushing charges of seemingly insane men dying in droves until they have overrun their objective, how much of it actually occurred? Many of the contemporary reports seemed to suggest that it was happening all the time But Andrew Geer, the Marine historian, writing in 1952, enters a sharp dissent

"Human sea" frontal assaults are rare and are ordered as a last resort when the necessity for victory dictates such a high cost Newspapers have reported "human sea" attacks on United Nations positions on many occasions. Actually there have been few such attacks made by the Chinese forces in Korea Such tactics were reported as an excuse for the defeat suffered by United Nations troops.[153]

[151] *New York Times*, April 25, 1951
[152] *Saturday Evening Post*, January 27, 1951
[153] Andrew Geer, *The New Breed*, New York, 1952, p 221.

Did it come to be used more loosely, to describe, say, the infiltration tactics which the Chinese used so skillfully, or even, most simply, to describe the larger number of enemy troops in almost any operation? Did the phrase "human sea" come to have a life of its own? Did operations officers, communiqué writers, correspondents, editors, and headline writers add, through this phrase, their own mental images of what was going on? Did the phrase help evoke the strong sense of difference between one's own side and those fantastic masses of *gooks* or *chinks*, subhumans, indifferent alike in killing or in dying? Did it help rationalize later, in the counteroffensives which finally deadlocked the war, "Operation Killer"—the concerted design for the most massive possible killing of this innumerable and inexhaustible foe?

Before the Korean War ended, the new image of the Chinese as warrior and foe became something more than a vision of vast numbers, of massed barbarians kin to the Mongol hordes. These were Mongol hordes with big guns and jet aircraft and a growing number among them who knew how to use these weapons with considerable precision and skill. A new conception arose not only of the Chinese as warrior but the Chinese as technician. These were only yesterday backward semi-idiots who knew only how to kill or to die, people of an unindustrialized country not at home with complicated machinery, ingenious but essentially "not mechanical-minded"[154] But in Korea they began, as we have already heard, to impress some Americans as "better artillerymen than the Germans" and soon after that war the Chinese were being held responsible for the superior technical showing of Ho Chi-minh's Communist forces at the siege of Dienbienphu in the climactic battle of the Indochina war. On April 5, 1954, Secretary of State John Foster Dulles read to a Congressional committee a top United States intelligence report which he called an "ominous story." It recited these six points:

1. A Chinese Communist general is stationed at the Dienbienphu headquarters . . . of the Vietminh commander.

[154] The persistent power of these stereotypes in the face of contradictory evidence is illustrated by Hanson Baldwin's sentence "The Chinese are not mechanical-minded, their maintenance of vehicles and motorized equipment is poor, breakdowns are numerous, yet many trucks are kept running literally with baling-wire."—*Loc cit*, p. 58

2. Under him there are nearly a score of Chinese Communist technical military advisers . . . [and] numerous others at division level.

3. There are special telephone lines installed, maintained and operated by Chinese personnel.

4. There are . . 37mm anti-aircraft guns, radar controlled, at Dienbienphu which are shooting through the clouds to bring down French aircraft. These guns are operated by Chinese.

5. . . . there are approximately 1,000 supply trucks . . all driven by Chinese army personnel

6. . . . the artillery, ammunition and equipment generally comes from Communist China.[155]

The enormous irony of the change implied by the tone of this report becomes most apparent when we compare it to the despair with which American military men had regarded the Chinese army barely a decade before. Then it was the Americans who were the technical advisers, Americans who set up and operated communications systems, Americans who threw up their hands at the way Chinese artillerymen handled their 37mm guns [156] and the way Chinese drivers abused the trucks they had been given to drive. The Chinese were almost universally thought to be hopelessly backward and incapable of marshaling a military power dangerous to anybody but themselves Yet now these same people had become not only formidable foes themselves but "ominous" as mentors of their own lesser allies in Korea and Vietnam [157]

This transformation of the Chinese from a nonwarlike to a highly warlike people and of China from a weakling among nations to a major power was accomplished with remarkable rapidity. Under the heading "Aggressive China Becomes a Menace," *Life* said:

China's Red Army, a guerrilla rabble 20 years ago, had been built into a menacingly Russianized fighting force. . . .[158]

[155] *New York Times*, April 6, 1954

[156] Talking about 37mm guns, here is a sentence from a wartime despatch of my own: "New weapons are often abused I saw a 37-millimeter gun that had fired 100 rounds without ever having its barrel swabbed It was a total loss."— *Newsweek*, November 20, 1944

[157] At the beginning of the Israeli-Egyptian hostilities in November, 1956, Cairo radio news reported the rumor that Chinese pilots were coming as volunteers to fly Egypt's Russian-built MIG jets The appearance of this rumor was in itself a measure of the transformation of current images of the Chinese as warriors Individuals young enough to have received their impressions of the Chinese only since the Korean War would find nothing incongruous or even surprising in the availability of Chinese as pilots for these superadvanced aircraft

[158] *Life*, November 20, 1950.

General Douglas MacArthur, who had made the discovery at first hand, so to speak, told Congress on his return in 1951:

> The Chinese people have become militarized in their concepts and their ideals They now constitute excellent soldiers, with competent staffs and commanders This has produced a new and dominant power in Asia.... [159]

In his revised estimate of Chinese military power, Hanson Baldwin wrote:

> The "Yellow Peril" in the sense we once used the term cannot exist until China is organized, developed, and industrialized—a process that will surely require not years but decades . We are unlikely to see a Red China colossus emerge, fully helmeted and armored, in our lifetime More dangerous is the possibility—still only that—that the Chinese Army may gradually be Russianized. . . . Meanwhile these conclusions cannot be gainsaid. The Chinese Army, little regarded in the past, is now a major political factor in the Orient. . . . [160]

An American army colonel predicted to a Boston audience "The Chinese Communist army will be the world's most dynamic fighting machine by 1970," so much so that by that time the survival of the United States will "be in doubt.' [161]

In our present panel, the sense of this transformation of image is strong. The quality of it is but suggested, perhaps, by the words and tone of a Midwestern publisher:

> I never thought of the Chinese as belligerent I never thought we would be risking war with them A peasant country! It would have been inconceivable to me even five or ten years ago that we could have a war with China Now I see China as a formidable foe. . . .

From this picture the friendly, attractive, admirable individual Chinese has almost completely disappeared The shape of our new images waits, in the most literal sense, on the shape of things to come.

[159] *New York Times*, April 20, 1951.
[160] Hanson Baldwin, *loc. cit*, pp 52, 62
[161] *Boston Herald*, February 25, 1956

PART THREE

———————— ✿ ————————

# THE INDIANS

BY CONTRAST to the scratches on our minds about China, the marks left in the past by India are many fewer and much fainter. The difference, moreover, is not merely one of quantity but of kind, a difference that imposes itself on almost all the scattered pieces of the pattern as we discover them.

There are no Indian counterparts for the many familiar links to China or the Chinese, like digging that hole through the earth, firecrackers, Chinese checkers, Chinese puzzles, Chinatowns, Chinese restaurants, laundries, and laundrymen, nothing like the popularity of Chinese food or the familiarity of Chinese touches in home decoration and furniture. A large part of the reason for this, of course, is that Indians, unlike Chinese, never became such a visible part of American life, they never emigrated to this country in such numbers, never became familiar figures, never acquired any comparable role in the literature or lore of the land.

There is, in addition, the special North American ambiguity about the word "Indian." Thanks to the remarkable perpetuation of Columbus' historic error, the word *Indian* in this country generally suggests *American Indian*, the Apaches, the Sioux, Sitting Bull, Geronimo, Hiawatha. As such it is prefixed to a great many words in the American language, we all know Indian beads, Indian nuts, Indian file, Indian war whoops, the Indian sign, Indian givers, and so on. In the many columns of such words listed in the larger dictionaries there are a few which originate in some relation to India rather than to North America, but you are not likely to find familiar ones among them unless you happen to be a user of something like Indian ipecac (a milkweedlike plant, says Webster, used as an emetic). *India ink* and *India rubber* are more commonly known, although, as the dictionary discloses, neither one is actually of Indian origin. Almost everything *Indian* we encounter has no connection whatever with *India*. Thus at the very outset of any discovery at all about India, young Americans have to face and overcome this considerable confusion of terms. Indians who come to this country must frequently do likewise. In one home I know this difficulty was met when the youngsters were small by establishing the separate existence of what were called *American Indians* and *Indian Indians*, but this hardly has become a usual American practice.

Beyond all this, one looks almost in vain for anything in schooling, the common speech, or environment to fix links to India in the time of our minds' growing up. There is nothing from school days to match the evocative power of the Marco Polo story, no phrases from the ordinary parlance of the later years like *damned clever, these Chinese* or the later *Confucius say*, no villain like Fu Manchu, no hero like Charlie Chan. How many know that the game parchisi is called "the royal game of India"? Not a single panelist mentioned it. How many would think of India in connection with *Cashmere* wool? The phrase *sacred cow* is common, but it appears to have become so fully naturalized as an American colloquialism that it has lost all touch with its Indian origin. There are some words we use—though not too commonly—which in themselves suggest their Indian origin: rajah, nabob, yogi. But many more familiar words from the Hindi and Sanskrit sources have largely lost their Indian identity: mogul, thug, khaki, pajama, pundit, calico, bandanna, etc. There are some other phrases of limited currency: some Western cattlemen doubtless know the relatively recent ancestry of the *Brahman* breed, and in New England and among literary folk the term *Boston Brahmin* has become fairly well established since it was first used this way nearly a century ago (apparently by Oliver Wendell Holmes in his novel *Elsie Venner*) to describe the Boston upper crust.[1] None of

[1] It is rather striking to note how many of these borrowed Indian words refer to ultrahigh status in society—rajah, nabob, mogul, pundit, Brahmin—and that these all have a certain negative flavor as used in American parlance.

Lon Chaney played an early murderous Chinatown villain in *Bits of Life* (First National, 1921)

Ugly Eastern evil has handsome Western virtue temporarily in its power in *Mr Wu* (M-G-M, 1927).

Boris Karloff characterizing the most famous of all fictional Chinese villains in one of many films, *The Mask of Fu Manchu* (M-G-M, 1932)

And the most famous of the Chinese heroes who displaced him, Charlie Chan, played here by Warner Oland in *Charlie Chan at the Circus* (20th Century Fox, 1936)

Pearl Buck's *The Good Earth* (M-G-M, 1936) brought real Chinese landscapes and plain Chinese folk to American screens for the first time.

Paul Muni as Wang Lung and Luise Rainer as O-lan, the two principal characters of *The Good Earth*, fixed film images of Chinese peasants in the minds of a whole generation in the United States and many other parts of the world where the film was shown Below, in a group, they look out over the lands they till

The exotic and gem-encrusted character of the Indian maharajah (as shown here in *Lives of a Bengal Lancer*, Paramount, 1936) was a familiar feature of numerous films over the years, creating a powerful stereotype which is only now slowly receding in the wake of the disappearing originals on which it was based

Indians in Hollywood pictures usually had mysterious, mystical, or magical powers, even when they were maidens played by Myrna Loy, shown here with a disguised Victor McLaglen in *The Black Watch* (Fox, 1929).

Three British troopers in the hands of a band of fanatic Thugs in *Gunga Din* (R.K.O., 1939) led by a man (at left) gotten up to look much like Gandhi. The troopers (McLaglen again, Douglas Fairbanks Jr and Cary Grant) got away.

East-West romance, shown here in one of its earliest and most famous tragic outcomes (*Broken Blossoms*, Griffith, 1919), invariably had to end in death or renunciation, or in the discovery that through some Gilbertian happenstance he (or she) was marriageably non-Oriental after all.

Love was a hopeless dilemma in *Son of India* (M-G-M, 1931)

It is less hopeless nowadays though still a dilemma and certainly more daring, as in this advertisement for *The Rains of Ranchipur* (20th Century Fox, 1955)

these seems to qualify as a reasonably universal or even widely familiar American association with things Indian. Perhaps the nearest thing to such a phrase in our common speech might be *the Black Hole of Calcutta*, which is used to denote a dungeonlike pit or a pitlike dungeon. I suspect, however, that a great many people who use the phrase would be unable now to locate the original as fact or fiction or to fix it in time or identify who originally put whom into any such place.

The most common currency in our Indian associations appears in the surviving fragments of our inheritance from Kipling. Of the 181 individuals interviewed for this study, 69 spontaneously mentioned Kipling as a source for early impressions relating to India, and it seems reasonable to guess that many more would have recalled him if specifically jogged on the point. It became clear in any case that Kipling's India was still part of the mental baggage carried about by a great many Americans of youthful maturity or older. On closer examination, however, the Kipling associations with India often turned out to be vague, blurry, or not *Indian* at all. The mention of India might evoke the name Kipling, but a majority, when they thought of Kipling, went on to think of the *Jungle Books*, which became and have remained children's classics divorced from all time or place, or of Kim, who was, after all, a European, or the lama in his story, who was Tibetan, or of the array of English characters building, keeping, or impeding the Empire in a hot, difficult, dangerous land peopled, especially at its fringes, by turbulent tribes which periodically had to be punished for their recalcitrance. Virtually no recognizable Indians swim up in memory out of Kipling. With rare exceptions, they remain faceless, the *lesser breed* for whom England had assumed the *white man's burden*, perhaps the best-known of all the tag lines associated with Kipling's name. Oddly few individuals mentioned Gunga Din, considering the fact that the line *You're a better man than I am, Gunga Din* did move in its time from the status of a classroom declamation piece into the common speech. Indeed, it might even be possible to say that Gunga Din was the Indian name best known to Americans until the advent of Gandhi, although just how *Indian* it remained is at least open to question. The resurrection of Gunga Din in a moving picture of that name produced by RKO in 1939 and revived for showing in 1954 introduced post-Kipling generations to the cringing and rather pathetic creature whose doglike devotion and ultimate sacrifice for his British masters might have pleased the bearers of the burden but could hardly have made him a folk hero in India.[2]

The elusive character of these fragments in our lives touching upon India goes as far back as we can take the matter. India too figured in the romantic clipper ship trade of the early days of the Republic but always more vaguely, somehow, than China, even down to the matter of its identity as a geographical fact. The terms *India, East India, East Indies,* or *the Indies* seem to have been used more or less interchangeably. Boston's India Wharf, a last relic of that trade, was destroyed by fire only recently, in March, 1955. The name had been associated with the spot since 1804 when, the news accounts said, "clipper ships laden with spices and other cargo from the Indies tied up there." Other relics of the time remain in the museum at Salem, in some art collections, and in occasional literary references. But there was a fine vagueness about terms and identities which often makes it appear that India was usually blended with the blurrier "Indies" or even confused with China, or lumped with China and all the rest in an amorphous "East" or "Orient" that was blurriest of all

This blurriness was very much part of the common currency of the time Typically, little Rosa, in Louisa May Alcott's *Eight Cousins* (1874) was taken to the harbor to visit a ship named *Rajah* and she gloried in an herb pillow, dress, and trinkets brought back by an uncle "from Calcutta" which enabled her to imagine herself an "Eastern princess making a royal progress among her subjects." (She went aboard the *Rajah*, however, to visit "China" in the persons of two "Chinamen" who had just arrived on the ship from Hong Kong.) The prominence of the British East India Company in the affairs of that part of the world had long since made *East India* or *India* highly borrowable adjectives. That is how *India* ink got its name, although the black pigment of which it was made came from China. When the United States Navy sent a flotilla to Asian waters to look after American maritime interests there it was given the name, in 1835, of the *East India Squadron*, although most of its activities were along the China coast.

Actual American trade with India remained minor and official American interest in the country minimal. Although consuls were appointed in several Indian ports to look after trade and shipping

[2] *Gunga Din* was, in fact, banned in India when it first appeared.

matters, at no time during the whole of the nineteenth century was it ever part of their function to report on Indian affairs. It has been noted that events like the Sepoy Mutiny in 1857 or the Afridi insurrection of 1897 were scarcely even mentioned in American consular dispatches. Such matters reached the press via England. But in sharp contrast to the lively official American involvement in China from 1844 onward, these events in India "might just as well have transpired in the land of Prester John as far as the consuls were concerned." [3]

Still, we can trace to these fragments of the past, both remote and more recent, a whole series of ideas and images of India which in varying forms are very much with us, even now: the cluster of colorful and vivid notions of a fabulous, mysterious India; the first appearance of Indian religious philosophy in New England via Europe, the simultaneous movement of evangelical missionaries to India which helped produce the still immensely powerful cluster of pictures that have to do with the very benighted heathen Hindu; the Kiplingesque images of the "lesser breed," and the contents of the "white man's burden." All these and others feed into the more recent associations and impacts of Gandhi, Nehru, and the Indians encountered in most recent years by an increasing number of Americans. As we sort out the images we found in the minds of 181 such Americans, we will often find it necessary to make excursions into the history, literature, and experience of the past, in search of antecedents and illumination. The chronology in time will give a certain progressive order to the emergence of these images, but they all coexist in the present. In the gallery that we now enter, they are all very much alive.

## 1. *THE FABULOUS INDIANS*

THE IDEA of exotic fabulousness attached to India from the distant past still has a firm place even in minds where it has to compete with the increasingly more varied, more complex, more sobering

[3] Bernard Stern, *American Views of India and Indians, 1857–1900*, Ph.D. thesis, University of Pennsylvania, 1956, p 6.

knowledge of contemporary India, its problems, and its peoples. This idea goes all the way back to the visions of splendor and wealth connected with the vague and unsituated "Indies" of the exploration era and the glamorous mythology of the American clipper-ship trade and Europe's empire-building days. Ultimately these notions seem to have transferred themselves from the "Indies" to India, rather than to China. For it was of India that there were dazzled accounts of bejeweled potentates, maharajahs, and princes, marble palaces, heaps of treasure, a bizarre and fearful animal world of tigers, of elephants decked in gold and silk, of snakes and snake charmers, a glitter of wealth and magic and power all alive in some distant realm of light and shadow not quite rooted in the real earth. These images have been kept in view over time in an unending procession of travel tales, talks, and films, pictures of regal scenes, of princes draped in gems, a vast literature of cheap adventure in which the central role is usually played by some jewel without price, newspaper stories and Sunday supplement accounts of princely excesses, the unending attraction of the bizarre forever jostling the larger reality out of its way.

Today these are dimming pictures, but they are still quite clear and are still evoked by the simple mention of the word "India." They might be summoned up apologetically, be deprecated or disavowed, or more freely attributed to others than to oneself, but in one form or another in more than half of the interviews, mention was made of

> maharajahs, jewels, wealth, snake charmers, elephants, tigers, tiger hunts, cobras, snakes, monkeys, mongooses, pig sticking . . .

Far from belonging only to the past, these images are still widely and vigorously promoted, they are pictures being flashed on our mental screens almost constantly, even now.

They still figure in popular children's books, where the intent is almost always wholly sympathetic.[4] They continue to be brought to life by every picture of the Taj Mahal, every view of a man in a turban (including professional magicians) and continue to provide staple fare for titillating or comic entertainment. They are standard

[4] Examples: Christine Weston's *Bhimsa the Dancing Bear*, New York, 1945, or J Kiddell-Monroe's *In His Little Black Waistcoat to India*, New York, 1948, cute and charming, both of them, but neither misses many tricks in the maharajah-tiger-snake charmer department.

THE INDIANS 245

for films, past and current· e.g , *The Rains Came* (1939)—recently remade as *The Rains of Ranchipur* (1955)—which featured a classic maharajah, sympathetic version, in his classic and sumptuous white palace, or *The Bengal Brigade* (1954) which features a classic maharajah, villainous version, in *his* classic white and sumptuous white palace. It is still considered newsworthy to report to the world that the Maharajah of Mysore has shot a 900-pound tiger, and no news item about the Nizam of Hyderabad can avoid mentioning that he is "one of the richest men in the world." The periodic items about the late Aga Khan, his bath water and his weight in gold, were standard fixtures in the feature columns, although, one must add, the Aga Khan was probably identified as vaguely "Oriental" rather than as Indian

The proliferation via television, radio, and the press is all but beyond measure. *My Little Margie* (NBC-TV) in one episode features a small band of those toothy, turbaned, popeyed, soft-footed emissaries of an Indian prince recovering that jewel again, this time a jewel that serves as a talisman for the prince's exercise of power Or Groucho Marx, greeting an Indian girl contestant, asks "Tell me,

Carl Rose © The New Yorker Magazine Inc

I've always been curious about India. Is it still all snakes, elephants, jungles, or sacred cows?"

Here is the result of some monitoring across a few days of November and December, 1955, most of the items occurring during the Thanksgiving week end:

• *People are Funny*, NBC-TV, November 12: An Indian student at UCLA, costumed like a rajah, delivers a gift of hay and peanuts to an astonished Los Angeles housewife Another foreign student, similarly gotten up, delivers a baby elephant. These were presented as gifts from "the Maharajah of India." Asked if she was acquainted with the Maharajah, the victim replies, quite seriously, that no, she has never met him.

• *New York Times*, November 23· A North American Newspaper Alliance item on the movie page begins: "A new Indian movie, a great success in the land of rope tricks and fakirs . . ."

• *Our Miss Brooks*, CBS-TV, November 25: Our Miss Brooks, overdosed with a sedative, is transported in a dream to the palace of a maharajah in India. She is carried into his presence on a litter by four slaves. A hootchie-kootchie girl is doing a dance. A huge department-store-type rack laden with dresses, coats, furs, is wheeled before her as a gift from the maharajah Says the maharajah: "I have also bought you a town for your town house." Overwhelmed, Miss Brooks replies· "And only last week you bought me a country for my sausages." The maharajah: "It is nothing, only a matter of 64,-000 rupees." Miss Brooks complains that she has been kept sleepless by the serenading of the chief of the harem guard. Harem guard is summoned to his doom by a huge turbaned slave striking a gong. Guard denies he has been serenading Miss Brooks, explains he has been trying to train his snake. He has failed with the snake, he moans, but succeeded with his necktie, which is rolled up to his neck, curled like a cobra. Dream fades

• *Longines Symphonette*, CBS-Radio, November 27 Announcer "We shall now take you to the land of temples and tigers with the playing of 'India Caravan'. . . ."

• *Assignment India*, NBC-TV, November 24· A contrasting ninety-minute documentary in which Chester Bowles attempts to present a serious picture of contemporary India and in doing so feels the necessity to put some of these popular images in their proper proportions. Thus, among much else, a scene of regal splendor, elephants, a camel cart, a snake charmer. . . .

● *New York Times*, November 27. The editorial cartoon of the week pictures Nehru sitting on top of a rope flung into the air and curlicueing upward to spell out the word "neutrality" with a puzzled world looking on.

● *Time*, December 5: About its New Delhi correspondent: "At his New Delhi home sacred cows browse in the flower beds, snake charmers with their cobras, fortune-tellers and holy men with begging bowls crowd the veranda, push in on him. 'I feel them at my shoulder as I work,' says Campbell." [5]

During the last year or so, a new, large, and quite receptive audience was created for some of these images by the vogue for ladies' fashions on themes borrowed from India. Herewith some examples of actual advertisements that could be duplicated from almost any daily or Sunday paper:

> Our lovely nylon sari nightgown . . . sleep like a maharanee . . . in opulent eastern elegance! It's our enchanting sari gown alight with golden glitter!

> The oriental look in sari slippers . . . light as air and foam, cushioned (like traveling on a magic carpet), sari slippers twinkle at your feet with gold coins . . . Exotic Oriental multicolor print. . . .

> Sari purse . . . exquisite Sari-print of tiny beads on gold cloth is opulent-looking. . . . Gold and silver sari scarf provides Oriental glitter. . . .

> Only at Bergdorf's will you find these dresses . . . fashioned of fabulously fine fabrics, hand-loomed of silk and cotton for the saris of

---

[5] These items were selected in the week that I happened to be working on this material. The weekend that I happened to return to this section of the manuscript to make some revisions, my labors were interrupted by the TV presentation of Laurence Olivier's "Richard III" (NBC-TV, March 11, 1956). One of the General Motors commercials on this occasion had someone ask the announcer if he would like to be a king. "I would rather be one of those fabulous maharajahs who can get anything he wants by snapping his fingers," he replies, and is forthwith transported into a palace scene, complete with silks, slaves, and gold. A magician with a series of finger snaps materializes a succession of sumptuous damsels proffering jars of powder out of which he produces glinting gems. The last one, of course, produces a spark plug, which comes from the same rich dust and has the same everlasting qualities.

aristocratic Hindu ladies . . . cloth of gold-yellow with scattering of leaves and border embroidered with thread not unlike molten gold. . . .

The Maharani—our fabulous watch glittering with Eastern opulence . . . imports from India, bags laden with silvery and golden-rich bullion . . . Bonwit's introduced these opulent silk stoles . .

Nylon sari lounger, lavished with golden-rich print . . . combines the glamor of the mysterious East with the nylon practicality of the West . . . captures many splendors of the East . . . jewel-like brilliance . . . opulent fabric . . . Golden-metallic prints of India . . . the glamor, the color, the excitement of India!

It seems likely that before the advertising copywriters get through with words like *opulent, glittering, exotic, gold, silver, oriental, eastern, fabulous,* all the wealth of India will be reduced to the manageable proportions of a $3.98 bargain item at the department store counter. But the glint of the remotely imagined reality will just as surely shine from new scratches on a great many more minds than ever before. In other types of advertising, especially for airlines or travel agencies, the stress on the *exotic* tends to run to the theme of mystery and magic, often featuring some treatment of the rope trick, the snake charmer, or the magic-carpet notion recast in Indian dress. The Indian Government's own travel agency contributes to the fine blur. Its window display on Fiftieth Street in New York for a long time bade the traveler come to "India, the Land of Pageantry" and featured the festival-dressed elephant, in that same ever-glinting gold.

By now most moderately well-informed people, including those interviewed for this study, are aware that there is a good deal more than extravagant opulence in Indian life. They know that the maharajahs, princes, and all their trappings have been displaced from power if not from most of their pelf, that they are passing from the scene, and were always, in any case, only one among the myriad facts of Indian life. This awareness does not, however, of itself divest the image of its strength. Enough survives, both in the reality and in the stereotypes rooted in people's minds, to preserve it as one of the more persistent images in thinking about India. To the extent that they are absorbed into a more realistic appreciation of present-day India, these pictures of the princes and nabobs tend to become part of the sense that many people have of the immense disparity in India between the lushly wealthy few and the poverty-stricken many.

By themselves, moreover, images of jeweled opulence ordinarily

THE INDIANS 249

find a place in the mind along with the fairy tales; except for those suffering from some special psychological misfortune, they have no emotional specific gravity. In fact, they generally have no gravity at all but float in mental space, occupying a given area but carrying virtually no weight. We find images of quite a different order and substance in a second major area of associations with India the whole range of things having to do with Indian religion and religious philosophy.

## 2. *THE RELIGIONISTS AND PHILOSOPHERS*

IMAGES OF INDIA as a land of religion, of Indians as a people deeply and peculiarly concerned with the religious life, are among the most commanding of all that appear in the course of this exploration. Indeed, the whole notion of the "mysticism of the East," if it is located anywhere at all, is more generally attached to India than it is, certainly, to China, Japan, or any of the Moslem parts of Asia The subject of religion came up seldom or not at all in connection with China In relation to India, it came up soon and often and for many was uppermost and controlling. Whether their knowledge or experience of it was extensive or slight, firsthand or second, vague or particular, recent or long past, people had strong and decided reactions to it These derived from an array of factors of background, education, intellectual and emotional commitments, and, more elusively, of particular personality traits.

In our panel of 181, there were 44 attracted by some aspect of Indian religious beliefs and attitudes Of these a majority coupled their admiring and respectful responses with a variety of critical comments and reservations, and a much smaller number had unmixed feelings on the subject. For some it was a sense of the quality of Indian thought.

> deep, contemplative, tranquil, profound, full of wisdom about life and its meaning; Indians are people more philosophical by nature than we are, people who think rather grandly. . . .

A few reacted responsively to their view of

> the mystic quality in Indian religion, a great radiant faith; the capacity

to depersonalize, to identify with animal life; some Indians are truly in love with God, more truly concerned with God; I admire their contempt for the immediate. . . .

Others admired

> the devotion of Indians to their religion; Indians are motivated by spiritual and religious considerations far more than we are, they really respect their temples, they take their religion more seriously; religion plays a large part in their lives. . . .

Or, speaking of particular Indians and sometimes of Indians in general:

> the high-minded moral content of their behavior; ethical, noble, idealistic qualities; Indians have a burning desire to be good, they are more anxious to be good than we are, the Indian ideal of the irreproachable life, disdain for acquisitiveness or cupidity; the desire to do what is right regardless of severe consequences. . . .

For a considerable number all of this bore a single symbol:

> I think of the figure of Gandhi.

We move here in a highly sensitive area in which most people react out of feelings and ideas that lie deep within themselves, deeper than it was usually possible to probe. Instead of attempting here, by gleaning and inference, to penetrate farther into these individual minds, let us take a brief journey into history, for which a visa is so much more easily obtained, and explore some of the cultural roots or ancestors of some of these reactions, or at least their counterparts. For if they are not always discernibly or directly linked to a continuous tradition, they are certainly reproductions of intellectual and emotional postures that can be identified from experiences of the past, no matter how elusive, slender, or widely separated these might be in time and space.

It is not too widely known that the exchange of ideas, images, and experience in the realm of religion and philosophy between America and India was a two-way passage which began long ago. The first American missionaries went to India to begin preaching evangelical Christianity to the Hindus, two pioneers in 1813, and several score of them by the 1830's. This enterprise was launched by Americans spurred in the first instance by coreligionists in England. It began in a time when, first in Europe and soon in America, the inclusiveness, uniqueness, and superiority of Christian faith had come into question. In Europe this departure from the old paths took one direction that led, through scientific naturalism, to Darwin; it took another that led, through the minds of the German idealistic philosophers, to transcendental mysticism and thence all the way back to . . India. Translations and expositions of the main works of Indian thought and scripture by Max Muller and other European Orientalists crossed the Atlantic. In this form they became known to the ranging, eclectic, unorthodox minds of Ralph Waldo Emerson, Henry Thoreau, and the small band of Concord intellectuals, founders of the Transcendentalist movement which so profoundly influenced American thought in the middle decades of the nineteenth century. These two groups, the New England missionaries and the New England philosophers, are the parents of two quite different sets of reactions to Indian religion and religious philosophy For the ancestral counterparts of those who have responded positively to Indian religious thought, let us turn first to the similar response evoked more than a century ago in Emerson and his friends.

The influence of Asia on Emerson, to begin with, has attracted scholarly attention only in recent years. In his *Main Currents in American Thought* (1927), Vernon Parrington could devote a whole chapter to an acute analysis of Emerson without ever mentioning it. On the other hand, Frederic Ives Carpenter is ready to regard Emerson's assimilation of Oriental literature as "perhaps his greatest distinction." [6] From the work that has been done on this subject by Carpenter and Arthur Christy [7]—often a labor of veritable sleuthing in the realm of ideas—it is clear that Emerson was certainly the first important American man of ideas to drink from Eastern as well as Western founts of wisdom It is also clear that from all, whether Indian, Chinese, Greek, German, French, or English, he took freely and eclectically whatever reinforced his own ideas and impulses and simply rejected or ignored what did not. In Emerson there was no systematic adoption, translation, or reconciliation of these systems of ideas, but a highly selective culling, adaptation, and borrowing, sometimes merely of what he called *lustres* or illustrations put to his own many different uses.

As a youth, Emerson first encountered India through characteristic

[6] *Emerson Handbook*, New York, 1953, p 210.
[7] *The Orient in American Transcendentalism*, New York, 1932

missionary impressions which led him to remark (in 1818) on the "immense goddery" and the "cruelty and sensuality" of Hinduism. Emerson's later discoveries, however, had nothing whatsoever to do with the substance of contemporary Indian life or religion but with the ancient texts of India. These came under his eye when he and his friends were already reacting both against eighteenth-century rationalism and the responding defense of lifeless dogma which offered so little to parched and questing spirits In these texts they found reinforcement for their own mounting emphases on inner spiritual resources, the universality of spirit and truth, agreement and identity in all religion These were books, exulted Emerson, "like rainbows to be thankfully received in their first impression and not examined and surveyed by theodolite and chain...." Thus Emerson the poet and mystic gleaned what he willed from the Hindu cosmic Brahma to enrich his idea of the "Oversoul," from Karma, or fate, what he called "compensation," from the Hindu Maya, or veil of ignorance, his "illusions" His famous poem, *Brahma*, recalled by one of our present interviewees, was a direct borrowing from the Bhagavadgita, both in its central theme and in the misty imagery in which he delighted to cloak it [8] There was little for Emerson to respond to in Islam, but he warmed to the mystic Sufi poets of Persia He responded to the idea of the "union with the beloved," which he read

[8] The poem.

>If the red slayer thinks he slays,
>  Or if the slain think he is slain,
>They know not well the subtle ways
>  I keep, and pass, and turn again.
>Far or forgot to me is near;
>  Shadow and sunlight are the same;
>The vanished gods to me appear,
>  And one to me are shame and fame.
>
>They reckon ill who leave me out,
>  When me they fly, I am the wings;
>I am the doubter and the doubt,
>  And I the hymn the Brahmin sings
>
>The strong gods pine for my abode,
>  And pine in vain the sacred Seven,
>But thou, meek lover of the good!
>  Find me, and turn thy back on heaven.

Carpenter notes what he chooses to see as a somewhat homelier example of Emersonian Hinduism in an unexpected place in the words of the preacher in John Steinbeck's *Grapes of Wrath* "Maybe it's all men and all women we love, maybe that's the Holy Spirit—the human spirit—the whole shebang Maybe all men got one big soul everybody's a part of."

and understood in his own way, and borrowed from them a style which, when he desired, he could make as blurry as a cloud. On the other hand, it was the "urbane Emerson," when he was interested in "observations on men, not the universe," who drew what he chose from Confucius and other Chinese sages.

Emerson said he wanted none of the metaphysics of these works—he had his own—but wanted "only the literature of them." Similarly, Thoreau, who absorbed from these sources a sense of their "mystical love of nature," made it quite clear that he cared only for the meaning he chose to read into the poetry under his eye. Neither cared for nor sought coherence or a resolution of contradictions in what they read, but only for the glints that illuminated their own intuitions. Emerson and Thoreau were, then, "mystics," but mystics who were, in Carpenter's phrase, "distinctively occidental, protestant, modern." They rejected the traditional assumptions that the mystical experience was an end in itself and that all other experience was valueless. On the contrary, Thoreau foreshadowed the strategy of civil disobedience adopted so much later by Gandhi (who read Thoreau in his South African days). Emerson, far from trying to escape the world, sought to become the most penetrating critic of his society and in his "stress on the need of action for the true understanding of ideas and the instrumental value of ideas for rebuilding the world," foreshadowed in his own way the pragmatism of William James and the instrumentalism of John Dewey.[9] Emerson's doctrine of personal intuition, Carpenter goes on, provided a "halfway house between religious dogmatism and the methods of scientific investigation." Finding that any religion afraid of science "dishonors God and commits suicide," Emerson rejected ordinary morality. "To science there is no poison, to botany no weed, to chemistry no dirt." Emerson reached for the ultimate conception of a disinterested, impersonal God, to whom human life and death, good and evil, shame and fame, are all one or all nothing. For these themes, so alien to the central ideas of the Judaic-Christian tradition, he found some reinforcing sanction in the ancient Indian texts. They form a bridge between him and many modern men of science who share similar thoughts and among whom also there are not a few readers of the Vedic scriptures.

It remains difficult to identify a specifically Indian thread in the multipatterned fabric of Emerson and his friends. Some Hindu writers have enthusiastically claimed Emerson as one of their own, but

[9] Carpenter, *op. cit.*, pp. 166 ff.

the facts seem to be that he and the other Concordians rejected or ignored much more than they took from these sources and, in any case, absorbed their gleanings into wholes of many different parts. Emerson found himself at home among some passages from which he freely borrowed, while to others, and to the heart of the philosophic system, he remained alien, attracted by the Infinite but too deeply committed to the Individual ever to travel too far from the world of men. But unlike most of their contemporaries and unlike a great many important people today, the Transcendentalists did not, at any rate, restrict their view of man's world or its intellectual treasures to the shores of the Mediterranean and the Atlantic. At least in the realm of ideas, they pioneered the breaking down of the parochialism of American man. When it comes, however, to tracing survivals of the Indian influence in their work, the showings become wispier than ever.

In the realm of ideas as such, it simply disappeared. Professor Norman Brown says that Emerson "contributed Indian ideas to American thought but in the successive generations of transmission Americans lost sight of the Indian source." [10] Transcendentalism itself, which had shown no interest in forming a cult or fellowship to perpetuate or practice its beliefs, disappeared with the Transcendentalists. Their influence, however, did brush onto many others in many different ways, and sometimes their borrowings from Asia figured directly or indirectly in these encounters. One of Walt Whitman's biographers says that it was Henry Thoreau who led the poet to dip into Oriental literature. One visible effect turned up years later in the poem Whitman wrote to celebrate the opening of the Suez Canal, a song he sang to celebrate the meeting of East and West.[11] It has also been

[10] Brown, *op. cit*, p 264.
[11] An excerpt
    Passage O soul to India
    Eclaircise the myths Asiatic, the primitive fables . . .
    The far-darting beams of the spirit, the unloos'd dreams,
    The deep-diving bibles and legends,
    The daring plots of the poets, the elder religions,
    O you temples fairer than lilies pour'd over by the rising sun!
    O you fables spurning the known, eluding the hold of the known, mounting to heaven!
    You lofty and dazzling towers, pinnacled, red as roses, burnished with gold!
    Towers of fables immortal fashion'd from mortal dreams!
    You too I welcome and fully the same as the rest!
    You too with joy I sing!

said, for another example, that Mary Baker Eddy, founder of Christian Science, developed at least an acquaintance with some Indian texts and ideas, either from her contact with Bronson Alcott or from other Transcendentalists. Some quotations from Hindu sources appeared in the first editions of her work *Science and Health*, but these subsequently disappeared and do not figure in the texts used by the Christian Science Church today.[12]

In Hindu literature, especially in the Bhagavadgita, the Emersonians had found a measure of flexibility which enabled them to choose freely among many alternative interpretations. They appear to have seen Buddhism as a somewhat "chillier" doctrine more single-mindedly committed to the negation of life. But somewhat later more became known of Buddhism. Its distinction from Hinduism was more clearly seen and its real or alleged similarities to Christianity noticed, discussed, and argued. In time, Buddhism, rather than Hinduism, became the focus of interest and controversy far wider than any ever provoked on this subject by the Concordians. It was one of the Concord group, however, Bronson Alcott, who contributed to this popularization of the issues by promoting the American publication of Sir Edwin Arnold's famous poetical narrative of the life of Gautama Buddha, *The Light of Asia* This work, published in England in 1879, appeared in the United States the next year [13]

By this time, the searching of souls, the redefinition of religious values, the re-examination of the idea of a single revealed truth through Christianity had spread to much wider circles. The appearance of Max Muller's essays on comparative religion and of James Freeman Clarke's *Ten Great Religions* (in 1871) had already done a great deal to spread the discussion to broader segments of the more literate publics on both sides of the Atlantic. Arnold's long poem, colorful, vivid, dramatic, learned, was high in the literary style of the period. It helped carry the whole matter widely beyond the precincts of scholarly discussion to the pulpits and the public prints Its particular appeal and the arguments over its implications for Christians gave this book a stunning popular success During

[12] Cf Wendell Thomas, *Hinduism Invades America*, New York, 1930, pp. 229–31 I am indebted for a careful check of this fact to Robert Peel, Committee on Publication, First Church of Christ, Scientist, Boston, Massachusetts

[13] A detailed discussion of this work and its historical and intellectual setting will be found in Brooks Wright, *Sir Edwin Arnold, a Literary Biography*, Ph D. thesis, Harvard, 1950, Part III

the next twenty years, *The Light of Asia* went through eighty-three countable American editions, regular and pirated, representing, Brooks Wright estimates, somewhere between 500,000 and 1,000,000 copies. By the end of the century, a good deal less diligence was going into soul-searching The changing spirit of the times sapped the issues of their relevance and stripped Arnold's poem of its popular appeal. It remained a matter of interest thereafter for much smaller numbers of interested persons and for the tiny groups which formed themselves at the fringes of the controversy to embrace theosophy or other like cults. We learn from Wright that it was made into a cantata and opera in Europe in 1891, into a play produced in California in 1919 and repeated on Broadway for twenty-three performances by Walter Hampden as late as 1928, and into a moving picture made by a German company in India that year, which had one private showing in the United States, in Boston, a year later. The poem has remained in print,[14] but its fame and the renown of its author, so great and wide in their day, have in this time almost completely evaporated. It may or may not be a salient comment on *The Light of Asia*'s durability to report that among the 181 people interviewed for this study it was mentioned by only one.

Religious preoccupations aside, intellectual interests relating to India remained extremely limited through this entire time. The American Oriental Society, founded at Boston in 1843, was the continuing center for the work of a tiny, though often highly distinguished group of scholars whose fields lay in the antiquities, the languages, the philology, and philosophy of the ancients In other fields there was no interest at all. Bernard Stern reports that between 1846 and 1900 the file of Smithsonian monographs included not a single title relating to India In the volumes of the American Historical Review between 1895 and 1900, there were no articles on India and only two book reviews [15]

Out of the religious controversies, however, our own century inherited a number of small cults of devotees to various versions of Hinduism and Buddhism. One of the first of these movements was the Theosophical Society, founded in 1875 by Mrs Helen Blavatsky

[14] It appears in its entirety in Lin Yutang's Modern Library compilation, *The Wisdom of China and India*, New York, 1942 A paperback edition, published in the United States in 1949, has appeared on American bookstalls under the imprint of the Jaico Publishing Company of Bombay and Calcutta

[15] Stern, *op cit*, pp 13, 14

and Henry Olcott, a group which not long afterward transferred its activities to India, where it later came under the leadership of Mrs. Annie Besant. Another more direct and more persistent Hindu countermissionary effort began with the visit of the Hindu leader Swami Vivekenanda to the Parliament of Religions held at the Exposition in Chicago in 1893 An obscure and rather turgidly controversial literature exists about this visit and the claims made for it. Vivekenanda made a colorful impression on some people at Chicago and lectured elsewhere in the country to small and avid audiences. After his return to India, his conquests were somewhat extravagantly described. He was quoted as saying that his doctrines were well on the way to winning a majority of English-speaking people, indeed, were "flooding the world." This provoked angry rebuttals by American churchmen. Various American dignitaries called Vivekenanda's claims "preposterous . . . simply silly." The recriminations passed into an exchange of compliments about the contending religions themselves. The swami was quoted as saying that Christianity was but a "patchy imitation . . . a collection of little bits from the Indian mind." Americans called Hindu India "the most stupendous fortress and citadel of ancient error and idolatry now in the world," and charged that Hinduism "benumbs the religious faculty, deadens the conscience . . ."[16] Hinduism did not quite conquer America, but the Vedanta Society, founded here by Vivekenanda at the time, has survived and maintains small groups and publications in a few large American cities.

Vivekenanda was followed to the United States by other touring swamis, not all of whom confined their efforts to the upper planes of spirituality. This was a migration of Indians, said an Indian writer in 1910, "who went in for the trade of spiritualists, clairvoyants, mind readers, professors of psychic knowledge, astrologers, and palmists."[17] Such individuals became somewhat more familiar fixtures in parts of the American scene, finding a place among the cultists of southern California, in some big cities, in side shows and carnivals, where sometimes it was not necessary to be an Indian but simply to have a turban, a robe, and a facile mind, to play the

[16] Cf. *Swami Vivekenanda and his Guru With Letters from Prominent Americans on the alleged progress of Vedantism in the United States*, Christian Literature Society for India, London and Madras, 1897.
[17] Quoted by E R Schmidt, *American Relations with South Asia, 1900–1940*, Ph D thesis, University of Pennsylvania, 1955, p 277

necessary role. These antics have made most thoughtful Indians wince, but the success stories of these individuals, filtering through the gauze of great distance and ignorance, are said to have added to the notion in India that Hinduism enjoyed a considerable success in America. If this is true, it becomes another of the many cruel little paradoxes of this history: what some Indians were seeing as evidence of India's spiritual conquest of America was in reality the stuff of a stereotype, still strongly held by many today, of Indian fakirs as fakers, as phony mystics, charlatans parading as swamis preying on the gullible, counting their victims mainly among "hyper-susceptible women" or, in another writer's phrase, among "the disconsolate and the mentally unemployed."

Such, virtually in the sum, were the bits and pieces of Indian religious or ideological influence brought to bear on Americans by Indians directly or by Indian thought via translated texts from the earliest contacts until the advent and impact of Gandhi and Gandhism in the last thirty years. In its more serious aspects, this influence—in the form of any direct heritage from the past—was all but invisible in the minds of the members of our present panel of interviewees. The relatively small number who reacted positively to Indian religious ideas did so not because they had learned about it through Emerson or Arnold but because, in varying degrees, they reacted in the same way or at least in the same spirit to the same stimuli. Such individuals were relatively quite rare, and much less common than those with strong impressions of the phony cultists and swamis, so many of whom are still with us and some of whom produce reactions of quite a different order. Here we begin to approach the edges of a quite different source of ideas about India and its religions: the American missionaries who tried through all these same many decades to bring the Christian Gospel to India and whose impressions were communicated constantly and over a long period of time to the parishioners at home on whom they depended for support. The picture they communicated in the main was not of the high-minded and spiritual Indian philosopher, it was a picture of the very benighted heathen Hindu.

## 3. *THE VERY BENIGHTED HEATHEN*

THE IMAGE of the very benighted heathen Hindu is perhaps the strongest of all that come to us out of India from the past and it retains its full sharpness up to the present day. It appeared, vivid, clear, and particularized, in the minds of a large majority of our interviewees, 137 out of 181. It was evoked from distant memory or from the last week's issue of *Time*, from pictures and captions in the *National Geographic*, the Ripley cartoons or the Sunday supplements of years ago or of yesterday, out of remembered things that people somewhere said or wrote, or the sharp recall of things and people seen or pictured in India itself.[18]

It could be visual:

> sacred cows roaming the streets; mobs of religious fanatics hurling themselves into the Ganges; naked ascetics, scrawny fakirs on nails, the multiarmed goddess; the burning ghats; the skull-laden figure of Kali; Benares, obscene Hindu sculpture, phallic symbols and erotic carvings on the temples. . . .

It could be a judgment:

> a debased, hopeless sort of religion, a complicated, alien mess; mystic nonsense; stupid taboos, horrible practices in a clutter of cultural dead weights, a benighted, superstitious, fatalistic philosophy; fanatical, barbarous religiosity, the elevation of animal life above the human. . . .

It could be a social commentary:

> caste system, untouchability, child marriage, purdah, suttee; religion as a dragging burden on growth and development, terrific waste from the animal cult, cows and monkeys sacrosanct amid starvation; oppression of ignorance, of religious and caste prejudice; a ridiculous idealization of poverty; religion as a sanction for barriers between people,

---

[18] Robert Ripley, creator of *Believe It or Not*, visited India to offer $100 to $500 for oddities delivered and accepted for display at the Century of Progress Exposition in Chicago of 1933–34 He asked particularly for "the Old Horned Man of Tibet, Fire Worshippers, a troop of fire walkers, ascetics and fakirs, men who hold up their arms, sit on beds of nails, gaze at the sun, hang upside down, etc" Quoted from a consular report, by Schmidt, *op cit*, p. 256. All of these and many others figured prominently in the famous Ripley cartoons seen daily by millions.

between clean and unclean, making for crippling social differences and divisions. . . .

In the panel as a whole, there is probably no single set of views more widely or commonly held than these reactions to popular Hinduism. They can be and are shared by the atheist, the agnostic, and the believer, by the rationalist who rejects mysticism and religiosity wherever he finds it, and by the committed believer who finds in Indian beliefs and customs features that outrage his own. In differing measures this reaction appears in the pragmatist and in the practitioner of (his own) common sense, in the idealist who might value the lofty abstraction more highly than the earthier reality, in the seeker, alienated from his own culture or religion, who finds virtue in another without being quite willing to accept its grosser forms, in the humanist who believes that man's emancipation lies only within himself. This takes in nearly everybody, undoubtedly including a great many of the Indian counterparts of these Americans or Western types. The best-known of these would be Jawaharlal Nehru himself, who has written:

> The spectacle of what is called religion, or at any rate organized religion, in India and elsewhere fills me with horror, and I have frequently condemned it and wished to make a clean sweep of it. Almost always it seems to stand for blind belief and reaction, dogma and bigotry, superstition and exploitation, and the preservation of vested interests . . . Organized religion, whatever its past may have been, today is very largely an empty form devoid of real content. . . . And even where something of value still remains, it is enveloped by other and harmful contents This seems to have happened in our Eastern religions as well as the Western.[19]

There are a few people who consistently believe that *all* roads lead to God and who therefore withhold or temper judgment on human foibles different from their own. There are a few who believe that *no* road leads to God, and that therefore one set of foibles is as good, or as bad, as another. These aside, it seems fair to guess that only the practitioners of a given set of religious practices fully approve or admire what they believe and what they do. No practicing Hindu was included in the present panel, and even if any were, the showing would depend on what kind of Hindu, for there are almost as many different kinds of Hindu as there are, say, kinds of Protestants. A given Indian's attitude toward these aspects of Hinduism, moreover,

[19] *Toward Freedom*, New York, 1942, p 240–41.

may be one thing, and his reaction to Western criticism of them quite another, as the example of Nehru amply indicates.

The religious ideas and practices to which these reactions are addressed are the features of Indian culture which seem to be the most different from our own, so different, often, that the normal culture-bound reaction to a difference-in-kind is more than usually sharp Of course even in the case of popular Hinduism this inevitably involves a certain cultural myopia. The American whose common sense is outraged by Indian superstitions may be far from outraged by the superstitions which persist in his own society. He may find some Hindu rites strange beyond acceptance, even though he may find nothing odd (much less laughable or ridiculous) in his own not uncommon piety toward the mystic, mysterious, or simply garish rites and trimmings of some of our secret or public fellowships and societies or of some of our religions. It does not require extraordinary detachment to discover irony in some Americans' criticisms of the marriage customs in other cultures, of religious or caste prejudices, or of religion as a sanction for barriers making for conflict between people, or in a Christian's scorn for a "ridiculous idealization of poverty," for the rite of baptism as practiced on the Ganges shore, or for the concept or practice of unquestioning faith, resignation, renunciation, self-denial, and even asceticism. It may indeed be precisely the intrusive sense of these parallels, of values somehow deformed, that accounts for some of the violence of the reaction.

These reactions to popular Hinduism nevertheless do have a wide currency. They are rooted in deep cultural beds They recur in all kinds of people and reappear in generation after generation. The Americans with whom we deal here faithfully and strikingly reproduce the responses common among the Americans who began to go to India nearly a century and a half ago, taking with them all their strongly fixed cultural and religious convictions and bent on persuading Indians to accept these convictions in place of their own. A comparison of our current collection of reactions on this subject and the record written by others in the past shows quite arrestingly how an entire complex of attitudes and feelings occurs in like groups of people widely separated in time and circumstance.

This body of views is almost unanimously negative in spirit in both past and present. But a few counterparts of a different sort do also emerge One study quotes, for example, the remarks of a former Chicago mayor named Carter H. Harrison who toured India in the

1880's. Hinduism seemed to him "a slavish faith, blind and superstitious," but, on the other hand,

> it started before history, in the mysterious and fantastic realm of the past, it was eternal and fascinating. Who can say my way is right and yours is wrong? One thing we can determine—that charity to the opinion of others and kindness and goodwill are included in the teachings of all religions which acknowledge a supreme ruler

Here, for comparison, are the remarks of a businessman in our panel:

> I was opposed to any attempt to Christianize Hindus. I was happy if they stayed good Hindus. There must be something in a religion that gets people to worship as they do . . I remained a good Baptist through all this and did not attempt to reconcile all these things. Whether a man is Buddhist, Hindu, Muslim, if he's a good one, that's all right with me. I get something out of my religion, they get something out of theirs

These are unusual examples, and it is not accidental that one comes from a politician and the other a businessman. The record made by American missionaries in India in their letters, books, sermons, and lectures, from the beginning down almost to our own time, is in large part dominated by a powerful sense of revulsion at Hindu practices. A mild example would be the complaint, in 1852, about "the deplorable ignorance and stubborn prejudices of the Hindus, together with the caste system, their entire absence of all correct principles, and finally their moral degradation" The Hindus, one might more commonly have heard, were "lifetime liars and worshippers of a stupendous system of carnal idolatry." Their temples would be "ornamented with all the orders of infernal architecture, displaying all the sins in the human figure and exhibiting evil spirits under the significant emblems of serpents, toads, etc" Letters prepared for Sunday school children stressed "mountains of superstitions," "the heathens in darkness," and "the Hindu mind." The whole literature was filled, Bernard Stern remarks, "with a positively morbid preoccupation with temple prostitutes and lingamites," with lurid illustrations, and in general with material more titillating than inspirational. Indian religions, said a writer in the *Christian Century* in 1905, were "debauched with deeds of lust and blood. . . Many of the Indian deities, given to lustful amours, are especially worshipped by the people... It is not surprising that religion in India is not only divorced from morality but married to vice . . . much indecency exists in India

## THE INDIANS

under the guise of religion, many of the temple dancing girls are merely consecrated prostitutes, and in many cases respectable women are led to lives of shame." [20]

The continuing missionary stress on this image of the horror and evil and sexuality in Indian life and religion was rarely challenged until well after the turn of the century. In 1907, a YMCA report suggested that "the idea of Christian superiority and consequent degradation of everything that was 'heathen' was having a detrimental effect on missionary work." Missionaries were urged to avoid these disparaging contrasts, "however true in themselves." Churchmen were feeling the impact of the "higher criticism" of the time, of increasing pressure for a less evangelical approach and greater stress on good works, and most of all, of the dawning awareness of political and economic problems of the Indian people. Certain shifts began to occur in missionary emphasis, at least in some quarters and for some individuals. There were notable persons, Robert Hume, Jabez Sunderland, Bishop Frederick Fisher, Eli Stanley Jones, who sought common grounds with Indians on the basis of a more sympathetic grasp of Indian feelings and problems. But Robert Hume came into conflict with most of his fellows for developing an early sympathy for burgeoning Indian nationalism, a sympathy which the majority of missionaries hardly shared. Bishop Fisher had to resign his bishopric to fight for his belief in the more rapid Indianization of the church in India. Eli Stanley Jones had to part company with many of his coreligionists to maintain that the Sermon on the Mount gave him sanction for sympathy with non-Christian religion. His ashrams made most Christian missionaries acutely uncomfortable. For a committed religionist to yield the principle of the exclusiveness or at least the superiority of his particular truth is to yield a great deal and to gain in return much painful confusion, a state of affairs not unfamiliar in some of the history of Protestantism.[21]

[20] Quotations from various missionary sources are from Stern, *op cit*, Chapter VI See also his extensive bibliography, Schmidt, *op cit*; and from Robert I. Crane, "The Development of the American View of India, as Seen in Certain Religious Periodicals Published in the United States, 1897–1931," MA thesis, American University, Washington, D C., 1943

[21] This situation among the Protestants brought a sharp though unwittingly ironic jibe from a writer in *Catholic World* in 1924 "Hinduism like Protestantism doesn't know its own mind, it knows neither what it is nor where it stands. ... Like the Protestant, the Hindu can give no positive definition of his religion, he does not know what to believe and what not to believe Moreover, the Indian is proud of his culture and does not want to admit that any part of it could be at

Soon it became necessary, at least for some, to ask the odd question: Was the heathen vile or not? Bishop Heber had written back in 1819 and numberless churchgoing generations had since sung the famous lines about the call that had come "from Greenland's icy mountains, from India's coral strand" to "deliver their land from error's chain " And the second verse said:

> What though the spicy breezes
> Blow soft o'er Ceylon's isle;
> Though every prospect pleases,
> And only man is vile·
> In vain with lavish kindness
> The gifts of God are strown,
> The heathen in his blindness
> Bows down to wood and stone.

Editors of some hymn books now looked twice at these lines and began to wonder about their appropriateness. The heathen in his blindness was still bowing down to wood and stone in the 1916 edition of the Episcopal *New Hymnal,* but he ceased doing so in the revised edition issued in 1940. The offending lines disappeared from the 1912 edition of the Congregational *Pilgrim Hymnal,* reappeared in 1931, and in a forthcoming new edition will disappear again, along with the whole hymn, regarded by the present committee of editors as reflecting an "old-fashioned" concept of the church's mission.[22] To be sure the matter could not be settled in the hymnbooks. It seemed to remain, for individual missionaries, a function of age and outlook

Generally speaking, one is told in missionary circles, the older the missionary the viler the heathen. But some of the elders and most of the more youthful carriers of the Word are now much less sure or hold distinctly different views. In the vastly changed times of the present, they have trouble defining their missions, often to themselves All the certainties of their fathers, the rectitude and

---

fault, therefore he will not renounce his religion Then, too, the Indian is bewildered by the babble of Christian sects in India Each one claims to be right and it is obvious that all can't be. This is the great obstacle to Catholicism in India." Quoted by Crane, *op cit*, pp 108–09

[22] An examination of hymnals, undertaken at our suggestion by John D. Raciappa, a student at the Episcopal Theological Seminary of Cambridge, Massachusetts, disclosed the interesting fact that "From Greenland's Icy Mountains" appears in its entirety in fifteen hymnals still currently in use, appears with the offending verse omitted in seven hymnals, and does not appear at all in nine

self-assurance—doctrinal, personal, or political—have largely disappeared, casualties of the collapse of Western superiority that accompanied the collapse of Western power. Missionaries who continue to work in India, if many do, will transmit to their constituents at home images of India and Indians, it seems sure, quite different from those of the past.

But the past remains unerased and its cost still unpaid. We have still to ask how much of the missionary imprint of these years was actually found on the minds of the Americans tapped for this study The only answer we can make to this question has to be based on limited though clear evidence· the amount and kind of missionary-linked memories brought to the surface in the course of the interviews themselves.

American missionary enterprise in Asia reached its peaks during the childhood or young years of most of the present group of interviewees. The larger and certainly the more widely known part of this enterprise lay in China, but the mission establishment in India was not much smaller. The number of American missionaries there rose from 394 in 1892 steeply to 1,025 in 1903 and on up to its peak of 2,478 in 1922.[23] Of the total estimated American investment in India of $50,500,000 in the 1930's, $22,858,000 lay in mission and religious institutions, schools, hospitals, and churches [24] This money had come, dollar by dollar, penny by penny, from the folks at home. To raise it, mission societies, councils, committees, and traveling missionary envoys carried on an unremitting program of education and appeal in all the churches open to them. It would be in this setting that young Americans would hear, often for the first time, something about India, its peoples, its religions, of the needs they had to help meet, of the work to which it became their duty to contribute. When they were asked what they could remember from years past that was linked in any way to Asia, a certain number of our panelists almost instantly uncovered the scratches left on their minds on those Sunday mornings long ago. They showed up small, but by no means invisible.

We have already mentioned the fact that of our total of 181, 137 indicated that they had been repelled in some degree by Hindu

[23] Figures supplied by R. Pierce Beaver, Missionary Research Library, New York
[24] Schmidt, *op cit.*, from government sources, p. 393.

religious ideas, practices, customs. This number was larger than the total put together of all who remembered missionaries in any connection whatever. It includes, of course, a certain number who because of their own particular religious backgrounds would have had little contact or none at all with missionaries or mission work. An uncertain discount must no doubt also be made for those who may simply have forgotten, who may have so ardently wished themselves elsewhere on those dim Sundays that they never heard or registered the things that were said. Whatever the size of this allowance, it would still seem clear that much the larger number of those repelled by Hindu religiosity did not receive their impressions from missionaries, at least not directly. Other sources were ample, in print or picture, person, or personal experience. It seems reasonable to write down the majority of them as Americans reacting with the same general cultural and emotional dispositions to the same things in the same way as their predecessors and counterparts did in the past.

At the same time, in our remaining cases there is some plain evidence of continuity and connection. There were altogether 123 individuals who mentioned missionaries or talk about the mission world among their early associations with Asia. Of these only 48 specifically linked this missionary recall to India. Of these 48, 23 remembered simply that the matter had to do with India and no more than that; they attached no quality to their remembered impressions. In the last group of 25, the recall from the past had all sorts of phrases and feelings trailing after it. It is here that we catch a glimpse of the way in which some missionary attitudes were transmitted with sufficient vigor to create impressions that could survive a lifetime of other preoccupations and could be touched to life by a single question.

Four of these recollections were neuter, or almost neuter, in feeling-tone. One remembered hearing of the Indians simply as "a people in great need of help"; another the mention of "great poverty, human misery, suffering" Another called up a reference to "Gandhi" and the "tremendous hunger of a great mass of people." The last recalled simply an impression about "heat."

Four others—and only four—remembered positive, friendly, or admiring remarks by missionaries. The Indians, one recalled hearing, were "poor, needy, good, simple, hardworking, worthy people," another that they were "fine deserving people." A third had gathered a feeling of "appreciation of Indian culture." The last remembered a missionary who had told him that Indians "didn't wear shoes," that the country was "hot, wet, and dry," and that he "liked India."

Seventeen, by contrast, brought up from their churchgoing memories images that were largely bizarre or terrible, horrifying or evil, or at least unbelievably odd:

> talk of poverty linked to filth, dirt, disease, superstition, a people oppressed by a backward religion, the evil caste system and the untouchables; different, not good in the Christian way, idol-worshippers, snake charmers, leprosy, child marriage, darkness, ignorance, turbans, a bed of spikes, mystics, can throw a rope up and climb it, ride elephants, tigers invade villages every other night and run off with people; snakes, forests, wild animals, woke up one night to find a cobra on his bed, benighted mystics, famine, poverty, wealth, India more heathen than China. . . .

To recapitulate in more tabular form:

| | |
|---|---|
| Total number of interviewees | 181 |
| With negative attitudes on Indian religion, customs | 137 |
| Total with some measure of missionary recall | 123 |
| With missionary recall pertaining specifically to India | 48 |
| Missionary recall without descriptive phrases | 23 |
| Missionary recall with negative images of India | 17 |
| Missionary recall with positive images of India | 4 |
| Missionary recall with neuter images of India | 4 |

It does not seem impossible to suggest that in the proportion of 48 to 123 we get a rough approximation of the *amount* of missionary communication about India to reach churchgoers in the generation just past; and that in the proportions of 4 neuter to 4 positive to 17 negative, we get a glimpse of the *kind* of communication that passed along these channels and, for better or worse, left its mark. These figures are of course wholly inconclusive, but their essence is not.

There have been many sources other than the missionaries for American impressions of the benighted heathen Hindu. In the second half of the nineteenth century, long before all but the oldest of our panelists were born, there was a large and popular literature of travel accounts, novels, and diaries touching India.[25] In a chapter reviewing this literature in detail, Bernard Stern finds that with rare exceptions, their "observations identically paralleled those expressed

[25] E.g., Mark Twain, *Following the Equator*, Hartford, 1897, pp. 345–609.

in missionaries' works." The earliest known American film about India was a Thomas A. Edison documentary reel called *Hindoo Fakir*, first shown in 1902.[26] The literature of the time reproduces all the types and outlooks we know much more familiarly from more recent times, from the distinguished public servant like William Seward—who concluded after a visit in 1871 that until India grasped the belief in Christianity's one God, it would remain "incapable of a firm advance in knowledge and civilization"—to two earnest ladies who visited India in 1890–91 and compiled a widely noted report on "organized vice and trafficking in women" in India. This last was almost a direct antecedent of a similar work that appeared some thirty years later and is familiar to many members of our present panel: the once famous—or infamous—*Mother India*, by Katherine Mayo.

*Mother India* appeared in 1927, the product of a six-months' stay in the country. It was a scalding and horrified recital of examples of child marriage, extreme caste practices, the plight of the untouchables, backward conditions of health and sanitation. Written on a single plane of total revulsion and narrowly focused bias, it had no room for qualifications, for examples of other aspects of Indian life, or indeed, for any other side of the story whatsoever. The most salient point made by the book's more thoughtful Indian and Western critics was that while it did not lie in its main particulars, it lied monumentally as a whole. It made or allowed the reader to make the most sweeping generalizations from its selection of examples. Any reader of the book was justified in coming away from it, for example, with the notion that every female in India above the age of five was the enslaved and brutally maltreated victim of the male population which consisted in its entirety of active, frustrated, or exhausted sex maniacs. This is what led Gandhi to call it a "drainpipe study," although he advised Indian readers of the book to take some of its facts seriously into account. Katherine Mayo wrote out of an unrestrained Anglophilism; the only decent people she encountered in India were the British and those few Indians she met who had been made over in the British image; the only decency she discovered was British in origin, inspiration, and practice. She also appropriated a number of the cruder British attitudes: she loved the princes, admired the Muslims, especially those hardy

[26] Dorothy B Jones, *op cit*, p. 51.

THE INDIANS 269

fighting men of the Northwest Frontier, and utterly despised the Hindus; and she made absolutely no bones about any of this at all.

Katherine Mayo died in 1940, so it has been impossible to seek from her directly any clues to the sources either of her Anglophilism or her Hinduphobia. She is described as having grown up with the "anti-British" notions associated with life in the shadow of Bunker Hill Her view of England was radically changed by a visit there during the First World War, when she acquired a permanent admiration for the virtues of British society, especially at its upper levels. She was obviously a woman of great restless energy, a spinster with a penchant for riding her prejudices into battle wherever it conveniently offered Her earlier career was marked by controversies over writing she had done on such varied subjects as state police systems, the YMCA's role in France in wartime, the political reforms of the Wilson administration in the Philippines and the role of the Catholic Church there. The trip to India was more or less accidental, and neither she nor her lifelong companion, Miss Moyca Newell, had any previous notions about the country, unless you count the fact that they had been sorely irked by the anti-British statements of various Indian lecturers in the United States in the early 1920's Miss Mayo went to India to look into conditions for herself, and in what obviously struck her as fetid sexuality on a vast scale, she found her most congenial and successful subject

*Mother India* became a sensation in the United States, in Great Britain, and in India It became the center of a storm that raged for half a dozen years, in the newspapers, the periodical press, and on the lecture platforms in all three countries. It provoked some ten books in reply by Indian authors who tried, with varying success, to turn Mayo's technique on the United States, focusing exclusively on some of the more grisly features of American life. In self-defense, Miss Mayo went through the nine volumes of testimony taken by a commission of inquiry into child marriage which sat in India following the furore raised by her book In 1931 she published another book, simply called *Volume Two*, devoted mainly to excerpts of testimony by Indians saying, in *their* way, many of the same things she had been so bitterly attacked for saying in *her* way. She simply could not understand the difference.

The controversy created an embarrassing dilemma for many American missionaries associated with work in India Some leading church figures instantly denounced the book as a libel. In fact, a great many missionaries found to their great discomfort that the book simply said what they had been saying for years and presented what they believed to be an essentially factual picture of Indian life. The Mayo issue was made peculiarly painful for missionaries because for many Indians, Mayo's India was indistinguishable from the missionary's India and the Englishman's India. As one writer shrewdly comments. "Had it appeared before 1900 a large body of missionaries would have approved of Miss Mayo's book." [27] The editor of the *Indian Social Reformer* saw the Mayo book as "nothing more than a reflection of the state of the Western mind with regard to India. The Western mind has scarcely ever viewed India in the light of truth and reason . . . The myth about India being the place of untold treasure has been exploded. The current one is that India is the land of strange mysteries, contrasts, peoples, and civilizations. This myth can be blamed on the missionaries and the British." [28] Attackers and defenders of *Mother India* continued to throw hardened missiles of ill-digested and regurgitated charges and countercharges at each other in a melee that lasted for years, generating ill feeling that has long survived the book itself or the arguments about it. *Mother India* was gradually forgotten everywhere but in India, where its name became and remains a shorthand epithet for whatever Indians regard as Western slander and dishonesty about Indian life, a symbol, as an Indian colleague describes it, for "what *they* think of *us*." [29]

In the course of all this history, *Mother India* went through 27 editions in the United States for a total of 256,697 copies,[30] by far the most widely sold book about India in our century. The wordage in press and pulpit on *Mother India* must have been immense, and its word-of-mouth fame, if sparked only by its more titillating pas-

[27] Schmidt, *op cit.*, p 265
[28] May 11, 1929, quoted by Schmidt, *ibid.*, p 262
[29] Just how painful the Mayo episode was for missionaries with the "newer" orientation was indicated by the discovery that a study of missionary writings covering that period simply omitted all mention of the Mayo controversy I wrote to the author asking him why this was so His reply "I cannot say that I recall the circumstances surrounding my omission of comment on the Mayo incident I was skimming very quickly over the 'typical' articles with the 'older orientation' and was concentrating my attention . on the articles that indicated a different kind of interest in India It is possible that I had an unconscious block on Mayo and therefore didn't 'see' mention of her As you know, India-wallas snarled at the mention of the Mayo name and I was no exception. Thus it is possible that I didn't 'see' the articles or that I refused to 'dignify' them with mention "
[30] Figures from Miss Moyca Newell and Harcourt, Brace & Co , publishers

sages, must have carried far indeed. All this occurred twenty-five to thirty years ago, when most of our present interviewees were between the ages of fifteen and thirty. For whatever it may be worth as a comment on the transit of glory, our showing is that 46 of our 181 interviewees, or roughly one-fourth, mentioned *Mother India*. Their recall of it ranged from the dim to the precise. Some remembered only the name: they had heard of it but did not know exactly what it was One of these individuals who felt he had to guess, guessed that it was some sympathetic portrayal or other of India—what else was one to think of a book with the word "mother" in the title? Others knew it had been a highly controversial book but were not sure what the controversy had been about. A larger number automatically associated *Mother India* with *child marriage* or with a generally critical attitude about Indian customs. Among these there began to appear a few who suggested that *Mother India* might have been responsible for some of the notions they had acquired or retained about caste, untouchability, and the low status of Indian women. Finally, there was a small group—and here we are among people directly and specifically concerned with India—who remembered quite precisely what the book was about and spoke of it either approvingly or disapprovingly according to their general predilections.

Sparse as it was, this awareness of *Mother India* was greater in the group as a whole than of any other literary source relating to India except for the work of Rudyard Kipling.

## 4. *THE LESSER BREED*

THE *benighted heathen* and the *lesser breed* are one and the same. The difference lies in the view of the beholder and depends on the relative sizes of the religious and secular peepholes through which he looks upon the rest of humanity. It is presumably plain that the propositions are twin: only a lesser breed could be so benightedly heathen; heathen so benighted must necessarily be of a lesser breed Indeed, if there is any nuance at all, it disappears in the source of the phrase itself. It comes from Kipling's "Recessional," his hymn to the God of our fathers "beneath whose awful hand we hold/ Dominion over palm and pine." It is in this poem that the most widely heard of all tumult and shouting in our language dies, that the best-known of all Captains and Kings depart. Here too, sinning in their failure to hold Kipling's God in awe, are *the lesser breeds without the Law.*

Kipling is not best remembered for the posture of religious humility he strikes in this poem. But even this humility is not a denial but an affirmation of the whole sense and spirit of the White Man's Burden; he demands only that it be borne with a proper respect for its divine sanction. Where it occurs in the "Recessional," the phrase *lesser breeds without the Law* may not even have meant what anybody would expect Kipling to mean by such a phrase. George Orwell has suggested that he was "almost certainly" referring here to the Germans who had embarked at that time (1897) on a peculiarly lawless jag of imperialist expansion [31] It almost does not matter, for the phrase has passed into our language in terms wholly in tune with Kipling's essential spirit: it expresses for all whom it fits the assumed attitude of social, racial, and physical superiority of the white Westerner toward the nonwhite, non-Christian peoples whom he subdued and held under his power in the years ending now.

Kipling's well-known contempt for the Hindu has been shared by a great many Westerners, both English and American, before Kipling's time and since, including a certain number of our present panelists. To a certain extent there has been a borrowing or an absorption of some of these attitudes by Americans from Englishmen, prominently including Kipling himself. But Bernard Stern's sharp-eyed culling of the writings of American travelers, journalists, and officials, as well as missionaries, during the nineteenth century long before Kipling shows that the record is too long and too full for any easy acceptance of this explanation. The same ideas, the same images, the same reactions, and often even the same words in Stern's century-old quotations from scores of works recur again and again in our notes of interviews with Americans held only yesterday, Americans who almost certainly never read any of these old books and whose recall of Kipling is usually too dim and sparse to account wholly by itself for the coincidence and the sharpness of their views.

The picture of the despised Hindu assumes many forms and particulars It can be expressed with easy contempt, as in the long-lived limerick.

[31] George Orwell, "Rudyard Kipling," in *Dickens, Dali and Others*, New York, 1946, pp 141–142.

> The poor benighted Hindu,
> He does the best he kin do,
>   Sticks to his caste,
>   From first to last,
> And for trousers just lets his skin do.

It also comes blistered and blistering from a collision of cultural values, habits, ideas It has to do with all the emotionally charged judgments and reactions toward the benighted heathen with which we have already dealt. It reproduces, in the Indian setting, most of the features of Westerners' reaction to the faceless mass already described in relation to the Chinese. It has to do with the conquered Indian, seen as unvital and weak as well as backward and all but subhuman It also has to do with the Indian as a dark-skinned man.

THE FACELESS MASS: In India, as in China, an overwhelming impact is made by the sheer numbers of people. Here are its constantly recurring terms.

> teeming masses, teeming cities, teeming population, teeming millions; swarming masses, great masses, vast, tremendous, enormous masses; crowds on the streets, on the Ganges, in the cities, numbers, density, multitudes, swarming, immense, dense population; people, mobs of people, sea, hordes, millions of people; nobody knows how many there are on this human anthill. . . .

Some see it as a problem, *the population problem*, sometimes *challenging*, more often *staggering* or even *insoluble*. A great many others attach to their view of the mass their own vividly fearful images of terrible poverty:

> emaciated people, diseases, ribs showing, shriveled bellies, corpses, children with fly-encircled eyes, with swollen stomachs, children dying in the streets, rivers choked with bodies, people living, sleeping, lying, dying on the streets in misery, beggary, squalor, wretchedness, a mass of semiaboriginal humanity. . . .

In some cases the direct impact of this massed misery is emotionally intolerable. The first impression especially strikes a hard blow, it comes most often in memories of the gateway cities of Calcutta and Bombay:

> that ride from Dum Dum into Calcutta; the streets of Calcutta made

me physically sick; after seeing the slums of Bombay I felt only horror at the luxurious life led by myself and my Indian friends, I broke down and cried on my bed after the first shock of poverty in Bombay. . . .

Adjustment has to follow, and it could assume forms as various as the varieties of personality. It could involve a sense of guilt that would never wholly recede and might even reshape a person's whole life thereafter. It could cause shame that sooner or later had to be rationalized into some other emotion in order to be tolerated. It could provoke only pity, and sometimes, for some people, the line between pity and contempt is thin, fine, almost invisible, often not there at all:

> I almost despise the people, have contempt for them; feel irritation, impatience, aversion, disdain, resentment . . .

For others, especially those at a greater distance from this great faceless wretched mass, the impact is much less felt because its existence is a fact beyond acceptable reality. This unbelieving rejection, whether close at hand or remote, often leads to the same result, to the same need to place these faceless masses beyond the knowable human pale, to see them, in short, as the lesser breed without the Law.

THE CONQUERED INDIAN: This is the Indian whom Kipling saw as "new caught, sullen . . . half-devil and half-child." This is also the Indian as a few (3) of our interviewees see him, who has

> always been conquered, always ran away, the country that had never shown strength to defend her rights and herself.

Seen primarily as a servant (by 8), he is

> obsequious, servile, cringing, submissive.

More generally he is marked (for 15) by

> passivity, inertia, docility, despair, lacking vigor, stamina, persistence, lacking initiative, industry, vitality, enterprise, enthusiasm.

The same figure is further particularized (by 23) in these terms.

> like slaves, inert, whipped cur, avoid your eye, hopeless, just stand stoically; masses lying on streets not moving, people lying in gutters who have just given up, accept their fate, starving to death without lifting a finger, beaten down, no spark of gumption, the poorer Hindu

buckling in at the knees, leaden overwhelming misery, only Indians accept suffering like this, no dynamism, no feeling of energy, a broken-spirited people. . . .

Here it is primarily the impression of *weakness* that provokes rejection and contempt Indians (it was said by 13) are

effete, soft, weak, unresilient, timid, no muscles, effeminate, lack virility, are not very good fighters

For some this is strictly an impression of the Indian as a physical being, for others it involves their rejection of the ideas of passivity, negation, submission which they see as central to the Hindu religious and philosophic outlook.[82] Sometimes it extends all the way to a more or less conscious rejection of the idea of Gandhian nonviolence, sometimes it is seized upon as the essential explanation for the Indian policy of so-called "neutralism" in current world affairs in which the American is interested. But it clearly goes farther back and deeper and relates to the value placed in Western society (and especially in Anglo-American society) on power, on strength, on physical prowess.

Until only the day before yesterday, it was always understood and assumed that a small Western military force was more than a match for an Indian (or Chinese, or other Asian) force many times its size. Similarly, the individual Westerner was a muscled giant who could invariably take on whole mobs of puny Asians singlehanded. This superior virtue has been sung and pictured in poem and film over the years· in a moving picture like *Gunga Din*, Victor McLaglen and Cary Grant, as tall, brawny British troopers, are engaged for a good part of the total footage in brawling free-for-alls with dozens

[82] In *Come, My Beloved* (New York, 1953) Pearl Buck writes of an American industrialist visiting India about one hundred years ago who sees how an Indian potter, threatened by an approaching cobra, sits motionless in an attitude of prayer The cobra eventually glides away, and the potter explains that the snake is a god and that it is sinful to kill one. "All the way back to Poona he kept seeing the flattened devilish head of the snake, and between him and it the slender graceful figure of the potter, a good man as even he could see, but one who did not dare kill the snake, the curse, the menace even to his own life, because of his religion. . Religion! Was that religion, being willing to wait for a snake to strike, passive and waiting, no protest, no self-defense? No wonder the people sat upon the barren land, waiting for the rains . ."—pp 29–31. By contrast, Bishop Frederick Fisher, in *That Strange Little Brown Man, Gandhi*, (New York, 1932) tells reverently how Gandhi's mother calmly refused to kill a scorpion that crawled upon her as the frightened boy Gandhi watched.—pp. 8, 9

and scores of Indians whom they hurl around like so many dolls. In pictures like the recent *King of the Khyber Rifles* (1954) it is made clear that one Englishman, even a half-Englishman, is more of a man than a whole recalcitrant tribe. This illusion of superiority dies very hard indeed. In the surviving figure of the weak and puny Indian those who mourn its passing keep alive the ghosts of their own past.

THE LESS LESSER BREED. The built-in Anglo-American reverence for physical prowess has often been generous enough in times past to extend to the foe or subject who proved the rule of Western superiority by being an exception to it. The admired attribute of strength could cancel out or neutralize much else that was despised, especially when the exceptional showing occurred either in the Westerner's service or in an episodic victory over him. East and West might never meet, but there was neither East nor West, sang Kipling, "When two strong men stand face to face, though they come from the ends of the earth!" ("Ballad of East and West"). When Sudanese warriors broke up an English square, they earned a Kipling salute: "You're a pore benighted 'eathen but a first-class fightin' man." ("Fuzzy-Wuzzy"). And of course, though he'd been "belted and flayed," it was Gunga Din's ultimate act of sacrificial heroism for his belters and flayers that made him such a better man This special recognition of vigor and strength is conferred from time to time on Indian troops who loyally served under the officers of the Crown, on warrior castes like the Rajputs and the Mahrattas In our interviews it has occasionally turned up in the form of compliments for the *upstanding Sikhs* or the *Gurkha fighting men*. But most often it appears as part of a generalized prejudice in favor of the Muslim as compared to the Hindu. This generally has to do with the Muslim seen as the more aggressive, more upstanding figure, readier and abler to meet the Westerner on Western terms, willing and able to fight It runs from this to a notion of greater alikeness and to the feeling that compared to Hinduism, Islam is a religion much closer to Christianity. These ideas emerge in 21 of our interviews in the following terms·

> Even the poor Muslim is a vigorous man, while the poor Hindu is buckling in at the knees, Pakistanis seemed energetic Western types, easier to talk to, had a partiality for Muslims, perhaps because, like the British, I felt they were "more like us"; I hear from people that the

THE INDIANS 277

Pakistanis are up and coming, good people, good fighters, whereas the Hindus are said to be mystics, dreamers, hypocrites, I was brought up on Kipling, i e., all Muslims fine, all Hindus unattractive; I like the Muslims better, we have the Old Testament in common with them; Muslim faith is more dynamic, the Muslim believes in one god; never had the disadvantage of the caste system, eats better diet, more masculinity, Muslim is very close to the Christian in faith and loyalties . . .

Some of this language clearly indicates that many of these remarks are quite recent impressions of *Pakistanis*, i.e., citizens of the country that is so much friendlier than India to current American views of the world situation. Several make this quite explicit:

The Pakistanis are ready to stand up and be counted as our friends, the Indians are not, officials here [in Washington] say Pakistanis are much friendlier, personally and politically. . .

These more immediate affinities run quite easily into the older grooves, i e., the Muslims are our friends *because* they are more vigorous people, better fighters, etc., confirming common British impressions that go a long way back and received such explicit form in the works of Kipling [33] The idea of the Muslims as stout, hardy, doughty, superb fighters owes a great deal to the Kiplingesque picture of the Muslim warriors of the Northwest Frontier, wily, treacherous, vicious, but also brave, foolhardy foes who made it possible to sing the praise of the British mettle, an image reproduced after Kipling by a small army of lesser writers and multiplied many times on movie screens by Hollywood.[34]

This strongly stereotyped British preference for the Muslim,

[33] Kipling's sympathies in general, remarks Somerset Maugham, "lay with the Muslims rather than the Hindus . There were qualities in the Muslims that aroused his admiration, he seldom spoke of the Hindus with appreciation. . The Bengali, for instance, was to him a coward, a muddler, a braggart . . ." *Maugham's Choice of Kipling's Best*, New York, 1953, pp vii–viii

[34] E g , *The Black Watch* (1929) in which a British officer, a Muslim aide, and a Muslim force save the Khyber Pass for Britain during World War I The theme of British glory in the frontier wars against the hill tribesmen has all but dominated American film treatment of India ever since the American Mutoscope and Biograph Company in 1903 made a picture called *Charge of the 1st Bengal Lancers* Those Bengal Lancers or their equivalents have charged continuously across American screens year after year, decade after decade Through all the years of the Gandhi-led Congress movement against Britain in India, the only rebellions recognized by Hollywood were those of the hillsmen on the frontiers, in which the British always won for India's greater good and safety Cf Dorothy Jones, *op cit*, pp 55–59.

adopted or reproduced by many Americans, is rooted in a rather complex history of relationships. The British conquered India by breaking the power of the ruling Muslim Moguls, and it was among Muslims that the British in the early days recruited most of their Indian troops. From among these came some of the rebels of the Sepoy Rebellion of a century ago, and while that bloody affair ran its course they were pictured in avidly read British and American accounts as brutish, cruel, and even more wickedly heathenish than the Hindus Seen in this setting, the Muslims were the kind of people, wrote one American, who would "assuredly crucify Jesus afresh on the streets of Delhi were he to come down from Heaven and fall in their power.[35] Said another: "While Hindus are superstitious and credulous, they remain pacific and courteous and intelligent Muslims are the direct opposite in character They are insolent and sensual, the very essence of their religion being hate and malignity. In fact they would have put all non-Muslims to death if it were not for a strong Christian power." [36] But after the British had blown a considerable number of them from the mouths of their cannon as examples and then brought the rest to heel, the Muslim soldier again became a faithful servant of the Queen. Although other martial Indian types were recruited into Britain's Indian army, the Muslims occupied a special place in British affections. Their wilder opposite numbers in the hills of the frontier likewise, in the romantic good-show tradition, could often command the ready or grudging admiration of the British officers who sallied out against them from their remote border forts After the turn of the century, when Hindu-Muslim hostility became a factor in the rise of Indian nationalism, the leadership of the Muslim minority was often cast, or cast itself, in the role of makeweight for the British in their effort to cope with growing Indian recalcitrance. As Indian nationalism became over the years a movement infinitely more formidable than the vest-pocket frontier rebellions, Muslim differences with the Hindu became a major asset for the British and British favor became a useful lever for Muslim leaders. The upper-class Indian Muslim often adapted himself readily and acceptably to the British mold. Both sides profited considerably from a complicated relationship over the years, culminating in mutual pledges and policies that ulti-

[35] Stern, *op cit.*, p. 166.
[36] *Ibid*, p 121.

mately helped bring about partition of the country and the creation of Pakistan.

The "good chap" status won by many Muslims was also achieved, to be sure, by Hindus as well; the Indian civil servant who became more British than the British is a figure that has only now begun to fade. But to achieve this status and this state of mind, the Hindu had to alienate himself from his own traditions to a far greater degree than the Muslim, and the wrench often made him into a good deal less of a pleasant fellow at various stages of his development. Here, from one of our interviews, is one rather unusual man's reading of this relationship:

> When I came to teach in London (in the early 1930's), I was violently pro-Indian and anti-British on general political grounds relating to the status of India. Then I experienced a certain disenchantment Found among the Indian students a top 10 per cent who were first rate but found among the rest an unusually high proportion of twisty, shifty individuals, liars, lacking in dignity in the circumstances of university life However, more contact and reflection made me realize that the Hindu had never really recognized white supremacy, while the Muslim always looked to the British for protection from the Hindu The Muslims were therefore "easier to deal with," i.e, they accepted more of the Britisher's terms of behavior and were therefore, mistakenly, seen as "more honest" I saw, for my part, that the Hindus were more difficult to deal with, were more unpleasant, for reasons I actually valued, their lying and behavior was part of a self-conscious process of resistance.

THE VILLAINOUS INDIAN. There is only one important real-life source for any current image of the Indian as a man of cruel and ugly violence. This is the truly terrifying image of the Indian in the setting of fanatical mob violence and fratricidal massacre, as in the Hindu-Muslim clashes before and during the partition of India and intermittently in mob outbreaks since.[37] Almost all other images of

---

[37] A M Rosenthal, the *New York Times*' able correspondent in India, has reverted often in his dispatches to the "strange flashing stream of violence in Indian life" Cf. "Violence Mars Nehru Mission of Reform" (June 10, 1956), "Nehru Bids India Give Up Violence" (August 16, 1956), and "False Gandhism Plagues Nehru," *New York Times Magazine*, November 4, 1956

The film version of John Masters' *Bhowani Junction* (1956) devotes a good part of its footage to Indian mobs engaged in pillage, arson, murder, and meaningless destruction, all in lurid color

the Indian as villain are synthetic and a good deal less than lifelike.

Mentioned a few times out of snatches remembered from history books, or, more likely, from the pages of George Henty, we hear of the Black Hole of Calcutta or the murderous villains of the Sepoy Rebellion, an event which has been kept alive hardly as history but rather as the setting for innumerable adventure tales or films. The evil or treacherous rajah was already a fixture in American moving pictures when George Arliss played the part in *The Green Goddess* in 1923. He is usually either trying to betray the British (and the best interest of India) by conspiring with the wild men of the hills, or is the leader of some viciously cruel and mysterious secret cult, or has evil designs on the lovely white girl who falls into his clutches, or, often enough, all of these together. There is the villainously savage tribesman himself, wily and bloodthirsty, whose greatest joy is to hurl his spear from the saddle of his galloping horse into the breast of a prisoner, preferably British, waiting tied to a stake for his brutal end. This pastime, known as "pig-sticking," was reproduced in meticulous and gory detail as recently as 1954 in the film *King of the Khyber Rifles*.

No one at all, oddly, mentioned the standard Indian villain of the genre of English literature represented by Conan Doyle's *Sign of the Four*. He is the turbaned, silent, soft-footed avenger come to England to recover the lost gem acquired by our retired hero in some romantic or—no matter—shady adventure. This has been the theme of a thousand stories and films. Almost the first feature-type American movie ever made on an Indian theme was Universal's *Bombay Buddha*, which concerned the theft and recovery of a golden Buddha figure. That was back in 1915, and it has been repeated interminably ever since. Likewise unsummoned from the innumerable paperbacked pages in which he has dwelt all these decades was the lascar, the "East India seaman," crewman aboard the British tramp lying in Singapore harbor or moving slowly up the Thames in the fog. He carries a knife in his teeth and his oiled body glistens as he goes about his business of thievery, murder, or the more staple occupation of jewel recovery. More modern paperbacks appear to prefer glistening bodies of the other gender, like *Woman of Kali*,[38] featuring "Sharita, high priestess of the cult of death, mistress of forbidden rites" in "barbaric India, land of languor, intrigue, strange appetites,

[38] Gold Medal Books, 1954

exotic women, cruel and scheming men!" Sharita commands an army of Thugs, the cult of villainous stranglers featured in so many thrillers of an earlier day when murderers did not have to be lascivious, merely murderous. It has all been for naught, as far as our present panel is concerned: none of these avengers, turbaned or oiled, or stranglers, male or female, turned up If they had ever passed through any of these minds, their passage went unacknowledged, or else they had moved softly, as befits their role, and had left nary a scratch.

THE DARK-SKINNED INDIAN: For certain people, it is villainy enough in the Indian that he is a man with a dark skin. The black Gunga Din had to be "white, clear white inside," when he acted like a brave man, and black all the way through the rest of the time when he was his cringing pathetic self. Nothing quite so crude as this turned up in our interviews, indeed direct evidence of prejudice based on "race" or "color" was extremely scant It has become bad taste, to be sure, to express such feelings openly. In the case of the Indians, moreover, there were so many other grounds, religious, cultural, political, for overt hostility that feelings about "color" or "race" could easily have remained safely submerged. About this no certain statement can be made, I can only report what the interviews did show·

Only 12 individuals mentioned color directly as an Indian attribute. Two did so admiringly

> That good-looking bluish-brown or bluish-black color, their dark skins and brilliant dress. . . .

Six simply mentioned

> skin color, dark, dark-skinned

as part of their mental picture of the Indian. These could have been obscure suggestions of prejudice or quite simple statements of fact. In some of these cases, the skin color of the Indian apparently served as a "label of primary potency," Gordon Allport's term for the most highly visible impression of a person or a people. Only 4 became explicit about color as a negative factor One confessed uneasily that

> skin color causes a certain tension in meetings with Indians

and another said

> in dealing with Indians you feel you're dealing with colored people, the same way you feel in the presence of Negroes. . . .

A third, speaking not of himself but of others in his circle of friends, said.

> The Indian with his darker skin perhaps consciously or unconsciously suggests the Negro in the United States That is why some Indians get refused by some hotels. Some friends of mine, one of them a Southerner, have said so in so many words: "They're just damn niggers to me!"

A fourth, when asked what he thought the American man-in-the-street might mentally associate with Indians, instantly answered: "*Nigger!*"

This is as far as the interviews go on this matter, and it is obviously not very far The association of the Indian and the Negro in these references does suggest, however, the value of attempting a look at the place of the Indian in the characteristic American color-prejudice pattern Gordon Allport has said. "A person with dark brown skin will activate whatever concept of Negro is dominant in our mind If the dominant category is one composed of negative attitudes and beliefs, we will automatically avoid him, or adopt whichever habit of rejection is most available to us " [39] Actually the position with regard to the Indian is rather less simple than this suggests. In some major respects, American color prejudice indiscriminately embraces everything non-"white." But there are also shades of prejudice as various as the shades of color, and they flicker often according to place, person, and circumstance Except for certain Californians of a certain mental or physical age bracket, "yellow"—as in Chinese, Japanese, Korean—tends to register rather mildly on the screens of "white" American color sensitivity; "brown," even a non-American brown—as in Indonesians and Filipinos—is a good deal less mild, but it is "black"—wherever it comes from—that sets the racial-color counters clicking the most violently. The Indian, shading along a wide spectrum from fair to brown to black, arouses these reactions in varying measures The experience of Indian visitors to this country, depending on their looks and on where they go, is likely to vary in this regard from nothing to the galling rudeness which is still the stuff of daily life to so many American Negroes in so many places.

The theme of sinful or tragic interracial love between Americans and Asians of different colors has been a recurring one in films and

---

[39] *The Nature of Prejudice*, Boston, 1954, p. 21.

popular literature. In order to have a happy ending, such stories usually contrived to turn the Asian involved into the long-lost child of suitably white parents and thus make possible the consummation in the sunset. Otherwise, it was necessary to kill off one of the ill-starred pair One way or another, it was agreed they could never live happily ever after. Only recently has a slightly more mature or casual note been struck about such affairs, although it is still extremely tentative and cautious.[40] As the son of an Indian mother, Tyrone Power nevertheless wins the general's daughter in *King of the Khyber Rifles*, and in *The Purple Plain* (1955), set in wartime Burma, Gregory Peck goes the distance with the beauteous Burmese girl. But both Tyrone Power and the Burmese beauty are fair. Garish advertisements for *The Rains of Ranchipur* (1955) daringly showed a really dark-skinned Indian planting a kiss on Lana Turner's lily-white throat, and the suggestion was left that this was "the great sin that even the heavens could not wash away."

The issue of color in relation to Indians rises now in a setting of great mutual self-conscious sensitivity· Indians watch for it to come up, Americans are embarrassed when it does But this American embarrassment is quite new, and this very newness is often an unrealized factor in Indian-American encounters. It was only a few years ago, well within the lifetimes of most of those present, that without any embarrassment at all, American lawmakers and American courts were officially relegating Indians to the status of lesser breeds where, it was felt, they rightly belonged There were so few Indians visible on the American scene before these last few years that the degree of Indian involvement in American immigration laws and practices is a matter now remembered, it would seem, by very few Indian immigration never did approximate the levels of the Chinese or Japanese; it began as a trickle in 1895 and reached a peak of 5,000 entries at San Francisco in 1910. These Indians, first as railway laborers and then as farmers, formed tiny enclaves in California that were gradually reduced in size as pressure against them grew Indian immigration had never been made easy by supervising American officials and was finally cut off altogether by the Immigration Act of 1917 In 1922 there were 2,600 Indians in the United States, 2,400 in 1940, and more than 3,000 in 1950, including 1,500 students. The small communities of Indian farmers in California, composed mostly of Punjabi Sikhs, became one of the smaller tar-

[40] Cf. Dorothy Jones, *op cit*, p 54

gets, along with the Japanese and the Chinese, of recurring "anti-Oriental" agitation. A 1920 report to the governor of California on the Hindu settlements complained of unsanitary conditions· "The Hindu standard of living is so vastly different from ours that it is difficult to present it properly "[41] Called "ragheads" by their contemptuous fellow Californians, these Indians kept their heads down, worked painfully hard, and from among their number began to send some of the first Indian students ever to enter American universities Some even became naturalized citizens of the United States until their claim to be "white persons" as defined in the prevailing American statute was challenged in the courts.

The claimant in the case, a Punjabi Sikh who had entered the country in 1913 and served with American forces in the First World War, claimed to be "a descendant of the Aryans of India, belonging to the Caucasian race (and, therefore) white within the meaning of our naturalization laws "[42] In a decision handed down on February 19, 1923, the United States Supreme Court disallowed this claim. Justice Sutherland, who wrote the majority opinion, found that a Hindu was not, after all, a "white person" in terms of the common understanding: "The words of the statute are to be interpreted in accordance with the understanding of the common man, from whose vocabulary they were taken." It was not a matter of racial superiority or inferiority, he went on, but of acknowledging a racial difference which, in the case of the Hindu "is of such a character and extent that the great body of our people instinctively recognize it and reject the thought of assimilation." Since the Act of 1917 had excluded all Indians as immigrants, it was "not likely that Congress would be willing to accept as citizens a class of persons whom it rejects as immigrants " The Sutherland decision, says the *Literary Digest* summary, "was hailed for the most part with delight by the California press and that of our Western seaboard." It was promptly followed by steps to force the Hindus off their little landholdings. Elsewhere in the country, the whole issue drew little attention. In India, however, it became one of the sources of a deeply biting and long-lasting grievance against the United States and against Americans.[43]

[41] *California and the Oriental*, Report of the State Board of Control of California, June, 1920
[42] *Literary Digest*, March 10, 1923
[43] Anup Singh, "A Quota for India Too," *Asia and the Americas*, April, 1944

This grievance was dramatized in 1929 when Rabindranath Tagore, the great Indian poet, arrived in this country for a lecture tour, was received insultingly by an immigration official, dropped his tour plans, and abruptly left the country Tagore wrote of this incident:

His insulting questions and attitude were deeply humiliating. . . . I was not used to such treatment. . . I came into the country, but my mind was not at ease. I went to Los Angeles, stayed there and lectured. But all the time I was impressed by the spirit in the air. The people seemed to be cultivating an attitude of suspicion and uncivility toward Indians. I did not like it at all. I could not stay on sufferance, suffer indignities for being an Asiatic It was not a personal grievance, but as a representative of all Asiatic peoples, I could not remain under the shadow of such insults. I took passage without delay. . .[44]

In various experimental studies of group prejudice patterns begun by pioneering social psychologists in the 1930's the Hindu seldom figured because few ever thought of the Hindu as playing any role at all in American experience. Where he was included, he invariably turned up at or near the bottom of all racial or social preference lists, usually rubbing shoulders there with the Turks at "the extremes of unfamiliarity" Since few if any of the Americans tested had ever seen, much less known, a Hindu, it was observed that it was "the ideas about the Hindu" that governed[45] Unfortunately these ideas about the Hindu were never examined, but it does not seem rash to guess that they would resemble many of those which have appeared in the course of the present inquiry

The official or legal view of the Indians as a *lesser breed*, at least insofar as it was expressed in immigration and naturalization bars, was not replaced until 1946, when an act of Congress restored—to a quota of 100 Indians annually—the privilege of entering the United States as immigrants and permitted them to become, if they desired, naturalized citizens of this country. This act was part of a broader action relaxing American bars against several Asian nationalities Still limited, it was nevertheless the beginning of an American response to the changing patterns of world power relationships. These changes were making it difficult for Americans—at least in the person of their federal government—to indulge their prejudices

---

[44] *Indian Review*, July, 1929, quoted by Schmidt, *op cit*, p 291
[45] Krech and Crutchfield, *Theory and Problems of Social Psychology*, New York, 1948, p 483

quite as freely as they could in the past. Changes abroad had become more compelling than "the understanding of the common man" at home or even—as so much of this study shows—the understanding of the not-so-common man, which has hardly changed at all in these respects.

It is the experience of this not-so-common man which leads peculiar relevance here to this brief review of the place of the Indian in the American color-prejudice pattern. Those few who have a long past of contact with India and Indians know and have felt its impact on themselves and on Indians.[46] But the greater number encountered India and Indians in a serious way only yesterday. Few of these show any awareness of this history. Many seem to have believed that the heritage of the past could have produced nothing but a benevolent and admiring attitude among Indians toward Americans. The discovery instead of bitterness, resentment, hostility was often a shock. Even then, it would frequently be assumed that this was something new, a product of current misunderstandings and differences rather than old hostilities cropping out in new settings. To many such Americans, reacting defensively with counterirritation and counterhostility, it would come as a surprise, I am sure, to learn that the American color bar has been a sore issue among many Indians for at least fifty years, that twenty-five years ago Indians in various local governments were trying to match American legal barriers imposed on Indians by imposing counterrestrictions of a similar sort on Americans in India.[47] The great majority of the Americans who figure in our present study are certainly not guilty of any of the cruder racialist attitudes and earnestly want to wipe the past slate clean; they simply underestimate the extent to which they must

[46] In her novel about an India missionary family, Pearl Buck makes this the nub and the ultimate irony of her story. The third-generation missionary, who has given his life to work in a remote Indian village, is brought face to face with the limits of his own belief in the brotherhood of man when his daughter falls in love with an Indian doctor who comes to ask for her hand. "His fervid eyes, his glowing words, the impetuous grace of his outstretched hands, the long fingers bending backward, the thumbs apart and tense, the white palms contrasted against the dark skin, were all too Indian, and in one of the rare moments of revulsion which Ted considered his secret sin, he was now revolted and sick. What—his Livy, his darling daughter? Was she to give up everything for this alien man? For a moment his soul swam in darkness. No, and forever, no!"—*Come, My Beloved*, p 284

[47] E. R Schmidt, op. cit., p. 351, says that G B Pant, now Home Minister in Nehru's cabinet, was the sponsor of one such piece of legislation in the 1930's

still carry the burden of the sins of their fathers now visited upon them.[48]

THE LESSER BREED'S LESSER BREEDS: The Indian as the dark-skinned object of white racist prejudice is only one-half of the story; the other half is the Indian, in all his many hues and groups, who has divided his own people and his own society into a complex hierarchy of greater and lesser breeds. The view of this side of the profile emerges no less sharply etched from a comparable number of interviews. It becomes more or less explicit in the large majority of interview references to the caste system and untouchability. It is present in references to racial and religious fanaticism and violence in India, especially in connection with the Hindu-Muslim slaughters at the time of the partition. It comes up most directly and specifically in 20 interviews as follows:

> strong color feeling; race prejudices; the caste system is based fundamentally on color; they hate each other as well as us; internal color difficulties in India, they prefer lighter-colored skins. . . .

In this connection two of our Negro panelists recalled their own experiences with Indian fellow students in their university days:

> the Indians wore turbans so as not to be identified with Negroes; they kept their distance, wanted nothing to do with Negroes.

Here is a larger excerpt from the remarks of a third, a Negro scholar who spent a year much more recently at a large Indian university:

> I definitely did not like the arrogant Punjabis I met in Delhi. Think I disliked them because most Punjabis are very light, consider themselves Aryan, always refer to "aryan culture." They would always refer to South Indians in a sarcastic manner, ridiculing them as would-be intellectuals, called them "pseudos," were contemptuous of them because they were so black. Must stress that this was one small group, even of the Punjabi group as a whole. Suppose attitudes on this ques-

[48] On the other hand, very few Indians can probably appreciate the dramatic speed with which these patterns can be upset in American life. The Indian community in the United States is still tiny and its rights to citizenship are only a decade old. Nevertheless in November, 1956, in California, the ancestral home of "anti-Oriental" prejudices, Dalip S. Saund, a Sikh who became a citizen in 1949, was elected to Congress from an Imperial Valley district, defeating Jacqueline Cochran Odlum, one of the country's most famous women fliers and wife of a wealthy industrialist. Saund was elected as a Democrat, moreover, from a normally Republican district. He had served since 1952 as elected justice of the peace in the valley town of Westmoreland.

288                     SCRATCHES ON OUR MINDS

tion would be decisive in determining my attitudes. . . . Once at school when I sat down to talk to a dark girl from Madras, she told me she thought I would never talk to her because she thought I didn't like "dark" people! She told me she had been rejected as the bride of a lighter fellow of her own caste and that his mother had said to her intended fiancé, in her presence: "You can't bring a black one like this into our family!"

The historical relationship between caste and color or "race" among Indians has been a matter of some scholarly controversy. In one recent work which argues for a minimal role of color in the origins of caste, the author nevertheless remarks. "The racial theory of the

Ed Fisher © 1956 The New Yorker Magazine Inc

"*More controversy in Alabama! You'd think those people were being asked to send their children to school with Untouchables!*"

origin of caste has tended to give new meaning to some Hindus' conception of themselves. Castes are now claiming to be 'true Aryans' with a recently discovered sense of tentative Nordic arrogance." As an example he quotes Swami Abhendananda:

"This noble pride has prevented the members of different communities from holding free intercourse and from intermarrying with foreigners and invading nations, and has thus kept the Aryan blood pure and unadulterated If they had not . . we should not find in India today the full-blooded descendants of the pure Aryan family" [49]

Attitudes about "race" and "color" have become a delicate and often embarrassing subject for some Indians in more recent years, especially when they have to explain the matter to Americans who are surprised to find long columns of matrimonial advertisements in Indian newspapers specifying the color shades desired in prospective spouses Members of the New Delhi Rotary Club were a good deal more embarrassed and appalled in February, 1955, when five African students studying at Indian universities told them, according to *The Times of India*, that they found "the prejudice of Indians almost as bad as that of South African Europeans," that "if India is against colonialism it should not discriminate against colonials of a darker hue" The charges were discussed at a further meeting and brought a flurry of explanations and disclaimers and countercharges of exaggeration One university official said that "in the rough and tumble of university life differences were bound to occur" and that "the African students, familiar with colour discrimination in their own country, were inclined to accept any exhibition of bad manners as an insult to their race" Others explained that the Africans were interpreting the "reserve" of Indian social life as "a display of prejudice against them." Another pointed out that whereas European South Africans were rigidly enforcing their color attitudes, "Indians were trying to rid themselves" of the "relic of colour consciousness" deriving from "the ancient system of caste." In a letter to the editor, M S. Radakrishnan said the African charges should be "an eye-opener to every Indian" He warned: "To show any colour discrimination against [the Africans] will mar our international reputation and will defeat our policy of universal brotherhood The

[40] Oliver Cromwell Cox, *Caste, Class and Race*, New York, 1948, p 82
For a brief discussion of some of the obscurities connected with "Aryan" prehistory in India, see Ralph Linton, *The Tree of Culture*, New York, 1955, pp 478–485

African students will carry with them memories of bitter experiences in this country. It may soon be too late for us to make amends." [50]

The ironies in all this are, of course, multiple Among Americans, the "common understanding" on this subject has undergone considerable development No American judge, certainly, could stand today on Justice Sutherland's 1923 grounds In social practice, however, the idea of "white superiority" still protrudes sufficiently to become part of the experience of many Indians traveling in the United States, or to form part of a more generalized Indian conception of the United States as a whole or Americans in general. But not all of this Indian reaction is necessarily based on any consistent humanism. I refer here to those Indians—and they are numerous enough to be part of the experience of Americans encountering Indians in recent years—who really think of themselves as more "white" than the "whites," indeed, as descendants from that "pure Aryan family" of prehistoric times. This endows them with a sort of Mayflower status in relation to "whiteness" or "Aryanism" which they deny to many of their own darker-skinned countrymen. This Indian, peculiarly outraged, is not challenging the white man's racism as such. He is crying· "How dare you assume your air of Aryan superiority over me when I am just as Aryan as you, even more so!" This was the substance of the Indian claim in that 1923 court case to which we have referred, and it is still the substance of many an Indian response to American racism. Out of these assorted motes and beams comes no small part of the confused ill feeling generated by so many recent individual American-Indian encounters.

## 5. *THE GANDHI IMAGE*

THERE ARE PLACES in all of our minds where images sit tight, secure, immovable, like monuments on battlefields long quiet. They brook no challenge; we live by what they mean to us. In some minds this is the whole scene, undisturbed, impenetrable, unstirred by intruders against whom all entry is barred. In most others, fortunately, the

[50] *Times of India*, February 6–12, 1955

neighboring fields of the imagination are open and lively. Here all the many images of varied ideas, experiences, and people seek and find their places, maneuver for position, struggle for status and primacy, jostle each other for the central spot like a cast of jealous actors on a stage. They can clash head on too, sometimes to a confused draw, leaving the scene a foggy maze of unresolved contradictions But once in a while a single image looms above all the rest; the light follows it, and all the other figures grow dimmer, and all the clatter of contradiction dies down. Something like this seems to happen in a great many of the minds we are presently exploring when all this array of bizarre or grim or unattractive images of Indians we have been describing is confronted by the single greater image of the figure of Gandhi.

The Gandhi image is overwhelmingly triumphant. Only a few dissent. He is acknowledged as a man to be admired virtually by all, whether friendly to India or hostile, attracted by Indians or repelled by them Freely or grudgingly, with or without reservations, even the most critical and the most prejudiced pay him some measure of respect To be sure, the accents and stresses range widely, from the unreserved to the perfunctory and even to the inwardly rebellious. Still there is a palpable weight of a nearly universal feeling that now leads even the most dubious man, asked if he admires Gandhi, to answer *yes, but*—— rather than *no, because*——. There are very few who care little enough for social disapproval to reject out of hand a figure who seems to get identified with every nation's national heroes, every religion's saints and prophets, every man's desire to be good, or better than he is.

To 144 members of our panel, the question was put: "Do you think of Gandhi as a man to be admired?" One hundred forty-one answered *yes* or *yes, but*, only 3 said *no*. Sorting out the traits and facets of Gandhi which commanded these reactions, we find a range that goes all the way from Gandhi the politician to Gandhi the saint. There were 8 who saw him as

> a skillful astute politician and negotiator, one of the cleverest, shrewdest politicians that ever lived; a politician of integrity who knew how to transform principles into mass action; a politician who brought high ethical standards into politics. . . .

Twenty-eight saw him mainly as leader of the struggle for freedom:

> a great leader of his people, of his country, worked incessantly, devot

edly, gave his life to the cause of Indian freedom; a tremendous leader who achieved British withdrawal and the peaceful liberation of India through the power of his personal influence on huge masses of people; one of the great political instruments of history, he moved more people in his lifetime than any man who ever lived .

Thirty-four, as the symbol of nonviolence and spiritual force in politics:

> his doctrine and practice of nonviolence, impact of his spirituality on all men, universal idealist; symbol of moral leadership in human affairs; a revolutionary leader who placed high value on means as compared to ends; great religious leader, moral force, came closer to the religious ideas in which I believe, created the admirable ideal of leadership of the spirit; preached a social gospel, demonstrated by his whole life the power of an idea; achievement of political goals without violence was divine conception, his concepts were basically Christian, i.e., goodwill in action, he was a politician-saint . . .

Forty-two who thought of Gandhi the man:

> his conviction, force of character, vision, courage, selflessness, steadfastness; devotion, dedication, patience, intelligence, self-sacrifice; his personal charm, magnetism, his power to capture the imagination . . .

and eleven as a transcendent religious figure

> think of him in same way as Christ; almost as deviant as Christ, clean, great, like Christ, genuine saint who devoted his whole life to truth; combines George Washington, Lincoln, Jesus; one of the saints of the earth, most powerful spiritual force to appear on earth in 1,955 years .

There is obviously a long and wide gap between the image of Gandhi as an astute politician and the image of Gandhi as the most powerful spiritual force to appear on earth since Jesus But the heavy clustering of the large groups of individuals who admired Gandhi for his character, his identification with nonviolence, and his role as the successful leader of his country's fight for freedom establish the essential substance of his image In the total of all our answers, there were 98 given entirely without qualification; whether as politician or politician-saint or just plain saint, these individuals viewed Gandhi in a single piece There were 43 who said *yes, but*—— and offered a great variety of afterthoughts and reservations Some of these were reflections on Gandhi's political and economic ideas.

his solutions for the country's problems were unrealistic; his social and economic views were contradictory; yes, as leader of the independence fight, but for his way of life? No! Rousseau, antimachinery, would have turned the clock back!; admire him but don't accept many of his ideas; don't agree with passive resistance though I respect it; Gandhi was a traditionalist and conservative, didn't really have workable political or economic ideas. . . .

Some were oddly varying choices of the different Gandhis:

admire him as a person but not as a political figure; as a philosopher, but not as a political leader, admire him much less as a human being than as leader of the independence struggle, for his morality, but not for his politics; as a formidable, astute, and courageous leader, but not especially for his spiritual qualities, an admirable but alien figure. . . .

There were some specific doubts:

the strange dualism about a man as good as he who was also a shrewd politician; a cross between Jesus Christ and Frank Hague, admire the one but not the other, think he damaged India in 1946; he had some less admirable qualities, as husband and father, for example, some theatrical exhibitionism, some stage-acting . . .

or wondering half-acceptances:

in some ways, of course Stuck to his principles under hell or high water, can't help admiring this whether I agree or not, but a lot of his stuff was phony stuff for the masses, the business of salt, spinning was a lot of public relations fluff . . .

or just plain wondering:

his influence over millions, he must have had something on the ball, whatever it was!, just don't understand him, don't know what makes such a man tick, like Christ, not really of this world . . .

or wondering half-rejections:

don't think he is to be imitated, admire but don't adulate; wouldn't go for the idolatry of Gandhi that some people express. . . .

These were all expressions of yes-but which still add up to yes. There were several yes-buts which really added up to no:

yes, but he's beyond my comprehension, was hard to understand, for example, his saying let the Japanese come in but don't cooperate. I couldn't go that far or rise that far. Just can't see it; yes, but less than

Nehru Like Gandhi's insistence on ideas, but he was a curious mixture. Don't like to be preached at by a man who took so long to get preached at as he did in sex matters, as he tells in his autobiography; he was a great man in a sense, a curious but not really an admirable one. His philosophy, i.e., passivity, breeds submission to totalitarianism. . .

There was 1 response, finally, which was clearly in a class by itself:

I'm afraid so [i.e., that I do regard him as a man to be admired] but have my old prejudices. I thought that what he was about was ridiculous Saw no reason why Indians should be independent But of course it was inevitable, and Gandhi's accomplishment was really extraordinary.

This brings us to the 3 lonely individuals who flatly and firmly said no, they did not admire Gandhi a social scientist with some background in India in Gandhi's time; a journalist with a China background; an historian with neither. They said.

Can identify with Nehru but cannot identify with Gandhi; am prejudiced against him, can't accept nonviolence, don't think it won India's independence, don't go for the "spiritual" approach to life, never suffered from the Tolstoyan school and it's surprising how much of Gandhi is Tolstoy, not worth much in troubled times, pacifism is a luxury of good times.

But the rejections are so few and the qualifications so largely muted that they remain marginal, leaving the essential picture intact. Out of these interviews, taken as a whole, one gets a strong sense of the Gandhi image, motionless and slightly smiling, a face for the faceless mass, simply staring down all the other images of the Indians, all the fabulous, the benighted, the puny, the dark-skinned, the lesser men.

This great and powerful Gandhi image climbed but slowly to its present eminence, and it climbed, moreover, right out of the troughs in which we have been wallowing. In the earlier years and decades of Gandhi's lifetime he appeared to many as the quintessential figure of the puny Indian, ribs showing, naked but for a loincloth or draped in a dhoti. He was the odd, the strange, the incomprehensible Indian, with his dietary peculiarities, his fasts, his mystic hold on the masses. his religiosity, his sainthood. He was everything, even to many of his Western admirers, suggested by the title Bishop Frederick Fisher gave to his book in 1932: *That Strange Little Brown Man, Gandhi*. He was also, to some of his opponents and critics and to many onlookers, not only puny and strange and brown, but comic. Typical American cartoons of the time show him as a ridiculously tiny figure, shaking salt on the tail of a huge and rather kindly British lion, or as an emaciated baby in a diaper being walked by a broad, harried, father-image John Bull, with the title: "Walking the Floor Again"; or again, he is a gaunt bony little figure performing as a weight lifter, facing the obviously preposterous task of lifting an enormous weight several times his size which is labeled: "full independence." The cartoon is titled· "The Strong Man of India."

Some Americans, especially religious liberals, had begun quite

Walking the Floor Again
—Hungerford in the *Pittsburgh Post-Gazette*.
1932

early to view Gandhi "as a saint, a holy man, a great soul, comparable to Saint Francis of Assisi or even Christ" As he rose to the unchallenged leadership of the Indian nationalist movement, newspapers began to call him "a commanding figure" or even "the most amazing figure of the age." When he came more closely into view at the London Round Table Conference late in 1931, much was made of his "odd appearance and strange ascetic ways," but a *New York Times* correspondent wrote· "Saint and social reformer, politician and propagandist, he has now shown himself to be a diplomat with one of the subtlest minds that ever came out of the East." He was seen as a peculiarly skilled politician who was somehow bringing the whole weight of the religiosity of the Indian masses to bear upon the bonds of British rule This was not always an admiring view. Some felt that his "nonviolence" inevitably bred more violence. Some of his more captious critics were calling him an opportunist, more rarely a phony, and one American newspaper even called him, in 1931, "the evil genius of India." [51]

As we have seen, some reflections of almost all these views of Gandhi have survived and came to light now and again in the course of our current set of interviews. But where they were critical, they were in all but a few cases muted There were always—and there still are—a great many serious questions to be asked about the role, ideas, and impact of Gandhi What was the real effect of his strategy of nonviolence on the course of the Indian independence struggle? What did it mean for the British, for the Indian upper classes? How did his social and economic ideas weigh against the needs of a modern India? What did his philosophy mean, for the Hindu, for the Christian, for the humanist, for the twentieth-century man in his world? What were the roots of the Gandhi personality? What, in sum, was the nature of the man and his impact? A serious approach to these questions has hardly been begun, even now Some of the answers are implicit in what has happened in post-Gandhi India (68 of our interviewees think India today is directed by Gandhi's influence, 53 think not). But in Gandhi's lifetime the logic of such questions steadily yielded before the aura of the man. The smaller, comic or odd, and more contradictable image of Gandhi gradually grew larger, more laden with the imponderable, increas-

[51] Quotations are from Harnam Singh, *American Press Opinion About Indian Government and Politics, 1919–1935*, Ph D thesis, Georgetown University, 1949, pp 386–405.

THE INDIANS 297

ingly difficult to challenge, much less to ridicule. Gandhi pooled religion and politics in a manner disconcerting and eventually rather frightening to Westerners, who generally think of such a union as ideal but not very practical.

Despite large public notice over the years, he remained a distant figure to most Americans until after the beginning of the war with Japan, when there was suddenly something dangerously less remote about the man who chose prison for himself and his adherents rather than join the struggle on any terms short of immediate freedom, who appeared quite serenely ready to meet not only British force and obduracy but Japanese attack with the same readiness to die unarmed, a test which never had to be made. But then came the greatest Gandhi of all, walking on his bare feet over the blood-sloshed

PATIENCE AND STATESMANSHIP MAKE GOOD
*St. Louis Post-Dispatch*, 1949

stones of Calcutta's streets at the height of Hindu-Muslim fury, bringing to a pause by his presence the incalculably insane violence of the people he had not been able to win, after all, to his doctrines. This was the Gandhi who said with infinite sadness that he had lost, that he no longer wanted, as he had often said he did, to live on to the age of 125, and the Gandhi, finally, who was murdered by a Hindu fanatic in the ultimate irony of the history he had made This was the Gandhi, as depicted in a Fitzpatrick cartoon in 1949, no longer puny, odd, or comic, but a giantesque figure looking down from the mists on the newborn Indian republic which the whole world by now saw as the product of his peculiar genius. It is this Gandhi, already a towering universal legend, for whom such general admiration and respect is now universally shown. It is piously shown, and piety asks no difficult questions. One interviewee remarked: "Gandhi is a hero to millions who have no idea of what he's really like." But others imply that the perceived greatness of Gandhi transcends reservation, inquiry, or disagreement: "I do not go along with many of Gandhi's ideas, but——"

It is not easy now to sort out and separate the Gandhi image from notions of the Indian independence movement in the minds of most of our individuals. For many the two are wholly identified, and for a majority of these the picture did not acquire shape until after the event. Only for a very few did it project very far into the past. Asked what events in Asia had first made a serious impact on them, only 4 persons mentioned the Indian independence movement, or the first trickle of memory of the name of Gandhi appearing in the press, the salt march and the civil disobedience movements of the 1920's and 1930's. Americans in India and Americans at home had reacted quite differently to these events. American missionaries, as already noted, either adopted or adapted themselves to the British view; indeed the British required of them a formal pledge to this essential effect The few dissidents who chose to identify themselves with the Indian interest remained mavericks almost to the end. The old guard saw Gandhi in the beginning as "a fanatic, a has-been, a man of violence, a reactionary, a Bolshevik."[52] Bishop Fisher was still expressing a minority view in 1930 when he wrote. "Gandhi is living and acting the thing we dream of."[53] On the other hand, those Americans at home who developed a sympathetic interest in

[52] Cf Schmidt, op cit, p 199 ff
[53] Crane, op. cit, p 127–128.

the Indian struggle reacted out of the much broader base of liberal humanism, to say nothing of the Spirit of 1776 and the strongly surviving bias against Britain, especially imperial Britain.

Long before there was a serious Indian nationalist movement, William Jennings Bryan, passing through India on a world tour, publicly opined that Britain ought to give India back to the Indians and was angrily denounced by the British as a seditionist. A good many years later, but still before the appearance of Gandhi, Americans had begun to interest themselves in the Indian cause. During the First World War, the India issue was dramatized in the United States by the arrest and imprisonment, at British request, of a number of *émigré* Indian revolutionists. Their cause was taken up by a small group of American liberals and Socialists [54] whose interest continued and spread in the following years The names of John Haynes Holmes, Roger Baldwin, Robert Morss Lovett, Norman Thomas, John Dewey, Oswald Garrison Villard, and others appear on repeated appeals for the Indian cause. Some of them formed organizations which devoted themselves to promoting the cause of Indian nationalism A prolonged tug-of-war went on between these groups and various official, quasi-official, or wholly nonofficial pro-British spokesmen for the ear of the American public. Events in India spurred by Gandhi's civil disobedience campaigns commanded considerable attention in the American press General interest remained marginal, but those few papers with enough interest to take editorial positions were, in the broad, sympathetic with the Indian cause For most of them this meant agreeing with the idea of Indian freedom in principle while agreeing in fact with the British in most current particulars Almost all news about India printed in American papers came from British sources, and this colored much of the editorial opinion expressed. At one end of the spectrum stood the few consistently pro-British papers, and at the other stood the liberal weeklies which, in the absence of adequate reporting, tended, in the words of an Indian study, to give the Indian freedom movement more "sentimental appreciation" than "critical appraisal." [55]

But the issue never became a major one for Americans. The Gandhi figure, though growing in stature, continued to be regarded

[54] Cf Robert Morss Lovett, "The United States and India, a Footnote to Recent History," *The New Republic*, April 1, 1931.
[55] Cf Singh, *op cit*, pp. 232 ff

as odd, though often uncomfortably so.[56] This was the time of the cartoon view of the puny Gandhi David challenging the British Goliath. The sympathy went to David, of course, but the edge of ridicule was sharp enough and visible enough for Gandhi himself to be acutely sensitive to it. When Bishop Fisher urged him to visit the United States after he attended the London conference in 1931, Gandhi reportedly refused because "he felt his appearance in America would only result in laughter." [57] In the 1930's the depression at home rather fully absorbed the attention of most Americans. For those who looked abroad the rising Hitler filled much the larger part of the foreign sky. For the few who looked in the opposite direction, Japan's attacks on China were the focus of concerned interest. Not until Pearl Harbor rudely wrenched American attention toward the Pacific did India's fate become an issue of sudden concern to a much wider American public. The Japanese sweep through Southeast Asia early in 1942 produced visions of a Japanese march into India toward a meeting with victorious German forces coming, as so many feared they might, eastward from Egypt. The position in India became the subject of proddings from Roosevelt to Churchill. The unprecedented missions to India of Colonel Louis Johnson and William Phillips on Roosevelt's behalf in those anxious months communicated a sense of anxiety to some of the newsreading public, sighting for the first time in the country's history the

[56] E g, when Gandhi was jailed again in 1930, Will Rogers, America's top humorist-philosopher of the time, wrote in one of his daily paragraphs: "They've got Gandhi in jail in India He preached 'liberty without violence' He wanted nothing for himself, not even the ordinary comforts He believed in 'prayer and renunciation' Well, naturally a man that's holy couldn't run at large these days. They figured that a crazy man like that was liable to get other people wanting those fanatical things Civilization has got past 'truth and poverty and renunciation' and all that old junk Throw those nuts in jail"—Quoted by Singh, ibid., p. 364

[57] Schmidt, op. cit, p. 305

It would never occur to any cartoonist today to depict Gandhi as the odd, funny little figure which represented him so generally at that time But the odd, funny little figure lives on, transferred from Gandhi to other Indian images that are still even now fair sport for the humorous cartoon strip E g, in a recent sequence, Al Capp's Dogpatch characters were being thrown into an uproar by a pair of visiting swamis—"Swami Riva and assistant Olman Riva"—featuring "Hindu magic" at a visiting carnival They get into trouble because they magically raise one of Capp's exaggerated hillbilly females fifty feet into air—Capp's twist on the rope trick—but forget the "proper procedure" for getting her down. The interesting thing here is that "Swami Riva" is drawn directly from the Gandhi model of twenty-five years ago, a tiny squatting man, with sunken chest, a large head, and with horn-rimmed spectacles over a great hook of a nose See *Boston Globe*, December 4, 1955

specter of military defeat The Cripps mission, its failure, Gandhi's fast, the launching of civil disobedience, the veritable insurrection of August, 1942, all made India, suddenly, top news, anxious news. Gandhi's defiance of the British and apparent indifference to the Japanese threat was for a time almost as incomprehensible and angering to many Americans as some of the more recent acts and policies of Nehru

This turning of American eyes toward India is mirrored quite clearly in the opinion polls of the time In all the crowded 1,911 pages of Hadley Cantril's huge compilation of polls taken between 1935 and 1946 there are only sixteen entries relating to India. Of these six are British or Canadian and the rest are American poll questions on the issue of Indian independence, the bulk of them between the critical months of March and August 1942, one again in 1943, then a last in 1946. The most remarkable figures shown by these polls are the percentages of a national sample of the American population who between March and August, 1942, said they had heard or read about the independence negotiations in India. the range was between 69 per cent and 78 per cent, a degree of awareness common only to issues of the utmost public interest. The great weight of opinion, as shown by these polls, favored quicker British action in granting freedom to India—43 per cent for full independence (with a majority of these calling for immediate action to this end) and 37 per cent for immediate dominion status. Other views favored firm promises for postwar action. Only a tiny 2 per cent opposed independence for India at that time or at any time The next year, in April, 1943, when the feeling of pressure was still great but more familiar, a National Opinion Research Center poll showed 62 per cent favoring independence for India, though widely divided between those who favored it at once and those who were willing to see it deferred until after the war. Three years later, with the war over and the public preoccupied with much else than India, interest had flagged. Barely half of a national sample in a Gallup poll (48 per cent) said they had followed the discussions of the issue in India; and about three-quarters of these (32 per cent of the total sample) felt that India should be set free at once [58] Americans were still interested but were no longer anxious about the matter India was, once again, rather far away

When independence finally came in 1947, and with it the partition of India, all news about it was unavoidably dominated by the

[58] All polls from *Public Opinion,* pp 326–328

tragic holocaust of Hindu-Muslim massacres with which that historic change was ushered in. The sympathetic image of Indians as fighters for their freedom was blurred in the terrible pictures of mutual slaughter that so deeply shadowed the transfer of power. The new image of the fanatically violent Indian in mobs suddenly overlay all the older pictures people had of the weak, unvital, unaggressive, passive, nonviolent Indian. The contradiction between the two was staggering and, to judge from the impressions of our present interviews, has not even yet been absorbed or firmly placed anywhere in the gallery of Indian images. But none of these massacres of the nameless produced anything like the impact of the news, six months later, that a single burst of this same fanatical violence had ended the life of Gandhi. I happened to be in a small town far in western Kansas on that January 31. Even there the news, reported in huge black lines in the local paper and read out solemnly from the local radio station, caused an odd hush among people who could hardly have explained why it did so.

Independent India rose in the wholly new circumstances of the following years. The image of Gandhi faded, growing larger and mistier as it receded. New in the foreground stood the much smaller and earthier figure of his successor, Jawaharlal Nehru, the fighter for freedom become the man of power, the new—and for many Americans now almost the only—identifiable symbol of the new India. New pictures were shaped out of the changed and changing setting in India and in the world. Around Nehru we begin to discern the images of people trying to face gargantuan tasks of growth in an old land, images of neutralists in the world struggle, images of touchy, sensitive, difficult people emerging to meet Americans on the new basis of equality of which they had dreamed for so long. It was a meeting for which not many Americans nor many Indians were very adequately prepared by all that had gone before.

## 6. *THE NEHRU IMAGE*

IN THIS GALLERY of images, Jawaharlal Nehru is a much smaller, more human, more complicated figure than Gandhi, closer to view and better known. Compared to most other important world figures of our time, he is even almost familiarly known. A remarkably large number of those interviewed for this study met him and talked to him, either in India or during his 1949 visit to the United States, and thus have some basis, even if limited, for a direct personal impression. All have seen him pictured in photographs and cartoons, seen and heard him in newsreels and on television, or read about him in innumerable news reports, interviews, articles, and books, and perhaps most meaningfully of all, in books he has written about himself.

Like Gandhi, though for different reasons, Nehru commands enormous and sometimes adoring admiration, as a leader, an intellectual, a sensitive, complex, gifted, and even tragic man. Nehru may symbolize the conscience of the West for its past role in Asia, it is not easy to justify a history in which such a man could be so long imprisoned or held to be inferior. But he has no saintly aura about him to deter criticism or temper dislike, many see him also as vain, arrogant, unwise, naive, or even plain foolish Agreement with Nehru requires no spiritual commitment, scorn for him need not be defensive or disagreement guilty By his own frank and self-searching accounts, Nehru always stood across a certain gulf—sometimes a painfully "vast distance"—from Gandhi, whom he revered but with whom he could rarely agree except blindly, a violation of reason that never came easily to him in all the long years of their relationship. The transfer of leadership from Gandhi to Nehru placed it in the hands of a twentieth-century secular-minded man, for Nehru is a citizen only of this world, subject to all the more normal fallibilities as man, politician, and statesman. His ideas and acts as leader of India, and for Americans especially, his role as "neutralist" in world affairs, are matters of sharp, controversial, and often angry opinion. His influence over his own countrymen is great, but quite unlike Gandhi's; his impact abroad is subject to all the clashing views of contemporary politics.

It is one measure of this impact that reactions to Nehru among Americans are so numerous, so strong, so varied, and often so downright personal Nehru had become a commanding figure in Indian nationalism, second only to Gandhi, long before he became known in any wider circles abroad, especially in this country. He came more insistently into the view of most of the members of our present panel only during the past decade, the period of his undisputed personal leadership of his country, the time in which he has come to personify India in its new relations with the rest of the world. Hence images of Nehru as an individual personality are now not easily separated from images of Nehru the man of power, prime minister of India, and Nehru the "neutralist."

But the impress of the earlier Nehru—the aristocratic rebel, the sensitive intellectual, the dauntless man who spent thirteen years of his life in British prisons and passed most of that time writing memorable and revealing books about himself and his country—lies strongly upon the fresher and stronger images of the Nehru we encounter today No important world leader now alive has given as candid and detailed a self-picture as Nehru did in those prison-produced volumes.[59] Only 18 interviewees spoke of reading any of these books, but many more, certainly, were reached by admiring review articles [60] and by the mounting volume of writing by Nehru and about Nehru in the periodical press over these years [61] His own reflections on himself, on religion, on philosophic and political outlooks are the direct or indirect sources of many of the judgments many people now make of his behavior and his ideas. Here, on almost every page he ever wrote, are to be found reasons why his admirers think of him as intelligent, honest, committed to human emancipation, a man with a widely ranging and inquiring mind and spirit, a sensitivity mirrored in his face, and luminous gifts revealed in the rich flow of the English language which so paradoxically became his own By the same token, Nehru himself anticipated many of the misgivings that are now felt about him. Long before

[59] His autobiography, *Toward Freedom*, was first published in England in 1936. Its first American edition appeared in 1941 and as of December 31, 1955, had sold 19,458 copies, *The Discovery of India* (1946) 13,555, and *Glimpses of World History* (1942) 12,095 Five other Nehru titles, including several collections of speeches, have had a total sale of 8,173 Figures supplied by the John Day Company, New York

[60] Like these on *Toward Freedom* "A many-sided personality who can turn aside from the heat and dust of political struggle to comment on the beauty of a glacier or to discuss a general philosophical idea "—*Atlantic Monthly*, March, 1941, "Noble, temperate, serene . apparently effortless expression of truth and purpose "—Vincent Sheehan in *Books*, February 16, 1941, "A synthesis of all the liberal traditions of the past and the best hopes of mankind for the future "—Hans Kohn in *Boston Transcript*, February 15, 1941, "Liquid lucidity of its prose . a sensitive spirit whose integrity completely identifies him with the oppressed . "—*Christian Century*, March 26, 1941

[61] *Readers' Guide to Periodical Literature* shows for 1929–32, 1 article by Nehru, for 1932–41, 5 articles by Nehru and 38 about him, for 1949–55, 10 by Nehru and 135 about him, for the year 1956, 6 by Nehru and 64 about him.

most of his present-day critics, he was speculating about his vanity, his "formidable conceit," the danger of his love of power, his fear that "only a saint, perhaps, or an inhuman monster" could survive "unscratched and unaffected" the adulation which became so big a part of his life.[62]

These attributes of the Nehru image impose a peculiar discomfort upon his critics. It is distinctly more difficult to see "foolishness" in a man reputedly so intelligent, "naivete" in a sophisticate, "opportunism" and "hypocrisy" in one believed to be so deeply committed to the highest form of secular morality, to charge appeasement of antihuman totalitarianism to a man known as a humanistic liberal. To be charged with dishonesty or ignorance, he has to be seen as a "cheap politician" and not as the philosopher-statesman that his admirers believe him to be From all these real or fancied contradictions comes much of the defensive uneasiness of his friends and the acute irritation felt by so many of his critics and foes.

The complexity of the reactions to Nehru among the members of the present panel emerges plainly from a sorting of the answers made by 156 of them to the question Do you think of Nehru as a man to be admired?

[62] In 1937, Nehru wrote an anonymous attack upon himself in order to help prevent his own re-election as president of the All-India National Congress. He acknowledged authorship in a section added to the American edition of his autobiography and included a long excerpt as an appendix Some excerpts of this since oft-quoted passage

"Is all this [his conduct in a crowd] natural, or the carefully thought out trickery of the public man? Perhaps it is both, and long habit has become second nature now The most effective pose is one in which there seems to be least posing, and Jawaharlal has learned well to act without the paint and powder of the actor

"Is it his will to power that is driving him from crowd to crowd and making him whisper to himself, 'I drew these tides of men into my hands and wrote my will across the sky in stars . '

"He calls himself a democrat and a socialist . and yet he has all the makings of a dictator in him—vast popularity, a strong will, energy, pride . . . and with all his love of the crowd, an intolerance of others and a certain contempt for the weak and inefficient His flashes of temper are well known . . . His conceit is already formidable. It must be checked We want no Caesars."—*Toward Freedom*, p. 437. "Today," said *Time*, quoting these words in a cover story (July 30, 1956), "Nehru is very close to being Caesar" C L Sulzberger quoted them once more, to Nehru, in an interview (*New York Times*, February 27, 1957) and asked his present views "It should have been perfectly obvious," replied Nehru, "that any man who detected in himself such character weaknesses could never possibly have succumbed to them."

| | |
|---|---|
| Admirers (Yes, with little or no qualification) | 41 |
| Friendly Critics (Yes, but with mixed feelings) | 49 |
| Ambivalent Critics (Yes, but really No, No, but with mixed feelings) | 44 |
| Hostile Critics (No!) | 22 |
| TOTAL | 156 |

Roughly partitioned, we have here 90 individuals—in degrees ranging from the highly persuaded to the extremely dubious—who show some admiration or sympathy for Nehru, and 66 who—in degrees ranging from doubtful to vehement—do not admire him at all

Attitudes toward Nehru do not always conform to attitudes about the policy of "nonalignment" (i e, with either Russia or the United States) with which he is so closely identified. Some of the shadings in this relationship will soon become apparent, but there is, first, one rather simplified but quite direct bit of evidence which we can interpolate here by comparing the answers about Nehru to the answers given to another question· Do you think Nehru's policy of nonalignment is good or bad from India's point of view? The results·

| | |
|---|---|
| Good | 101 |
| Bad | 42 |

A sorting of the two sets of figures produces the following results:

| | |
|---|---|
| Admire Nehru and approve idea of nonalignment | 75 |
| Do *not* admire Nehru but approve idea of nonalignment | 26 |
| | 101 |

| | |
|---|---|
| Admire Nehru but do *not* approve idea of nonalignment | 15 |
| Do *not* admire Nehru and do *not* approve nonalignment | 27 |
| | 42 |

It appears from these groupings that there are 41 individuals who discriminate quite sharply between the man and his policy. But it must immediately be added that there is a big difference between approving the idea of nonalignment and approving the way in which Nehru is carrying it out The fact is that a majority of those who approve the idea, including some of his admirers and almost all of his friendly critics, are unhappy with Nehru for being inconsistent in applying it, for failing to keep himself and India genuinely nonaligned. Most of them think that Indian nonalignment, wisely pursued, would be a good idea not only for India but for the United States as well. What worries most of Nehru's friends and angers all his foes is the way in which he seems to have let this good idea slip away from him. There are of course some ardent partisans for whom

THE INDIANS 307

Nehru can do no wrong. There are others in this group whose view of Nehru sits in a frame other than that of current world affairs. But we shall discover that the man and his foreign policy are never far apart in the minds of most of these individuals as we move along the range of the attitudes they have expressed about Nehru, from warm admiration, through a variety of mixed feelings, all the way to cold antipathy.

## The Admirers

The views of Nehru begin with those of a small group (12) who are most unreserved of all in their admiration for his character and role:

> Nehru is one of the three great statesmen of this century, alongside Churchill and Roosevelt, a man of great intellectual capacity, very high principles and intentions, great charm, and personality, man of great wisdom, integrity, dedicated to humanity, eloquent, volatile, sensitive; his extraordinary perseverance and qualities as an individual kept India from disappearing into xenophobia; captured the imagination of many people and reflects their aspirations, international outlook, passion for welfare of people of India, devotion to peace, superb mind, able, astute, self-giving, one of the ablest men in the world, one of the few morally incorruptible statesmen . .

To these add 11 more who also explicitly approve his foreign policy role:

> One of the few with a world view, playing an admirable role, integrating, attempting to be a balance wheel, saying some truths about the Western role which need to be said and he's right about a lot of things, a brilliant man with distinctly pro-West leanings who's playing a smart game, I think he's right, admire him for his neutrality, his ability to face both East and West, and to push through his five-year plan. . . .

Here is a fuller excerpt of one of these opinions:

> I have a high opinion of Nehru, who strikes me as being an intelligent man, acting intelligently despite the rabid Right-wing Senators in this country who have been yelling at him I think Nehru is honestly disturbed by Communism, is opposed to it, though not as violently as we are, but politically opposed. I would guess that Nehru's notion is to fight it, but not by a frontal attack, as we do It seems to me Nehru figures that India has to be able to get along with Communist China in order to be able to venture to win the leadership of Asia

There are 18, finally, who admire Nehru primarily as the effective leader of a country that could not survive without his leadership:

> He is peerless as a democratic leader; he is *the* leader who can push India toward democracy, the personification of Indian nationalism, his selfless, courageous leadership gives Indians confidence and a sense of stability, has achieved much against great obstacles in unifying India and holding groups together, Nehru is the chosen leader of 350 million people. . . .

## *The Friendly Critics*

Qualified admiration for Nehru begins—for a first group of 16—with the introduction of flaws perceived in the man, or a mild measure of disagreement with his course:

> His is a genius, with blind spots and weaknesses, has integrity, strength, but shouldn't lose his temper; has qualities of greatness but is very egotistical, do not agree with all his conclusions, but we must realize that Nehru is keeping the nationalist banner in his hands and is keeping it away from the extremes, if Chiang Kai-shek had acted like Nehru, he might still be in power . . .

In the next 10, admiration becomes more marginal, doubts about him stronger:

> His quality is charism, not wisdom, I doubt his political realism and leadership. admire his technique as a political operator but not his personality, he is never strong enough to do anything but compromise; he is doing a good job of looking after India's selfish interests but is very opportunistic, he is playing things quite canny, I admire him but wouldn't want him for a personal friend. . . .

Another 15, still friendly critics, are bothered by Nehru's

> inability not to make petulant, critical speeches; he should weigh very carefully his need to make arrogant and ill-informed statements about the United States, it would be helpful if he did not feel compelled to make condemnatory statements every other day; his speeches seem calculated to get our backs up . . .

And 8 find the contradictions in Nehru puzzling:

> Always did admire Nehru, but now I don't know, am trying to fathom what in blazes is going on in his head; am uncertain as to whether he's sincere in trying to steer a middle course and if he is well advised, his bewildering pronouncements are those of a man who is essentially a

diplomat on a tightrope, though a patriot by his own lights; am not sure I understand his position, think he's playing a dangerous game, see in him ambivalence, calculation, emotionalism, dedication, he puzzles me. . . .

## *The Ambivalent Critics*

As we move along this spectrum of gradually more reserved admiration, we come now upon 14 individuals who salute Nehru for many of the qualities already mentioned but who begin to challenge, in a distinctly less admiring spirit, what they see as basic flaws in his thinking and especially in his view of the world. Typically,

> Nehru is a great man of action, but is quite arrogant and has a total misconception of America and American capitalism and its impact on people, was quite impressed by Nehru when I met him here, but think his mind runs on its own track and only sometimes is this the track of reality as I see it, Nehru is a thoughtful man, sincere leader, who contradicts himself by his own actions, always regarded him highly as a friend of democracy, though his recent statements make me question this, he is motivated by India's welfare and the rest be damned and this is something we ought to understand, Nehru inherited an impossible role along with Gandhi's saintly toga and has managed to hold India together, but my concern is with his inability to see the difference between the United States and the U S S R. . .

Occupying the last stretch of the bridge between Nehru's admirers and friendly critics on the one side, and his hostile critics and foes on the other, are 21 individuals whose mixed feelings about Nehru are mixed to the point of genuine ambivalence. Nearly half of these (10) said yes, they admired Nehru, but then went on to express views about him in which any surviving tinge of admiration quickly disappeared, they really meant no, they did not admire him at all. Here, for example, was the reaction of an important publisher

> Yes, he has leadership, rectitude, but he is twisted I also have a certain feeling of antagonism to Nehru. I try to allow for his life's experience, but I think he's unrealistic. Talks pacific, but acts otherwise. When his own ox is gored—Kashmir—he uses the same weapons as anybody else Nehru may be hypocritical, though a softer word might fit him better. Maybe he doesn't see it. I know he's a fine man, but he's annoying on personal contact, supercilious, chip on shoulder. Like a Jew always looking for anti-Semitism, he's always looking for some

aspect of racial discrimination, he's color-conscious. I was ill at ease with him.

Even more strongly mounting irritation shows in these remarks by an individual prominent in Washington:

> Nehru is a scholar and leader, going through the anguish of unifying a huge country. When he came here, I was tremendously impressed, found him pleasant, sympathetic, admirable But in the last few years his policy has turned quite unrealistic. Have a great sense of hypocrisy as a product of his developing relations and policies I find it damned annoying to find Nehru, who is so important to us and to whom we are so important, being so half-baked in understanding what this country is getting at. . . .

Personal impressions grow markedly less complimentary:

> he has some earmarks of being quite small potatoes, his ego is a little more obvious than it needs to be or deserves to be, always lecturing the West on moral force, but look at his position in Kashmir, Nehru is in danger of becoming too strong-headed and vain, a man who has gone

THE ROPE TRICK.

*New York Times,* 1955

from being a disciple of Gandhi to having too much pride, he has become arrogant . . .

and judgment of his policies still sharper:

we cannot allow Nehru to get into the position of directing American policy decisions, he feels he can abuse us because he knows us, but is scared of the Communists and guides himself accordingly, Nehru has not followed a policy of neutrality, is not the No. 1 peacemaker, he is playing a double role, is intellectually crooked, a meddler. . . .

With the remaining 11 in this group, we come to the first who said no, they did not admire Nehru, and then went on to express mixed feelings like these:

He is a personal tour de force in politics, but I question how substantial his foundations are, I feel partly respect for him, partly annoyance, partly I fear his weakness, am repelled by adulation of Nehru but am equally repelled by the notion that he's like Nenni or Wallace; I don't think he would lie, but somehow I don't think he would tell the truth either, he has violence in him, and can be awfully unjust and prejudiced, I don't admire him, but don't agree with his critics either because they don't take into account the pressure he is under both at home and abroad. . . .

Mixed feelings begin to disappear from the remarks of a final group of 9, one of whom, a prominent Washingtonian, gave this account of an evening's talk with Nehru.

I asked him what he found lacking in American civilization He said he thought we had a materialistic attitude, weren't sensitive to the things he valued. He seemed to me a man who could be intimate with masses but not with an individual, or at least not with me What he got onto right away was Kashmir. He talked about it half-lightly, half-mystically. I found it difficult to understand He didn't want to let me behind his façade, his strong sense of privacy I got the same sort of feeling so often aroused by Vishinsky, the feeling that he was role-playing. . . .

Others in the group saw Nehru's limitations as crippling:

He has great intelligence, so that I don't see how he equates interest in freedom with being so critical of the United States. If Nehru really believes the American people are eager to go to war, are trigger-happy, he doesn't know what is going on, is misreading the real danger and the real state of mind of our people; as an Indian I could admire him perhaps, but not as an American. He has a strong desire for personal power, but as to genuine and deep understanding of human emotions and world philosophies, I see Nehru as somewhat naive and willful; Nehru strikes me as another Jan Masaryk. I don't think he understands what he's up against.

## The Hostile Critics

There are, finally, 22 members of the panel who are quite unreserved in their hostile criticism of Nehru, whether as man or as "neutralist".

> Nehru plays a power game like any other politician, takes a free ride on the prestige of Gandhi and the myth of the great spiritual power of India, am very suspicious of him, he can and does talk out of both sides of his mouth, i e., on Kashmir and on the Chinese Reds, I think he is getting scared, trying to buy time, but I hope he will be replaced by others who know more about the United States, carries water on both shoulders, is naïve, vain, ambitious, opportunistic, evasive, surly, never gave forthright answers, one of the worst hypocrites I've ever met, wishy-washy, no clear idea of where he stands, but has basic antagonism to the West and is playing into the hands of Peiping, Nehru is not honest, he is a fuzzy thinker, not really an idealist, just another practical politician keeping himself on top of his big dung heap; a neutralist policy can be canny and legitimate, like George Washington's, but Nehru's is not, he is trying to be a peacemaker as well as a neutralist; I don't know how much fear enters into his policy, but through fluffheadedness he accepts the idea that Communism will grow more solid and less aggressive, Nehru is a tightrope-walking pro-Communist; he is an arrogant, anti-American, pro-Communist, high class, aristocratic, stiff-necked Hindu. . .

If we look back at the individuals occupying the various segments of this spectrum, we find that

- People with more personal experience in India tend to be among Nehru's admirers, or at least among his more friendly critics,
- Individuals whose Asian experience has related to China are not to be found among Nehru's all-out admirers (there was only one, a missionary), but tend to appear among his less friendly or hostile critics;
- *All* of Nehru's all-out admirers are "liberals" while 17 of his 22 all-out critics are "conservatives," including a notable clustering of what we might call our ultraconservative Right wing, including

almost all the individuals in the panel who feel most strongly on the subject of American Formosa policy from a pro-Nationalist bias.

But these divisions, while visible and interesting, are by no means clear cut. The large middle group of friendly and unfriendly critics cuts across all these lines, and among Nehru's most hostile critics, 6 of the 22 are clearly "liberal" and 2 of these are individuals with extensive and sympathetic contact with Indian affairs. Consider this view by a well-known writer long identified by his strong sympathy for India and its leaders

> I did admire Nehru, until 1946. Through his autobiography, his role in the independence struggle, he established himself as an attractive, brilliant, progressive idealist But look at the things he has done since he got to power. He is moved by political expediency, is not always the idealist or man of principle. I now regard him simply as a politician. He is too vain, too much of an actor, too weak, and, I think, has a power lust. He is a transposed English intellectual, a Kingsley Martin in power.

Or, finally, this comment, by a former high-placed government official

> I am not an admirer of Nehru, though it took me a long time to conclude that the idea of Nehru as a great dedicated soul, motivated in all his acts by noble and virtuous sentiments, was a myth Nehru is really motivated by expediency He was quite ready to use force in Kashmir, Hyderabad, but not in the larger context where we have to operate If Nehru did previously possess these virtues, they are now corroded, changed I now have a great mistrust of Nehru's leadership There is too much information about the low level of his thinking and his motivations

## The Alter Image: Menon

Somewhere close to this end of the spectrum where Nehru's policies are most strongly opposed and his personality pictured in its least attractive light, we begin to come upon the image of another Indian figure, V. K Krishna Menon, long Nehru's principal roving ambassador and chief of India's delegation to the United Nations. Menon carries to a further extreme the policies and the personal traits for which Nehru is reproached by his admirers and attacked by his critics As Nehru's alter ego, he is also an alter image, a figure upon whom Nehru's friends can project the stronger feelings they cannot quite apply to their hero, and in whom Nehru's foes find reinforcement and confirmation of their most virulent charges.

The Nehru who begins to be seen by his critics as arrogant, supercilious, close-minded, contemptuous of Americans, of American society, culture, values, and sincerity, is an image constantly superimposed, as we have seen, on the Nehru known to his admirers as sensitive, intelligent, scholarly, deeply committed to democratic humanism. When Menon stands in for his mentor, there are no such confusing contradictions, no blurring of the picture's lines, for Menon is a man who has had a peculiar success in persuading almost everyone he encounters that he is really as obnoxious as he appears to them to be. Nehru's own speeches and statements often anger his foes and dismay his friends, but the charge of pro-Communism, anti-Americanism, or anti-Westernism in Nehru is always subject to some other knowledge of the man, his predispositions and his beliefs. There are hardly any such reservations about the views, presumably Nehru's, as they are represented by Menon when he speaks for his chief in public forums and international councils. There still seems to be some slight perplexity about Menon's personal political views, but he leaves no doubt at all about his acidulous contempt for everything pertaining to Americans and the United States Of the 26 interviewees who brought up the subject of Menon, all had encountered him personally, but only 4 offered marginal reservations in his favor One was a top American official who had often faced Menon in UN debates·

> He's a man of elusive values, able, but not frank or reliable, you always have to watch him carefully He's always patronizing. He seems to have to keep on reassuring himself. But I can overlook this. He has courage and nerve and I rather enjoy tussling with him He's never boring

The other 3:

> A Machiavelli with a swelled head, though he has his good side too; a pretty vicious guy, but you have to respect him; I even like Krishna Menon, we do get along, though he does with very few. He *is* a prickly character, but we enjoy scrapping, he lectures me and I lecture him.

These remarks fall somewhat short of being encomiums, but they are the only near-compliments to be found in our present record. The exasperation and repugnance which Menon appears more generally to arouse are shared in this group by 11 who are among

THE INDIANS 315

Nehru's most hostile critics and by 15 who can be classed as more or less friendly critics or outright admirers. One of the latter said of Menon:

> A devil incarnate. It relieves me to know that he lived most of his life out of India. He is vile in private relationships and in every possible way. I can understand ordinary anti-Americanism, but what disturbs me more in Menon are his personal traits and the terrible feeling that he is really sincere in all this. He has done enormous harm over here and I wish Nehru would send him back to India.

Other views of Menon:

> More objectionable than anybody I have ever met in my life, a poisonous fellow; rubs people the wrong way; always fighting to assert his masculinity, keen and lashing in a fight, a dangerous man, he was quite insulting to our delegates at the UN, I experienced it myself when I served there; a pro-Communist anti-American blackmail agent; Menon is actively inimical to Americans, he just doesn't like them; I feel no sincerity in him at all, can never believe a thing he says, Menon is the archetype of the kind of unpleasant people Forster described in *A Passage to India*, glib, unctuous, self-righteous, arrogant, if Nehru wants to improve relations, let him withdraw the loud-mouthed anti-American Menon . . .

Between 1955, when most of these interviews were held, and the spring of 1957, when these pages were being readied for publication, the Nehru image and the Menon alter image were brought closer together. At the end of 1956, Nehru's admirers were badly shaken by his equivocations and delays in taking a stand on Russia's armed suppression of revolt in Hungary. At the United Nations, Krishna Menon voted against demanding Soviet withdrawal and abstained from a proposal to send United Nations observers to the scene. In those same weeks, Nehru, Menon, and the Indian government were unhesitating in their quick denunciations of Anglo-French and Israeli actions in Egypt. The contrast was a painful one for Nehru's American friends and for many of his most ardent supporters in India. The near-revulsion was enough, after the passage of several weeks, to lead Nehru to make a number of offsetting public statements critical of the Soviet Union. But an insensible change had occurred in the Nehru image by the time the Indian leader came to Washington, in mid-December, to visit President Eisenhower. In his host he met a man who had far outdone the neutralist Nehru with the evenhandedness of his moral indignation, directed at all ill-doers regardless of nationality, political creed, or condition of alliance with the United States Nehru was in the unaccustomed role of moral-fence-mending, and he seemed to his hosts softer, friendlier, more responsive than before During this visit, Krishna Menon, like John Foster Dulles, was kept designedly out of sight, since both men, it was reported, were "peculiarly irritating to each other's government." Nehru's visit remained friendly, therefore, even "reassuring," the Washington spokesmen said

But in January, 1957, the Kashmir issue was again before the United Nations. Menon, reiterating India's stubborn stand against a United Nations majority in a series of marathon speeches, brought a nearly universal cry from the American press. "Two-faced moral standard!"[63] At home in India, he became a national hero, and Nehru helped him win a seat to India's parliament and, in April, elevated Krishna Menon to the post of Minister of Defense in his cabinet Menon now stood more prominently than ever at Nehru's right hand, and had nearly become a man of power in India in his own right. The space between the image and the alter image had distinctly narrowed, and this had come about, it seemed, not because Menon had drawn any closer to Nehru, but because Nehru had drawn closer, or perhaps because he now looked less large next to Menon

Back home from his travels, Nehru had betrayed an awareness of how he had come to look abroad during these critical weeks. Addressing a mass meeting in New Delhi, he said that his foreign critics were "happy because they think my stature has been reduced." But, he cried, "if I have any stature it is you, my countrymen, who have built it up and no outsider can detract anything from that!" And the crowd cheered. In one of his many searchingly thoughtful reports from India, A M. Rosenthal remarked that much of the world seemed to expect Nehru to stand not merely for India's national interests, but "for something a little extra "[64] This expectation, after Hungary, had shrunk, and it was by this much that Nehru's stature had changed, and that the difference between his image and his alter image had diminished.

[63] Cf Life, February 11, 1957.
[64] Cf New York Times, February 4, 1957, April 18, 1957 Cf A. M. Rosenthal, "Nehru—Still the Searcher," New York Times Magazine, December 16, 1956, and "Krishna Menon—A Clue to Nehru," ibid , April 7, 1957.

## 7. *THE INDIANS ENCOUNTERED*

These large and highly visible portraits of the arresting or the incomprehensible Gandhi, the attractive or less attractive Nehru, or the repellent Nehru-Menon serve with remarkable fidelity as models for the more numerous and smaller images of the many Indians encountered by Americans in recent years. In most of these Indians, almost all the essential features except the greatness of the Gandhi-Nehru enlargements are reproduced, refracted, or fragmented. In the Americans exposed to all these smaller images, the range of reaction is likewise the same admiration, respect, puzzlement, or antipathy, becoming only sharper, more personal, and therefore often more strongly felt.

More Americans have met more Indians in the last dozen years than ever before in the history of the two peoples. There have been at least two distinct chapters in this brief history of encounters. The first was the massive movement of about 250,000 American soldiers to and through India during the Second World War. Perhaps as many as half of these remained in India for periods ranging from three months to three years. For the great mass of these young Americans, this was an ordeal. The wartime conditions, the tea patches and jungles of Assam, and the fetid slums of Calcutta were no breeding places for educational or elevating experience. All the stereotypes of glamour that might have been brought to India by these men were swiftly enveloped by the squalid reality. The Indians were the *wogs*,[65] recognizably human only to the rare GI, India a country they were desirous only of leaving.

A few individuals who shared that wartime experience in India acquired interests that have since shaped their careers, several of them appear in our present panel But the great mass of their fellows seem to have left their memories behind them or let them dim away in the disappearing past. The experience has so far not only failed to produce any memorable literature, it has produced hardly any at all.

[65] Wog, sometimes translated to mean Wily Oriental Gentleman, is a British term many decades old, applied by Englishmen to nonwhites generally from North Africa eastward all the way to India During World War II it was generally adopted by American GI's in India, who kept it moving east until it met the term "gooks," similarly used to describe all nonwhites met in the Pacific area.

Leaving aside those few works which deal with strictly military affairs or with soldiers only within their military environments, I have been able to find actually only three books which deal at all with the impact of India on Americans brought there by the chances of war. The only one with any GI flavor is a justly obscure account based on the letters written by an air force chaplain to his wife. It is called *Lookin' Eastward—A GI Salaam to India* (by Thomas H. Clare, as told to his wife Irma M Clare, New York, 1945) and it is believable only if it is read as an intentionally gross caricature both of its authors and its subject. It does, however, fleetingly convey some of the impressions of India common among American soldiers, including a description of the Hindus as "a subcultural species." A second, somewhat more serious literary fragment of this time and place is *American Sahib* (New York, 1946), in which John Frederick Muehl (later the author of the much more memorable *Interview with India*, New York, 1950) describes his experiences as a member of a volunteer American ambulance unit attached to British forces in India It is primarily the young author's account of a rather shocked discovery of the mentality and habits of the colonial British

Of quite a different order is Edmond Taylor's *Richer by Asia* (Boston, 1947), in which an ex-correspondent of long European experience and a self-described "fantastic Occidental insularity" recounts the "adventures of the mind" which befell him when he found himself transported on a military assignment into the strangeness of India Taylor had acquired from his study of the Nazis in Germany some lively ideas about the role of delusion in human behavior, and he had become sensitive to the tricks of the mind which were capable of creating mass attitudes and affecting the course of history. His adventure in India really started the day he caught himself "unconsciously creating a picture of the Indian people in the image of my bearer." This shocked him into a searching examination of "the pathology of imperialism" and led him on a quest through Indian politics, history, philosophy, and religion, for the sources of "the impression of monstrousness which India always produces on the Western mind." His restless and oddly unpeopled odyssey led him to some striking notions about both Hindu and Western "anticulture" and to the conclusion that the successful self-reassertion of India would be helpful to the re-establishment of "the tribe of man." *Richer by Asia*, essentially a work of contemplation, was surprisingly successful—three printings and about 10,000 copies [66]—but it was mentioned by only 5 of our panelists as a book remembered

This was, as far as I have been able to discover, the sum of the literary legacy of the wartime experience of Americans in India. The impact of Americans on Indians or of Indians on Americans had not, as yet, appeared as the theme of any novel Nor was there any other form of any nostalgic recall in film or in print. no Indian war brides, no softening in afteryears of the memories of pain. One member of our panel, a constant lecturer before public forums, reported running into echoes of the GI reaction. "I often run into the influence of men who had been to CBI (Chinese-Burma-India Theater), all frightfully unfavorable. India was a stinkhole of a country they wanted no part of, seldom had a solitary good word to say about it." [67]

The second and still current chapter in these new American-Indian relations began after the end of the Pacific war, with India's climactic partition and separation from Britain, its rise to sudden new importance in a world dominated by the Great Power conflict as an emergent nationalism on the democratic path, a new repository for the hopes so painfully abandoned in China. Several major newspapers and both major American news agencies continued after the war to maintain correspondents and bureaus in India. There was a marked increase in the quantity—if not generally in the quality—of news reports from Indian appearing in parts of the American press [68] The new events and this new American interest produced a brand-new literature of reportage from India by American writers commanding a certain serious attention from critics and readers, e.g., Margaret Bourke-White's *Halfway to Freedom* and Vincent Sheehan's *Lead Kindly Light* in 1949, Louis Fischer's *The Life of Mahatma Gandhi* and Muehl's *Interview with India* in 1950, all of which were mentioned by scatterings of from 6 up to 12 of our panelists, and Chester Bowles' *Ambassador's Report*, in 1954, which was mentioned by no fewer than 30. Other travelers' reports ranged from the kindly view of Eleanor Roosevelt's *India and the Awakening East* (1953) to the more critical views of Saunders Redding's

---

[66] According to Houghton Mifflin Company
[67] Some vignettes of the GI experience in India will be found in Isaacs, *No Peace for Asia*, Chapter 1, under the heading "The Wogs"
[68] Cf. *The Flow of the News*, International Press Institute, Zurich, 1953, pp. 50–52.

*Saul Steinberg drew the Indians as many wartime Americans saw them, "no joy in life, beaten down . . .*

(From Saul Steinberg, *All In Line*, Duell Sloan and Pierce, New York 1946)
and the Chinese, full of inquisitive and acquisitive vigor. . . ."

*An American in India* (1954) and Carl Rowan's *The Pitiful and the Proud* (1956). There were small but highly interested audiences for some new Indian novels, a friendly reception for a sensitively admiring film about India, *The River*, great acclaim for visiting Indian dance troupes, a certain vogue for Indian fashions, and even a small fad for Indian cookery

Aside from the daily flow of news which made the newsreading public aware of the phenomenon of Indian "neutralism," the major source of new American impressions of India in this period was the experience of encounters between Americans and Indians The new relations established by the independence of India started first a trickle and then a widening stream of travel between the two countries, a flow of official and private visitors [69]

To their experiences and encounters with Indians in India, or with Indians traveling in the United States, these Americans have brought some bits and pieces of all the images of Indians that have so far found a place in our gallery The notions of mystery and of fabulousness, the religionists and philosophers, the benighted heathen masses, the varieties of "lesser breed," and the images of Gandhi and Nehru have all mingled in the kaleidoscope But with direct contact, the frame narrows The visual and visceral impact of India and of Indians in the mass is still powerful, but even the traveler in India experiences it only at a certain distance The more personal and more typical encounter between Americans and Indians now occurs for the most part as a meeting between similars, between and among officials, diplomats, business men, scholars, educators, journalists, publicists, and politicians, for these are by and large the kinds of people who have journeyed between the two countries in the decade following Indian independence. Whatever else they glean from their travels, their sharpest personal impressions are likely to be of each other, of their own elite counterparts

This is all quite new to nearly all concerned· almost the only exceptions are a few scholars and the missionaries The missionary has tended generally in the past not to mix with the Hindu intelligentsia, but this has been changing. In his schools in India his contact has been quite largely with Indians who belong to the educated classes, and especially since Indian independence, the

---

[69] Just over 6,200 American travelers visited India in 1953, according to *International Travel Statistics, 1953*, London, 1955 An Indian Embassy official has estimated for us that Indian visitors have been coming to this country at an annual rate of about 1,500 There are an estimated 1,500 Indian students in the United States, and an estimated 5,000 Americans resident in India

newer, younger missionary has had to become more a man of affairs, he has had to seek broader and more satisfactory relations with Indians on the new basis, much like the diplomat, official, journalist, or scholar. For the whole new body of contacts, there are few precedents in history to draw upon for insight, no literature to give any clues or illumination We have little more than the raw material of what we have learned in this study. the impressions these Americans have had of the Indians they have encountered in this time

Before starting out among these unmapped crags and crevices, it might be well to check some of our bearings The first is a reminder that we are dealing here with the impressions of 181 Americans. They all occupy important places in various spheres of our society, and 99 of them have been to India They are in many important respects representative of their various environments But in many no less important respects they remain 181 unique individuals with their own patterns of experience, personality, and response The Indians who figure in their impressions are generally, as indicated, their opposite numbers in Indian society. If we were to hazard an extremely rough guess based on the information at hand, we might venture to say that these impressions were gained by these 181 Americans from encounters of longer or shorter duration with perhaps 5,000 such Indians These too would be unmistakably representative in many ways, at least of the small segment of college-educated leaders of Indian society Equally, they must also be regarded as so many single personalities, particularly individuals about whom many particular things are said The recurring patterns of impression and reaction will have to provide, as they unfold, their own measure of discrimination between individuals and types.

There is also the bearing of the time and its atmosphere. Except for the small group of missionaries and businessmen and one or two scholars, all this contact dates from the Second World War and the great bulk of it since Indian independence in 1947. In much the smaller number of cases, professional, official, or other assignments have involved several years' residence in India, or constant contact with Indians in this country. Much more commonly, the contact consists of encounters during brief and swift journeys of a few weeks or months by Americans to India or by Indians to the United States These have taken place in the atmosphere of these first years of Indian-American relations, an atmosphere neither salubrious nor kind There have been conflicts of interest and outlook between governments, which have inevitably communicated themselves to individuals, for they have been on political issues which are deeply felt by most of the people of the sort who figure in this study and whose reactions are whetted almost daily in the pages of the press and the periodicals which they read. A meeting between individuals strongly caught up in this atmosphere was not often likely to be the beginning of a beautiful friendship

We have seen, moreover, that neither party to these encounters started with an empty slate The Indian of this class had seldom acquired either under British tutelage or from his own experience an admiring or a friendly attitude toward Americans and American culture. On the other hand, the bits and pieces from the past that made up the characteristic American awareness of India and Indians were often not, as we have seen, of a kind to flatter Indian sensibilities. There was, on the whole, little blessing in the portents for the encounters of these years. The measure of mutual regard that did develop out of so many of them can be gratefully regarded as a triumph of men over circumstances.

## Profiles

Out of the notes of all the interviews, we sorted some 4,000 words, phrases, or remarks made about Indians Like heaps of metal shavings clustering to the poles of a magnet, they paired off in diametric opposites along a wide range of reactions and attributed traits and qualities Listed by the number of panelists who mentioned them and arranged by their contrasts, here is an initial picture of how they said they found Indians to be

| | | | |
|---|---|---|---|
| Charming, friendly, hospitable | 104 | 90 | Unpleasant, uncomfortable to be with |
| Easy to communicate with, to be with | 64 | 52 | Difficult to communicate with |
| Generalized positive reaction ("like, admire," etc) | 108 | 44 | Generalized negative reaction ("don't like," etc) |
| Intellectual qualities, positive | 98 | 91 | Intellectual qualities, negative |
| Competent, able | 65 | 28 | Impractical in workaday affairs. |
| Spiritual, high-minded, moral | 44 | 48 | Holier-than-thou, hypocritical. |
| Westernized, in positive sense | 41 | 42 | Anti-Western |
| Physically attractive | 40 | 35 | Physically unattractive. |
| Devoted, dedicated | 32 | 24 / 19 | Lacking social responsibility / Self-seeking |
| Articulate | 31 | 25 | Garrulous |
| Sensitive | 29 | 92 | Superiority-inferiority complexes. |
| Vital, good sense of humor | 28 | 52 | Unvital, no sense of humor |
| Reliable and honest | 22 | 61 | Unreliable, dishonest. |

From these matched or unmatched pairs of views, we can begin to discover some of the varying features given to the portraits of the Indians encountered, as well as of the Americans encountering them. Some are uncomplicated examples of the influence of the general on the specific Most of those, for example, who said they found Indians physically attractive were people who indicated that they liked Indians generally and most of those who did not like the way Indians look did not like much else about them either This was even more explicitly true with regard to certain other marked traits. Thus we had 31 individuals, all but 3 of them warm admirers of Indians, who said they are

> articulate, fluent, facile, eloquent, vocal, fine conversationalists, able and outspoken debaters . . .

while 25, of whom only 2 could be classed as admirers, described Indians as

> talkative, wordy, chattering, voluble, glib, garrulous, great foolers with words, talk you to death, argue uselessly . . .

Humor, on the other hand, was a somewhat more elusive matter than sight or sound In this matter there is certainly a wider gap between, say, a Bombay intellectual and a Bengali farmer than between the intellectual and his American counterpart. Here the difference was likely to be not between Indian and American notions of humor but between the English and American varieties. Actually, most of those who referred to the Indians as humorless were talking rather about an absence of laughter, merriment, or joy of life, a certain torpid listlessness among the masses of people they saw around them in India as they traveled. Only a smaller number (23) said they had missed the quality of humor in Indians they had met and talked to·

> humorless; unable to laugh at themselves, didn't dare tell a joke for fear I'd be misunderstood, can you imagine kidding an Indian?

Whereas there were 16 who had quite a different view, finding that Indians

> have a good sense of humor; enjoy life, humor is more akin to the British, same as ours . . .

In the difference between those who saw the Indians as *high-minded* and those who saw them as *holier-than-thou* we come to a major issue. A special spirituality and morality is freely conceded to Indians by some admirers. On the other hand, the frequent Indian claim to possess these qualities in some unique measure is perhaps the most aggravated of all the reasons others give for disliking the Indians they have met From the first group (44):

> Indians have a profound philosophical bent, deep, contemplative thinkers; more philosophical by nature than we are; are truly concerned with the idea of God, are in love with God; have a great radiant faith, are spiritually minded, take their religion more seriously, motivated by spiritual and religious considerations more than we are; are concerned with high moral principles in human relations, the Brahmin ideal is the irreproachable life, disdain for wealth and acquisitiveness, are more anxious to be good than many others; have great moral, ethical values, noble qualities; above our kind of materialistic culture, are more idealistic, more tolerant than we are, greatest honor in renunciation, bear life and suffering with fortitude. . . .

But for others (48):

> the claim of moral, cultural, spiritual superiority is infuriating, holier-than-thou, full of offensive moral pretense; assumption of spiritual superiority is untrue; there is no link in action between their philosophy and their behavior, their moral and spiritual preoccupations are an empty shell, the great dedicated Indian soul is a myth, there is great talk about ethical-spiritual-moral values matched against great private yearning for material things, emphasis on philosophy and principle which they completely fail to follow themselves; hypocritical, ready to argue any side of a question, am annoyed by this harping on American materialism, they play up the line of deep humanistic attitudes, but are all things to all men; can and do talk out of both sides of the mouth, they are not sufficiently embarrassed by these disparities, the spiritual-materialistic business is a joke that gets me very sore, they are unaware of discrimination in India or willing to rationalize it; are severely critical of our race problem while they are probably the most racially biased people in the world; don't know anybody who chases a dollar worse or does worse things to get a dollar than the Indian businessman, Indians take a free ride on the absurd Western image of the soul-like character of Indians. . . .

These contending pairs are not at all as evenly matched as the numbers suggest The 48 individuals on the negative side of the question are all quite explicitly and emphatically repudiating what they see as specious Indian claims to a higher spiritual and moral stature.

There is no such uniformity on the other side. On the contrary, a closer examination of the positive total of 44 rapidly melts it down to a much smaller number who seriously accept the idea of a unique Indian spirituality The total includes many who are placed here because they said some Indians are "idealistic" or "deeply contemplative" or "take their religion seriously."

Not a single academic specialist on India nor any of the academic panelists with "secondary" involvement with India concede any part of the idea of moral or spiritual superiority in Indians. There are actually 10 individuals with extensive India experience included in the total, but an examination of what they said shows in almost all a much more perfunctory kind of acknowledgment 4 businessmen who expressed a conventional kind of respect for other people's religion or religious attitudes, a diplomat who conceded the Brahmin "ideal," and 3 missionaries whose respect for Indian spirituality has a certain unavoidably hollow ring Only 2 in this group showed stronger feelings, one a missionary-scholar who saw the Hindu reform movement as the cradle of a true Christianizing of the country and its religion, and a woman writer who was deeply impressed by the idea of "right action" even though, she added, Indians don't live up to this idea themselves very often. Aside from these 2, there are perhaps 6 others who responded in some deeply personal manner to the nonrational, inclusive, or mystical qualities of Hinduism, some of them seeing it in the shape of a kind of universal religion with an essentially Christian spirit, some stating simply that they felt a certain affinity between Indian spirituality, mystical beliefs, or impulses, and their own. These were all individuals with very little experience in India and scanty contact, on the whole, with Indians.

The weight of opinion in the panel on this subject is perhaps most clearly indicated by the answers to a specific question later in the interview which called for comment on a set of common Indian stereotypes about Americans One of these was. "Indians are more spiritual, while Americans are only interested in material things." Only 6 individuals said they thought this statement was "justified"; 43 said it was "partly justified", 100 said, often with sharp accompanying comments ("hogwash!"), that it was not justified at all

Vivid as they might be, these paired groups of disembodied phrases, marching two by two into the ark of judgment, cannot convey the tone, tenor, and individuality of the separate interviews. They cannot show how these pairs mingled in constantly changing company in single minds. In our whole panel there were only half a dozen individuals who had nothing at all adverse to say about Indians and only 13 who had nothing whatever good to say about any of them. Some talked of particular Indians, some of Indians in general. Some held their views lightly, some with passion. Some spoke out of long experience, some out of none at all. The shadings away from the most strongly felt views were numberless in their kinds, varieties, and combinations, depending on the meanings different people read into their experiences or the weights each gave to various attributes in his own particular scale of values. To retrieve these many individual varieties, we depolarized all the words and phrases, put them back into the sentences from which they had come, resettled them in the environment of each particular interview. Here they could recover the elements of tone and feel, manner, quality, and relationship which make up a total impression of an individual's attitude. Out of all this sorting and re-sorting, dehydration and rehydration, we arrived at certain rough classifications of members of our panel in terms of their attitudes about Indians. We indicate these groups here by numbers which are not meant to be taken as absolute digits but as a means of suggesting their proportionate sizes within our panel.

There were 51—28 per cent of the whole panel—who expressed a predominantly favorable view of Indians. We called them *Pros*.

There were 73 with a predominantly unfavorable or negative view of Indians, 40 per cent of the panel, whom we called *Cons*.

A third group of 43, or 24 per cent of the whole panel, held views made up of mixtures of Pro and Con, leaning in one direction or another, whom we called *Mixed*.

There was, finally, a small clustering of individuals with views so particularized or so balanced that it seemed necessary to classify them by some criterion other than that of bias. There were 8 of these individuals, 4 per cent of our panel, and we called them *Differentiators*.

One major fact about these assorted groupings leaped to view almost at once: very few individuals with substantial or extensive experience *in India* appeared either as Pros or Cons. They bulked most largely among the Mixed and accounted for 7 of the 8 Differentiators.

Brought together in a single tabulation, this profile of our panel looks like this:

|  | Total | Extensive | Brief | None |
|---|---|---|---|---|
|  |  | *Experience in India* [70] |  |  |
| Pro | 51 | 3 (6%) | 21 (41%) | 27 (53%) |
| Con | 73 | 4 (5%) | 31 (42%) | 38 (52%) |
| Mixed | 43 | 18 (42%) | 18 (42%) | 7 (16%) |
| Differentiators | 8 | 7 (88%) | 1 (12%) | 0 |
| Insufficient information | 6 |  |  |  |

## Full Faces

But to tabulate is to simplify. To put all the warts and irregularities back on this profile of the panel as a whole, we have to go back textually to the interviews themselves and quote excerpts long and varied enough to communicate the infinity of their mixtures and contrasts and qualifications. This we now propose to do, and at some length. We shall present them grouped by degrees of Pro, Con, and Mixed Many of these passages may often also suggest why these particular Americans see their Indian counterparts in the particular ways that they do Except for some identifying information, especially about extent of contact with Indians, these excerpts will be offered without comment As we rub, gently as we can, on the surface of what was said, let the portraits of Indians and Americans both come into view by themselves.

## Strong Pro (6)

Here at the positive extreme are those individuals who are most emphatic and least reserved in their admiration for the Indians they have encountered. Five of the 6 are pre-eminent figures in their respective fields, 2 as scholars, 2 connected with metropolitan newspapers, and 1 a noted publicist. The sixth is an official of a national women's organization. None has been connected with India in a lifetime career sense, in fact, for all of them contact with India and Indians has been a quite marginal experience. Three have never been to India at all, two have visited briefly, and one spent nearly one year in the country on an academic assignment. The latter said:

---

[70] As previously defined, "extensive" means primary career involvement For the present purpose we have added in some with "secondary" experience with India which has been relatively substantial, involving some years' residence in the country, as contrasted to the "brief" experience of a few months or weeks

Educated Indians are almost carbon copies of educated Westerners. They have the same perspectives. Their attitude toward their own culture is about like mine toward my own. They have great aesthetic and intellectual interests, are eager for all the West can offer We mutually appreciated our cultures and felt the similarities outweighed the differences. There was charm, gentleness, humor, very little fencing for position. In the United States you are always fencing not to put your foot in it In India they said clearly what they think. Many seemed almost British, talked British English, had British ways of academic thinking and working. We talked of philosophy, architecture, sculpture I made a lot of good friends Those I met were eagerly picking up as much Western social science and psychology as they could. Communication was clear and full I always got intelligent questions from student groups. Some students asked me about anti-Semitism, Negroes, etc., but most of the heckling was moderate.

The second scholar reacted more explicitly on a somewhat different level:

I admire their sensitivity, their great awareness of you and your spirit. Many have the qualities I associate with sensitive women, that is, the ability to listen actively, not only on the surface but in depth This is rare, but less rare in Indians . . I am attracted by the idea of a great radiant faith that I associate with Indians The fact that they don't kill the cows despite their economic need to do so impresses me They have great moral and ethical values, a long historical view. I think of their traditionalism as benign Perhaps I see through Western manifestations of this kind of thing because I know it better, but somehow I think of nonviolence as being integrated in the Indian tradition, so that outbreaks of violence acquire a schizophrenic character.

. I haven't actually met many Indians of this spirit It is more a collective idea I have, an emotional feeling associated with Gandhi and with what I think of as the fundamental Indian attitude to man. I do not consider myself governed only by rational impulses. . . .

A similar accent appears in both newspaper editors The first·

I like Indians enormously. Always have the greatest sense of affinity with what seems to be the Indian way of looking at things, i e., a neutrality that views things as from a considerable distance. I see an affinity between Nehru and Woodrow Wilson. . . Gandhi was always vivid to me, made sense to me. The Indian type of pacifism accepted all the consequences, while Western pacifism always seemed more sentimental Hinduism seems to me free of sentimentalism, while

Christianity is full of it. That is why I have always thought I would fall in love with India. It responds to some of my own basic tendencies.

And the second:

> Remarkable cultural richness, cultivated people in depth. . I'm probably a curious kind of mystic myself, so we do get some communication I try to rationalize my religious concepts, but I do believe all reality is spiritual, so obviously there is a certain bond between me and them I see Gandhi as a most realistic mystic

The focus of the publicist is quite different, his experience with Indians occurring almost exclusively in a political context:

> I think of them always as individuals of all sorts My interests have always been primarily political, but have had warm personal friendships as well as a political bond. The Indians can be relied on to take the most advanced view on human rights, colonialism They are the strongest and most insistent in these matters . . . About Indian intellectuals, a lot of my friends don't like the Cambridge-Oxford veneer. I do hear of rudeness, argumentativeness, an air of superiority But this has not been my experience. They are plain-spoken people, much less likely to be politic, argue with you more quickly, and this is thought to be a display of superiority. I think a lot of Americans are like this too

The one woman in the group comes closest to having an almost totally undiscriminating attitude Her experiences occurred in one brief visit to India on an exchange mission:

> I loved them very much, intelligent, stimulating, love to talk, very articulate, love to argue. I enjoy their argumentativeness Friendly, wonderful, interesting people Very philosophical, always challenging our materialism. Village workers, imbued with great enthusiasm, doing all kinds of exciting things. Indian art is beautiful Indian religion a liberal kind of thing, not at all dogmatic, the required things about food and cleanliness all seemed very practical to me, all sensible rules . .

It is worth adding here, if only parenthetically, that of these six individuals who liked Indians so well, three did not like the Chinese at all.

## Moderate Pro (25)

The person with moderately positive views about the Indians is usually somewhat less emphatic in his admiration, or begins to introduce some qualifying impressions on the negative side, or seeks to counter more hostile views by offering explanations. Among these 25, we find only three with relatively extensive experience in India, a scholar and two businessmen. One of the latter makes a distinction between Indian types that occurs quite often in these interviews:

> I have intense admiration for the Indian as a gentleman, administrator, and businessman. The men I met would compare very favorably indeed with the better-than-average in the United States. Integrity is not one of his greatest virtues, but when the Indian businessman gives his word, clearly understood, I'd just as soon deal with him as with anybody. The ICS [Indian Civil Service under the British] people are a fine able group of men, but unfortunately they are a dying species. People now being trained may not have the breadth of vision they acquired under British training The politician is a quite different type; I find myself opposed to him most of the time... Many things Indians do, of course, are downright filthy. Betel-chewing is repulsive as the devil, even in the nicest friend I also didn't like the servants' attitude that the European is fair game for cheating . . .

The second businessman, a banker:

> Excellent to do business with, proud, honor their loans, could almost always depend on their reliability. Almost in the same class with the British, whom I put at the top as to reliability of the spoken word. . . . Of course there was the caste system and all that, which I guess India will outlive After all there are caste systems all over the world, even here in our own country. I must say, however, I never really had a great deal to do in any very intimate way with Indians and those we did business with were necessarily highly selected.

The scholar takes a friendly view, low-keyed and quite impersonal:

> Of course there are as many SOB's among Indians as in my father's Masonic lodge. Lots of misunderstandings, but all minor Some showed bad manners, and here and there, like anywhere else, a few stupid and unintelligent people But I found Indians always receptive and always had good experiences They are articulate and friendly, always ready to share food and shelter all over India . .

Among the 9 moderates who have toured in India briefly in their various professional capacities, a Midwestern newspaper editor said:

> The spiritual side of many Indians I have met has impressed me and I have liked most of them My own Quaker background helps me appreciate the Gandhi point of view One Indian I know is a heel, intel-

lectually dishonest, but he is so untypical that he's irrelevant. I think them attractive, but nearly all people seem so to me on one ground or another. Among some Indians I have noticed a certain touchiness, chips on their shoulders about their national or cultural superiority. But I understand this as part of their present situation It didn't bother me greatly. I don't go in for strong emotional feelings about people. . .

A well-known writer mixes some of the same views with a rather stronger emotional ingredient.

> Of course I know that many people have said they strongly dislike the Indians I find this especially true among the news people I have thought sometimes this was true because the Indians have not put out for them the way other [Asians] have They expected the Indians to come to them, and they haven't done so. Of course there is a lot that feeds this feeling India is messy, Indians are more guarded, and of course there is too this business of Indian arrogance I encountered plenty of it, but it seems to me quite obvious that it is a product of the imposed sense of inferiority against which so many Indians are still struggling. and when you have been kicked around as much as they have been, how can you blame them for reacting this way? I have found the approaches really open if you persisted. As far as I am concerned, I like Indians as I like Chinese or Japanese or anybody else for that matter. . . . Actually I am a bad person to ask about a thing like this because I am probably the most undiscriminating person in the world when it comes to liking people I will admit often being irritated, but even with those who got me very mad, I found I could break down the hostility and achieve some friendly mutuality.

Or this from an economist who once taught in a missionary college in India·

> They are intellectually brilliant, smarter, cleverer, sharper than American students. Some strange contradictions, highly trained medical men tolerating old superstitious practices in their own homes This led to the death of one doctor's wife in childbirth. . . They suffer from inferiority attitudes, have strong irrational reactions to any critical statements about Indian things, extreme touchiness Often this made for a real problem in communication which bothered me, puzzled me, but gave me feeling of sympathy when I came to understand it. The superiority-attitudes of some of the missionaries made me feel almost the same way as the Indians did.

Finally a Catholic writer·

> Ones I've seen are all extraordinarily high-class people Of course,

they were all Catholics, so they had their religion in their favor as far as I was concerned . . . But I can see where I would like Indians less if I knew more of them I think their greater knowledge of English lets the differences come through more easily Since they know English, we expect them to be less different than they are.  But those I've met are well educated, gentlemanly. I think of Indians as quite spiritual, with deep-seated traditional beliefs and practices I never heard of any common immorality among them, like you hear that Greeks are slippery customers. . . .

## Mild Pro (21)

The quality of "mildness" can be simply one of mild and friendly acceptance of interesting people briefly encountered, as in the case of a Chicago editor

> The Indians we see are intelligent, sophisticated, self-possessed, and like people generally, I find them attractive enough . . .

or a Midwestern public opinion specialist:

> My impression is of people well poised, quite articulate, well educated, mild, neat, courteous, college-trained, just like their similars here in America, just like you and me . .

or this Washington correspondent who sees Indians there frequently:

> I find in them a high degree of intellectualism. Have often argued with them over pacifism or foreign policy They are brilliant arguers and I generally like them. Disagreement has nothing to do with whether I like or dislike anybody. I guess I like people generally. I have trained myself not to have generalized opinions, and I am quite aware that all the Indians I have met have been of a particular group, all cultivated and extremely articulate.

A more cautious and somewhat more critical detachment occurs in the remarks of 2 Negro panelists, both prominent publicists. The first introduces an element we shall encounter in stronger terms later on·

> Indian visitors I see now tell me the British taught the Indians to keep away from the American Negro, but now that India is free this attitude is changed Those I've met seem quite intelligent, interested, proud of their country, assured, confident. They also have this color identification on a global scale That's why they come and look us up. They deny that a greater value is placed on a fairer skin in India, although I had recently read about internal color difficulties in India.

But the Indians I have met are pleasant enough on casual acquaintance. Who knows what might develop out of closer knowledge?

The second, a major national figure in race relations affairs, carries us to the bridge between those with mildly positive views and those who begin to be more clearly mixed·

> Much impressed with them. They seem competent, intelligent. Educated like the English and get more maturity and knowledge out of their education than we do. They seem to be pretty stubborn in their conviction that the plight of the Negro in the United States is very much worse than we say it is. They insist, despite what they see with their own eyes. They seem pretty thoroughly indoctrinated before they get here, and it's pretty difficult to root out a lot of things They may not always be wrong. There are some things, perhaps, to which the American Negro has adjusted so far that he thinks them unimportant Of course when you try to talk about Untouchability, they bridle right away People are pretty much the same—they like to see what's wrong in the other fellow's back yard. I never heard any Negroes complain about treatment they got in India, but they all report the same stubborn refusal to believe the facts of Negro life in the United States as Negroes describe them I spoke to some Indian students once who accused me of being "paid by the State Department" for saying what I did. They simply cannot understand the diversities of this country . . .

## Mixed Pro (18)

A "Mixed" view in what the phrase itself implies. a set or blend of contrasting or differing observations and reactions. It marks out traits in different individuals or distributes them to types or groups. It usually has more than one focus, distinguishing more clearly among personal or emotional, or intellectual, political, or religious reactions at varying levels. It contains some mixture of Pro and and Con The Mixed view usually has a great deal more to go on and is therefore almost always associated with some greater measure of experience. As our previous nose-counting has already shown, the 43 grouped as Mixed include virtually all in the panel with substantial experience in India and about half of those who have at least visited India more or less briefly.

Among these 43 there is a first group of 18 whose mixtures of views retains a certain bias toward the Pro. Among these there are only two who have never visited India One is a social psychologist who is often visited at his university by Indians working in the same field:

> Little as I know about India, I am pretty sure that the Indians I see have very little more contact with the people in the lower sections of their own society than I have, and I simply suspect their judgments where these people are concerned I feel they do not really reflect India to me. I usually get a feeling of competence and charm from the visitors I see. My only negative reaction is to some of their views I feel that they are unrealistic, that they do not realize the implications of modern technological development. I feel a certain complacency in these people about their own social responsibility I mean by this that if I were an Indian I think I would be lying awake nights thinking about what I as a social scientist could best do to help cope with our problems. Nevertheless I liked them immensely .

The other nontraveler is a former government official of high rank who encountered Indians frequently in various international bodies:

> They are as diverse as we are, more so. I do get an impression of considerable unrealism from my experience with them in the last five or six years in UNESCO and elsewhere Radakrishnan, for example, was just as unrealistic after as he was before his experience in the Soviet Union. There is a disconcerting vein of unrealism in their general line of argument about the Communist world. In other matters I feel a blend of practicality and fuzziness . I am always quite comfortable with Indians They seemed quite straightforward, even as I tried to be. Always seemed truthful to me In official contacts less so, but then that is generally the case in official relations . . .

There are seven in this group with brief experience in India One is a Negro sociologist

> I liked the ready friendliness, even when there were disagreements. But what I disliked was an unreasoning hostility to America, especially since I moved only among intellectuals. There was much stress on color, partly a reaction to me as a Negro, but this was common with everybody I would often refer to newspaper advertisements seeking brides of "a wheatish color" or "clear light complexion." They would insist this was like Americans preferring blondes or brunettes, not a matter of color discrimination Of course among American Negroes too we have some attitudes like this I don't know whether I found their answers reasonable or not. They certainly took a self-justifying attitude . .

A Jesuit missionary official:

> A great deal of friendliness and hospitality in my brief contact. But I felt a certain difficulty in getting my own point of view across to them. They seem to have been nurtured on some sort of party line. I found the same opinions, the same way of looking at things and at current political problems. This struck me because Hindus are supposed to be so tolerant of other opinions and this behavior was quite a contradiction of this idea. I felt irritated at times, though I tried not to show it. I rather liked the people I met as individuals.

Among these Mixed Pros we also find eight persons with extensive India experience. These included an anthropologist who said "I do not separate personal from professional qualities." And an economist: "With Indian economists I feel much more common ground on a professional basis, while among noneconomist Indians I have a certain feeling of apple-polishing." A political scientist in this same group was a good deal more willing to react to his Indian encounters as human experiences:

> I found them all very full of themselves and their problems, but extremely friendly, frank, and open. No hesitation about criticising the United States and Americans. In Europe people do not do this until they are more familiar with you. The students were argumentative but not very substantial. I was shocked at their attitudes toward their own people. One young official said "Any Indian who can't speak English has nothing worthwhile to tell you." I felt a deep gulf between the educated people and the mass. They were much closer to me than they were to their own lower classes... Servants jumped up for high officials and for me too without even knowing who I was. These elite attitudes and relationships are very dangerous. Could lead to Fascist attitudes about the dumb masses.... In manner of judgment, the students were quite impersonal. I had no complaint about manners, but they seemed to need very little basis in fact for their statements. Many had absorbed elementary Marxist theory and held rigid and formalistic stereotypes in their minds instead of ideas. I often felt their antagonism was based on envy of our wealth. I tried to put them straight with facts about U S poverty, slums, struggles, unions. They had no picture of this at all, and the information did not appeal to them. As people, I reacted very favorably to them. Their open frankness appealed to me. I note certain differences between Indians in the United States and Indians in India. Like almost all people, they will defend abroad what they will attack at home. But in India I always felt they were quite sincerely frank.

We encounter missionaries for the first time in this group. They really belong in a class by themselves in this panel, if only because they have generally lived in the different milieu of the Indian Christian community and because they have had a much longer history of evolving attitudes and experiences. Here are samples from this first group which expressed the most favorable views about Indians of any given by India missionaries in this study, first from the remarks of an older man who originally went out to India, rather reluctantly, in 1917:

> We were pretty isolated in a small place Knew our students and faculty and some people in town. They varied so much, as people would anywhere. Friendliness and courtesy everywhere Ran into dishonesty and lack of punctuality but when I came home after my first term, I found the same things here. Our servants were faithful and reliable, dishonest, but very disarming about it. Otherwise all degrees, quarrelsome and meek, honest and dishonest, devoted and not so devoted Our Indian faculty did not contribute much to our curriculum but some of them had keen minds, intensely logical, and marvelous memories. One was very difficult, very touchy, would fly off the handle if he thought he was slighted. I was politically unsympathetic in the beginning toward Indian aspirations for freedom but began to change in the mid–30's. Thought of Gandhi as a politician but came to think of him later as combining social responsibility with political acuteness Indians today try to compensate for injuries to their pride and this leads to some amusing claims, especially about Hinduism. That is why so many students who come to the United States are so self-assertive and, I understand, make themselves obnoxious

Another prominent missionary figure who spent twenty-five years in India.

> I liked the farm life; I think of some devoted Indian pastors and their infinite patience The Christians I dealt with were as potentially able as anybody Limited by their social heritage but not by anything innate Their caste system leads to group conflicts and tends to create inequities and nepotism... Most of what Katherine Mayo wrote was true, but too selective. She played up the seedy side and overlooked the nobler aspects. I did not like the dirt, smells, sordid surroundings These are all physical, but physical facts get attached to men too Often I felt I did not know what Indians were thinking about, didn't know what to expect Their inscrutability may have been a matter of language or of difference in social, economic, and religious backgrounds.

It all added up to a lack of understanding gradually dispelled by more contact and knowledge

Finally, a younger missionary who spent his career years in India overcoming prejudices:

> Although to begin with I was pro-British, I gradually became very sympathetic to the nationalist cause. Had thought of Gandhi as something of a schemer, but as time went on my attitude changed . . . I expected the villagers to be hostile, instead they were hospitable. When I went to India I expected to find many abhorrent things of which I had heard and read, snake worship, extreme asceticism But they did not upset me as I expected. I kept an even temper in the face of these things. I did feel a strong sense of injustice to the outcasts Am still disturbed by the fact that many Indians can combine an enlightened approach and superstitious practices College graduates in cow protection societies! Always baffled me On the other hand, saw good features in the joint family, in the social cohesion provided by the castes in some respects, in the fine family relations I am still annoyed by the Indian habit of bringing outside influence to bear on you if they want something, some of our missionaries have adopted this habit But I liked their friendliness, always had agreeable relations with Indian neighbors, never had a bad moment with an Indian. . .

The last of our Mixed Pros is a noted writer on international affairs whose focus is political with strong emotional and rather personal biases His views, which bring us close to many which will feature more largely in the more negative attitudes to follow, are certainly the most fully stated.

> I like Indians They have interesting minds. There is a quality of loveliness among them, a mellowness, a lack of bitterness among the people, a kind of softness, gentleness, meekness, which I find most attractive. Many of them are limited by their sensitive nationalism, and suffer from a sense of inferiority and the compensations they seek for it. Some are easily wounded. Others are one-sided, superpatriotic. Occasionally they are arrogant But even in the same person who is arrogant and narrow, there is often a kind of tolerance. They do seek a greater inclusiveness of points of view Many have been touched by Gandhi, though not all are Gandhian in any full sense of the term. Both the good and bad qualities seem to me to be very specially Indian There is more of all these things in India than elsewhere The negative qualities are more in evidence among upper-class officials and intellectuals, but still they have a quality that makes them companionable and pleasant to associate with  . . I feel ferociously hostile to all the trap-

pings of Indian religion and the whole system of caste and Untouchability. Most of my friends share this intellectually, but some do not, and this gets in the way of our friendship. I condemn their attitudes on Russia and China and we exchange mutual charges of ignorance and prejudice. I tax them with their color attitudes and they either regret them or say they don't share them These things spoil our relations, and when I want to keep things pleasant, I avoid talking about them. They claim to be ignorant about Soviet Europe and insist they don't accept dictatorship, but they just go along blindly with their prejudices and won't even read things about it. Of course in the last few years all this has modified my relations with many Indians. I think a lot of old friends of India in America are sick and tired of the smugness and the holier-than-thou attitude, the claims about their spiritual quality and our materialism Arthur Lall and Krishna Menon rub a lot of people the wrong way. Mme. Pandit makes a beautiful impression, but those who know her know she is arrogantly superior in her outlook The closer you are to Indians, the more you are likely to be disenchanted with Indian politicians and Indian attitudes.

## Mixed Con (25)

From the Mixed Pros we move across a sort of divide in this topography of attitudes toward Indians encountered. The divide itself is not unpeopled, and we will eventually return to it for the views it offers. But we cross it now to follow first the currents of feeling as they begin to flow in the opposite direction. This shift starts with a group of 25 Mixed Cons, individuals whose views are mixed but with a weight of reaction that is essentially negative.

There is a heavy concentration of India experience in this group 10 with extensive contact with India, 11 with briefer experience on the ground, and only four with none at all. The striking thing about the India-experienced group is the large number among them whose judgments tangle, often in a deeply troubling way, with their committed personal and professional sympathies. We find among them a journalist of several years' experience in India, a woman writer who has devoted much of her time to the Indian cause in America, a professional man who has achieved international repute for his work in India, a foundation official wholly concerned with Indian interests, 2 India-born men, one of whom followed the parental missionary path, the other now a scholar exclusively concerned with Indian matters, and a missionary official whose job it is to advance the Christian cause in the new Indian conditions.

The journalist came out of a three-year stay in India with a great sense of triumph over having won "acceptance" from Indians against great difficulties:

> There is tension in all relations. You are constantly forced to prove yourself to him in a way he does not have to prove himself to you. Your bona fides are constantly being questioned. The problem of color sensitivity plays a large role in this. You discover the Indian's own color attitudes and also his acute consciousness of color issues in the world. The color problem is always present in a friendship between Indians and Americans It is hard to put your finger on, but you feel a certain absence of rapport, with the Indian always probing you. . . In exchanging ideas, they tend to overstate their views in order to make sure there's no question about their asserting themselves, quite aggressive and belligerent But this conduct does not upset me I have had my own good faith accepted, so I feel satisfied .

The foundation executive feels the same one-sidedness of the relationship

> Get a great variety and a whole range of types You almost always do run into some form of inferiority complex and defensive posture. They try to find my vulnerabilities and attack whatever I represent They have a great sense of insecurity, many conflicts over family relations and social status, an underlying lack of confidence and a certain cynicism. They are self-seeking, quite importunate in selfish personal matters. . . . Actually, though, I have liked most of them. I have been readier to see their good qualities than they have been to see mine But I do have a sense of a persistent distance between us. I have never really had time for real leisurely relations with Indians I think if I did there would be very few Indians I would want to see very much of. . . .

The India-born missionary, who ardently defends India's foreign policy against its American critics, spoke of the difficulties of relationships in India itself

> I think this whole complex of attitudes derives from the well-imbedded Indian expectation that the white Westerner is going to think the Indian is inferior Therefore the Indian is hostile and rejects the white Westerner. I feel you get over this barrier only after long association, but even in my own experience—and I was born in India and identify quite fully with it—I am subject to this acute sensitivity and have had some very painful experiences. . . I think it is this inferiority complex which is directly responsible for the great arrogance of a great many Indian intellectuals It seems often that they cannot abide any

comparisons. Personally what I feel most strongly about is their lack of social consciousness and responsibility for the well-being of people they do not know or are not connected with personally Indians are most generous and friendly with those whom they know, but they seem almost not to comprehend that others are human beings too. I have been greatly struck to observe that Indian teachers are not interested in their pupils as individuals, are not sensitive to individuality or character. . . .

The mixture of identification and exasperation emerges perhaps most fully in the reaction of the India-born scholar:

Indians make me think of many different things. I like them as friends I like their point of view on politics They are more intelligent than most Americans I know about what's going on in the world. They are too sophisticated to believe that everything we do is holy, everything the other side does is unholy They realize more subtle shades of gray This may reflect Indian philosophy, which does not construe the world in blacks and whites The Indian claim of moral superiority is just an outer layer. If you know them well, they speak differently. They only half-believe it You can get onto other levels if you are able to break this barrier down Some really believe it, and this of course limits their sophistication They are loyal people—loyal to their country and their culture, quite admirably so . . But I now realize more than I did before that the Indian mind is fundamentally unscientific, i.e., as we understand the scientific concept in research I am also much more aware of this ambivalence, between the white culture they cannot accept because of what it has meant to them, while at the same time they cannot fully accept their own. So they are full of conflicts, difficulties Anybody who knows Indians well will tell you they have very insecure traits This is illustrated by their silly use of titles, titles, titles The Babu mentality, a sort of petty clerk arrogance toward all who are inferior, together with servility to all one's betters. This is sometimes maddening You can see it right here in Washington at the embassy—how they treat each other in terms of status. It is carried to the point of rudeness They are also irresponsible, will promise to do things and then don't do them Continuously, always, not just once in a while, and even when it is to their advantage to be more cooperative This happens again and again. I attribute this to a lack of organized minds, lack of concept of method There are of course notable exceptions, occasional, but certainly not frequent. Their scholarship rarely reflects any quality Their Ph D. theses would not qualify for entry into graduate work here. Same thing among businessmen, although perhaps not so much irresponsibility. But businessmen combine even more superstitious beliefs with modernism than the intellectuals. But given half a chance, they are warm and friendly, polite, and helpful, until the European expresses some racialist attitude. Then the curtain drops. It is the primary touchstone. Bending over backward, patronizing, is just as bad as the opposite... Their irksome qualities do get in the way of liking many of them It depends on the degree to which any particular individual has them. Among "old India hands" there is, I am afraid, a fair amount of covert contempt, the unspoken sentiment is· We know how tedious and trying and silly they can be, even though we know how nice they can be too...

Among those whose involvement with India is still considerable but of much more recent date, a great measure of detachment tends to appear. The effect of one brief trip to India appears in these remarks by an economist:

Before I went to India my impressions of Indians were aggressive, insecure, humorless, verbally facile, quite often bright. I no longer feel they are without humor. I also found many more with genuine self-confidence instead of aggressiveness due to a lack of confidence. Still think of them as verbally facile. Before I went there, I had on balance a minus feeling, bright and competent but rather unpleasant and unadmirable as human beings I tend now to classify them more as person-to-person, fewer national characteristics than before Also realized my earlier contacts had always been scanty and unmotivated. In India I found it took quite a while to get through to a person, but once you were through, it was all right. They were certainly more secure, perhaps because I was now seeing them on their home grounds. I had images of mysticism, lack of practicality, religious fervor, hideous poverty. Now some of this is not as strong as before. It is not effaced, but greatly reduced, especially on the mystical side. . . .

The professional businessman made a conscious effort to avoid emotional involvement in his rather extensive Indian associations:

I don't "live" India, I'm just very interested in it In India you get into closer sympathy with people than you do here where things are less intimate. They call more for that put-your-hand-in-mine relationship. Many seemed to me frustrated people who don't see what path to follow. Great deal of professional jealousy, are never satisfied with their prestige or economic returns, suffer from a sense of unreality, tend to equate the possibilities with their wishes They are educated to conformity rather than to experiment or questioning. They very rarely write critical or self-critical reports . . . Certain Hindu doctrines, especially renunciation, appeal to me very much, but I do not believe they have really permeated Indian life People there are really quite indifferent to the ideas of Gandhi or the Gita They are really very callous about life I think we are more humanitarian than they are, while the more sensitive among the Indians are generally more sensitive than any of us.

A missionary official of fairly recent India experience:

Ascetic, sensitive, intelligent, articulate, but with a certain aloofness. It is very difficult to get close to Indians, to share experience or understanding with them Felt a kind of bottled-up resentment under the surface while outwardly they were trying to be polite and calm. I felt uncomfortable and apologetic because I was so well off, secure, in contrast to all that poverty Had a feeling they sensed and resented this. Maybe I just imagine it . Indians are helpless in practical matters Those who come here have to be nursed along. Have to take care of them every step of the way. Same kind of childlike dependency in finances Many are unable to be completely straightforward or honest with you Much petty maneuvering and dishonesty. Have had some very unhappy experiences. . Indians are opinionated Maybe this is the British influence because I've always had the notion that Britishers are opinionated too. But when we have Indians to a meeting of fifteen or twenty well-informed people, the Indian will tend to dominate the whole business. Has opinions on everything and is very uninhibited about expressing them. I keep wondering whether I feel this because I am not particularly opinionated, always holding my judgments in abeyance, so maybe I notice it more . . I like Indians, and I admire them, and I try to see their point of view on controversial matters like politics. But I am a little uneasy in their presence. I feel I am suspect. I am inclined to think that some people who have spent their entire lifetime in India feel this same way . . .

Four present or former top American diplomats and one rather important member of Congress appear among the Mixed Cons To a far greater extent than most others, their preoccupations lie primarily in the field of politics, and all of them share a more or less hostile impatience with Indian political outlooks. One of the diplomats:

Those I had contact with were very superior people. However there is a great gulf between these Indians and the rest. It is enormous, like two different races. The British-educated official class, the ICS [Indian Civil Service] people received their better education and values from the British, and a sense of public responsibility The Congress people did not have the integrity of the ICS. They carry the scars of the past, full of inhibitions and prejudices It is so difficult to get them to see your point. They just close up in certain things The press people lack honesty and candor, and the business people are even lower in the scale. Double-faced, wily, squirming mentalities, always twisting and embarrassing you, try to trap you and confuse you and catch you up, rather than try to get at the truth. India is a madhouse of confused leaders . . .

The second said:

> Communication is easy because of their use of the English language, and their training under the British gives the same quality to the words used But there is a different mental approach that gets in the way It has taken me years to understand this There is extreme race consciousness They are guilty in their own country of the strongest race prejudices and caste system in the world, but they solidarize automatically with other colored people, even the Mau Mau, simply because they are colored. Whatever the white man does is wrong Many Indians have risen above this, and Nehru seems genuinely to want to overcome these distinctions in India

A third, who had visited in India but whose principal meeting ground with Indians was as a member of the American delegation at the UN, sees them in the back of his mind in these terms:

> I think I have an insight into some of the spiritual qualities of Indians, their fine and noble qualities, but also some of the dreadful distortions of their religion. From members of my family [involved in missionary work in India] I have gotten the idea that Indians have a different view of honesty than we have. Also a greater courtesy and politeness than ours and a certain serenity. Some a joy to be with, but in general a negative reaction My [missionary] relatives share a sort of Britisher's white-man's-burden view of Indians and tend to look down their noses at Indians more than I do I think I have more charitable feelings and greater sympathy for Indian religious ideas than these missionaries have But I do see them as somewhat inferior Part of this is the feeling that you are dealing with colored people. . . At the UN I and my country were insulted by Indian representatives, and this has helped form my mental picture of Indians.

## *Mild Con* (21)

Almost all the colors, features, and accents of the encountered Indian have been sketched in by now, even though all our more critical portraitists still await their turn at the easel The additions to come, however, are almost entirely a matter of lighting, and lighting is a matter of intensity and placement. Beginning very early among the Pros and accumulating among the Mixed, attributes seen as less attractive have mingled with the attractive in varying schemes and touches. Now as we move among those whose view of the Indians is predominantly negative, the more attractive features begin to disappear into the shadows and the light falls more and more exclusively on features reflecting dislike, distaste, and hostility. With strikingly few exceptions, the harsher judgments are the products of much scantier contact and experience

In contrast to the high frequency of India-experienced people among those with Mixed views, we find in this first of our negative groups, the Mild Con, 21 individuals of whom only 1 had any moderately extensive experience in India—less than a year's time on an academic assignment—and only five who had been briefly in the country—1 only for an overnight plane stop—and 15 who have never been there at all. Some of the latter have had almost no contact whatever with Indians anywhere The sparsity of contact with counterpart Indians seems in some cases to leave the mind free to retain many of the earlier, cruder images An example in a public opinion specialist:

> I think of impoverished, ignorant fanatics, teeming masses, no education, bizarre religious practices These are probably my own earliest impressions, out of the *National Geographic*, and I am probably attributing these to people now—fakirs, beds of nails, hot coals, that sort of thing I still retain this picture although I realize of course its extreme forms are now more rare. I think of India now mostly in a political context.

Others offered various fleeting impressions fleetingly gained E g, a social psychologist:

> From my experience with students in my classes, I have one strong stereotype· the Indians seem to be philosophical and abstract rather than empirical and scientific A recent study made in Durban [in South Africa] showed that Bantus were very concrete and Indians very abstract This fits my impression of all the Indians I have met. Two I remember as extremely oily. I had one who filled his pocket with my cigars and then had the audacity to offer me one I have known lots of Americans like this too. . . .

# THE INDIANS

A professor of psychology:

> Have met only a few Indians and most of these I have felt unable to reach I really mean a difficulty of getting good first impressions, never can get an impression of what the pitch is, what kind of fellow he is, his interests, quality of mind. This seems to be my experience with Indians; rarely with others. . Because the brother's-keeper concept doesn't have value in the Indian value system, I distrust it . . .

A prominent Negro journalist:

> Have long known the caste system is based fundamentally on color and that Indians have color prejudices. Have read and heard lots about it from people who have been there. A friend of mine who went to India in 1948 remarked on advertisements he saw in the papers seeking light-skinned wives Once he commented on the beauty of Indian women and was shocked when an Indian acquaintance said. "You ought to go up north, we have some women there you can't tell from white!" Indians I meet here seem critical of our color line but I frequently thought that these people don't see the beam in their own eye, especially on this matter I am sometimes annoyed too by their harping on American materialism Everywhere I've ever gone, all people are materialistic.

A government official:

> They are very intent and voluble people. At FAO conferences always the first and last to speak. Gave me the feeling they were neglecting their own problems and thinking about theoretical world problems. Have heard from others who have dealt with Indians, who say Indians are quick to learn but more in theories than in practical accomplishments. They said the Indians never relaxed with them on a man-to-man basis. . .

One of the travelers in this group was a Congressman who made an overnight stop in Calcutta in 1947:

> Had a glimpse of the crowds. The religious and political tension was on. It was a depressing sort of experience. Thought of it later when the head of WHO asked me how public health could be helped in India when cattle roam freely and religion prevents any proper sanitation I think Nehru has stultified India in American eyes by being so footsey with Russia and the Chinese Communists. I used to be very sympathetic but I now feel highly critical. . . .

Another was a United States Senator who toured in 1953:

I found Indians inscrutable Such an enormous number of them and it was a handicap not to be able to meet many run-of-the-mill people Just because Nehru or Menon says something it doesn't mean they reflect the people's thinking How do we get at it? Pakistanis have no use for the sincerity of Indians, and I was more impressed with the sincerity of the Pakistanis. . .

A third was a major political figure who came away from a brief visit the same year with these impressions:

> There was an aggressive intellectualism and a sort of curious self-confidence that they really know, overeducated people, preoccupied with the ethics of modern society, and with highly discolored pictures of the West I have met these types before, and I don't think my impressions are inaccurate. There were no vast surprises when I went to India On the whole I found it less frightening and miserable than I had foreseen Saw some ghastly things but not as bad as I had anticipated. . .

The last of this group stayed longer, an economist who spent nearly a year in India.

> Great latent ability but need formal training. Suffer from basic rootlessness in their value system. Are at sea in their own minds between reverence for traditional Indian culture and the feeling this does not serve them in the industrialization of India or in making India a first-rate power A marked sense of inferiority, national and personal, a tendency to think they know the answers. Insufficient humility before problems Quite materialistic Didn't like the Indians as well as I liked the British in India . .

## Moderate Con (20)

The distinction between "mild" and "moderate" is a matter of both quantity and intensity. Here more is said, and the judgments are as a rule more strongly made. In a good many cases, they are based on considerably more experience. In contrast to the travel experience of the Mild Con group, we find that half of the Moderates have been to India, 1 for fairly extended visits of up to a year, and nine for briefer periods. They include rather substantial representatives of every professional type and category in the panel as a whole. Several of these, both travelers and nontravelers. lend the predominantly negative feeling its most important weight precisely because they are individuals not given to easy or superficial judgments and their remarks cannot be taken in any simple or single dimension. Here are the reactions of a highly trained scholar and observer:

> Have a great impression of verbosity They are most talkative, voluble people. . . You expect to have a rational conversation up to a point, then a barrier They move into a mystical, noncoherent kind of world that is fantastic to me They escape my ability to interchange Certain emotional sets become more important than rationality or coherence. It has the nature of what we call prejudice, they are a singularly prejudiced people. Emotions ride high in many things, e g., race problems. They are quite unable to see that they are in the same box on this matter. They suddenly escape you when you call attention to it The unmarried, professional, aggressive modern women are like their counterparts in the United States Met a few beautiful, well-groomed upper-class girls who leave a great sense of emptiness. Gracious, but disappear into thin air, like the same type here.
>
> Don't think of Indians as people I enjoyed, but only as people who interested me Not like in Southeast Asia where areas of incomprehension are just as great or greater, but where relations are more relaxed With Indians there is a dark intensity, a malaise, a self-consciousness, intense, full of hostilities and insecurities, no sense of enjoyment or pleasure. Southeast Asians don't touch at sensitive subjects, while Indians pick at their souls. Indians are really more accessible in this sense I admire the great achievements of the last seven years and for India as a place I have the warmest aesthetic feelings, exciting, endlessly colorful and varied Many Americans there see the poverty, squalor, are overwhelmed by it and find it an offense They find their own helplessness intolerable Many took harder than I did the arrogant, supercilious, superior, hostile Indians, who disconcerted and amazed them no end, and they met hostility with hostility In my case, I was resentful, but tried to keep resentment on an individual basis and not to project it to India as a country . .

Consider, on the other hand, the view of a writer who has never been to India and knows very little about it, but judges Indians primarily in terms of their role in present-day world politics and by the individuals he encounters in Washington and other international centers

> I observe primarily the power of British education and its influence on them, and their vast capacity for hypocrisy which they have taken from the Anglo-Saxons, I suppose. They are playing the role Americans played in the nineteenth century, standing off and lecturing the world This critical neutralism rather amuses me. They are hypocritical even

when they discuss their neutrality, which is based on the very power they are criticizing They emphasize philosophy and principles which they completely fail to follow themselves I think they are hypocritical in international affairs and deeply prejudiced They fiercely criticize this country for its prejudices while in their own life they are so fiercely prejudiced. They talk to us about the Negroes but do not apply to themselves the principles they recommend to us. They do not apply to Pakistan the ideas they would have us apply to certain other countries I have had a growing irritation with Indians in recent years, and this is quite unique with me. I do not have any such feelings about any other people.

An ex-professor whose recall of Indian students goes back to the 1920's:

They are prize go-getters, will insinuate you out of your eyebrows Not always consciously guileful, though sometimes they are. They have axes to grind and they grind them. Will not only remember you on waking and retiring as a favorite teacher, but will let you know it. Maybe guile is not a good word because it is not so much deliberate as it is part of their nature. Only two or three exceptions to this but these have all been extremely Westernized types The Hindu students respond quickly to Western culture and then have a revulsion against it Back in India they become lost souls. Have lived through some tortured experiences with some of them, for the revulsion is very powerful I became extremely fond of several, who had the run of my home But I suppose I come nearer to having a prejudice about Indians than about any group whatever If it is not a prejudice, it is a strong set of reservations I reacted also against their tendency to mysticism, which seems to give them a sense of their own holiness and smugness about their messianic character. I have noticed this particularly in scholars I have met in recent years, even in a leading Indian statistician who visited us here, in manner and way of saying things, the questions they ask, and their reactions to the answers. Talking about this exaggerates it—I am talking primarily about experiences with about five among many dozens But there it is, and I don't have this feeling about any other people I know. . . .

Finally, from one of this country's most respected older public figures.

I must say that I do not find it easy to like Indians. I am not sure what it is. Maybe it is because I don't like the holy man idea and I don't like the caste system. I have felt at much greater ease visiting other countries than I did in India. Some intellectuals I met I learned to really like, but I confess that even among this most friendly group I found some pretty hard to take. Many of the professors I met, for example, seemed to me to be great foolers with words They struck me as people who lack the capacity or desire to take hold of life vigorously.

Among the Moderate Cons we also find an official with considerable responsibility for an international exchange program that brings him into frequent contact with people of almost every nationality on earth. His account.

I go on the assumption that under the skin all people are almost alike I like to feel I can break through any reserve, and I do it all the time, except with Indians. They are smart and intellectual but also volatile and unstable and often petty and irritating. I don't ever quite know where they stand, and I feel distrustful of them. Maybe these words are too strong I like them all right, but I have learned not to be surprised if they give the opposite impression twenty-four hours later They are something of a problem. . . . They are often unpleasant, annoying, and frustrating. I think everybody around here would tell you: "Of all the peoples we deal with, the Indians are the most difficult. ." Other Asians are much easier and more pleasant to get along with, Indonesians, Burmese, Thais. I felt this within fifteen minutes of landing in Rangoon from India The whole previous week in India had involved a great sense of strain in all my contacts In Rangoon it simply disappeared I could laugh and expect the Burmese to laugh too In India I didn't dare tell a joke for fear I'd be misunderstood.
. I observe that people who have a great deal to do with India, some of the political boys and many specialists on India, have even stronger feelings, personal and political, than we do and are harder on the Indians than we are though they have been working with Indians all their lives.

And here is the account of a young exchangee who went to India for several months·

They are very sensitive about everything, themselves and their country. Had to be awful careful about the way you talked They were very hospitable. I somehow felt they were not happy to see me but were hospitable anyway They would ask your opinion about something, but as soon as you said anything that rubbed the fur a little bit, they would jump you on it. They weren't very tactful. They would just about meet you and would soon be demanding to know why the United States is so terrible, its morals so bad They have big misconceptions Naturally I resented this It burns you. They wouldn't believe my explanations, they had their own ideas It was pretty hard to talk. You'd try to explain and three or four of them would talk you down... To put it in plainer words, I found them pretty two-faced. They would tell you one thing and tell others another thing, about us and about each other. They weren't frank I would say this about almost all the Indians we got to know. They have a sense of humor, but it's different. It is harder for Indians to laugh at themselves. . . .

A novelist:

I think of moral arrogance in connection with Indians Something about the rightness of Gandhism as the way of solving the problems of the world. The various Indian intellectuals, writers and others whom I meet seem to me to try to rationalize what they already believe, traveling around just to confirm their own generalizations. I do think of them as having a certain abstract idealism, a kind of goodness, but I regard the spiritual-materialistic business as a joke that sometimes gets me very sore. . . .

Finally, these views from a social scientist:

I have met several who have showed extraordinary intelligence and superior proficiency in their fields, but generally Indians seem to me chattering, full of grievances, full of their spiritual superiority. I don't like people who talk about their injuries and oppressions, Negro-preoccupied Negroes, Jew-preoccupied Jews, self-preoccupied selves With Indians you are always walking on tiptoe to avoid giving rise to crankiness.

## Strong Con (32)

Antipathy for Indians and India is heavy in the panel as a whole, and among those with negative views the heaviest weight in sheer numbers falls among those with the strongest views on the subject. At this end of the spectrum we find no fewer than 32 individuals who share the most unqualified, the most sharply expressed, and the most intensely felt attitudes of rejection, criticism, or dislike of Indians in general and in particular.

This group is drawn from every professional category in the panel and from every degree of Asian experience and contact But it also has one most remarkable feature  here among the total of 32 we find 14 people identified with China backgrounds. These 14 comprise nearly the entire China group in the panel as a whole; they include 13 of our 16 China specialists and 1 other who is not listed as a specialist because his experience dates back so far and his interests have been engaged elsewhere since. Of the three other China specialists, two are in the Mixed Con group, holding views of Indians which are hardly less critical than in the present group but expressed in a more moderate or more qualified form. The 1 remaining, a missionary, is the only person of China experience who views Indians favorably; he appears among the Moderate Pros This virtual unanimity among the China people with regard to Indians cuts across all other lines of politics, philosophic outlook, or personality. They appear here whether they are ultraconservative admirers of the pro-Chiang Kai-shek school or "liberals" who have been accused of being soft on Communism because of their hostility to Chiang and the Kuomintang. Maligners and maligned, bitter foes on China issues, they come together in a tight cluster on the subject of India and Indians. Some examples·

A government official.

> The startling contrast between the Chinese and the Indians in the mass The Indians showed no joy in life, beaten down, no spark of gumption, the equivocal shake of the head that says neither yes nor no, the retreat into vagueness. I am not speaking of intellectuals or political leaders, whom I did not meet much, but the others one passed among and worked with  Was repelled by the submissiveness of Indians, no sharp, clean twinkle such as you see in the eye of a Chinese shopkeeper Every time I went back to China [during the war] I would sigh with relief and feel that here are *people* again The Chinese would look at you, respond to you Indian laborers avoid your eye. Maybe there has been a change since independence, for I always equated this attitude to British rule But I don't know . . .

A well-known diplomat

> Have never found Indians agreeable. They're humorless, sorry for themselves. After seeing and being with Chinese, the Indians never seemed happy What makes the Indian such a cantankerous soul? . . . Any group of Chinese and Americans seem to belong together With Indians you never get this feeling. Can you imagine kidding an Indian?

A noted journalist·

> I judge by history. India—insofar as it has a history that we know—is a debased and contemptible kind of place. You can't even call it a nation with a history. Its ideas and religion are based on a mess of

mystical nonsense. No resilience, no strength, never could really stand up for itself. . . Since Indians are a very irritating people, it is going to take an irritating kind of American to get along with them . . . Why, the Indians burn their dung! I am Chinese enough to consider this a crime, the ultimate in foolishness An unpleasant country, an unpleasant people I don't like half-baked Westerners . . . The Chinese, on the other hand, have the greatest and most unique history in the world. . . . You don't often find a Chinese who is a fool . . .

In this entire group with extreme negative views, there are only two who have had substantial experience in India itself. One is a journalist who has served there for lengthy periods during the last decade:

They are people who tend to worry too much about how many angels can dance on the head of a pin without worrying about the character of the angels or the location of the pin They carry the act of argument to the point of enervation and are more interested in argument than in substance. It is a diseased state of mind in which any possibility of constructive action is vitiated by an intensely detailed and intricate analysis of motives Saps all the energy out of any operation I think they are like this because of the uncertainty of the Hindu religion, which means all things to all men, a mass of superstition gathered over time and applied differently to different classes. There is a basic insecurity in their religion which is no damned good at all and they must recognize it. So they discuss! There would be more to talk about with a Hindu on a desert isle than with a Catholic! I think this explains why they are so defensive I am really fond of them generally—some of the nicest people I know annoy me—but I have no high opinion of them. What I really feel is an amused tolerance. . . .

The second case is the quite different one of a missionary, born in India of an old missionary family, and who spent several decades there in mission work beginning before World War I. He left India in 1939:

There is a lack of integrity and straightforwardness Indians themselves, I think, admit this when their hair is down. By integrity I mean intellectual honesty I have often felt and said that an Indian can harbor in his mind two opposite views and seem to do it with equanimity. This is almost illustrated by their lives: Western clothes and manners in a traditionalist family and household. They become almost two different personalities. This is not quite everything I mean The fact is that they lie One of my friends used to say that Indians will tell the truth only as a last resort The same sort of thing exists among us, but the percentages and attitudes are different Stealing and lying come together. I was always warned against placing responsibility for money on any of my Indian associates I am talking about people all the way from high court judges and professors down to the village Indian They are willing to cheat. It is very common at the upper levels It is taken for granted, so there is a lack of trust in each other. . . . We used to do our best not to prejudice the younger missionaries coming out The Indians used to say these young fellows were fine until the older missionaries got to them But it was their own experience that changed them. . . . It is almost impossible to give a well-balanced picture Every missionary learned about these elements of Indian character and his job was to help Indians improve and overcome these characteristics. We were criticized for doing too much too soon In my father's time missionaries were much more dominating, they dealt with the lowest-caste people, but their estimate of the Indians was the same lack of honesty Indians also lack tenacity Have short-term enthusiasms, then give out, don't persist in things There are economic reasons for this but also character reasons They are still lovable, though. Find yourself indulgent You make allowances for all the lapses . . . I am probably too critical. I haven't been back in India for a long time, so I am quite ignorant about conditions now. . .

Except for these two, all the members of this extreme group are people whose personal experience with India or Indians has been quite brief and incidental. This includes the entire China contingent. Among them we find a certain number who are peculiarly exposed, by their jobs, positions, or interests, to the pressures of current international relations. They all tend to have certain latent prejudices about Indians stemming from some of the familiar sources we have been encountering all along, and these are clearly activated by the current political tensions and differences. Here are the remarks of a former high-ranking official in the present administration in Washington:

Read *Mother India* a long time ago. Fascinating Pretty shocking state of affairs I was interested by the Indian outcries against the book, but I rather believed it, don't know why, but I did . . Had some idea from Kipling long ago that the Indians loved the British The *Life* piece on Hinduism is the closest I've ever gotten to Indian religion. Theoretically interesting, but I wonder how a people who think a cow is their mother are ever going to get on in the world A strange mixture of brutality and asceticism. Think of the events at the time of the partition of India. They are more brutal than we are—and they think *we* are brutal! In the government people were either against the Indians—just plain disliked them, the goddamned Indians—or were for them, thought them remarkably intelligent, dedicated people with great capacity for philosophical thinking. . . I personally just bristle at Indians. A generalized bristling. Never personally involved, although in UN negotiations frequently ran into it. Could always count on unreasonable Indian opposition, was never at ease with Indians. Pathologically obsessed with obsolescent Western colonialism and disregarding Soviet colonialism that is on the way in. . . .

The editor of an important magazine:

The Indians seem to be a very conglomerate foolish race by Western standards. Notion of cows and scanty crops, nobody to kill the cows. It's insane. I don't feel called upon to worry about them. If that's the way they want it, caste system and all, it's their business. But why should we feed and build up anything like this? Nehru, as far as I am concerned, is an arrogant anti-American, all his speeches indicate that he's pro-Communist and anti-American, Menon the same or worse. That's all I know.

One of the country's most prominent publishers:

English-speaking Indians speak with a beautiful flow of language but half of what they say amounts to nonsense or at least high-grade muddleheadedness. I am offended by it. Maybe muddleheadedness is not the word. Need a politer one, maybe high subjectivity . . . An Anglo-Saxon gets embarrassed by the disparity between the beliefs and ethical code and actual behavior of Indians. The Indian is not sufficiently embarrassed by this disparity.

The UN correspondent of a major newspaper:

They and they alone are right and know what is right. Self-righteous. They alone hold the key to successful diplomacy. Arrogant, Menon especially. They have a tendency, when in positions of power, to be extremely exacting masters. They see the whole world moving around India. Benegal Rau was a better-balanced type of man, although not exempt from this kind of thing. Madame Pandit is a twisted person, all things to all men and able to turn any way according to needs and calculations. . . Met Nehru when he was here in 1949 and was fed up by the way American newspapermen pushed him to choose sides and I felt sympathy for his irritation. But since then I have gotten more and more irritated by his speeches. . . .

A Midwestern Congressman·

Dark people, queer religion, fetishes, sacred cow Indian civil servants were surly and unpleasant. Only ones like them I've ever met. In Calcutta on the street you almost despise the people, you want to help them but you can't respect them My meeting with Nehru didn't help He was very evasive about Kashmir, never gave a forthright answer. He was the only foreign head we ever visited who expressed no friendly sentiment at all.  .

A nationally prominent scholar:

I made a trip to India with my father when I was sixteen, and I think of Gandhi, Nehru, and Indian intellectuals now with mixed feelings against a background picture of squalor, caste, and a cringing, broken-spirited people. The Indian intellectuals I have met in recent years seemed to me abstract, repellent, always making verbal approaches, unable to shift the level of discourse to something practical and relevant Back of this I have the whole Babu-British stereotype, the undereducated Indian making an ostentatious display of knowledge. Nehru's neutralist policy does not arouse my strong antagonism —look at our own history!—but I do get mad at Indian self-righteousness about it.

In certain other cases that appear in this group, current political tensions or attitudes have little or no bearing. The hostility centers on other characteristics. One of the most common of these is associated with the quality of being "Westernized." As we have seen, this is quite often the basis, or even the only basis, for high approval of Indians encountered But for some, it is quite the opposite. An example

The Indians are Anglicized in dress, manners, and speech to a degree that is sometimes irritating. Indians are much less pleasant to be with than Indonesians, and I can only ascribe this to this feeling I have of unpleasant artificiality They present themselves to you in terms of your own culture, yet without having to go very far, you find their own culture traits and not very admirable ones, fatalism, superstition In contrast, Indonesians translate their own culture into Western dress and manners but remain essentially what they are. With the Indians it is more of a veneer they are consciously imitating the British manner, whereas the Indonesians are not trying to be like the Dutch. They merely adopt certain exteriors without aping I think this must go back to my boyhood resentment of English affectations among

Canadians, and I felt the same way in England about Central European refugees who became more English than the English. This involves an escape from a sense of inferiority by acquiring the forms of social superiority Few Indians, despite their efforts, are wholly successful at being Englishmen.

In a distinguished Negro scholar, the focus is directly on racial attitudes and relationships.

> I had some Indian fellow students when I was at Harvard They kept away from Negroes, wanted nothing to do with us. They were "Aryans" despite their color . . . It was a standard joke among us that all you had to do to get away from unpleasantness was to put on a turban and pass as an Indian I had no contact with them, certainly did not push myself on them. All they had was a selfish desire to improve only their own status . . Other Negro intellectuals had similar experiences and it created strong anti-Indian feeling among many Negroes After independence, Nehru publicly chided Indians in Africa for exploiting Africans, and Indian attitudes toward Negroes in this country were reversed. They began to court Negroes here. We had one visiting professor who told us how India felt about the world color conflict, but I have always felt that somebody like Madame Pandit does not think of herself as belonging to the same race as black Indians Nehru's statement came after the Durban riots of 1949, and it was the first of its kind Indians now come looking for examples of American prejudice and feel complete rectitude about their position See themselves as having such a noble spiritual attitude that they can't have race prejudice themselves I am rather cynical about this wherever I run into it.

By contrast, something of the same kind of preoccupation turns up in the form of what might most charitably be called an exasperated Anglo-Saxonism, both personal and political, in the reaction of a State Department official·

> I became aware of having a pronounced anti-Hindu prejudice as far back as 1935. At various gatherings and discussions in Chicago, fanatical independence chaps among the Indians got me exasperated, and the same later when I went to Harvard—suave, objectionable and biased presentations, unfair to the Western world. Ramaswamy Mudaliar came to Ohio State and was blandly and suavely rude to everybody. Just plain nasty, hard to take. He felt extremely superior to all us proletarians laboring at the university. In 1935 ran into Indians in Paris and London. My wife's a blonde and they are interested in blondes. She thought them interesting and I thought them terrible

This intensified my prejudice against these buzzards Knowing what irrational, objectionable guys they were, I wondered how they would ever build a country This is still a sizable component in my attitude toward Indians I share and understand those who get up in the Senate and say let's give no dollars to Nehru

By far the most deep-seated of these intensely personal reactions turned up in a man of great intellectual attainments and personal sensitivity in whom the question about Indians touched off these small explosions

Indians? I think of fakiry, spelled both ways It's the same thing. It means deception, swindling, sleight-of-hand, illusion, as opposed to reality Insincerity. From the first time I ever heard about the Indian rope trick, I felt that anybody who said he could throw a rope up into the air and climb it was a damned liar and I wouldn't believe anything else he said. Somehow I am almost tempted to use the word feminine I feel a certain effeminateness about Indians that bothers me, although I am not bothered in general by homosexuals I think of the rope climber, fakir, magic, illusion, large scale ignorance and superstition—this all comes from somewhere way back . . . Skin color has something to do with this too Now let me make this clear. I have no such feeling about color in others. Color as such makes no difference to me, and as you know, I have lived my life that way. But I *am* irritated by Indians as a physical type, and it has to do with color or maybe a certain oiliness. Maybe I am mixing this up with my thoughts of Indians as insincere and unreliable Maybe the elusiveness of their personality and character adds up for me to a sense of their lack of grasp of reality . . I never felt it odd that other colonial people of various lands should speak English, but somehow Indians speaking English always made me feel that they were affected. . . .

I am quite ashamed of this whole feeling. It is the only one of its kind I have in relation to any group as a group. I know that it goes back somewhere to my earliest reading experience and that these were reinforced by later experience and contact In India they were reinforced although narrowed down to the Hindus and Parsis, not the Sikhs and Muslims The only exception I can remember was a purely visual one. When we were being taken across India in a hot, stinking train crowded with soldiers, I remember stopping in a station where a saintly-looking old man just released from prison was being welcomed as we went through I can remember that the quality of that man impressed not only me but the crudest of the GI's who were with me. On the other hand, pictures of Nehru repel me, that is as a physical type, although I have found his writings not bad. For all these reasons I never could really get interested in the Indian nationalist movement. I never met an Indian yet whom I instinctively liked and wanted to make a friend of I even think the sari is affected. Effete is a word I think of. I think of Indian civilization as unproductive and in a blind alley. I know all this to be a completely irrational prejudice pattern, and I know how stupid it is It has diminished somewhat over the years but mainly because I have made a conscious effort to control it.

Though we sought them for many hours, we never did get close to the sources of these strong feelings. They were much too deeply embedded behind impenetrable defenses

## *The Differentiators* (8)

Far, far back up the slope we have been descending, we spoke of crossing a divide, or an open space between the positive and negative poles in this crackling field of inquiry. We said then that this space was not unpopulated and that we would return to it. Back there now, we meet the 8 individuals whose views and feelings about Indians are so mixed and so differentiated that it would do them or the subject no justice to try to locate them at any particular point along a positive-negative scale, in their reactions we find varying blends of almost all that has been said on all sides.

Here are the visible features of this group.

● Four are scholars, 2 journalists, 1 an ex-journalist, and the last a businessman. All except the businessman have had long professional and personal involvement with India, have visited there frequently, or have lived in the country for some or many years. All except 2 are still deeply committed, as a matter of their life's work, to India.

They all share a general outlook that may be vaguely characterized as "liberal" in the loose political and social sense of that term as it is used in the American environment.

● Seven of the 8 can also be characterized as having primarily intellectual interests.

● Three of the 4 scholars are identified with missionary backgrounds, although only 1 is still connected with a missionary institution. All 3 expressly disavowed any interest in the evangelical aspects of mission work, all became teachers, and one has become a distinguished scholar in his chosen field.

● Two are women.

• Two have family links to India, one of them with recent English antecedents long connected with India, and one as the son of a missionary family long established there.

We shall forego any attempt to guess what common pattern of personality brought these people together in this place. Let it emerge, if it is there, from some of their own accounts, which we shall quote extensively, beginning with one of the scholars:

> I think of very warm, deep, lasting affection on both sides. Hospitality of almost an exaggerated caliber, reliability and integrity to the utmost degree But I also feel a skepticism of their roots, of the depth of the values they hold. Their ability to compartmentalize, the lack of relationship between philosophy and behavior, used to annoy me. This is so universal among Indians that I felt that maybe it was my understanding that was wrong, that an apparent contradiction might not be as unique or as contradictory as I thought. I have had to suspend my judgment, though I still react emotionally against it You can't often take what they say too literally With some you get some tortuous rationalizations of things like caste, or others will make the obviously nonsensical statement that it has been "abolished" This makes it difficult for me to like Indians indiscriminately. There are times when I can't stand speaking to any of them and I seek out others, Europeans, who somehow seem to speak the same language I do
>
> The grandeur of their past is a barrier through which one has to pass, a barrier of well-meant self-righteousness When I do not encounter it, I am almost cautious, feeling that this individual's explanation of Indian experience might lack some degree of authenticity. I often think I am getting something objective about India when I see an Indian's report in a Western journal, but that means it's been acceptable to a Western editor, 1 e, the insights come from those whose ideas are closest to our own Those I have liked are those with whom I have gotten over this barrier because we have known each other so long It is a kind of façade to make the outsider think India is great, but the longer you know a person, less and less of the façade is presented There are also those who acknowledge at least the existence of their contradictions. I have gotten to the point of discussing this with perhaps twenty people, without resolving it in any way It usually ends up with a discussion of *my* contradictions alongside theirs I do not think the parallel is exact They think it is .
>
> I don't find it easy to live in India. I feel the poverty. I once stopped a man who was beating a bullock People laughed. This makes it hard. All of it often makes my life a hell, because I identify myself with problems I see in a way that makes it difficult for me to be a good social

scientist. The fact is that although I like Indians as an intriguing people, and I feel at home in India, it is a constant mental and emotional experience for me while I am there You can never be passive. It asks for action, for thinking More so than in the United States. I feel more a part of it, as I do not in the United States, where all is self-satisfied I like the country and am most illogical about it. I do tend to think of the negative factors because I react to things that need something done about them. .

Here are the judgments of a woman who first went out to India as a missionary college teacher thirty-five years ago.

Everyone is different, some good, some bad, some this and some that, and I knew hundreds of all kinds Yet I do believe there are some characteristics that are Indian, certainly more Indian than American. I can draw a sort of composite that may not be *real* but is certainly *true*. There is a certain gentleness that is peculiar because it is combined with a kind of cruelty They are insensitive to the suffering of people whom they do not know or are of lower status than they are. They have plenty of brains and love to talk. Never saw such talkers, they love to argue, it gives them great pleasure. They are exceedingly generous within certain limits. At the same time pretty bigoted and prejudiced. This is due to their Hindu upbringing, even among people who like to claim they are emancipated but really aren't, prejudices about living, eating, doing things a certain way, about approaches to people. This has a lot to do with caste, even for those who believe they don't pay attention to these things Some are very conscious of status and those who want to push push a lot, not through merit but through influence or any way they can. There is great loyalty, but mostly communal. My Indian friends, I think, would be ready to do anything for me with less calculation than Americans would. The reverse is true; my Indian friends would ask for things an American would hesitate to ask, even of a friend They give and expect, regardless of cost. They have often told me, of course, that I can't generalize about these things

There is plenty of humor. But here again Indians are extreme, I mean uninhibited, extremes in joy and sorrow, extravagant, say anything, many things that would be embarrassing to an American. They get very emotional If they want to cry, they cry, the men too. If they want to wail, they wail If they have pain, they don't conceal it from anybody. Don't discipline their children. Americans are prone to think that the lesser breeds without the law don't have virtues. But they do They love their children. On man-woman relationships, among those who keep Indian traditions, it is astounding for so often educated men have illiterate wives and I have been astonished to see how good their relationship often is. Like here, it is sometimes very bad too

The Indian is not as religious as we think he is We greatly exaggerate this. I don't think the Indians are any more spiritual than the Americans The idea of the meditative Indian on the riverbank is silly. He is just as interested in his daily bread and material things as we are. I don't think religion occupies the whole horizon of the Indian, it only seems to ...

I like Indians, my composite Indian too. It happens to be my temperament that I don't expect my friends to be perfect. I see faults in all of my friends. I am very fond of India and Indians but that doesn't mean that I don't sometimes feel amused or a little superior or irritated by some things And sometimes I feel inferior in others, especially in the matter of generosity, the capacity to give oneself, loyalty Many Indians, for example, do not have the same standards of honesty and integrity that we have Americans think Indians are such liars But my Indian friends are just as critical of other Indians for this sort of thing. Some Indians are finaglers We have that among us here too. Indians don't admire losing one's temper. They might think this is worse than lying as a characteristic. I have learned, while keeping my own standards, that there is such a thing as having a different emphasis. ...

Another woman who lived five years in India:

I get a diffusing sense of warmth. Some I loved very much. I keep these memories to prevent bad temper and irritation with Indians from carrying me away They can be damnably irritating people I come to their defense when others attack them, but I think they are very negative, ornery . With some friends you get very close, although they cross you up sometimes too. They are self-conscious people, always conscious of how they are impressing you But I can only think of them as individuals I liked their sense of humor Some newspaper people told me I'd never hear anybody laugh or make a joke, but this is completely untrue Their humor is more delicate or subtle, in the villages quite bucolic and ribald. .. Their attitude of moral superiority, however, is infuriating, although maybe in some ways they are superior I was converted to the Indian idea of "right action" even if the Indians don't live up to it themselves. Indians are more anxious to be good than any other people I've ever met. Their emphasis on life and its meaning is something we've rather forgotten. My feelings are not quite mystic, but sometimes I felt something, felt carried in a stream of humanity, not of individuals, just life in a crowd of people animals, an endless flow of humanity I never get this here

When I first went to India in 1947, I discovered murderous hatred, ugliness, urge to kill, hysteria. I hated the whole bloody country that year But I began to meet gentler people, and found many different sorts, as well as many I didn't like. I didn't think much of the Gandhians after I saw them in action Coldness to everybody outside their fold, arrogant attitude toward everybody else. They do not have a true sense of love Perhaps not even Gandhi himself. One of my friends called him a "hypnotizer, charlatan, and minor archangel " I thought this was pretty good I can't get explicit Corruption, messy outrageous things. But also a feeling of great, good power . . Tempers flared easily in Indians I knew, but so did my own In the time of the riots, even my friends were unable to be dispassionate. They would almost deny what was happening, and after that I was always a little distrustful of the Indians' concept of the truth They usually exaggerate or else minimize, they are not interested in the importance of the actual fact. I did feel an underlying hysteria in Indians, but while I was in Kashmir I happened to pick up a history of the Thirty Years' War and realized the behavior of the people in that time was worse than that of the Indians in the riots People are oppressed so much by ignorance and circumstances. . Social conscience has yet to grow in India, where there is no real sense of the brotherhood of man. They don't really give a damn about others. Of course Indians can hold two contradictory points of view I can too I think Nehru is hypocritical about Kashmir, yet I also think Nehru is a sincere man. . . .

A long-time student of Indian affairs in general and politics in particular

There is a great capacity in Indians for friendship, but often a fairly sharp line beyond which it is impossible to penetrate or understand. We find blanknesses in each other which are mutually unsatisfying With one after another of my Indian friends, I found I could go astonishingly long distances, only to hit a road block at the end In general this is true of all human relationships, but in our own society I can have some sense of what the impenetrable areas are and can make some assumptions about them But the unease in Indian relationships comes from the fact that I know that the area I cannot probe includes a lot of potent forces of culture, tradition, and superstition, all along quite different lines from my own This is all asking a lot of a friendship, of course, but the Indian pattern is to resist the casual association to which we are accustomed and to concentrate on the deeper association It was obvious to me quite early that if I was going to have friends, the American pattern was inadequate. Had to give a lot more to receive a lot more

My feelings about Indians are strong, warm friendships and rather sharp antipathies, discrimination of individuals and traits. No blobby emotional reaction either way. About the only generalization I can offer is that except in the most Westernized group, I have to go farther out of my own cultural patterns to establish good communication with Indians than I would have to with a good many other national groups. This unease about Indians may be a special feature, resting in their basic insecurity and frustration. It is often dissipated to a large extent but it comes up again and again. . . . I think it stems from the fact that their lives no longer parallel the lives of their fathers and that more broadly, since 1947 and independence, they have lost a sense of a clear-shining goal.

Finally, a senior scholar whose interests embrace both India's ancient past and her troubled present·

Of course I have a high opinion of the achievements of India in the arts of civilization and ethics After all, you are asking me about the subject of my life's work, and if I didn't have some such feelings what would I be doing in it? Of course I say these things with selectivity Many things in India and Indian literature are stupid, that is to say they are not consistent logically with the principles the authors lay claim to, but this of course is true in all literature. It strikes me that when you come across people who are like that, it may very well be difficult to talk to them. Nobody likes his own society to be judged by such people, who exist everywhere. Many non-Indian intellectuals are irritated by this kind of Indian, but they are also irritated with the logical Indian It is of course when the premises seem unreasonable—like Nehru's— that irritation results Of course Indian stereotypes like the one about the materialistic West are very irritating The whole pattern of inferiority complex with its twin aspects of arrogance and timidity enters into these attitudes I think Indians carry a very strong sense of shame out of the 1947-48 experience—shame, rather than guilt. They are also highly sensitive to the notion that most Americans still have the "Mother India" point of view and are basically patronizing It seems to me obvious that Indian stereotypes about Americans are as wrong as most stereotypes are. Actually on this spiritual-materialist plane, there is very little difference between the two. Indians simply do not accept the hundreds of references in the Rigveda to wealth, lineage, victory over one's enemies as the rewards for right doing and the good things which you ask from your gods. Of course in a more transient way our current obsession with Communism feeds some of the hostile attitudes, but this seems to me a phase that can't last forever. It is necessary to keep remembering that neither we nor the Indians like to be told that our prejudices are wrong.

## 8. *THE GALLERY REVISITED*

OUT OF ALL THIS one thing at least seems reasonably clear: the reactions produced by most American-Indian encounters are rarely casual Strong emotions get involved. They are perhaps aggravated but are not caused by current political differences. Neither are they in their essence specious or superficial, the product of crude "misunderstanding" or of the confrontation of simple-minded stereotypes The recurring patterns are too protruding and too insistent and are repeated too far back in time to allow us the ease of any such cushioned interpretations. The uniqueness of all these individuals, Americans and Indians both, could dictate the many varieties and particular combinations of traits, attitudes, and feelings. Yet these many different kinds of Americans, mirroring in their reactions so many different kinds of Indians, were very often speaking of precisely the same things, whether they were reacting to them favorably or otherwise The Indian compositely pictured here is not the whole man or every man, each has his separateness But he is a sum of all the resemblances seen in so many by so many Americans. These make him no mere creature of these American perceptions. He is in some part truly this Indian himself, with his charm, his generosity, his intellectual qualities, his capacity for friendship, and also with his many nettles, in his mixture of "good" and "bad" recognizably a part of the contemporary Indian reality. This is the Indian encountered, the elite counterpart of the American who figures in this study and who also, by his recurring reactions, offers some clue to some of the qualities he holds in common with his fellows In the major features of his portrait of the Indian, as we have already tried to suggest, there are many keys to the American's portrait of himself.

In the first and most all-embracing of these recurrent themes, this Indian is seen as the product or the victim of two warring cultures, the Western and his own This is, of course, the great theme of modern Asian history In the broadest sense it is the theme of all the history of our time. A vast literature, not all of it illuminating, already exists on this subject of the "East" and the "West," much of it soaring far from the human reality into stratospheric generalization. Let us say here only that this conflict has shaped the history of every Asian country in the last three centuries, that it has been part of the life story of every Asian wrenched by circumstance out of the traditional molds of his past Only now is Western man beginning painfully to realize the extent of his own involvement in this process, because only now is he being called upon to pay history's price for his brash and brutal assumption of overlordship of the world and all the other races of man inhabiting it.

There have been many differences in the way this history has influenced the social character of the people concerned in each of the affected Asian cultures But one common result among upper-class types in almost all of them during the last three or four generations has been a fluctuating pattern of superiority and inferiority feelings, of overacceptance and overrejection, of deep resentments and frustrated striving. In few places have these become as marked as they have in India, perhaps precisely because in India these resentments were the most deeply internalized, force was not met with force but passively, and even in the end, emancipation was sought not by physical means but by the assertion of an idealized doctrine of nonviolence. The eruption of force that did occur was not directed at the foreign ruler but was internal and fratricidal. In Indians of the elite classes the carry-over of this experience in the makeup of individuals who shared in it has assumed especially acute forms. It breaks upon the encountered Westerner, especially the American who thinks of himself as having had no part of the Indian's past, with a peculiarly aggravating impact Out of this, then, at least in part, comes the defensive arrogance noted by so many admirers and critics alike, the inordinate self-love, self-preoccupation, self-glorification, and a considerable confusion of values. To all of this some Americans are sympathetic, either because they accept the claim to superiority, or because they feel a share in the guilt which helped produce it, or—most rarely—because in their friendships with Indians these strains are overcome and disappear. But much more frequently, as we have seen, especially in brief acquaintance and discovery, the effect is annoyance, antipathy, and even outrage.

One set of these consequences has to do with the fact that this Indian's exposure to the West took place through British lenses. On him, therefore, we can find the marks of the blind and brutish acquisitiveness of the days of the East India Company, the imperial and racial arrogance that Kipling celebrated, the incredibly stuffy pukka sahibism speared so mercilessly by E. M. Forster in *A Passage to India,* with the converse of the toadyism in Indians which both these authors, in their separate ways, so clearly memorialized.[71] From his mentors this Indian received too the concepts of law and of democratic institutions which the British honored so well at home and so much less well abroad From British—and other European—Orientalists he even also received the gift of a new view of his own Indian past, a glorification of his own religious and philosophic traditions. All of these things and many more show through to the American in his present-day encounter with this Indian, and, most important of all perhaps, they are communicated in the Englishman's language which is also, more or less, the American's own.

The fact that this Indian usually speaks English so fluently has a curiously mixed role in the impact of these encounters. Thus a great many remark the unique ease of communicating with Indians encountered, in contrast to so many other Asians. But a few perceive that the sharing of a tongue makes it easier for differences and difficulties to make themselves felt "Because he speaks English," shrewdly observed a panelist, "you expect him to be more like you than he turns out to be." The differences that are often discovered through the fluency of talk can often be not so much Indian as English in source, for this Indian has borrowed more than a language. His identifications often extend to a whole range of British values, judgments, and even manners If, as often happens, the particular American is more or less Anglophile, the more "British" he finds an Indian the better he likes him; you will readily recall those for whom the "best" people in India are the Indian Civil Service or other types who show the greatest British influence in their appearance, manner, outlook, and behavior. On the other hand, in a great many other Americans quite the opposite effect occurs It is precisely this Anglicized quality in the Indian that they find the most irritating, either because they are something less than Anglophile or because they react against what they see as the "veneer" of the "half-baked Westerner" parading as something he is not.

This irritation often becomes especially sharp if this Indian's adoption of British outlooks includes, as it frequently does, the borrowing of some of the cruder British stereotypes about American values, education, culture, and even intelligence. It was, after all, no

[71] For an unusually provocative discussion of Forster's *A Passage to India* see Nirad C Chaudhuri, "Passage to and from India," *Encounter,* London, June, 1954

part of the British system of education for Indians, whether in England or in India, whether in schools or in the news and publications made available to Indian readers, to render America attractive On the contrary, Indian students acquired from their British mentors a rather dim view of American culture From the news selectively circulated by British agencies in India about America over many years, Indians learned much more about the seamier sides of American life than they ever did about any of its other aspects. The total effect in creating a pattern of attitudes is rather well illustrated by a passage from the autobiography of a British Labor member of Parliament in which he describes an episode on a preindependence visit to India:

> One night I was at a small party where there were a number of Indians and British and two Americans The Americans were not the best examples of their country They were loud, hectoring, naive, and somewhat foolish in emphasizing opinions of little value They left before the rest of us When they had gone the Indians and the British looked at each other, smiled, and continued the conversation. The look and the smile were exactly the same as those which would have been exchanged among the British if there had been no Indians present, or, I am sure, among the Indians if there had been no British present Understanding was unspoken and complete [72]

When this particular kind of Indian does not successfully conceal from an American, say a Harvard scholar, his opinion of Harvard's (or any American university's) inferiority as compared to Oxford or Cambridge, he is quite unlikely to kindle the American's affection, especially if the American happens to be one who himself retains a vestigial inferiority complex about Oxford or Cambridge. Indian snobbism plus English snobbism is not a mixture calculated to arouse American enthusiasms except in the American who is willing to accept a quite low valuation of himself, his country, and all its works Only the most secure among Americans can view this behavior more tolerantly, like the individual of high place and attainments who said he could bear with Krishna Menon's patronizing air because he could see that Menon had to assume it to satisfy some deep—and rather pathetic—need. But few Americans have this much assurance More often the American of this class still feels himself one of a "new" people—almost everyone in the present panel

[72] Woodrow Wyatt, *Into the Dangerous World*, London, 1952, p. 93

occupies a place in society different from his father's—too "new" to have formed the thicker crust it takes to feel assuredly superior to the vagaries of all others He may sometimes be able to concede some measure of this superiority to the Englishman, especially the upper-class Englishman, for the English do after all stand in so many ways in a parental relationship to the American But in the Indian it is seen as an unwarranted and usually intolerable assumption, for in every way that is important to him, this American feels if not superior certainly not inferior to the Indian

The American who feels some share of responsible guilt for this experience—in its racial aspects, for example—is likely to react more understandingly He is the American, you may recall from the examples given, who was made to feel that it was up to him in India to prove his bona fides to the Indians and who could not feel it unjust that his Indian friends felt no need to prove themselves to him. But most Americans do not think of themselves as bearing any responsibility for the colonial past. They come into the new situation expecting to be liked and even admired, perhaps often feeling that as Americans they deserve a certain benevolent gratitude for being different from other Westerners and for what they feel to have been the American record of always being on the side of the angels where the issue of freedom was concerned. Many are taken rather aback to discover their self-image bears little or no resemblance to the Indian's image of them. "Joe likes to be liked," said the wife of one of our panelists, "and when he discovered that the Indians didn't like him, he disliked them right back " The clash of personalities indicated in so many of these impressions is in great measure a clash of ego involvements and insecurities on both sides.

The psychological consequences of the colonial experience, here so briefly glimpsed, are heavily marked indeed on this Indian with whom we are concerned. In his frequent impatience and lack of sympathy, the American very often fails to appreciate how deep and abiding these consequences are and how long it is going to take for them to fade. But the heritage from the colonial past is not the whole story. The Indians were not the only people to have this experience. Many others, including the Chinese, shared it and suffered the same consequences of ambivalence, of schizoid cultural exposures, of profound repression and dislocation, of subjection to senseless and infuriating dominance by "superior" Westerners. In the postcolonial period, the urbanized, Western-educated elite intellectual in all of these countries also shares with his Indian counterpart the often remarked apartness from his own society, the gulf of ignorance, impotence, and sometimes even contempt between him and the masses of his own people. He has also often shared a certain upper-class indifference or a greater acceptance of the squalid and degrading poverty of the mass, to which the American may sometimes react with mere fastidious distaste but more often and more characteristically with shame and indignation and a strong sense of the need for somebody to *do* something about it Many in these countries have now begun the enormous task of bridging the gulf, of raising their social and economic sights and of budging the villages from their changelessness. But all alike they are individuals faced with overwhelming tasks and responsibilities to which, most often, they feel hardly equal There is no uniqueness in the Indian in this respect, except perhaps in the larger size of the demand made upon him and the effect upon his particular personality of his sense of inadequacy.

But in all these respects the comparable middle- and upper-class types among such peoples as the Burmese, Indonesians, Vietnamese, and others have gone through the same deforming history and show many of the same stigmata as the Indians do Yet contact between them and Americans rarely seems to produce the pattern of reaction created by contact with their Indian counterparts. On the contrary, individuals in the panel repeatedly insisted upon the uniqueness of their experience with Indians. If anything like it ever occurred with other Asians, it was exceptional or much less intense. There is even considerable evidence to suggest that a great many of these other Asians react to their Indian counterparts much as these Americans do.

What then, beyond the colonial experience and its effects, is peculiarly "Indian" about the figure who emerges from this great array of impressions? Obviously we are not equipped here to attempt any full or systematic answer to this question or to enter into any discussion of the "Indian" personality, if, indeed, such a thing exists. We shall deal only with some of the major features that come into view on the portrait our Americans have drawn.

To begin with, there is the shape and substance given to this Indian by the whole unique Indian complex of which he is a part. Behind and around this figure of the urbanized, college-educated, English-speaking individual stand all the crowding figures of Indians in the mass, all the peculiarities of caste and Untouchability, of Hindu religiosity, practices, and customs. Toward the "benightedness" of popular Hinduism, this Indian may often take a view not too different in essence from that of his American counterpart. Only he is less indignant, more passive, rejecting in the abstract what he may tend to accept more or less involuntarily in real life. His identifications with it all are strong enough often to lead him to defend against the Western critic what he might not ordinarily defend and perhaps might even attack when the Western critic is absent and the sensibilities which the Westerner can so easily touch are not aroused. This is no simple situation for this Indian, since his community, his family, his parents, and even his wife as a rule still piously accept much that he might sometimes feel tempted to reject. Except in the tiny grouplets of the most thoroughly "Westernized" people, he has had little external sanction or support for such open rejection. Only to a very moderate extent and only for a very few was any such rejection involved in embracing the nationalist cause. Gandhi himself was a foe of Untouchability and he decried some of the excesses of caste practice, but he did not confront the inertness of Indian society and beliefs as an apostle of a Westernstyle modernism Few were ever as sweeping as Nehru in denouncing common Indian religious practices as superstition. But most Indians of this class have been much more bound than Nehru by the ambivalences in their life situations Hence the common experience of encountering the Westernized Indian whose home and family are still strictly traditionalist and rarely entered by the foreigner Hence the anomalies noted by some of our panelists, like Westerntrained physicians whose own wives are delivered of children in the old manner, or like "college graduates in cow-protection societies" Whatever the degree of conflict created by these situations, this Indian—if he is not Parsi or Muslim or Christian—remains a Hindu of some sort without necessarily feeling at one with the man who lies on a bed of nails The permissiveness of Hinduism offers him wide latitudes in which to dwell with his beliefs, a space perhaps larger but not too different from the range in American Protestantism from agnostic humanism to ultrafundamentalism, or in our society generally from atheism to Roman Catholicism.

As it appears to most of our present Americans, the "Hinduism" of this college-educated, English-speaking Indian assumes more intellectualized forms. They have to do largely with the way in which this Indian seems to the American to think. The American would note again and again that the Indian he encountered seemed given to certain nonrational habits of thought, perhaps even to a kind of mysticism, which would take the Indian into areas where the more pragmatic-minded American could not follow him. This was the notion of the oft-mentioned "barrier" in communication, the sense the American so often had of being left behind at this barrier where it was still anchored in reality while his Indian interlocutor took off into extraintellectual space Here, many noted, were the limits not only of friendship but even of ordinary conversation. It would be suggested that beyond this barrier, the Indian floated free among abstract categories visible and graspable only to him, his own farther reaches of philosophy or his private platform for communion with the Infinite One can readily suspect a certain element of exaggeration both in this Indian posture and in the American's reaction to it, but the core of a truth is here, attested by too many witnesses friendly and unfriendly to be dismissed as imaginary. A few Americans, perhaps heirs to Emersonian mysticism or German idealism, felt they could pursue their Indian friends at least part way into this void; a few others of more inquiring bent sometimes viewed this evaporation of their more normal categories with at least a curious respect But the more typical American product of a "common sense" culture or of the James-Dewey era in philosophy and education was much more likely to react with exasperated incomprehension, and most often he did. To him this Indian's evanescent philosophic garb was no more substantial than the emperor's new clothes. When he put them on, the Indian was simply escaping from reality, from problem-solving, from all the hard demands of existence

Here in this setting appear all the many observations that this Indian is largely given to abstractions and is a stranger to empirical thought, that he is readier and abler to talk than to do, that he is happy among large and smooth generalizations and acutely uncomfortable among smaller thornier facts, and that at many levels of interest—political, administrative, or scholarly—this makes effective communication difficult and sometimes impossible. But of all his habits of thought, the most baffling and often the most aggravating is often described as this Indian's peculiar capacity to house unresolved contradictions in his mind, not only without feeling the need for resolution but often even without acknowledging their contrariness. This was the way he seemed to manage to live in two worlds

This was how he might often claim simultaneous allegiance both to Marxist and to Gandhian economic ideas. This was how he could seem so often to see himself as "holier than thou" when it seemed plain to the American that there was at least as much common clay in the soil of Indian culture as in his own. This was how the Indian could righteously abhor the white man's racism while denying or rationalizing his own. This was how he could wear the mantle of Hinduism's principle of universal toleration while displaying what appeared to the American to be an acute degree of intolerance. This appeared in large areas of tension in Indian life, religious, communal, caste, and linguistic, and especially in the great disputes that today divide the world It is this "housing of contradiction" that so often looks to the American like plain self-deception, patent insincerity, or downright hypocrisy. This was the business of the Indian "talking out of both sides of his mouth" and his unreceptivity to the views of others. On all these scores the American has most often and most strongly felt that his readiness to differ respectfully with the Indian has not in the least been reciprocated. Perhaps above all else in the experience of these encounters, these mental and moral acrobatics produced the strongest hostility in those disposed to be unfriendly and produced the most defensive explanations among some of this Indian's warmest friends and admirers.

There is always in such reflections the danger of a certain presumption, no matter how dispassionate the purpose or good the will involved Certainly the refractions from a group of Indians perceived through the minds of a group of Americans leave wide margins for distortion, no matter how representative the groups on both sides. The possible unreality or at least the incompleteness of this portrait might be suggested to the American reader by these adjectives applied by Indians to Americans.

> materialistic, pragmatic, arrogant, smug, frivolous, condescending, intolerant, self-righteous, insular, morally loose, lacking in family institutions. . . .

Such characterizations, which can be duplicated from innumerable Indian sources, happen to come from a group of Indian students in the United States and occurred in a series of interviews with an Indian psychologist who was studying the process of their adaptation to American life.[78] From this same source, however, we also get a few unaccustomed glimpses of Indian self-images. These same students applied to themselves, among other more favorable terms, the following adjectives:

> prejudiced, cynical, hypercritical, jealous, arrogant, fatalistic, apathetic, passive. . . .

One of them enlarged on a familiar theme:

> We are at the stage when we are reacting against things. . . . These reactions lead to a certain arrogance, which is an overcompensation for a felt inferiority, and it hinders a sane outlook. We try to cover it up by saying, "We are as good as you" instead of remedying the specific error or lack This is not so pronounced among Indians at home as among Indians here.

Another said:

> Few people among Indians seem to manage themselves in such a way as to show that they are quite confident of their activities and can react to Americans as persons.

From another, an echo that we have also heard before:

> The Indians love talking for the intrinsic enjoyment of it and not for any specific purpose Anglo-Saxon people do not talk much but they mean what they talk They use language as a medium to convey their thoughts. The Indians use language for the enjoyment of the language itself or conversation.

Finally, a reverse twist on the matter of religion.

> Religion is taken seriously here, even by scientists . . . I did not expect [this]. . In India students do not care too much about religion or even think about it or analyze it . . .

These glimpses from Indians suggest how helpful it might be if we knew more than we do of this kind of Indian's self-image and if the process of mutual discovery could take place in a kindlier or less strained atmosphere than usually surrounds the typical American-Indian encounter at the present time.

But even as we write these lines, there comes to hand a rather

---

[78] George Coelho, "Acculturative Learning A Study of Reference Groups," unpublished ms , 1956 Cf Khushwant Singh, "What Are the Dominant Traits of Indian Character," *Illustrated Weekly of India*, Bombay, December 18, 1955, and letters to the editor in the issues of January 8, 15, 22, 1956

376                                      SCRATCHES ON OUR MINDS

authoritative Indian self-analysis which reproduces much of the detail—if not the feeling-tone—of the portrait that has emerged from the experience and impressions of these Americans. Many have said that the Indian encountered, when confronted with some of his contradictions, often reacts defensively, suggesting that the American simply does not understand the subtlety of the power to straddle two planes in mental space. But not so Jawaharlal Nehru writing for his own countrymen. Here, to place side by side with the more synthetic portrait these Americans have created, is Nehru's picture of exactly the same subject:[74]

> The fact that India was for long a closed land gave it its peculiar character. We became as a race somewhat inbred. We developed some customs which are unknown and not understood in other parts of the world Caste, in its innumerable forms, is a typical product of India Untouchability, the objections to inter-dining, inter-marriage, etc., are unknown in any other country The result was a certain narrowness in our outlook. Indians, even to the present day, find it difficult to mix with others Not only that, but each caste tends to remain separate even when they go to other countries. Most of us in India take all this for granted and do not realize how it astonishes and even shocks the people of other countries
>
> Thus, in India, we developed at one and the same time the broadest tolerance and catholicity of thought, as well as the narrowest social forms of behavior. This split personality has pursued us and we struggle against it even today. We overlook and excuse our own failings and narrowness of custom and habit by referring to the great thoughts we have inherited from our ancestors. But there is an essential conflict between the two, and so long as we do not resolve it, we shall continue to have this split personality.
>
> In a more or less static period these opposed elements did not come into conflict with each other much. But as the tempo of political and economic change has grown faster, these conflicts also have come more into evidence... We are compelled by overwhelming circumstances to put an end to this inner conflict.... The industrial revolution is coming rapidly to India and changing us in many ways It is an inevitable consequence of political and economic change that there should be social changes also if we are to remain as integrated human beings and an inte-

[74] From "The Crisis of the Spirit in India," written as a preface to *The Four Phases of Culture* (in Hindi), by R D Sinha Dinkar. The English text was issued by the Government of India Press Information Bureau on February 21, 1956 It also appeared in the *New York Times Magazine,* March 11, 1956, under the title "Nehru Explains India's 'Split Personality.'"

grated nation. We cannot . . . imagine that we can continue unchanged in the social sphere The stresses and strains will be too great and, if we do not resolve them, we shall crack up . .

We talk still, as of old, in the highest terms, but we act differently. It is extraordinary how our professions run far ahead of our practice We talk of peace and nonviolence and function in a different way We talk of tolerance and construe it to mean our way of thinking only and are intolerant of other ways We proclaim our ideal that of a philosophic detachment even in the midst of action . . . but we act on a far lower plane, and a growing indiscipline degrades us as individuals and as a community

When the Westerners came here across the seas, the closed land of India was again thrown open in a particular direction The modern industrial civilization gradually crept in in a passive way. New thoughts and ideas invaded us and our intellectuals developed the habit of thinking like British intellectuals That shaking up and opening out was good in its own way and it began to give us some understanding of the modern world But this cut off these intellectuals from the mass of the people, who were little affected by the new wave of thought Our traditional thinking was displaced and those who still clung to it did so in a static and uncreative way, totally unrelated to modern conditions Now this faith in Western thought is itself being shaken and so we have neither the old nor the new, and we drift not knowing whither we are going
This is a dangerous situation and if not checked and improved is likely to lead to grave consequences

Thus Nehru, no ordinary Indian or ordinary man, says in his way what so many of these Americans have said or glimpsed, with more or less sympathy and understanding, in their many particular ways We can perhaps at least sense from these juxtapositions the realities in these two portraits, the Indian and the American, both men living in a time of great transformations, the Indian faced with the need to change not only his society but himself, and the American confronting the enormous demands of his new role in human affairs and his need to win new relationships for himself among people in a world no longer dominated by the Western white man

To their encounter in this time, this Indian and this American bring, as we have seen, not only their strong transient feelings about current affairs, but also a whole mass of clustering influences and attitudes often rooted in their different histories and cultures. This is why so many of the resulting reactions echo those which can be traced far back in time. But there is much in this encounter, too, which is crude and new and tentative and shifting. It can be said almost certainly that any examination of American-Indian relationships even a decade or two decades hence will show how profound the changes are that are beginning only now. From that point in time, this report may serve at least to suggest how the matter stood when it all began.

PART FOUR

———————— ✿ ————————

# SOME REFLECTIONS

THE REPORT ENDS HERE. We have summoned up these many images of the Chinese and the Indians. We have described them as they appeared in a number of American minds. We have traced origins, measured historical dimensions, and examined their relation to the experience and contact of individuals. This has been a many-sided exploration and, as best we could, we have carried each part to its own conclusion. There are many other aspects of the matter to be explored, many observations still to pursue, and a great many questions which this inquiry has left in my own mind, and, I hope, in the reader's. I would like, in the manner of a postscript, to muse about some of these in some final pages.

## What is Image, What is Real?

Certain Chinese artists had a way of painting mountains which I had always taken to be an artistic convention until once, in northern Kwangsi, I came down among just such mountains as I had seen before only on parchment or on silk. They were unbelievably sorted in cones and knobs and a great host of unmountainly shapes rising at random from the flat valley floor and threaded together by fine curls of white mist. These mountains and the paintings of them come back to mind now as I think back over all the images that have crowded through these many pages and I hear a troubled reader asking: What is real? What is shadow, what is substance?

There is no tidy answer to this question. None of these images seems to me wholly a creature of pure fantasy. Each represents the effect of somebody's experience, the "truth" of somebody's perception. However fleeting, every perception is still an encounter of some kind between perceiver and perceived, one of that endless succession of interlocking observations that never quite tell the whole story. I know it would be simpler if it were otherwise, but I have no set of models, no certified genuine original portraits to which I can compare these many vignettes, no master answer sheet on which I can now tick off, true or false, any of these many images we have glimpsed through these American eyes. By unanimous—or nearly unanimous—consent, we can doubtless crop a few absurdities from the fringe, e.g., the rope trick Indian, Fu Manchu, the nerveless Chinese. But very little can really be excluded from the great host of particulars The jeweled maharajahs were real enough, and so were the fakirs on nails, the bodies, alive or dead, on the streets of Calcutta or Shanghai, the Indian saints, and the Chinese sages. I would not be surprised to learn that there were sliding doors and secret passages in some American Chinatown establishment, and I have little doubt that somewhere, sometime, some Chinese cook did take off after juvenile tormentors with a meat cleaver in his hand. There is no end, as Ripley showed, to what can be believed or not. The trouble begins with the unwitting or witless process by which we generalize from the small fact or single experience.

The mind's bent to make much out of little is, of course, part of the secret of human genius. This is how children learn not to play with fire and how men, gradually marshaling and sharpening their wits with increasing rigor and discipline, have learned most of what they know about the universe, about the earth, about each other, and about themselves. Once in a great while, the act of the mind that turns some particular picture into a universal symbol is an act of creation: great perception, great humor, great art. Not with greatness but with a decent respect for the needs of our common understanding, many people of course employ the normal devices of generalization every day of their lives. But equally every day these are checked for relevance and validity against the realities with which they must cope In a great many matters, however, in a great many minds, what goes on is a kind of mental trickery, a process of enlargement whereby we people our worlds with caricatures which appease some private or social needs. To distinguish between myth and reality in what we think and see requires effort and discipline. To do this we have to examine, each of us, how we register and house our observations, how we come to our judgments, how we enlarge upon them, how we describe them, and what purposes they serve for us. Even if a man discovers all this about himself, his reality need not be uniform with any other man's, for in each man substance can end and shadow begin at some different point. This point is located by the endlessly different combinations of a man's culture, education, and place in society; the time and place of his particular experience, the traits and drives of his individual personality. By examining the images we hold, say, of the Chinese and Indians, we can learn a great deal about Chinese and Indians, but mostly we learn about ourselves and about how, in each of us, this process of triangulation takes place. It is in some way unique in every man.

On this passage of inquiry through these many minds, I was heavily reinforced in my appreciation for the unending variety of individual uniqueness. But along the way I was also impressed by the influential accumulation of attitudes, images, and notions held in common by large groups or commonly attributed to others I fear that I learned only a little about the specter of personality that makes men unique, but I was led by this experience to look at their common holdings with a new eye There was obviously a clustering of more than one kind of uniformity among these individuals. A man *can* be an island, but islands are not often isolated atolls or lonely rocks. They lie mostly in archipelagos or at least in groups, and have many features alike. In this relation to each other, too, stood many members of our panel.

## Some Common Holdings

It is quite plain, to begin with, that large groups in our panel of 181 Americans shared a great many biases concerning the Chinese and the Indians Here are the bare bones of a summary of what we found

• Ninety-eight, or 54 per cent, expressed more or less strongly negative views about Indians. Some of this antipathy was attributable to feelings over foreign policy differences. But it clearly had deeper roots, reproducing in some respects much older American reactions to Hindu life and culture. The antipathy was directed most particularly, however, toward Indians in the same professional classes as these Americans, and with but few exceptions these were Indians encountered by these Americans during the last ten years, the first decade of Indian independence

• One hundred twenty-three, or 70 per cent, expressed predominantly positive or admiring views of Chinese, applying these views to China as a nation, to Chinese culture as a whole, and to Chinese people of all sorts and classes, as known, encountered, or in some way discovered most generally in the years between 1920 and 1940 Changes reflecting the more recent circumstances have only just begun to weaken these attitudes, especially in individuals in whom they were not too strongly lodged

• Thirty-nine individuals in our panel "liked" both Chinese and Indians, 17 "disliked" both There were 17 who "liked" Indians but did not "like" Chinese. But there were 72 who "liked" Chinese and "disliked" Indians.

• This pattern of reaction held with remarkable consistency no matter how we sorted these Americans, by the kind and amount of their contact, by their policies, by their degrees of involvement in Asian affairs, or by their professional groups In every grouping there was a predominantly positive view of the Chinese and either a roughly even division or a preponderantly unfavorable view of Indians. The Chinese stood highest in the esteem of those who had most contact with them and lowest (though never very low) among those who knew them least. On the other hand, Indians scored better among those who knew them little—who tended to polarize to the extremes of "like" or "dislike"—than among those who knew them well—who tended to be more moderate or more mixed in their reactions Thus 12 of our 16 China specialists were strongly positive about Chinese, 4 were "mixed," and none was negative. Of the 25 India specialists, 9 were positive about Indians, 9 negative, and 7 "mixed"

• China-identified individuals had notably uniform attitudes about Indians. Of the 16 China specialists, 15 were strongly antipathetic, and only 1 was not. India-identified people were much less uniform in their reactions to Chinese, but there is a faint flavor of reciprocation about some of the figures. Of the 6 individuals, for example, who were most strongly admiring of the Indians, 3 distinctly did not

## SOME REFLECTIONS

admire the Chinese at all. Of our 25 India specialists, 7 had negative views of the Chinese, a higher proportion (28 per cent) than appeared in any group within the panel. Of 65 panelists who had visited India but had never been to China, 13, or 20 per cent, were cool about the Chinese, while of 32 panelists who had visited both China and India, only 3 "disliked" Chinese while 21 "disliked" Indians.

From all the information and all the impressions at hand, I can say that I would expect this general pattern to be confirmed, reproduced, and reinforced by any wider or more systematically stratified inquiry in the same general milieu at this time. The evidence for this is strong and is multiplied in my own knowledge by instance after instance going far beyond the numbers of our present panel or the period of time in which these particular interviews were conducted. We are obviously confronted here with a community of views and reactions that extends far beyond these individual digits and derives from a body of common holdings covering a quite large area of experience.

Much about the character of these common holdings has already been suggested in the body of this report. It has been shown in many ways, for example, that many of these images and attitudes are products of their time and place and circumstances. It has been shown that dominant American reactions to China fluctuated widely during the 170-year history of American-Chinese contact, while American-Indian experience is connected only by thin strands to any distant past, and that this suggests that much is subject to change in the present patterns relating to Indians. True as this may be, it does not tell the whole story. For it is usually not the attributes that are changed by circumstances, but the way they are seen, a matter, again, of those lights shining at different times from different directions on different facets of what there is to see. Even under this constantly flickering and moving light, moreover, it is plain that some parts of the picture have always been in view. The lines of admiration for the Chinese, and of fear and mistrust as well, have been there from the beginning, have never been quite wholly effaced at any time since, and will not disappear wholly from any new views the future may disclose. It is similarly plain that the Westerner's capacity to be shocked and repelled by the Indian and his culture goes far, far back—there are intimations of it even in

Marco Polo's brief account of his Indian travels—deeply underpinning and long antedating the irritation felt by so many Americans over so temporal a matter as Nehru's foreign policy, or by the behavior of Indians attributable to the newness of their independence.

How else may we, then, begin to define any of these common holdings? I bring no ready set of answers to this question, only some discussion These are, by definition, large matters. They take us into a region of large and normally careless generalizations, a place where one ordinarily hunts for intellectual prey, but where now I warily seek some food for thought One of the largest beasts rumored to be native here is now referred to in some social scientific dialects as "national character." Many hunters seek him in the belief that they will find hiding in his coat some of those bits of lively truth that are said to inhabit all popular national stereotypes. But like the Abominable Snowman, he has never yet been clearly seen, much less trapped and exhibited The chances are that he never will be until he is much more precisely and narrowly located and identified. He may not, indeed, be like the Abominable Snowman at all, but more like the giraffe before which that man in the cartoon stood and declared: "There ain't no such animal!"

I do not propose to enter any abstract discussion about "national character," Snowman variety or giraffe But I do want to consider here—much more seriously than I would have when I embarked on this inquiry—the possible meanings that attach to the single words "Chinese" or "Indian" or "American." All other identifying details apart, what might these adjectives alone suggest by way of common holdings of the people of all three nationalities who have figured in our study? These nationality labels are words that vibrate at many different frequencies for different people. To me they signify certain large geographic and certain very broad cultural identifications within which the possible varieties of individuality are without number Yet I find myself now somewhat more willing than I was before to consider the possibility that they can be somewhat more descriptive, that they can suggest the presence of certain cultural traits, modes, even ideas. These can vary enormously in expression from individual to individual, but remain nevertheless in some form the common holding of large universes of people As such, they can exert some particular effect on members of other large groups of people when contact takes place across cultural boundaries

As one possible example, I offer the phenomenon of *li*, the Chinese code of correct manners. Our panelists gave especially high marks, the reader will recall, to the special Chinese brand of courtesy, sensitivity, charming manners. Now the Chinese code of correct manners is as precise as a manual of arms or of court protocol. It is a system designed to assure within certain clearly defined limits that every man's ego is decently respected, or at least not publicly diminished. There is nothing uniquely Chinese about the business of gaining, saving, or losing "face"—it goes on in some form in every human society. But the Chinese acquired a special reputation in this matter because they acquired a high skill for it, turning it almost into an art form, full of formal convention, yet often extraordinarily satisfying in its effects. Chinese politeness was designed to smooth away all surface frictions. It established orderly priorities for almost all human relationships and the proper form of behavior for each one. Systems much like this exist in other societies but none, seemingly, with the patina and quality of the Chinese at its best. This is why Chinese amenities were always so charming, Chinese hospitality so attractive, and almost all encounters with Chinese so pleasantly memorable. In most of the ordinary business of human intercourse, this system accomplished its purpose admirably. Since over most of the period of American contact with Chinese in China, the foreigner almost automatically enjoyed high status and a high degree of deference, it was especially successful with foreigners and particularly so with Americans.

The system was fine so long as it was never tested for depth. It was based on the notion that most human contact is superficial and should be kept that way. Designed to preserve smooth surfaces, it did not allow much room for the free play of greater intimacy or interplay and expression of any deeper emotions. In times of stress, this politeness screened all sorts of unruly and unpleasant contradictions. In such circumstances, Chinese behavior could and did look to the foreigner like insincerity or downright dishonesty. This was the familiar judgment on Chinese manners in the difficult decades of the nineteenth century, and it has cropped up again in our own century whenever the going between Americans and Chinese got rough, especially during World War II, and since. The "deviousness" or "dishonesty" or "untrustworthiness" of the familiar negative stereotypes are, after all, only the undersides of good Chinese manners as they appear if the basic relationship is one of conflict. No American now is likely to mistake the well-known charm of

Chou En-lai for a quality of inner virtue. But over the long period of time when the foreigner's superior status was acknowledged in fact as well as in form, it was a good deal easier for foreigners to believe in the sincerity of Chinese charm and the reality of Chinese deference. Many foreigners in China, especially teachers and scholars and masters of crafts, like ship captains or engineers, had every reason to feel they were being genuinely respected, especially in the years when so many Chinese were so seriously engaged in learning all they could about Western ways from Western tutors This deference was, to be sure, often overdone and was associated with weakness; it sometimes became obsequious and generated contempt and patronage. This was not an uncommon form of the foreigner's experience and behavior in China, especially in the treaty ports But in most cases, even when Chinese deference was understood to be a formal posture, I suspect that it was difficult for most Americans not to respond to it with eager self-appreciation All other things being more or less equal, it is a rare ego that is proof against inflation, a rare man who will not believe that deference shown him is well merited. On this sure and shrewd knowledge, the Chinese built their code for interpersonal relations. As our present study and much other evidence shows, it has helped them make friends and influence people for a long, long time

It is quite difficult to suggest any example of a similar single common holding of Indians or Americans comparable in character and effect to conventional Chinese manners Much was said of Indian courtesy to travelers and hospitality to guests, and there was testimony to a subtle, even delicate sensitivity in many Indians met, known, and admired. But in most accounts the accent was much heavier and more frequent either on the obsequiousness of servants or the aggressiveness of Indian intellectuals, an outspokenness carried often to the point of rudeness Now except for the item of obsequiousness, many of the things some of these Americans said about some Indians have a familiar ring, because they are the same things that some Indians (and many other foreigners) have been saying about some Americans, i.e., that they are brash, know-it-all, arrogant, unmannerly, and above all, morally self-righteous. To the extent that these qualities or manners do appear in significant numbers of individuals on both sides, the result is a collision of alikes, a repulsion between poles not because they are different but because they are the same. A meeting between two apostles of righteousness is not often the beginning of a beautiful friendship. But however unpleasant the frequency of their appearance, these are still not peculiarly "Indian" or "American" qualities. They would not on either side be enough by themselves to explain the nature of so many of our present encounters. As irritants they seem rather to compound the effect of a whole series of more important differences that have a much longer history, differences in religious and philosophic outlooks, in the manner of relatedness to other men and nature. Some of these certainly do suggest common holdings on both sides that do in profound ways mold the social character of the individual members of both cultures But whether these holdings are distinctively "Indian" or "American" is quite another question which is not simply or quickly answered.

It does not seem at all accidental that with respect to "Chinese" it is easier to summon up such a distinctive identification, and that it turns out to be related to the Chinese system for maintaining the smoothness of surface contact, counterpart in the sphere of human relations to the Chinese preoccupation in art with exquisite form. It seems to me equally not accidental that in the attempt to summon up any comparable generalization for "Indian" or "American" we run at once into matters that are quite different, more substantial, more complicated, more difficult, and probably less truly distinctive

Thus in seeking examples of something distinctively "Indian" and something distinctively "American," I found myself thinking of the Indian institution of *caste* and the American idea of *the totally mobile society*. I offer myself at once a dozen valid objections to accepting either one of these as truly unique attachments to the unamplified adjectives "Indian" or "American." Still, I think the collision of these elements plays so great a role in Indian-American encounters that I take the license to pursue them here at least for a short distance.

Echoes of this collision are heard from as far back in the past as we have the written record of American discoveries of India. The nineteenth-century American traveler to India, who much resembled the twentieth-century Indian traveler to America in his thorough appreciation of his own moral and political virtues, was uniformly horrified by the rigidities of Indian caste.[1] He was likely to see it as the most complete antithesis of his own culture's belief in total social mobility. Caste set up for this American, and for his counterparts down into our own time, an immediate barrier of incomprehensibility, a first and powerful impulse of rejection By the same token, this same American reacted with identifying approval to the discovery in Chinese society of a mythology akin to his own, the idea that long, long ago, the Chinese system aimed to make it possible for the lowest farmer's son to rise by individual merit to the side of the Heavenly Throne. This won marks for the Chinese among Americans, as we have noted, all the way back to Thomas Jefferson's time

The belief in total social mobility, the inherent right and opportunity for all to proceed through merit and achievement from rags to riches, from log cabin to White House, is a peculiarly American article of faith. It may be a myth contradicted by much in the American actuality. It may explain many American postures of self-congratulation, righteousness, superiority, hypocrisy Yet, as I have suggested before in connection with the American relation to Western imperialism in Asia, it has the power to overlay many of these contradictions. Every man who is a product of the American culture stands in some relation to this central dream of his society, whether in his view of himself or his view of his nation's role and behavior, in his own clusters of personal or national pride or guilt Burdened as it may be with clichés and fatigue and failure, and despite all the great range of individual variations—one thinks of the much-caricatured American yearning after European aristocrats, or of the easy relish with which so many Americans adopted the modes of the lords of creation in Asia—the democratic dream still provides the yardstick by which the "American" measures his experience of other cultures more formally stratified than his own.

In current American-Indian encounters the issue of caste plays a complicated role. Taken by itself as the symbol of ultrastratification and also as a symbol for all the elements in Hindu society which retard the country's advance, it arouses the traditional American reaction. Only now this reaction of rejection and bafflement is multiplied by frustration, for this American is usually interested

---

[1] Caste, observed Mark Twain in an account of his Indian travels sixty years ago, "separates people into layers, and layers, and still other layers, that have no community of feeling with each other."—*Following the Equator*, p. 399

either in helping or in seeing Indians "do something" about their problems. On the Indian side the response to this is defensive. Almost every Indian carries the mark of caste upon him, whether he counts himself a defender or a critic of the system It is connected with the special forms of Indian caste and color prejudice, and attitudes toward status and the relation of educated Indians to their own particular groupings, to the uneducated masses, and to Indian society as a whole If he is a conservative Indian, his response to the American reaction is a natural posture of defense. If he is a "modern" Indian, the matter grows more difficult, for every forward-looking Indian is himself today committed to ending the caste system and all its rigidities and all its extrusions in Indian life. Yet he smarts and struggles under the knowledge that he has not yet even emancipated himself from its grip.[2] His country, like a great part of the world, has accepted, at least as a credo, the dream of a democratic society which was for so long the unique possession of the new American culture that developed from European origins. This Indian, with all his accumulated sensitivities about himself and his own culture, cannot accept this without a certain resentment. He is in much the position that Cyrano took toward comments on his nose, willing to denounce its monstrousness himself at poetic length, but quite ready to deny at sword's point any untoward word by anyone else Unable to skewer his critic as Cyrano did, he impales him on charges of being a lyncher, a racist, a pelf-seeker sunk in materialism, or borrows from the fading images of his British heritage, and scorns the American as a vulgarian without art or good manners. The American, for his part, may be none of these things but still suffer from too poorly representing that great and elusive dream which he now shares with so many people all around the world.

Whatever clues these examples might offer as to the nature of the common holdings of these people, they all still remain uncomfortably large generalizations, blurred and fuzzy, like the view in a poorly focused camera's eye. The images evoked by the labels "Chinese" or "Indian" or "American" have to be more rigorously defined and more sharply seen by bringing into view the string of

[2] "We say we are against communalism, casteism, against provincialism and all that," said Nehru to a meeting of the All-India Congress Committee on June 1, 1957, "and yet you know well enough how poisoned we are to the very core by communalism, casteism and provincialism Which of us, I or you, is completely free of this?"—*New York Times*, June 2, 1957

other identifying adjectives to which they may be attached. Much more can be said in general about such a group as "American businessmen who lived in Shanghai in the 1920's," or "Indians educated in England in the generation before independence," or "Chinese college students at the time of the Japanese invasion." These or any of a great host of other such particulars fix these Chinese, Indians, and Americans in groups located in society, in time, in place, and often in particular circumstances Such groups not only have a great deal of experience in common They can also come to have many common characteristics, modes, manners, outlooks, and these are capable of producing an almost predictable effect on members of other particular groups. Among these common holdings, the nationality label adds only one meaningful item of identification to a great many others, for these are people who also share common professions, preoccupations, interests, and situations. They are people who are looking out at the world from much the same windows and who therefore tend to get much the same view of what they see

## Windows on the World

All images are shaped by the way they are seen, a matter of setting, timing, angle, lighting, distance Images carried about by some people for a whole lifetime may have been fixed by a single exposure dating, perhaps, from an experience deep in the past Or else they may emerge from a whole collection of pictures that a man takes with his mind over the years and which come out looking much the same because his mind's setting is fixed, like a fixed-focus box camera.

This aperture is set by the totality of what a man is. Primarily, of course, he is an individual personality with his own unique bundle of needs and forms of self-expression. These fix the most important conditions in which his images are shaped and seen. But we are trying here to see the image-shaping identities that many such individuals may hold in common as members of groups We have suggested that the first such group identity may be the fact that he is "American" with all that may suggest or imply as to his outlook But more graspably, he is a lot of other things too· he is a bachelor, master, or doctor of art, science, medicine, or philosophy, an editor, teacher, diplomat, businessman, writer, Congressman, or wearer of his church's cloth These identities establish for each man the area in which he functions and expends most of his energy, the interests which govern his behavior, the kinds of satisfaction or frustration he may derive from his experience with other people His images of the Chinese or Indian are clearly going to have quite different shapes according to whether he sees them as prospective customers, objects of his benevolence, souls to be saved, or digits in a population problem or exemplars of some sociological category. His attitude is going to be influenced to a decisive degree by what he seeks from his encounter with the Chinese or Indian (or anybody else, for that matter), by whether he wants to win acceptance of the product, the creed, or the policy he has to sell or promote, or whether he wants the person he meets to satisfy his scholarly, journalistic, acquisitive, or merely idle curiosity, or if he wants nothing at all but to meet and pass on by. All these shapes, outlooks, and purposes flickered in the many interviews of which this study is made

Sometimes this fixed focus could be narrow enough to produce extraordinary distortions, as in the case of the oilman who translated the whole complex of Chinese and Indian problems into the figures of their oil consumption, or the missionary who, when asked what India could do to improve Indian-American relations, instantly replied "India could remove restrictions on visas for missionaries." Perhaps the most striking examples of a special window on the world were provided by Negro members of our panel who uniquely described the Chinese as "Uncle Toms" because they catered to white prejudices by not serving Negroes in their restaurants But let me enlarge here one such an example, an impression I acquired quite freshly for myself in the course of this inquiry.

This concerns the businessmen in our panel, a small group of only 12, including 3 with long India experience, 3 similarly identified with China, and 6 others who had been in both countries and other parts of Asia on somewhat briefer tours of business duty. This is a small number of men about whom I draw no conclusion but simply offer an observation. I noticed that while they might express themselves quite strongly on politics or matters of business, their comments on the Chinese or Indians as people tended to remain generally moderate or mild. There were only two exceptions to this in the group, one the familiar case of an "old India hand" who liked Indians very well indeed. But all the others were much more casual about the Chinese or Indians, casting their images in more matter-of-fact lines than most other members of the panel I have reported the observation of one of these businessmen that to be successful one had to know what made the other fellow tick, at certain levels of relationship this tended to make for a certain shrewd insight, even a certain sympathy, and sometimes, perhaps, affection for the other fellow with whom one had to deal But more generally speaking, it seems fair to say that the businessman in China or India in the time of Western supremacy felt the least necessary involvement with the Chinese or the Indians as individuals In his favored primacy of those days, the foreign businessman did not have to deal with Chinese or Indians as serious competitors, he played with a stacked deck in this respect. He needed people mainly to serve him as agents or clerks, and when these were loyal and reasonably efficient, and faithful for a long time, they were valued affectionately as old retainers Even Asian businessmen or brokers or bankers who reached higher rungs of the business ladder never seriously threatened the places reserved at the top for the dominant foreigner. This foreigner might have found it occasionally useful to exchange certain minimum social amenities with Chinese or Indian businessmen, but these were rare and exceptional right up to nearly the closing years of the whole epoch. As late as the outbreak of the Japanese war, Chinese guests were normally welcome in neither the British nor the American clubs in Shanghai, to say nothing of Indian guests in British clubs in India If the businessman in this setting did develop any friendships or interests outside the circle of his similars or outside his business preoccupations, it was exceptional and accidental, and he was an unusual man. There were such unusual men—I ran into one of them—but they hardly set the general tone of the group

The group had established a fairly simple set of rules to govern relations with the people among whom it lived The businessman required only the assured security of his contracts, his profit and his comfort, and proper deference to his person and his position. Generally speaking, he did not care in the least about their immortal souls—he regarded the missionary with a glum eye—or about the state of their minds—he thought too much education was unsettling and dangerous. He was not interested in their social systems or customs except where they interfered with business or where, by adaptation (e.g., contract labor practices), he stood to profit. He was concerned with their politics only when these politics directly affected his interests and his position All this had certain consequences —ultimately fatal—for foreign businessmen in both China and India.

But in relation to the people of the land, my own particular little sample suggests that they may have been able to be much easier-going, less emotional, and on the whole more relaxed. It seems reasonable to suggest that they did not care as much, and that they were therefore better able to withstand the blows of outrageous fortune when they fell.

## The Specter of Personality

But how about that "unusual" businessman who was different? Why was he different? To answer this question, I would have had to learn much more about the individual than I could hope to learn in a single interview, for this was no longer a matter of his nationality, his profession or trade, his public window on the world. This was a matter of his private being.

Once, quite early in this inquiry, I had occasion for the first time to analyze a particular group of interviews. After poring awhile over the numbered cards containing these interview notes, I found that I wanted the individual's name attached to each one to help me in making my assessments I clearly felt the need to summon up in my mind a picture of the person, to revive my memory of *how* he said what he said, to re-evoke all the unspoken inferences and all my impressions of the *kind* of person he seemed to me to be. By this process I was able to weigh in the elements of his demeanor and his tone and the quality of his candor. But beyond all these there was something else I was taking into account without being sure what it was, that ectoplasmic presence, the individual personality, that specter, always on hand, always playing a role of whose nature I could never be sure. Indeed, this specter haunted the interviews so aggressively that I once tried to establish contact through several highly recommended mediums. I tried to discover from several psychologists if there was not some systematic way in which I could trap this ghost, make him materialize and take his place at the table. But I soon discovered that I was only making an amateur attempt to penetrate surfaces that the professionals have as yet barely scratched. In the presence of so much informed tentativeness, I was urged to tread freely where angels still feared to rush in. Out of modesty and caution, I have not accepted this invitation Instead, I will try here simply to note down a few of the things which, as I skirted the question, I thought I saw.

It was obvious, to begin with, that through a man's window we could discover *what* a man sees but very little of *how* he sees it We were still left also to wonder why two men sitting at the same window, or in the same bank of windows, often saw things so differently. Why did one scholar describe Indians as "articulate" and why did another say they were "talkative"? Why did one person regard the people around him with distaste and even fear while another regarded them mostly with a relaxed and quizzical curiosity? Why did one traveler remember only the squalor and the urinal stench of city streets, and why did another call to mind the high color, vivid motion, and the "pungent odor of dung fires burning at night" in the Indian countryside? Why was one diplomat made bitter and angry by policy differences, and why did another react much more matter-of-factly, even though both held substantially the same view of the matters in dispute?

One of the most marked of these examples concerned two of the Negro panelists who saw the Chinese in their role as restaurant-keepers who discriminated against Negroes. One reacted to this experience, which he knew of only by hearsay, by forming a strong prejudice against Chinese in general: "The Chinese are international Uncle Toms, bootlickers of the white man!" The second, a man of similar background, interests, and profession, reported *his* experience of this matter as follows

> Once back in the thirties my wife and I were on a driving trip and near Salt Lake City had some trouble finding a place that would serve us breakfast We finally entered a Chinese restaurant but the Chinese proprietor waved us away: "No serve colored, no serve colored!" My wife, who had an attitude of sympathy for the Chinese in the Sino-Japanese fighting, turned on him furiously. "I hope the Japanese really smash your country!" she cried at him. Back in the car driving away I said to her "Now what did you want to take it out on that poor beggar for? It's the Mormons who run things around here, and he's just going along with the system What else can he do? If you want to get sore at anybody, get sore at the Mormons for the patterns they have set up, certainly not at the whole Chinese people!"

Another prime example concerns two scholars, both of high repute in their respective fields. Neither is inclined to underestimate himself, both set high value on intellectual qualities and interests, both especially admire the way these values are exemplified in England, each, indeed, in his own fashion, can be said to be an Anglophile. This is a great deal for two men to hold in common. Yet one was impatiently contemptuous of Indian intellectuals and the other was warmly admiring. Both men made their first trip to India in recent years Both came away from the experience with all their previous notions powerfully reinforced, the one more than ever convinced of the ineffably surpassing qualities of his Indian friends and acquaintances, the other full of his confirming evidence that the Indians whom he observed, with notably few exceptions, were shallow and shoddy. It is true that they had somewhat different preoccupations, but the deeper reasons for differences lie locked up in these two individuals. One could start looking for them, probably, by trying to discover the nature and sources of each one's Anglophilism and going on in from there to wherever the search might lead. But that would be another inquiry, another book, indeed another book written by someone else.[3] I can deal here, again, only in some impressions.

Some of the most vivid of these impressions have to do with the uncovering in some interviews—often to the interviewee himself at the same time—of the great molding power of early experiences or environmental influences. In one way these help fix for us each individual's window on the world, but they are also windows through which we can look inward and catch glimpses of what made this person what he is, what caused him to see and react to the Chinese or the Indians as he did.

In some cases, this was the direct effect of a total early environment, as in the cases of individuals born to missionary families living in China or India. I have already remarked being struck by how little we know about the varieties of pain and pleasure produced by the experience of being a missionary's child in a strange land. The subject remains largely untouched and unscrutinized, whether by social scientist, novelist, or writer of memoirs In the present context I think particularly of an India-born woman (not, incidentally, a member of the present panel) who described to me once with wounding sharpness her childhood sensation that wherever she went, along the road, in the streets of the town, even in the mission itself, she felt that she saw all Indians as through a *glass wall* which

[3] The relation of individual personality to images of foreign peoples is explored with the instruments of social and clinical psychology by Howard V Perlmutter in his forthcoming *Personal Identity and the Foreigner*, Center for International Studies, M.I T.

wholly cut her off from all intimacy and all communication. Out of frustration over this separateness she came to hate them all, she said, and not until she returned to India as an adult did she begin the slow process of redirecting her feelings about the people among whom she moved

Some of these influences were more general, much less direct, but still powerfully decisive. I think of four different religious environments of four different individuals.

• A writer brought up in a strongly Methodist Ohio town where he took in the intense missionizing spirit of friends and kin linked to China by several generations of work there and who had, by the time of his boyhood, already translated their feelings into a highly sentimental regard for China and the Chinese people. Today, although he has had little personal experience with China, this individual is one of the most ardent of all Sinophiles;

• An editor raised, also in the Midwest, in a Unitarian family. From this background he acquired a skeptical view of all missionary work, and thence a skeptical reaction to sentimental attitudes about the Chinese. Today he is a man who discusses highly controversial matters about which he has strong opinions with a manner of sympathetically detached tolerance,

• A diplomat, product of the Eastern seaboard aristocracy, high Episcopalian, which seemed to mean that as a child he heard of missionary work, but only from afar, that he knew of missionaries, but as rather odd folk, and of the distant peoples they catered to as rather outlandish people who, for all he knew, inhabited another planet. When events and his career brought him, nearly five decades later, into urgent and even critical contact with some of these outlandish peoples, he reacted to them . . . like a man from another planet.

• A woman who came out of a liberal Quaker, pacifist, well-meaning, do-gooding family and had been molded by it into a person quite unwilling to have strong negative reactions except against political or social evils. She became like a mirror that registered all the impressions of her later years in India and retained them all. Unable to resolve the many contradictions that assailed her, she adopted the Indian mode of housing them all, and somehow lives with the jumble of pain and pleasure and uncertainty of her emotional biases.

Many an interview turned up a sharper, more particular vignette of some early experience that came into view, materializing almost like a genie as we rubbed the appropriate lamp Once in a while these were startling, even amusing One of our most distinguished newspaper writers reacted to "Indian" instantly: "Indian makes me think of the Sikh we had in our house in Cambridge. He was the only man there who ever left hairs in the bathtub, and so many hairs!" That young Sikh who simply assumed that some servant would clean the bathtub after him had been his schoolmate nearly thirty years before, and though he could properly disclaim that this experience had fixed his whole view of Indians, it was still worth wondering why this was the picture that peeled first off his memory after so many years. Then there was the highly conservative politician who had as a small lad seen an actual fakir on nails, brought all the way to Columbus, Ohio, to take part in a missionary exhibition, as an example, no doubt, of the horrors of Hindu heathenism. This sight aroused in our friend no powerful aversion to Hindu mysticism. It stimulated in him instead an interest in psychic phenomena that has remained with him all his life and shaped a great deal of his behavior "Why, I can lie down there," he said, pointing to the couch in his office, "and get more rest in twenty minutes than you get in a whole night's sleep! It is a matter of knowing how to relax." When he was not relaxing, this man was doing his best to promote the political tradition and principles of the late Senator Robert Taft of Ohio.

In other cases, the vignette was a sudden disclosure of self, a remark rising like a bubble of air in some deep emotional pool—the noted public figure, passing middle age, speaking with savage anger of a "saccharine Indian" to whom his highly regarded mother once showed unusual favor in his presence when he was a young man; or the Jew who grew up in a small foreign city smarting from anti-Semitic gibes and who, without any relevance whatever to any political views of his own, said of the Chinese Communists· "I like their militancy. They are doing for me what I can't do for myself, keeping alive a spirit of rebellion."

But perhaps my prize exhibit in this department of the power of early experience is the story that came out in several pieces during an interview with one of this country's ablest students of public affairs. Early in the interview he said:

I can remember feeling that I ought to go to Asia, especially after I began writing about it . . But there was something that made me not want to go to Asia I said to ——— the other day that he ought to go out there He said no I asked why He said it was on his conscience, but he guessed it was a fear of pestilence and disease I think my own reluctance comes from some of the same thing Asia was diseased, different, felt I didn't like it. How many villains in early movies were Orientals? I think that had something to do with it. The heathen Chinee, seaport scenes, Oriental villains, Chinese associated with all sorts of wickedness, opium smuggling, all this from the movies.

When we began to talk about his sources for "pestilence and disease" we moved rapidly back to his boyhood and this is what came tumbling out:

I was brought up in a fiercely religious family. My parents wanted me to go into the ministry and I was taken to church several times a week. I was told to say that I was going to become a missionary and teach the Gospel to the heathen. This is what a noble man would do with his life Go out among those teeming masses Got this from my mother and father all the time Heard missionaries in church, usually from China They told us of the poor wretched people to whom men of God brought civilizing qualities I thought these men of God were quite wonderful, but I didn't want to do the same as they did or get mixed up among these wicked, diseased, hungry, different people I didn't want to be a missionary

Musingly, he now contemplated this reason for his reluctance to go to Asia, to expose himself to the crowding, the pestilence, the difference, the people for whom he had not wanted to be noble, about whom he had to listen for dreary hours when all he wanted was to be out playing ball. The interesting thing is that he eventually did make a quick Pacific tour, but he did it aboard a freighter, visited only at the ports where it called, and used the ship as his hotel while he went ashore to get his glimpse of Asia and to meet some of its people. "In fact," he commented wryly, "it wasn't as bad as I'd thought."

With such vignettes we reach some of the anterooms, but not the inner sanctums of each man's personality, here we are left to try to guess from details in the foyer the nature of the man of the house I shall not attempt this about any single individual, but before leaving for more hospitable quarters, I would like to report a few other intimations of personality that emerged from numbers of these interviews. These are impressions that I could not by any stretch inflate into facts, but they recurred so frequently that I found myself mentally classifying them in some unlabeled or roughly labeled groups.

It is a common claim of folk wisdom that you learn most about a man in his off-moments, by what he's like when he plays or when he's drunk In somewhat the same way, I began to wonder how much one learned about a man's mind and his personality not by the way he dealt with what was most centrally important to him, but by the way he handled matters outside his inner core of interest, preoccupation, and knowledge. Students of the human mind have begun to give us some fairly vivid accounts of what the place looks like and what goes on inside, but it is impossible to catch a glimpse for oneself, even to look out over Xanadu, without some sense of fresh discovery Thus I saw for myself that in most minds there stands only one solid or rickety structure in which a man houses what he knows, where he keeps in some reasonable order the one or two things about which he feels able to distinguish beginning, middle, and end, to observe with some decent rigor the connection between cause and effect, fact and source, past and present. Here, in his chosen role, he has a measure of command, here he can expend much of his energy, here he can flick familiar switches, turn on familiar lights, and light up familiar surroundings. Here there is a certain order, a certain coherence. But beginning just outside, great masses of all sorts of miscellaneously shaped bits and pieces float, apparently quite free, in the surrounding spaces of his mind. Here in multitudes are all the things that had seemed to go in one ear and out the other but had actually left wispy traces behind, all the things caught sight of out of the corner of the eye and seemingly flicked away forgotten, but which nevertheless fell somewhere into the invisible orbits of this little mental universe, operating by its own peculiar laws of gravity and relativity.

I noticed that a man could behave quite differently when something (i.e., an interviewer's question· "When you think of India, what comes to your mind?") suddenly required him to step out across the threshold of coherence and familiarity into the looser, stranger spaces beyond He was likely, in our panel, to be a man who inside his own boundaries of coherence insisted upon a reasonable precision, a certain discipline of thought and fact, e.g., an economist wedded to concrete categories, a sociologist wedded to abstractions almost as rigid, at least a man whose responsibilities did not give him much room for fooling around He might, upon stepping outside, look blankly and suspiciously at all the space-borne flotsam and insist he had no way of making any sense out of it at all. But he might also throw all care for coherence to the winds, and like a boy let out of school, whoop for joy and take off into the bright air, leaping from bit to piece and from piece to bit in great fine swooping generalizations, falling back, when he had to, not on evidence, but on his prejudices or his poetic intuition Such individuals I came to tag mentally as Easy Generalizers, men who could fly through the air with the greatest of ease from the fragmentary fact to the universal—and usually final—judgment Opposite them were the Hard Generalizers, individuals with a greater regard for consistency who might also sometimes make a paralyzing dogma out of preserving the separateness of each scrap of information, whether it was floating free or tied down somewhere inside their heads.

There were other categories into which individuals seemed to fall I noticed, for example, that some men were embarrassed by the revelation of their ignorance of Asia—no matter how legitimately it was come by—and others quite indifferent to this discovery. I noticed that some men found it difficult to say "I don't know——" or "I haven't read——" while others did not mind saying so at all. I noticed that some individuals were acutely uncomfortable while they were being pressed to grope around in the attics of their minds to locate the reasons why they said some of the things they did, and that some of those who groped most blindly for the roots of their attitudes sprouted the most fully with strong and authoritative and readily expressed opinions on current affairs. I began to recognize also the Easy Relaters—prone to accept all comers at first face value and to discriminate among them afterward—and the Hard Relaters—those holders at arm's length, prone to reject all first comers and to discriminate among them afterward I was struck, too, by the varieties of what I came to call the Sure and the Unsure. In this panel, the Unsure were a distinct minority. Most people who think of themselves as intellectuals or communicators seem to become unhappy if they cannot assume an air of reasonable certainty about their knowledge and their opinions. But I noticed that Sureness and Unsureness could spring equally out of knowledge or out of ignorance, out of knowing too much or knowing too little, out of appreciating or ignoring how complicated a thing could be.

I fear there is not much I feel able to say about the relation between these personality traits as I so limitedly observed them and the various ranges of attitudes about Christmas and Indians that I have reported. My information on this score simply remains too meager. I could not predict from any of these traits or postures of mind alone what a man's images or attitudes about the Chinese or Indians would turn out to be. They only helped to suggest the particular route by which he had arrived at his views. In some cases they helped explain his manner of holding them, e.g., the Easy Generalizers, given to sweeping judgments, usually located themselves at the extremes of the scale, ultra-plus or ultra-minus, as the case might be. In this matter of the relationship of personality to images, however, I must unembarrassedly avow my Unsureness and declare with reasonable certainty that it arises out of my ignorance and my great respect for the complexities. I therefore abstain from Easy Generalizing. If this makes me seem a Hard Relater to any of my readers, I can only bow in apologetic humility, Chinese style.

## Images and Politics

How, finally, do these images and attitudes relate to politics, international relations, the making of government policy, the shaping of public opinion?

The first answer is, of course, that relations between nations are determined primarily by the large and highly material considerations of geography, resources, power, economics, and the somewhat less tangible quantity of the national self-interest as conceived by governing groups. These considerations consist mostly of hard facts harshly seen, and leaders are usually effective to the degree that they keep these facts unblinkingly in view. But even these large chunks of reality can often be seen in dimensions larger or smaller than life. Great events indeed can result from such "mistaken" arrangements and images and ideas in the minds of men in power, e.g., Napoleon's views of Russia and England, the conceptions of Russia and the United States on which Hitler based his course, the ideas about China that governed the thinking of Japanese military leaders in the 1930's, the belief of certain American leaders in 1945 that Japanese fanaticism would outweigh Japan's loss of capacity to wage war, the belief of British and French leaders that they could impose their will by force on Egypt in 1956. When the issues between nations are those of war or peace, the consequences of such "miscalculations" can, as we have all seen, be quite formidable.

The nature of these judgments is of course no simple matter. The leader's images of other peoples and nations is plainly only one of a large group of interlocking elements that come into play in the making of almost all decisions. It is not easy to sort these out sufficiently to see what role such images played in any single instance. The noted American historian Howard K. Beale recently re-examined the behavior of Theodore Roosevelt in precisely this context and arrived at this striking conclusion:

> The block to Roosevelt's understanding was the inability he shared with many Americans of his day to associate qualities and aspirations of "superior" people with the Chinese. His persistence in regarding them, because of military weakness and industrial underdevelopment, as a "backward people" destroyed the effectiveness of his policy in the Far East

Beale attributes in large measure to Roosevelt's "block" on the Chinese the failure of the United States to align itself effectively at that time—just after the turn of the century—with the "new spirit" of reform in China To this failure he ascribes, in the longer run, the ultimate failure of American policy in China half a century later.[4] It would be a task of no small magnitude and no small promise to examine from this point of view the images of Asian peoples—insofar as they can be retrieved—that governed the thinking and relevant behavior of such men as William Howard Taft, Elihu Root, Woodrow Wilson, Charles Evans Hughes, Henry L. Stimson, Cordell Hull, Franklin D. Roosevelt. The images of Asia and of Asian-Western relationships persisting in the minds of men educated and conditioned primarily to an Atlantic-Western-white view of the world certainly have a major place in the slowness and pain with which major American policy makers have reacted to the new realities in Asia since 1945. Different as they are in qualities of mind and character, this seems to apply both to Dean Acheson and to John Foster Dulles, i e., it appears at all extremes of competence in the leadership of our public life.

Generally speaking, we may assume that intelligent people who

[4] *Theodore Roosevelt and the Rise of America to World Power*, Baltimore, 1956, p. 251 and Chapter IV, "Roosevelt and China," pp. 172 ff.

deal with problems of international politics try to distinguish between their personal feelings or reactions to nations or peoples on the one hand, and their judgment of the merits or demerits of policy decisions on the other. This effort shows up clearly in our present panel, intelligent people all, and some of them heavily burdened with policy responsibilities In this group those who took a generally sympathetic view of India's foreign policy were about evenly divided in their reactions to Indians as people. They tended to accept Nehru's policies as sensible or wise, at least from the reasonable standpoint of Indian national interests, or even to hold that these policies for India were the better course from the American point of view as well Among those hostile to Nehru's foreign policy, the proportion was less even Yet even here, about one-third were individuals who were otherwise quite positively disposed toward India and Indians, but who felt that Indian foreign policy was damaging either to India or to the United States or to both.

Every government official or member of Congress who was interviewed stoutly denied that his feeling about India or Indians, whatever it was, had anything to do with his policy decisions or his votes affecting India A conscientious public servant could hardly make any other assumption or statement about himself Yet it is difficult not to speculate about the inner realities of the decision-making process One government official who was a member of several interdepartmental committees in Washington confessed that whenever an India item arose, a palpable sigh would pass around the table and somebody was quite likely to say something like "Oh God, here we go again!" Individuals operating exchange and public information programs found themselves confronted with this problem in a peculiarly acute form. They were supposed to generate good will through personal contacts which normally produced only irritation and ill will. The feeling of frustration over Indians in general and Nehru in particular became a familiar and recurring state of mind in policy-making quarters during this time in Washington. How far then, may one guess, did this feeling influence the making of critically important decisions? Perhaps the single most important one relating to India made in this period of time was the decision, made by the National Security Council and announced by President Eisenhower in February, 1954, to extend arms aid to Pakistan. Many factors no doubt entered into the taking of this step But it was so obviously going to have a major effect on American-Indian relations that the issue before the policy makers really came down to a choice between the real or alleged advantages of the Pakistan aid program and the further serious alienation of India. One cannot help wondering about the role of the underlying feeling about India, expressed in a remark attributed to one of the top policy makers at the decisive meeting: "This is a good thing to do if only because it will show Nehru where to get off!"

China policy of course occupied its own special place at this time in the business of American foreign-policy making. The extraordinary role of the special images, emotions, and attitudes connected with China has already been reviewed in great detail. The watchers on these ramparts, led in Washington at this time by such figures as Senator William Knowland of California, held back for several years the public development of a more hardheaded view of American needs and interests vis-à-vis Communist China and the Nationalist remnant on Formosa Yet by all accounts, in the summit of the Administration itself and in wide concentric circles of interested individuals, the consensus grew that Communist China was an accomplished fact of life that had to be accepted as the starting point of new American-Chinese relations, even if only for the purpose of more effectively pursuing American aims in the power struggle with the Soviet Union In our panel, 135 individuals said that they believed that some kind of normalization of relations with Communist China was going to be required. A total of 17 believed that the United States would sooner or later get into further hostilities with Communist China—these opinions were mostly expressed at the height of the Quemoy-Matsu tension early in 1955—but only 11 individuals thought that American policy should be aimed at forcibly overcoming Communist China through isolation and blockade, and only 5 bitter-enders said they thought that this policy should include the active preparation of Chiang Kai-shek's army for a return to the Chinese mainland. Not until the end of May, 1957, when the flare-up of an anti-American riot in Taipeh, the Formosa capital, brought a certain catharsis in the oddly artificial relations between Washington and Formosa, did the fear of offending special sensibilities on the Chinese issue seem to begin to relax. The facts of power and the needs of policy were imposing themselves. The older images and the older attitudes were being forced to give way to the new demands.

I make no categoric statement on the subject but merely report that I have never discovered any reason to credit the government policy maker as a type with any superior mental discipline, any unique capacity to separate his concepts of his own and other peoples from the so-called international facts of life. In fact my own image of the policy maker—based on numerous encounters with such in more than one country over the years—establishes him as a man quite like any man. Indeed, as I think of the American policy maker of the most recent years, I would amend this to say that I think of him as quite an ordinary man just like any other quite ordinary man, with eyes to see, ears to hear, who laughs when he is tickled, bleeds when he is pricked, and has images floating around loosely in his head, even as you and I. Events are shaped by social forces that are normally much larger and more powerful than any individual policy maker, but insofar as policy makers do play a role, then their images of the people concerned (like their images of themselves and their own nation) have some part in the process Just what part this is must be examined and understood in every particular case.

The effect of images on events remains an elusive matter hidden in the biographies of many men, most of them still unwritten, and a great deal of study, most of it still not undertaken. But the effect of events on images is a much more visible affair, especially of great events, like wars, that forcibly intrude upon the private lives of a great many people. Under the impact of such events, a rearrangement of some kind takes place in the assortment of "good" or "bad" images that we normally carry around in our heads, all coexisting in time but advancing or receding according to the call of circumstances. We seem to have at our disposal all we need to think sufficiently well or sufficiently ill of almost anybody, it is merely a matter of the provocation.[5] Sometimes events create images which remain stable for a long time because nothing happens to upset or contradict them Such, for example, was the image of the murderous Turk that was lodged in the European mind from the time of the Crusades and was reactivated, especially for Americans, by the Turkish maltreatment of Armenians immediately following World War I. That is why this unpleasant Turkish character turned up at the bottom of every scale of American images of foreigners assembled

[5] For references to a variety of studies on this point, see Cantril and Buchanan, *How Nations See Each Other*, Urbana, Ill , pp. 56, 96.

by early social science researchers a generation ago It was probably not budged from that position until after World War II, when for a fairly limited public the Turks began to appear in the more attractive role of staunch allies against Russia, and more widely, as tough and doughty fighters against our foes in Korea.

But in our time this process has been enormously accelerated Great events involving life-or-death for great masses of people, vast shifts in power, changes in the constellations of friend and foe have been taking place at a hitherto incredible rate of speed It seems to me like the earthman's mental picture of what happens when a plane breaks through the sound barrier the sound you make at this instant is gone before you can hear it and never does catch up with you. In this situation the sorting, shaping, and reshaping of our popular images becomes a somewhat frantic process Thus in a matter of only a few years, people were called upon to transfer their images of "Oriental cruelty" from the Chinese to the Japanese and back to the Chinese again. In a single generation, the dominant images of the German have moved from the *gemutlich* bourgeois to the booted militarist, to the Nazi mass murderer, and back again to older images of efficient, hard-working people divided between West (friendly) and East (unfriendly or captive). In an even shorter space of time, Americans have been called upon by events to leap from images of the wanton Japanese murderers of Nanking and the Bataan Death March to new images of reformed sinners and earnest democrats, from bloody-handed rapists and sadistic captors to the delicacy of flower arrangements and the color of a kabuki play In the same period of time, Americans have also been shuttled from the totalitarian monster of Stalin in the purge years to "Uncle Joe" of the war years and back to the crazed megalomaniac hidden behind the Kremlin walls until he died

These changed images are at every point so highly colored by propaganda that they become more grotesque than the truth For a time it became fashionable for sophisticated people to reject them, like the atrocity stories of the Kaiser's time Now it is better understood that the ends of propaganda—the use of information for interested purposes—are best served when biases, exaggerations, or plain lies are blended with large elements of truth There was certainly nothing mythical about Japanese barbarities during the war in China or in the Pacific, or about the ruthlessness of American retaliation. There was nothing phony about the Nazi gas chambers, nothing imaginary about the nightmare of the Russian purges under Stalin. The currency of truth has been debased not only because there has been so much lying but because so much of the truth has been unbelievable, especially for Americans who "saw" these events not as participants but as spectators from afar. Generally speaking, with notable exceptions, propagandists have found it necessary to lie more about their friends than about their foes But not often in history have friends and foes changed places on such a large scale so swiftly as they have in the affairs of nations in the years since 1939. Never has there been such a transmogrification of so many "goodies" into "baddies" and vice versa in so short a time. Just how this process, taking place along the swollen channels of communication that now fill every man's world with sight and sound, has affected the patterns and habits of popular ideas and stereotyping in American minds is another one of the many subjects that wants more examination.

The more relevant term for politics, and perhaps for much else, is not *image* but *relationship*. In terms of relationship, especially where Chinese and Indians and Americans are concerned, something a good deal more than transmogrification is taking place. Transmogrification means change with an absurd effect, and there can be no question that such effects abound in current world affairs. But laugh, cry, or gape, what confronts us is no more speedy change of scenery, flag, costume, posture, or facial expression, no frantic flashing of new pictures on the propaganda screens It is the beginning of a change in the underpinning of the total relationship between Western and Asian and African men For nearly three hundred years this underpinning was the assumption of Western superiority: a whole vast political-military-social-economic-racial-personal complex was built upon it Almost every Western image of Asian and other non-Western peoples was based on it. This assumption can now no longer be made or maintained. The whole structure based upon it is being revised All the power relations that went with it are being changed This is history in the large, a great continental rearrangement, bringing with it a great and wrenching shift in the juxtapositions of cultures and peoples. Western men are being relieved of the comforts and disabilities of being the lords of creation, Asian and African men can no longer merely submit, nor live on the rancors of subjection, nor revitalize their own societies by the ideas or sanctions of their own more distant past. All must move from old ground to new, from old assumptions to new ones, and as they move must constantly refocus their views. They will all be engaged, for some time to come, in more or less painfully revising the images they have of themselves and of each other.

In this revision, all the images and experiences of the past have some part. They are not effaced but are absorbed and rearranged in some new design. Much is relegated to the museums and to the memory and to the contending history books, but the greater part remains to bedevil the process of change itself. All the sounds, old and new, go on in our hearing at the same time, making the great din in which we live. All the old and new images flicker around us, giving our world and every individual mind the quality it has of a kaleidoscope. The problem for every man, be he Chinese, Indian, or American, would still seem to be to try to know the nature of this process, to sort out the sounds and distinguish among the sights, to understand their effects in his own mind and in the minds of others. It is at least barely possible that this knowledge can help make the new relationships, the new assumptions, the new images a little less unflattering to themselves and to human society. In the present work we have attempted a sort of natural history of a set of these images as we found them in the crevices of a number of American minds. If the results are such that the reader will recognize these images when he encounters them again, that will be good. If he meets them in his own mind and is led to explore their origins, so much the better.

# INDEX

## A

Abend, Hallett, 160n
Abhendananda, Swami, 289
Acheson, Dean, 191, 402
Aga Khan, 245
"agrarian reformers," 163
Alcott, Bronson, 255
Alcott, Louisa May, 242
All-India National Congress, 305n, 389n.
Allport, Gordon, 281, 282
Alsop, Joseph, 192
*America*, 16
*American Historical Review*, 125n
American immigration laws (See Immigration laws, U S )
American Indian, 103, 197, 239-240
American Institute of Public Opinion, 16, 25n., 173
*American Journal of Sociology*, 113n.
American Oriental Society, 256
American Universities Field Staff, 16
Americans in China, 69, 141ff , 194-209, 212-215, businessmen, 148-151, 159, 201, 390, 392-393, China-born, 153-154, soldiers during World War II, 103, 104n., 177-189, severance, 212-215, panel members, 352ff , (See also United States and China, "old China hands," missionaries, Sinophiles, etc )
Americans in India, 257, 261-263, 298, 317-322, 322n., businessmen, 262, 323, 332, 360, 392-393, during World War II, 317-319, after World War II, 319-322, panel, 324-365, passim (See also United States and India, missionaries)
Amherst College, 15
Arliss, George, 280
Army, U.S Department of the, 16, 177
Arnold, Sir Edwin, 255-256, 258

Aryans, 284, 287, 289, 290, 358
*Asia*, 146n , 147n , 170n
"Asian flu," 45n.
*Assignment India*, 246
Associated Press, 16
*Atlantic Monthly*, 21, 304n
Attlee, Clement, 213

## B

Baldwin, Hanson, 230, 233, 236n , 238
Baldwin, Roger, 299
"Ballad of East and West," 276
*Baltimore Afro-American*, 214n.
Bandung Conference, 214
Bataan Death March, 406
Beale, Howard K , 402
Beard, Charles A , 126n.
Beaver, R Pierce, 265n.
Belden, Jack, 80
*Bengal Brigade*, 245
Besant, Annie, 257
*Bhagavadgita*, 252, 255, 344
*Bhowani Junction*, 279n.
Biggers, Earl Derr, 91, 119
Black Hole of Calcutta, 48, 241, 280
*Black Watch*, 277n
Blavatsky, Helen, 256-257
Board of Foreign Missions, Presbyterian Church in the U S A., 16
Bogardus, Emory, 120-121
*Bombay Buddha*, 280
*Book of Knowledge*, 50, 90
*Books*, 304n
Boston Brahmins, 240
*Boston Globe*, 45n , 70n., 300n
*Boston Herald*, 238n
*Boston Record*, 218
Boston Tea Party, 67
*Boston Transcript*, 304n.
*Boston Traveler*, 108n
Bourke-White, Margaret, 319

Bowles, Chester, 25, 84, 246, 319
Boxer Rebellion, 49, 63, 69, 106, 107, 133, 139, 141, 142, 143, 144
*Brahma*, 252
Brahman cattle, 240
Brahmins, 240n, 326
brainwashers, 218
Brando, Marlon, 108n.
British East India Company, 242
Brooklyn College, 15
Brown, Norman, 18n, 254
Bryan, William Jennings, 299
Buchanan, William, 405n
Buck, Pearl, 50, 63, 77, 79, 80, 81, 85, 86, 106n, 120, 154, 155-159, 216, 275n, 286n
Buddhism, 35, 49, 107n., 255, 256, 262
Burlingame, Anson, 112, 159

C

Calcutta, 45, 48, 273-274, 298, 317
Caldwell, John, 130
California, 24, 26, 108, 111, 112, 122, 123, 282, Hindus in, 283-284
California-Texas Oil Company, 16
California, University of, 15
Cambridge University, 369
Cameron, James, 213
Cantril, Hadley, 87n, 107n, 174n., 301, 405n
Capp, Al, 300n
Carlson, Evans, 232n
Carnegie Endowment for International Peace, 16
Carpenter, Frederic Ives, 251, 252n, 253
Cartoons, 57, 100, 108, 175, 189, 210, 211, 221, 226, 227, 234, 245, 288, 295, 297, 310, 320, 321
Caste system, 259, 262, 268, 287-289, 332, 338, 340, 345, 347, 350, 357, 361, 362, 372, 374, 376, 387, 388
*Catholic World*, 263n
Catholics, 24, 121, 126, 128, 129, 135, 145, 206, 207, 333, 354, 372
CBI (See China-Burma-India)
Chan, Charlie, 80, 91, 119, 42, 240
*Charge of the 1st Bengal Lancers*, 277n
Chaudhuri, Nirad C., 368n
Chennault, Gen Claire, 177, 178
Chiang Kai-shek, 49, 82, 144, 160, 161, 162, 163, 170, 171, 176, 180, 188-190, 203, 204, 206, 231, 308, 353
Chiang Kai-shek, Mme, 87, 161, 162, 170, 171, 174-175, 176, 178, 183, 185, 203, 404
*Chicago Daily News*, 15
*Chicago Sun-Times*, 15
Chicago, University of, 15, 118

China-Burma-India Theater (CBI), 177-189, 319
*China Handbook*, 206n
China trade, 48, 86, 126
*China Year Book*, 145n, 202n
"Chinaman," 84, 93, 109, 110, 114, 115n, 118
"Chinaman's chance," 115
Chinatowns, 50, 65, 69, 86, 110, 115, 116, 117, 120, 122, 123, 239, 380
Chinese-Americans, 68, 111, 116, 124
Chinese art, 69, 79, 88, 90-91
*Chinese Characteristics*, 101, 137-140
Chinese Communists, 51, 53, 162, 163, 164, 189-192, 208, 209-238, 347 (See Communist China)
Chinese examination system, 96, 388
Chinese exclusion laws, 65, 113, 120, 142, 198, 212 (See also Immigration laws, U S)
Chinese food, 50, 69, 78, 117, 239
"Chinese homer," 70n
Chinese in the United States, 65, 68, 109-124, 197-198
Chinese laundrymen, 65, 109, 110, 115, 122, 123, 239
Chinese, panel-eye view of, 72-89
*Chinese Repository, The*, 133n, 134
Chinese-Russian alliance, 55
"Chinks," 101n, 115n, 123, 236
*chinoiseries*, 93-94, 98n
Chou En-lai, 214, 224, 386
*Christian Century*, 202, 304n.
*Christian Herald*, 16
Christian Medical Council, 16
Christian Science Church, 255
*Christian Science Monitor*, 15, 21
Christy, Arthur, 94n, 96n, 251
Chunch, Di Alfred, 48, 50n
Churchill, Winston, 178, 204, 300, 307
*Churchman, The*, 16
*Churchwoman, The*, 16
Clare, Thomas H, 318
Clark, Gen Mark, 233
Clarke, James Freeman, 255
clipper ships, 67, 242, 244 (See China trade)
Clive, Robert, 48
Coelho, George, 375n.
*Collier's Encyclopedia*, 103n.
Color prejudices, 45, 85, 87, 103, 110, 116, 117, 281-290, 341, 345, 347, 350, 357, 358, 359, 370, 378, 389, 394
Columbia Broadcasting System, 16
Columbia University, 28
Commerce, U S Department of, 16
*Commonweal*, 16
Communist China, 55, 108n., 105, 209-238, 307, 404 (See also Chinese Communists, Chou En-lai, Mao Tse-tung)

# INDEX

Confucius, 48, 49, 79, 86, 91, 94, 95, 253, "Confucius say—", 119, 240
Congress of Industrial Organizations, 16
*Congressional Record,* 30
Cornell University, 15
*Cosmopolitan Atlas,* 42
Cox, Oliver Cromwell, 289n
Crane, Robert I., 263n, 264n., 298n.
Creel, Herrlee, 94, 95
Cressy, Earl Herbert, 146n, 148
Cripps Mission, 301
Crow, Carl, 131, 132n, 151
Crutchfield, Richard S., 285n.
*Cumulative Book Index,* 66n, 177n
Cushing, Caleb, 68, 125, 201

## D

*Daily Alta California,* 111
Darwin, Charles, 137, 251
Daugherty, William E, 169n.
Davidson, Basil, 213
Davies, John Paton, 154
Delano, 67, 168
Democratic National Committee, 16
Democrats, 23
Dennett, Tyler, 125n, 142n
*Denver Post,* 15
Deodhar, Shyama, 48n
Dewey, John, 147, 152, 195-197, 201, 253, 299, 373
Dewey, Thomas E, 204n, 207n
Dienbienphu, 236-237
Dinkar, R D. Sinha, 376n
Doubleday & Company, Inc, 16
Doyle, Sir Arthur Conan, 280
*Dragon Seed,* 157
Dulles, Foster Rhea, 111n, 125n, 203n
Dulles, John Foster, 25, 39, 214n, 236, 316, 402
Dunlap, A M, 213n.
Durban riots, 358

## E

East India Squadron, 242
"East-West" struggle, 39
*Economist,* 21
Eddy, Mary Baker, 255
Edison, Thomas A, 268
Eisenhower Exchange Fellowships, 16
Eisenhower, President, 25, 178, 192, 226, 315, 403
Elgin, Lord, 134
Emerson, Ralph Waldo, 94, 96, 251-255, 258, 373
*Empress of China,* 67
*Encounter,* 368n.
Ennis, Thomas E, 94n.

Episcopal Theological Seminary, 264n
Exclusion laws (See Immigration laws, US)
extraterritorial rights, 112, 120, 135

## F

Fairbank, Wilma, 69n
fashions, 247-248, 322
Feis, Herbert, 172, 177
Ferno, John, 170
films (See moving pictures)
Fischer, Louis, 319
Fisher, Bishop Frederick, 263, 275n., 295, 298, 300
Fitzpatrick, D R, 170, 298
*Flow of the News, The,* 319n
Ford Foundation, 16
*Foreign Affairs,* 21, 230n., 231n
Foreign Operations Administration, 16
Formosa, 21, 64, 189, 204, 208-209, 313, 404
Formosa Strait, 38, 228
Foster, E. M, 367, 368n.
*Fortune,* 121n.
*Four Hundred Million, The,* 170
Fox Studios, 119
Franklin, Benjamin, 95
"from Greenland's icy mountains," 264
Fu Manchu, 84, 116, 117, 119, 120, 122, 218, 240, 380
"Fuzzy-Wuzzy," 276

## G

Gale, George S, 213
Gallup, George, 25, 173, 174n, 190n, 301
Gandhi, 49, 241, 243, 250, 253, 257, 266, 268, 275, 290-302, 303, 309, 311, 322, 330, 331, 332, 338, 339, 344, 352, 357, 364
Ganges River, 47, 259, 261, 273
Gannett, Lewis, 202, 204
Gauss, Clarence, 187
Geer, Andrew, 235
General Motors Overseas Corporation, 16
Genghiz Khan, 48, 50, 63, 99, 105, 227-228
Gibbons, Floyd, 228
Gilbert, Rodney, 150n, 160n.
Girl Scouts of America, 16
Glick, Carl, 120
Goethe, 93, 94
Goldman, Eric, 191n.
*Good Earth, The,* 77, 80, 81, 155-159 (See also Pearl Buck)
"gooks," 104n, 236, 317n.
Grant, Cary, 275

Great Britain, 96, 269, 278ff., 299-301
Great Wall of China, 44, 47
*Green Goddess, The*, 280
Greene, Robert W., 213n.
Guillain, Robert, 213
"Gumps, The," 84
Gunga Din, 241-242, 275, 276, 281

## H

Hampden, Walter, 256
Harcourt, Brace & Co., 270n
*Harper's*, 21
Harrington, Fred H., 126n
Harrington, Philip, 214n
Harrison, Carter H., 261
Harte, Bret, 50, 110, 113, 114
Hartford Seminary Foundation, 16
Harvard University, 15, 23, 77, 369
Hastings, Warren, 48
Hay, John, 49, 126, 141, 194
heathen, 45, 109, 113, 122, 147, 258, 259ff., 264, 267
"heathen Chinee," 109, 113, 122, 398
Heber, Bishop, 264
Henty, George, 280
Hersey, John, 130, 158n
*Hindoo Fakir*, 268
Hinduism, 49, 252ff., 255, 256, 257, 258, 259ff., 275, 276, 330, 354, 355, 372, 374, 382
Hindu-Muslim conflict, 278-279, 287, 298, 302
Holmes, John Haynes, 299
Holmes, Oliver Wendell, 240
Hoover, Herbert, 166, 168
Hornbeck, Stanley, 186
Houghton-Mifflin Company, 319n
Howard University, 15
Hughes, Charles F., 402
Hull, Cordell, 187, 402
"human sea," 227, 232-236
Hume, Robert, 263
Hungary, 228, 315
Hutheesing, G. P., 213
Hyde, A. M., 167n
hymns, 264

## I

*Illustrated Weekly of India*, 375
Immigration Act of 1917, 289
Immigration Act of 1946, 198, 285
Immigration Laws (U.S.), 65, 113, 120, 142, 198, 212, 283-285
India ink, 240
India League of America, 16
India rubber, 240
Indian Civil Service (ICS), 332, 344, 368

Indian immigration to U.S., 283-285
Indian independence, 51, 301-302, 323, 382, American attitudes toward, 299-301
Indian nationalist movement (See Gandhi, Nehru, Indian Independence)
*Indian Review*, 285n
*Indian Social Reformer*, 270
Indians in U.S., 257-258, 283-287, 299, 322, 322n
Indochina War (1954), 51, 56
Information Agency, U.S., 16
International Educational Exchange Program, 16
International Farm Youth Exchange, 16
International General Electric Company, 16
International Research Associates, 16
Interviewees, description of, 13-27
Interviewer, described 31-35
Interviews, description of, 27-31
Irving Trust Company, 16
Isaacs, Harold R., 104n, 231n, 319n.
Ivens, Joris, 170

## J

Jacoby, Annalee, 177n, 179n
Japan, 19, 38, 144, 171, 171, 201 (See Sino-Japanese War)
James, William, 253, 373
Jefferson, Thomas, 95, 388
Jesuits, 94, 95, 126, 337
Jews, 24, 83, 110, 117, 121, 122n, 123, 309, 352, 397
John Day Company, The, 156, 304n
Johnson, Louis, 300
Jones, Dorothy B., 66n, 116, 119, 120n, 156n, 157, 227n, 284n
Jones, Eli Stanley, 268

## K

Kali, 259
Kashmir, 309, 312, 313, 316, 357, 364
Kates, George, 153n
Khrushchev, Nikita, 224
Kiddell-Monroe, J., 244n.
*King of the Khyber Rifles*, 276, 280, 289
Kipling, Rudyard, 50, 241-242, 271, 272, 274, 276, 277, 355
Knowland, Sen. William, 25, 84, 209, 217, 404
Koestler, Arthur, 218
Kohn, Hans, 304n
Korean War, 38, 51, 58, 69, 82, 105, 191, 212n., 214, 225, 232-236

## INDEX

Krech, David, 285n
Kuomintang, 162, 163, 164, 179, 190-191, 194, 208, 353

### L

Lall, Arthur, 340
Lao Tze, 49, 91
Lasker, Bruno, 102
Latourette, Kenneth, 49, 95, 98n., 133, 134, 140n
Lau Shaw, 158n
Lawson, Robert, 109-110
League of Women Voters, 16
Lee, Rose Hum, 115n., 118, 119n , 120, 124
Legge, James, 135
"lesser breeds without the law," 272
Lew, Dr Timothy, 48
Lieberman, Henry R., 207n.
*Life*, 15, 21, 154, 167n , 223, 237, 316n , 355
*Light of Asia, The*, 255-256
Lin Yutang, 79, 120, 153n , 155n , 156, 256n
Linton, Ralph, 289n
*Literary Digest*, 118, 119n , 284
London Round Table Conference (1931), 296, 300
*Look*, 214n.
Lovett, Robert Morss, 299
Luce, Henry, 130, 154, 171

### M

MacArthur, Gen Douglas, 25, 107n , 178, 232, 238
Magruder, John A , 185-187, 230-231
Mahan, Admiral Alfred T , 171
Maharajah of Mysore, 245
maharajahs, 244-248
mah-jongg, 69
Malraux, André, 79
Manchu Dynasty, 98, 133, 142, 143, 144
Manchurian invasion (See Sino-Japanese War)
Mao Tse-tung, 63, 64, 99, 209, 224
Marco Polo, 48, 63, 66, 90, 93, 183, 240, 384
Marshall, Gen George C , 188, 191
Marshall, S L. A., 232-233
Martin, Kingsley, 213
Mary Victoria, Sister, 213n.
Maryknoll Seminary, 16
Masaryk, Jan, 312
Masland, John W , 169n , 170
Massachusetts Institute of Technology, 15
Masters, John, 279n.
Mau Mau, 345

Maugham, Somerset, 277n
Mayo, Katherine, 50, 268-271, 338
McLaglen, Victor, 275
Menon, V K Krishna, 55, 313-317, 340, 348, 356, 369
Methodist Board of Missions, 16
*Middle Kingdom, The*, 106n , 134n , 135-140
Midwest, 24, 26, 83, 110, 121n , 122, 131, 238, 332, 334
Millard, Thomas, 159
Miller, Jessie A , 142n , 143n., 144n.
*Minneapolis Star-Tribune*, 15
Minnesota, University of, 15
Missionaries, in China, 67, 69, 73, 77, 80, 81, 96, 105, 126-140, 144-148, 159, 161-162, 169, 194, 199-203, 205-208, 212n , 216, in India, 243, 251, 258, 262-267, 270n , 298, 322-323, 337, 338-339, 341-342, 354-355, 391, impact on panelists, 50, 106, 127-131, 266-268, 398, Jesuits, 94, 126, 337
*Mississippi Historical Review*, 126n
mobile society, 387, 388
Moguls, 278
Mongol hordes, 48, 48n., 63, 227-228, 233, 236
"Mongoloid," 103, 103n
Moraes, Frank, 213
Morgan, Lewis, 137
Morris, Robert, 67
*Mother India*, 268-271, 355, 365
moving pictures, 80, 66n , 80, 91, 116-117, 119-120, 156, 157, 170, 174, 245, 268, 275-276, 277, 277n , 279n , 280, 282-283, 303, 322
Muehl, John Frederick, 318, 319
Müller, Max, 251, 255
Muslims, 262, 268, 276-279, 359, 372

### N

Nanking, sack of (1937), 167, 406
*Nation, The*, 142
National Association for the Advancement of Colored People, 16
National Broadcasting Company, 16
National City Bank of New York, 16
National Council of Churches of Christ in America, 16
*National Geographic*, 50, 259, 346
National Opinion Research Center, 16, 216, 301
National Security Council, 403
Negroes, 23, 24, 83, 85, 87, 103, 110, 116, 117, 121, 123, 281-282, 287, 334, 335, 336, 347, 350, 352, 358, 391, 394
Nehru, Jawaharlal, 55, 243, 247, 260, 261, 279n , 286n , 294, 301, 302-316,

322, 330, 347, 348, 356, 357, 358, 359, 365, 372, 376, 377, 384, 389n, 403, 404
Nenni, Pietro, 311
New England, Chinese influences, 67, 69, 86, 126, Indian contacts, 243, 251-255
*New Hymnal*, 264
*New Republic*, 213n, 299n
*New York Herald Tribune*, 15, 21, 121n
*New York Post*, 214n
*New York Times*, 15, 21, 70n, 93n, 103n, 124, 207, 208n, 213, 218, 219n, 220n, 224, 235n, 237n, 238n, 246, 247, 279n, 296, 305n, 316n, 376n, 389n
*New Yorker*, 93n
Newell, Moyca, 269, 270n
*Newsweek*, 16, 21, 229, 237n
Nineteenth Route Army, 167
Nizam of Hyderabad 245
Northwest Frontier, 269, 277-278
Northwestern University, 124

O

Odlum, Jacqueline Cochrane, 285n
Office of Public Opinion Research, 107n., 174n
Olcott, Henry, 257
"old China hands," 74, 75, 149, 150-151, 201
Olyphant, D W C, 126
Open Door, 38, 49, 126, 141
Operations Coordination Board, 16
Opinion Polls, 25, 37, 107, 121n, 172-174, 190n., 216, 301
Opium wars, 49, 96, 98, 125
Oppenheimer, Robert, 35
Orwell, George, 218, 272
Overseas Chinese, 21, 80
Oxford University, 369

P

*Pacific Historical Review*, 169n.
Pakistan, 276-277, 279, 348, 350, 403, 404
Panay, U S S, 163, 168
Pandit, Mme., 340, 356, 358
Panel, description of, 13-27, views of Chinese, 72-89, views of Indians, 324-365, summary of views, 382-383
Pant, G. B, 286n
Park, Robert E., 118
Parrington, Vernon, 251
*Passage to India*, 267, 368n.
Pearl Harbor, 37, 38, 51, 52, 76, 120, 157, 160, 164, 165, 174, 183, 203, 300
Peck, Graham, 177n, 179, 192
Peck, Gregory, 283

Peking, 44, 151-153
Peking Language School, 152
Pennsylvania, University of, 15
Perlmutter, Howard V, 395n
Perry, Commodore, 48
Philippines, 52, 141, insurrection, 51n.
Phillips, William, 300
*Pilgrim Hymnal*, 264
Pitkin, Victor E, 65n
*Pittsburgh Courier*, 15
Portsmouth Conference, 49, 171
Powei, Tyrone, 283
Princeton University, 15
Protestants, 24, 121, 126, 128, 130, 135n., 145, 206, 372 (See Missionaries)
*Public Opinion*, 37n, 173n, 174n, 301n
*Public Opinion Quarterly*, 168n, 169n
"pumpkin papers," 191
*Purple Plain, The*, 283

Q

Quemoy-Matsu, 56, 58, 404
Quesnay, François, 94, 95
Quigley, Harold, 49

R

Raciappa, John D, 264n
Radakrishnan, M S, 289, 336
Radio programs cited, 246
*Rains of Ranchipur, The*, 245, 283
Random House, 164
Rau, Benegal, 356
*Reader's Digest*, 168n., 170n, 203n.
*Reader's Guide to Periodical Literature*, 66n, 304n.
"Recessional," 271
*Red Star Over China*, 155n, 162, 163
Redding, Saunders, 319
Reinsch, Paul, 49
*Reporter, The*, 16, 21, 195n
Representatives, U S House of, 16
Republican National Committee, 16
Republicans, 25
Ricci, Father Matteo, 126
*Richer by Asia*, 318
Riggs, Lt Col. Robert, 232n, 233n
Ripley, Robert, 100, 259n., 379
*River, The*, 322
Rockefeller Foundation, 16
Rogers, Will, 300n
Rohmer, Sax, 50, 116
Romanus, Charles F., 177n
Roosevelt, Eleanor, 319
Roosevelt, Franklin D., 168, 171, 174n, 178, 185, 187, 188, 201, 204, 300, 307, 402

# INDEX 415

Roosevelt, Theodore, 142, 144, 168, 171, 200-201, 402
Root, Elihu, 402
Roper, Elmo, 16, 121, 173
Rosenthal, A M, 279n, 316
Ross, E A, 101-102
Rostow, W W, 213n.
*Roughing It*, 114, 115n
Rowan, Carl, 322
Rowntree, Joshua, 134n
Russia, 183, 214, 219, 220, 221, 222, 223, 315, 340, 347
Russo-Japanese War, 49, 51, 141

## S

"sacred cow," 240, 245, 259, 330, 339, 355, 356, 357
*St Louis Post Dispatch*, 170
Sandmeyer, Elmer C, 113n.
*Saturday Evening Post*, 119, 192n, 235
*Saturday Review of Literature*, 16
Saund, Dalip S, 287n
Schmidt, E R, 257n, 259n, 263n, 265n, 270n, 285n., 286n, 298n, 300n
Schools, influence of, 40, 47-50, 65-66, 90
Schoyer, Preston, 181n
Schricke, B, 112
*Science Digest*, 103n
Sepoy Mutiny, 243, 280
Senate, U S, 16, 175
Sevareid, Eric, 105
Seward, William H, 125n, 200, 268
Shaplen, Robert, 93n
Sheehan, Vincent, 304n, 319
Siegfried, André, 79
Singh, Anup, 284n
Singh, Harnam, 295n., 299n, 300n.
Singh, Khushwant, 375
Sino-Japanese War, 51, 52, 81, 105, 120, 162, 163, 165, 173, 203-204, 216, 300
Sinophiles, 76, 88, 148-163, 207
"slopeys," 104n.
Smedley, Agnes, 80, 162
Smith, Arthur H., 101, 102, 115n, 137-140
Snow, Edgar, 80, 155n, 162, 163
*Social and Political Science Review*, 48n
Soong, T. V., 185
South (U.S.), 26, 82, 85, 121n, 282
Southeast Asia, 19, 21, 174, 300, 349
Soviet Union (See Russia)
Spanish-American War, 51, 141
Stalin, J V, 178, 201, 218, 228
Standard Vacuum Oil Company, 16
Starr, C. V., Company, 16

State, U.S Department of, 16, 141, 177, 186, 191, 193, 212n, 358
Steinbeck, John, 252n
Stern, Bernard, 243n, 256, 262, 263n., 267, 272
Stevens, Edmund, 214n
Stevenson, Adlai, 25
Stilwell, Gen. Joseph W., 177, 178, 179, 180, 188, 231
Stimson, Henry L, 166, 168n, 203, 402
Stone, John, 119
Stowe, Leland, 182-184, 203
Strong, Anna Louise, 80
Strunk, Mildred, 37n.
Stuart, John Leighton, 154
Suez Canal, 254
Sulzberger, C L., 305n
Sun Yat-sen, 49
Sunday school, 40, 50, 80
Sunderland, Jabez, 263
Sunderland, Riley, 177n
Supreme Court, U S, 284, 290
*Survey, The*, 196n., 202n
*Survey Graphic*, 118
Sutherland, Justice, 284, 290

## T

Taft, William H., 402
Tagore, Rabindranath, 285
Taipeh riot, 208-209, 404
Taiping Rebellion, 133
Taj Mahal, 44, 47, 244
Tawney, R H, 54
Taylor, Edmond, 318
Television, programs cited, 90n, 245-247, 303
"Terry and the Pirates," 50, 80
textbooks, treatment in, 42n, 47-48, 90
Theosophical Society, 256-257
Thomas, Norman, 299
Thomas, Wendell, 255n
Thoreau, Henry, 251, 253, 254
*Time*, 16, 21, 154, 171, 175, 247, 259, 305n
*Times of India*, 289, 290n
Tolstoy, 294
*Toward Freedom*, 260n, 304n., 305n
Transcendentalists, 251-254
*Treatment of Asia in American Textbooks*, 42n., 47-48, 90
Truman, Harry, 25, 192
Turner, Lana, 283
Twain, Mark, 113, 114, 140n, 267n., 388n

## U

U S S R (See Russia)
Union Theological Seminary, 16

United Nations, 59, 235, 314, 315, 316, 345, 356
United Press, 16
U.S. and China, early relations, 68, 125ff., 141-143, 200-201, boycott against, 143, reaction to Japanese attack, 165-170, end of isolationism, 171-174; wartime relations, 185-189, effect of Communist victory, 191ff (See also Americans in China)
U.S and India, early contacts, 242-243, immigration laws, 283, wartime experience, 317-319 (See Americans in India, Nehru, Menon)
U S News and World Report, 15
United States Catalog, 66n.
untouchables, 259, 268, 287, 288, 340, 372 (See Caste system)

V

Vandercook, John, 103n
Vedanta Society, 257
Versailles Conference, 49, 51n, 52, 201
Villard, Oswald Garrison, 142, 299
Vishinsky, Andrei, 311
Vivekenanda, Swami, 257
Voltaire, 94

W

Walker, Richard L., 213n
Wallace, Henry, 311
Waln, Nora, 77
war lords, 93, 143, 152, 159
Washington Conference (1921-22), 52
Washington International Affairs Seminar, 16

Washington Post, 15, 21
Welles, Sumner, 168n, 169, 184, 205
Westinghouse International Company, 16
Weston, Christine, 244n.
"White Man's Burden," 241
White, Theodore H, 177n, 179n.
Whitman, Walt, 254
Wilbur, R L, 167n
Williams, Frederick Wells, 49
Williams, S Wells, 106n, 134, 135-140
Wilson, Woodrow, 201, 330, 402
"wogs," 104n, 317
Woman of Kali, 280
World War I, 141, 147, 151, 159, 160, 269, 284, 299, 405
World War II, 18, 19, 31, 38, 69, 84, 89, 103, 124, 150, 317, 323, 385, 406
Worthy, William, 214n
Wright, Brooks, 255n, 256
Wu, Sherman, 124
Wu, Y L, 213n
Wyatt, Woodrow, 369n

Y

Yale Divinity School, 16
Yale-in-China, 130
Yale University, 15, 23
Yalta, 191, 201
Yalu River, 64, 215
"yellow" (cowardly), 97n
Yellow Peril, 68, 110, 115, 123, 226, 238
Yen, Maria, 213
Young Women's Christian Association, 16
Youth's Companion, 106

CPSIA information can be obtained
at www.ICGtesting.com
Printed in the USA
LVHW010353111218
599931LV00012B/319/P